LEARNING THE NEWS

MOSAICA PRESS

LEARNING THE NEWS

Halachic Perspectives on Current Events

RABBI SIMCHA LAUER

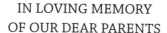

IN LOVING MEMORY
OF OUR DEAR PARENTS

JUDY AND DR. EDWARD L. STEINBERG

יהודה ליב בן יצחק גדליה ע"ה
יהודית ליבה בת שמחה הכהן ע"ה

DORIS AND GEORGE LAUER

גרשון בן אליעזר ע"ה
דבורה בת משה יוסף ע"ה

who would have enjoyed using this *sefer* and would have been so proud
of their beloved grandson's commitment to Torat Yisrael and his
accomplishment in producing this monumental work.
May their memory be a blessing for all of Klal Yisrael.

MARILYN AND ELIOT LAUER
Lawrence, NY

דוד קאהן

ביהמ"ד גבול יעבץ
ברוקלין, נוא יארק

מכתב ברכה

בס"ד

לידידי ש"ב ר' שמחה שליט"א

זה עתה קבלתי טופס של ספרך והנני אץ למלאות בקשתך מאתי לאמר,
ובלשון בני הישיבה, מעשה גדול ומעשה חבבא, מעשה הגבורה: הנך
קרוב לאנשי תמיד והלוא מקרוב מכיר הוא ומבדיל לא תמיד. אומנם המחי"ה
יותר הוא הטעם של חבבא שזכית לחבר ספר שייך לכל מאן עולם"מ
עם מבצבץ מאין השורות הסמכות של המאמ' שהנך מביא. גם הנך מקיים
מצות קידוש ה' ללמד שאתה מפרסם בשער בת רבים איך שכל מאורע
בחיים יכולים לדון עליו ע"י התורת חיים שלנו.

[אגב, מש"כ אודות נדירת חיים להפוגה, ישנה מעשה מפורסמת
שבתו של הצדיק רב אריה לוין זצ"ל היתה חולה אנושה וכשבאו לבקר
אסירי ציון כמנהגו ונודע להם המצב שלה, קריאת התורה, נדר
כל עולה משנות חייו ושאר האסירים נמשכו אחריהם ונתנו לה משנותם
נפש הצדיק לשיבה ונודע לו מהמעשה הזה, וזכתה לאריכות ימים ושנים]

והנני מברך אותך ולכל אשר לך שכל אשר תפנו תשכילו ונעשה
ותבשר אך ורק בשורות טובות ישועות ונחמות, אכי"ר

החותם לכבוד הגברא לכבוד המחבר
דוד
כד' סיון תשע"ט

20 Av 5778

Michtav Bracha

I have had the pleasure of reading a number of essays by Rabbi Simcha Lauer addressing and explaining contemporary halachic issues. Rabbi Lauer's treatment is outstanding in a number of respects: first, he chooses interesting questions that immediately grab the reader's curiosity, often using an item from a recent news story; second, he utilizes a wide range of sources to explain how halacha would address the particular problem, drawing on Gemara, Rishonim, Acharonim, all the way to the most recent Poskim and Teshuvos; finally, he presents this complex material in a clear, organized manner that can be understood even by people who have a somewhat limited background. A study of these essays will be of great benefit both to the novice and the seasoned talmid chacham. The novice will be exposed to the beauty, depth and complexity of the halachic process and will hopefully be stimulated to increase his own efforts in Limud HaTorah. The talmid chacham will be able to see a wide range of mekoros and psakim, some of which are not so easy to find, which he can then proceed to analyze and elaborate upon. The mechaber deserves our great appreciation for putting together this fine work. May his words reach a wide audience of acheinu bnai yisrael who are thirsting for the Dvar Hashem .

Bivracha ub'haaratza lichvod HaTorah vlichvod HaMechaber,

Yitzchak A. Breitowitz,
Rav, Kehillas Ohr Somayach

ב"ה, ער"ח אלול תשע"ח

מכתב ברכה

הביאו לפני כמה קונטרסים לעיון ממה שכתב מיודענו הדגול
הרב שמחה לאער שליט"א
בו עוסק בסוגיות חשובות שמתעוררות בזמנינו, ומעתיק ע"כ ממקורות
ההלכה בספרי קדמונים ואחרונים עד גדולי זמנינו בטיב טעם ודעת.

אין אני בקי בשפת הלע"ז, אך חזקה עלי דברי הרבנים הגאונים שליט"א שכתבו
על החיבור דברי שבח מעולים, ובפרט שיש להעמידו על חזקתו שהתורה
חוזרת על אכסניתה לבית של תורה שמוכר לנו הערכת חותנו ר' שרגא
פייבוש ברקוביץ הי"ו ללומדי תורה, אחר שזכינו להתאכסן בביתו ונוכחנו
לראות מקרוב את הבית המפואר של תורה, וכן משפחת הרב לאער ששמענו
עליהם כמוקירי תורה ולומדיה, ובע"ה גם הרב שמחה שליט"א ימשיך דרכם
בלימוד ואהבת התורה, ואנו מברכים אותו שיזכה לשבת באהלה של תורה
כל הימים, להפי מעינותיו חוצה על פלגי מים מתוך שפע ברכה ורב נחת .

בברכת התורה
ובברכת כהנים באהבה

הרב שמחה הכהן קוק

RABBI YITZCHAK SILBERSTEIN
Rabbi of Ramat Elchanan
Bnei Brak

יצחק זילברשטיין
רב שכונת רמת אלחנן
בני ברק

י"ד חשון תשע"ט

גם אני החו"מ מצטרף לברכת הכהן הגדול
רבי שמחה קוק שליט"א הרב הראשי לרחובות להרה"ג רב שמחה.
ויהי השי"ת עמו לכוון לאמיתה של תורה, והרה"ג
ר' שמחה לאער שליט"א יגדיל תורה ויאדירה, לשמחת כל
עם ישראל
מברך באהבה,
יצחק זילברשטיין

בס"ד, ט"ז בסיוון ה'תשע"ח

יוסף צבי רימון

רבה של אלון שבות דרום
ראש בתי המדרש ורב המרכז האקדמי לב
ראש מרכז הלכה והוראה

רחוב קבוצת אברהם 10
אלון שבות 9043300

משרד: 02-9933644
נייד: 052-5456060
פקס: 153-2-9933644

rimonim613@gmail.com

מכתב ברכה לרב שמחה לאער שליט"א

ראיתי חלקים מספרו של הרב שמחה לאער שליט"א. שמחתי מאוד לראות כיצד הרב המחבר שליט"א עוסק בעניינים חשובים ומעניינים בניסוח יפה ובהיקף מקורות מרשים.

פעמים רבות ניתן לזהות על פי הכתוב את מקומו של הכותב, לאיזה סוג אוכלוסייה הוא משתייך, מה הם דרכי הלימוד והפסיקה שעליהם גדל, והאם הכותב הוא מארץ ישראל או מארצות הגולה. בספרו של הרב לאער עיסוק רב בסוגיות ישראליות, סוגיות המתהוות מתוך המציאות הישראלית של מדינת ישראל, עיסוק הנותן תחושה שהמחבר גדל בארץ וגר בארץ. מצד שני ניתן לראות פסקים ופוסקים בני חו"ל שהמחבר מביא רבות מתורתם. כך שיש בספר שילוב מרשים של ארץ ישראל וארצות הברית, גם במקרים, גם בפסיקה וגם בניתוח הדברים.

זכיתי להכיר היטב את משפחתו של המחבר, המלאה ביראת שמים, ומתוך כך להבין מהיכן שאב המחבר את דרכו בתורה.

הנני לברך את המחבר שליט"א שימשיך ללמוד וללמד, לכתוב בעוד נושאים רבים, להגדיל תורה ולהאדירה.

ברכת ה' עליכם,

יוסף צבי רימון

TABLE OF CONTENTS

Acknowledgments XV

Introduction 1

A Tree of Forty Fruits 5
May one create a tree that produces forty different types of fruit?

Beware of Dog. 10
*Is a homeowner responsible for injuries that his pet causes to a
trespasser? And related questions.*

Chassid Goes Undercover 19
*May one act as an undercover agent, thereby endangering his life and
misrepresenting himself, in order to help the police apprehend drug
traffickers?*

Donating Years of Your Life 25
Is one permitted to give away years of their life to someone else?

Do Not Hate 34
*What are the parameters of the prohibition against hating another
person?*

How to Catch a Thief 40
*Are employers permitted to plant money to test their employees'
honesty?*

Intermarriage Intervention 47
*Is it permitted to violate Shabbos in order to save another from
spiritual danger?*

Interrupting Shemoneh Esreh for a Missile 55
*When an air raid siren rings, may one interrupt his Shemoneh Esreh
to run to a bomb shelter if he is in an area protected by the Iron Dome?*

Jewish-Gentile Music. 62
   What does the Torah say about using the tunes of secular music
   for Jewish songs and prayer?
Kareem and the Power of a Curse 67
   Is one ever allowed to curse another, and do curses have any effect?
Killing Insects 77
   Is it permitted to kill insects, and, if so, what are the parameters
   of doing so?
Lashon Hara—About Yourself. 83
   Is it permitted to speak lashon hara about oneself?
Modern-Day Slavery 88
   Is a person permitted to trade himself on the stock market?
Olam Haba for Gentiles. 94
   Do gentiles receive reward for the mitzvos they keep?
Olam Haba for Sale. 100
   Can a person sell his portion of Olam Haba?
Paying a Ransom. 108
   What are the halachos of dealing with a hostage crisis?
Raising What?. 115
   May a Jew raise pigs?
Removing Tattoos. 119
   Is a Jew with a tattoo required to get it removed?
Reneging on a Pledge. 125
   Is it permissible, according to halachah, for a donor to withdraw a
   monetary pledge from a law school if he disapproves of an event that
   took place after he made the pledge?
Revealing Your Sins 130
   Is it permitted to reveal past sins to inspire others?
Risking Your Life to Save Others 136
   Is a person permitted to risk his life to save another person?
Sand and Snow Sculptures 146
   Is it permitted to make human statues of sand or snow?
Seeking Berachos from Tzaddikim. 151
   Should one go to rabbis and tzaddikim for berachos?

Selling Kotel Stones 157
   Is it permitted to chisel off a piece of the Kotel wall?
Sheva Mitzvos Campaign in East Jerusalem 162
   Should we publicize and teach the Sheva Mitzvos Bnei Noach to gentiles?
Standing Up to Bullies 167
   What does the Torah say about standing up to bullies?
Steve Jobs and Yossele the Holy Miser 175
   Is it permissible to anonymously give tzedakah, but outwardly appear
   as a miser, causing people to suspect that one is not properly fulfilling
   the mitzvah of tzedakah?
Synagogue or Cyber-Shul? 181
   Is it permitted to conduct religious services through a cyber minyan?
The Apocalypse 188
   What is the Torah's approach to the apocalypse?
The Celebration of Sin? 194
   Is the celebration of sin also a sin?
The Dybbuk Exorcist 198
   According to the Torah, is there truth to dybbuks and exorcism?
The Honor Guards 207
   What is the difference between the security systems of the White House
   and those of the Beis Hamikdash?
The Kabbalah Phenomenon 216
   Is it appropriate to learn Kabbalah or seek advice and yeshuos
   (salvations) from Kabbalists?
The Kosher Shabbos Goy 222
   Is it permitted to make use of the services of a Shabbos goy?
The Lost Parakeet 227
   Can one rely on a parrot's recognition of its owner as evidence
   of ownership?
The Magen David 231
   What is the source of the Magen David?
The Real Competition 235
   What does the Torah say about competing and comparing ourselves
   with other people?

The UPS Matchmaker. 242
   Is there an obligation to pay shadchanus (a matchmaking fee) to a UPS
   driver?
Torah on the Moon. 245
   Is it permitted to send a Sefer Torah to the moon or to place mezuzos
   on non-Jewish edifices?
Unorthodox Collectors 251
   Has one fulfilled the mitzvah of giving tzedakah if he inadvertently
   gives it to a person who does not truly deserve it?
Who Chopped Down the Cherry Tree?. 258
   Is it prohibited to chop down fruit trees? Are there any leniencies?
Yearning for Mashiach. 266
   Is believing in the arrival of Mashiach a Biblical obligation, and are
   there any consequences for someone who doesn't have this belief?

צַיָּידֵי נאצים 1
האם אנו צריכים לתפוס פושעים נאציים? ואם לוכדים פושעי מלחמה נאציים
האם מותר להוציאם להורג?
תפילה על גויים 7
האם מותר להתפלל עבור גויים?
שימור מינים 11
מהי דעתה של התורה לגבי שימור מינים?

ACKNOWLEDGMENTS

I would like to thank Hashem for giving me the unbelievable opportunity to compile and develop the topics discussed in this book.

Also, many thanks to Rabbi Eliyahu Miller of JewishSelfPublishing for editing the manuscript and consulting on the wording. Suri Brand was very helpful in copyediting and providing overall comments to the manuscript as well, Chaya Silverstone did a great job proofreading, and Malka Breindel Unger did an excellent job translating the chapters into Hebrew. I would like to thank Rabbi Yonasan Rosman for reviewing the entire manuscript and providing corrections and insights. Additionally, Rabbi Moshe Pessin's close review of the text and his discerning insights on the Torah sources were very valuable to this work.

Thank you to Rabbi Elly Storch for his warm guidance over the years and to Rabbi Aryeh Lebowitz, whose *shiurim* have inspired me to appreciate the beauty in learning contemporary halachah.

It goes without saying that Mosaica Press brought this whole project to fruition. Rabbi Yaacov Haber and Rabbi Doron Kornbluth took on the endeavor and saw the book to print. Specifically, Rabbi Reuven Butler's discerning comments in the editing process truly sharpened the analysis of the chapters.

I am also greatly indebted to my parents, Eliot and Marilyn Lauer, who have encouraged me wholeheartedly to pursue my passion for Torah through this project and throughout my life. I also look up to my in-laws, Fredi and Debbie Berkovits, as true role models in *chessed*, in how they open their home to all those in need.

Finally, I want to thank my wife, Rena, for the tremendous amount of time she put into editing and upgrading the quality of the *sefer*—her contributions are invaluable.

INTRODUCTION

As educated individuals living in the twenty-first century, we encounter numerous forms of text and media every day. The *Rambam* writes that the prohibition of *chukas akum* (imitating the gentiles) means that not only must we act differently from non-Jews, but that we must also think differently from them.[1] The Torah provides us with the framework that guides our unique way of thinking.

We're all engaged in the world around us, but we cannot take what we read at face value. When reading the news, the Torah we learn enables us to bring the Jewish perspective to world events. Asking myself, *What is the Torah's perspective on these issues?* has always been a favorite practice of mine. This book presents news stories and offers the Torah's perspective on them, through the writings of the *gedolei ha'poskim*. It is important, though, to consult a *posek* before making halachic decisions based on this book.

The phenomenon of Jews reading newspapers is not new, and the opinions of Rabbanim on the topic are varied. Rav Shlomo Zalman Auerbach, *zt"l*, browsed the newspaper daily to check the headlines.[2] Rav Avigdor Miller, *zt"l*, "avoided listening to the news"[3] and said that "a glance at the headlines is sufficient."[4]

---

1   *Mishneh Torah, Hilchos Avodas Kochavim* 11:1.
2   Rabbi Shimon Finkelman, *Reb Moshe: The Life and Ideals of HaGaon Rabbi Moshe Feinstein* (ArtScroll/Mesorah, 2012), p. 173.
3   Rabbi Yaakov Y. Hamburger, *Rav Avigdor Miller: His Life and His Revolution* (Judaica Press, 2016), p. 239.
4   Ibid., p. 463.

1

While Rav Moshe Feinstein, *zt"l*, once remarked, "With one glance at a newsstand, one can lose all he gained in a week's learning,"[5] Rabbi Moshe D. Tendler, Rav Moshe's son-in-law, said that Rav Moshe did read some newspapers:

> *My shver was uniquely sensitive to society. Despite what they write in all the books about him, my shver never failed to read the Yiddish newspaper—either the Tog in the early years or the Morgen-Zhurnal later on—cover-to-cover every single day. People publish that he would walk down the street and avert his eyes when he passed by newspaper stands. There are a thousand talmidim of his who will testify, 'I bought the paper and handed it to him in the lunchroom in the yeshivah,' but it does not make a difference for some people—they do not want to hear that.*[6]

Although Rav Baruch Ber Lebowitz generally glanced at the newspaper headlines, he stoppped doing so in the late 1930s when the sufferings of the Jews in Germany became immeasurably worse. He felt that since he wasn't able to help these people, he wouldn't be able to properly participate in their pain. It was therefore preferable that he not be made aware of their misery.[7]

Rav Benzion Uziel, the Sephardic chief rabbi of Israel in 1939 to 1948, perused the paper each day.[8] Likewise, Rav Baruch HaLevi Epstein writes in his *Mekor Baruch* that his uncle, the Netziv, would read the Hebrew newspaper.[9]

In his book on the Lubavitcher Rebbe, Rabbi Joseph Telushkin writes,

> *There are people who lived in Crown Heights in the 1940s who recall seeing him [the Lubavitcher Rebbe, Rav Menachem*

---

5   *Reb Moshe: The Life and Ideals*, p. 164.

6   Shaul Siedler-Feller, "An Interview with Rabbi Dr. Moshe D. Tendler." *Kol Hamevaser*, Aug. 31, 2010.

7   *Taam Vedaas, Shemos*, p. 6.

8   Rabbi Marc D. Angel and Rabbi Hayyim Angel, *Rav Haim David Halevy* (Urim, 2006), p. 55.

9   Rabbi Baruch HaLevi Epstein, *My Uncle the Netziv: Rabbi Baruch HaLevi Epstein Recalls His Illustrious Uncle, R' Naftali Zvi Yehudah Berlin, and the Panorama of His Life* (ArtScroll/Mesorah, 1988), pp. 87, 90–91.

Mendel Schneerson] heading for the subway station in the morning, carrying four newspapers, The New York Times, the Yiddish Der Tog Morgen Zhurnal, a newspaper in French, and another in Russian (the newsstand special ordered these last two for him).[10]

We see, then, that many *Gedolei Yisrael* regarded being well-informed of the news as permissible, perhaps even necessary.

On the importance of religious newspapers, the *Imrei Emes* states, "I have spent a long time toiling and laboring to establish a newspaper written in the spirit of Yiddishkeit, free of words of heresy and *nivul peh*."[11] Rav Chaim Ozer Grodzenski also advocated for having a paper for the Torah community in Lithuania in 1924.[12]

In light of reading the news through a Torah lens, Rabbi Berel Wein writes about Rav Mendel Kaplan, who was just off the boat from the Mir after six years in Shanghai and unfamiliar with American culture. Rav Kaplan taught at Hebrew Theological College, a Chicago yeshivah, in Yiddish, to a class that spoke English. Rabbi Wein notes, "They were surprised when Rabbi Kaplan marched in with a copy of the daily newspaper, the *Chicago Tribune*. He opened the paper and told the boys, 'Today you are going to teach me English and I am going to teach you how to read the newspaper'... At the conclusion of each piece, Rabbi Kaplan would interpret the events from a Jewish point of view."[13]

When discusssing *Gedolim* who read secular papers, though, it is important to note that the value of reading the news would not have superseded the caution they took regarding the halachos of gazing at or reading inappropriate material.

Finally, Rabbi Joseph B. Soloveitchik once said that if it was up to him, there would be a fourteenth principle of faith: that whatever is

10   Joseph Telushkin, *Rebbe: The Life and Teachings of Menachem M. Schneerson, the Most Influential Rabbi in Modern History* (Harper Wave, 2014), p. 165.

11   *Osef Michtavim* §71. Quoted in *Yated Ne'eman*, Feb. 24, 2017, p. 14.

12   Rabbi Shimon Finkelman, *Rav Chaim Ozer: The Life and Ideals of Rabbi Chaim Ozer Grodzenski of Vilna* (ArtScroll/Mesorah, 2010), p. 164.

13   James David Weiss, *Vintage Wein: The Collected Wit and Wisdom, the Choicest Anecdotes and Vignettes of Rabbi Berel Wein* (Shaar Press, 1992), pp. 140–41.

written in the Torah applies to all generations and is relevant to everyone. Viewing current events through a Torah lens is one way of making Torah relevant to everyone.

A TREE OF FORTY FRUITS

IN THE NEWS

In 2014, the *Huffington Post* published a fascinating article about an American artist who runs a project called "Tree of Forty Fruit."[1] The artist, Sam Van Aken, grows trees that can yield forty types of stone fruit, including peaches, plums, nectarines, and almonds.

He begins by grafting a few different types of fruit-bearing trees onto the root system of a single tree. He allows this "working tree" to grow for two years, then adds additional fruit-tree branches to the limbs of the working tree. He calls this "chip grafting": he places branches with buds into cuts in the original tree and tapes the new branches in place.

Van Aken's method, as of the time the article was written, has produced sixteen such trees, with each tree taking five years to mature.

Is it permissible to create a tree that produces forty different types of fruit? Is one allowed to own such a tree and eat the fruit from it?

A TORAH PERSPECTIVE

Generally, land-based mitzvos apply only in Eretz Yisrael,[2] yet the Gemara says that *kilayim*, the prohibition of grafting, applies outside Eretz Yisrael as well.[3]

---

1   Katherine Brooks, "This One Tree Grows 40 Different Types Of Fruit, Is Probably From The Future" (July 24, 2014), www.huffingtonpost.com. This project has its own website too: www.treeof40fruit.com.

2   *Kiddushin* 36b.

3   Ibid. 37a; *Shulchan Aruch, Yoreh Dei'ah* 295:1; *Rambam, Hilchos Kilayim* 1:5.

In terms of what this involves, the Mishnah says that it is prohibited to graft together two different species of trees,[4] two different species of vegetables, or a combination of a tree and a vegetable.[5] The *Shulchan Aruch* rules that this applies not only when different trees and plants are merged together, but even when the roots of a vegetable are merged with the branch of a tree.[6]

The Torah also prohibits planting different types of vegetable seeds together—what is called *kilei zera'im*.[7] This prohibition is derived from the *pasuk*: "You shall not sow your field with a mixture of seeds."[8] The *Shulchan Aruch* maintains, however, that this prohibition only applies in Eretz Yisrael and that one may plant different types of vegetable seeds in close proximity to each other outside the land.[9]

The Torah also prohibits planting different types of vegetable seeds in a vineyard.[10] Although, Biblically speaking, this prohibition does not apply outside Eretz Yisrael, it is nevertheless prohibited by the rabbis.[11] The *Rambam* states that this prohibition is only violated outside Eretz Yisrael when the seeds of two species of grains or vegetables are planted together with grape seeds in the same hole.[12] It is important to note that while it is prohibited to eat or derive any benefit from mixtures

---

4   The Gemara in *Kiddushin* 39a says that it is Biblically prohibited to graft different fruit trees together based on a *pasuk* in *parashas Kedoshim* (*Vayikra* 19:19). See also *Chazon Ish* (*Hilchos Kilayim* 3:7), where he discusses whether all citrus fruits are considered separate species with regard to the *issur* of *kilayim*.

5   *Kilayim* 1:7.

6   See *Shulchan Aruch, Yoreh Dei'ah* 295:4. It was common practice to bend a tree branch to the ground so that it would merge with a vegetable plant. The *Shulchan Aruch* (*Yoreh Dei'ah* 295:5) there notes that this is not practical with regard to tree branches, which are hard and won't be penetrated by vegetable roots. It's different, however, with grapevines; vines are soft, and if the vine branches are buried less than a foot underground, planting another species on top of them would pose a problem.

7   *Shulchan Aruch, Yoreh Dei'ah* 296:1. See *Rambam* (*Hilchos Kilayim* 3:7 and 3:10) and *Chazon Ish* (*Hilchos Kilayim* 6:1) for how much space between different types of seeds is required when planting.

8   *Vayikra* 19:19; see *Kiddushin* 39a.

9   *Shulchan Aruch, Yoreh Dei'ah* 297:2.

10   *Devarim* 22:9.

11   *Kiddushin* 39a; *Shulchan Aruch, Yoreh Dei'ah* 296:1.

12   *Hilchos Kilayim* 8:13.

of grape seeds and other types of seeds,[13] this is not the case with seed mixtures that don't involve grapes.[14]

As for grafting two different species of trees, the *Rambam* rules that not only is this prohibited for Jews, it is also prohibited for a Jew to allow a non-Jew to graft onto his tree.[15] The *Derech Emunah*,[16] Rav Chaim Kanievsky's commentary to the section of *Zera'im* in *Rambam's Mishneh Torah*, explains that this fits with another statement of the *Rambam*, where he rules that non-Jews are also prohibited from grafting trees onto each other.[17]

The *Derech Emunah* notes, however, that even according to the *Rambam*, one would not be required to stop a non-Jew from grafting trees. He also notes that most Rishonim say that non-Jews are not prohibited from grafting trees.[18] The reason it is prohibited to allow a non-Jew to graft onto a Jew's tree, he continues, is because of the Rabbinic prohibition of *amirah lenochri*.[19]

Although they maintain it's prohibited to graft trees in the first place, both the *Rambam* and *Shulchan Aruch* rule that one may cut off a shoot from a grafted tree and plant it elsewhere.[20] However, Rabbi Yirmiyohu Kaganoff[21] cites that many *poskim*[22] prohibit owning a tree that was grafted, similar to the prohibition of owning *kilayim* in a vineyard.[23] The

---

13   *Chullin* 115a; *Shulchan Aruch, Yoreh Dei'ah* 296:3.

14   *Chullin* ibid.

15   *Hilchos Kilayim* 1:6. See also the OU Kosher Halacha newsletter, which rules like the *Rambam* on this matter ("Can I plant a fruit tree that I purchased from a nursery that was grafted onto the rootstock of another species?," Halacha Yomis, www.oukosher.org).

16   *Derech Emunah* on *Rambam, Hilchos Kilayim* 1:6.

17   *Hilchos Melachim* 10:6, based on the opinion of Rav Elazar in *Sanhedrin* 56b, 60a.

18   *Tosafos, Ritva, Rosh, Tur,* and *Ran,* to name a few. Similarly, the *Shach, Yoreh Dei'ah* 297:3, rules that non-Jews themselves are not prohibited from grafting trees. The *Shach* is based on the opinion of the Sages (*Sanhedrin* 56b). The *Shach* also believes that this is the opinion of the *Rambam* in *Hilchos Melachim,* ch. 9.

19   If an action is prohibited for a Jew to do himself, he may not ask a non-Jew to do it for him.

20   *Rambam, Hilchos Kilayim* 1:7; *Shulchan Aruch, Yoreh Dei'ah* 295:7.

21   Rabbi Yirmiyohu Kaganoff, "May a Non-Jew Own a Nectarine Tree? For That Matter, May a Jew?" (April 10, 2010), www.rabbikaganoff.com.

22   See, for example, *Pischei Teshuvah, Yoreh Dei'ah* 295:2, 295:4; *Rosh, Hilchos Kilayim,* chs. 1 and 3.

23   *Rambam, Hilchos Kilayim* 1:2, 1:3, 5:8; *Shulchan Aruch, Yoreh Dei'ah* 297:2.

Aruch Hashulchan, however, defends the practice of observant Jews who purchase properties with grafted trees.[24]

What about reciting the *berachah* of *Shehecheyanu* on a new fruit that came from a tree of *kilayim*? Rav Moshe Feinstein was uncertain whether it was proper to recite this blessing over such a fruit, since the blessing speaks of our happiness over having this fruit, and the fruit is the product of a prohibition.[25] However, Rav Hershel Schachter rules that if one is uncertain if the fruit was grown through violating *kilayim*, one may recite the *berachah* over it.[26]

SUMMARY

It would be Biblically prohibited to create a forty-fruit tree, which involves grafting different fruit trees together. While there is a dispute over whether one could own such a tree, one would be permitted to cut a branch or shoot from the tree and grow it elsewhere. One would also be permitted to eat fruit from the grafted tree, assuming there were no grapevines mixed in it.[27]

Regarding the reason the Torah prohibits crossbreeding in the first place, Rabbi Joseph B. Soloveitchik offered this beautiful explanation:

> *Each species of animals, fruit, or vegetables expresses itself in its own distinctive form. When man grafts two fruits together,*

---

24 *Aruch Hashulchan, Yoreh Dei'ah* 295:17–18. There, the *Aruch Hashulchan* cites the Gemara in *Kiddushin* (39a) and says that the prohibition of grafting trees is derived from the prohibition of crossbreeding animals. Just as there is no prohibition of owning animals that have been crossbred, there is no prohibition of owning trees that have been grafted. The *Aruch Hashulchan* also says this leniency explains the position of the *Shulchan Aruch* that permits taking a shoot or branch from a grafted tree and replanting it elsewhere. If there were a prohibition against owning a grafted tree, it should be prohibited to take a branch from a grafted tree as well. The *Betzeil Hachochmah* (vol. 5, §13), however, says one should be stringent and not own grafted trees.

25 *Igros Moshe, Orach Chaim*, vol. 2, §58. See *Yabia Omer, Orach Chaim*, vol. 5, §19.

26 OU Kosher Halacha Yomis newsletter, ad loc.

27 However, there is also the prohibition of *orlah* (benefiting from the fruit of a tree in its first three years) to take into account, which applies outside Israel as well (*Kiddushin* 36b). The prohibition of *orlah* applies even if one uprooted an entire tree and replanted it elsewhere (*Shulchan Aruch, Yoreh Dei'ah* 294:16). However, if the tree was uprooted with enough dirt that it could have survived without being replanted, then one does not restart counting the *orlah* years (ibid. 294:19).

the product takes on a different synthetic form, which does not express the characteristics of either form, but some of each. In grafting, man confuses the characteristics and appearances that Hashem implanted in each fruit at the time of Maaseh Bereishit (Creation). One who transgresses the prohibition of kilayim is actually confusing boundaries... [28]

The Rav added that the prohibition of *kilayim* also teaches that there are boundaries for all of us as well. Every individual has skills and abilities that are different from those of everyone else. [29] We must focus on our own unique capabilities in order to maximize our potential in this world rather than trying to imitate others. [30]

28   Aharon Ziegler, *Halakhic Positions of Rabbi Joseph B. Soloveitchik*, vol. 6 (Ktav, 2013), pp. 108–9.

29   Ibid.

30   For more great articles on the topic of *kilayim*, see *Living the Halachic Process*, vol. 2, pp. 193–95, 283–85.

BEWARE OF DOG

IN THE NEWS

An employee of CenterPoint Energy, a gas and utility company, entered the Willcox family's backyard in Houston, Texas, to disconnect their gas meter for not paying their bill. Also present in the Willcoxes' backyard were their two dogs, Flash and Shutter. When the technician saw the dogs, he went after them with his large metal pipe wrench, wounding both animals.

The dogs' owner, Mike Willcox, said about his pair of canines, "[They've] never bitten anybody [and are] very friendly. It was like the guy was swinging to kill." He said that his four-year-old son, who witnessed the entire incident from close range, now "thinks there are monsters in the backyard." Willcox demanded reimbursement for the resulting veterinary bills, which amounted to $2,000.

The technician, whose name was not released, claimed, "If they come at me, I can swing if I want." When asked about why he did not use the front door to enter the property, he responded, "I don't have to do that."[1]

The *Washington Post* noted that the utility company's workers have, in fact, been accused of similar incidents in the past. A family from Houston reported that in 2007, a CenterPoint Energy worker set foot in their backyard and attacked their dog despite their "No Trespassing" and "Beware of Dog" signs.

A spokesman for the Houston Police Department said that "in the state of Texas, if someone is employed by a utilities company...[and attempts]

---

1   Peter Holley, "'The guy was swinging to kill': Contractor caught on camera attacking dogs with pipe wrench" (April 12, 2016), www.washingtonpost.com.

to disconnect or repair a meter, [the employee is] basically there to conduct work. Per state law, they're in the right to defend themselves."[2]

In March of 2017, Yeshiva World News reported that an Arab terrorist broke into a Jewish community located in the southern Chevron Hills and tried to stab Shabtai Kushlavski in his home. The Kushlavski's dog jumped at the terrorist, giving Shabtai the chance to get his gun and fire at Ali Kaysia, killing him. Yekutiel Ben Yaakov, director of the Israel Dog Unit, said, "We continue to urge Jews to arm themselves with dogs, which have proven to be the most effective biological weapon. The proper use of dogs can save many Jewish lives."[3]

If a trespasser defends himself against the homeowner's pets, is the trespasser responsible for damages inflicted on the pet? Is a homeowner responsible for injuries that his pet causes to a trespasser? And, on a very basic level, is it permissible to own a guard dog?

A TORAH PERSPECTIVE

The Gemara says that if a person enters someone's property without permission and the homeowner's animal kills the trespasser, the animal is put to death,[4] but the homeowner is exempt from paying the required compensation—called *kofer*, or "ransom"[5]—since the trespasser had no right to be on the property.[6] The *Shulchan Aruch* codifies this as the halachah.[7]

The Gemara also discusses the case of a worker entering his employer's property to collect his wages and being killed by the homeowner's

---

2   Ibid.

3   "Sofie The Dog Stops Blood-Thirsty Terrorist in Mor Farm" (March 2, 2017), www.theyeshivaworld.com.

4   *Bava Kama* 23b.

5   See *Shemos* 21:28–30, where the Torah mentions that in certain cases, if an animal killed someone, the animal is put to death and the owner must pay a "*kofer*," a ransom, as a penalty. There is a dispute in the *Gemara* (*Bava Kama* 27a) about whether the *kofer* refers to the value of the deceased victim or the value of the owner of the ox.

6   See *Daf Al Daf, Bava Kama* 23b, for a discussion of whether the homeowner is *chayav misah biydei Shamayim*—whether he deserves to die at the hands of Heaven—for the person's death on his property. The conclusion there is that he is not *chayav*, as the Torah exempts the homeowner not only from paying damages to the trespasser (or, if he is dead, to his heirs), but also from the obligation of watching his animal.

7   *Choshen Mishpat* 389:10.

animal.[8] Is the homeowner exempt from paying the *kofer* payment in such a case? The *Rambam* rules that even workers do not have permission to enter their employer's property without permission to collect their wages, and therefore the employer is innocent.[9] The *Shulchan Aruch* seems to follow the *Rambam's* opinion.[10]

The *Rema*, however, states that workers who come to collect their wages are not considered trespassers and that the employer would be responsible for preventing his animal from harming his employee. Therefore, according to the *Rema*, an employer must pay for injuries caused by his animals to any of his workers.[11]

The *Rema's* opinion is based on the ruling of the *Rosh*,[12] who says that in the times of the Gemara it was uncommon for people to enter another person's property uninvited, so workers would seek their wages in the marketplace. However, in the times of the *Rosh*, circumstances had changed, and it became common for workers to enter another person's property to collect their wages. Therefore, records the *Rema*, the employer is guilty and obligated to pay for the injury caused by his animal.[13]

It would seem, then, that according to the *Rambam* and *Shulchan Aruch*, if a worker enters someone's property without permission and is injured by the homeowner's dog, the homeowner would be exempt from paying damages. However, according to the *Rema*, perhaps the homeowner would be obligated to pay for injuries inflicted by his dog, since it may now be common for workers to enter the homeowner's property to do routine work on his property. This is especially true in the news story above where the worker had permission from the state to enter the premises.

8   *Bava Kama* 33a.
9   *Hilchos Nizkei Mammon* 10:11. See *Maggid Mishnah* there.
10   *Choshen Mishpat* 389:10.
11   *Rema, Choshen Mishpat* 389:10.
12   *Bava Kama*, ch. 3, §12, cited by the *S'ma, Choshen Mishpat* 389:10.
13   The *Yam Shel Shlomo, Bava Kama* 3:25, argues with the *Rosh* and writes that only explicit permission granted by the homeowner is considered permission (see *Taz, Choshen Mishpat* 389, and *Pischei Choshen*, vol. 6, 5:12).

However, what if someone entered another's property without permission and injured the guard dog while defending himself from attack? Is the trespasser responsible to pay for damages he inflicted on the dog, since he entered the property without permission? The *S'ma* records a debate on the matter: according to the *Rambam* he would be obligated to pay, but according to the *Tur* he would be exempt.[14]

Nevertheless, if the person had permission to be in the yard—as in the example of the utility worker in the opening story, who was permitted by law to enter the property to disconnect the gas meter without the explicit consent of the homeowner—then he would be exempt from paying any damages he caused to the homeowner's dog in defending himself from attack.[15]

People generally assume that it's acceptable to own a guard dog, but let's examine this from the Torah's perspective. Rav Yitzchak Zilberstein[16] cites the Gemara, which says that one should not own a dangerous dog.[17] The Gemara derives this from the *pasuk*, "You shall not place blood in your house."[18]

The *Maharsha* remarks that the concern of having a dangerous dog on one's property is not that it will injure one's own family. It is presumed that the dog is accustomed to the family and that the purpose of having it is to prevent robbers from coming into one's home at night. Nevertheless, the Torah still tells us that one should not have such a dog on one's property.[19]

---

14   *Choshen Mishpat* 383:3.

15   Email response from the Business Halacha Institute. Obviously, he is only exempt from paying for damage inflicted on the dog if it was necessary to protect himself, not if he went out of his way to harm the dog.

16   *Chashukei Chemed, Bava Kama*, p. 399.

17   *Bava Kama* 15b.

18   *Devarim* 22:8.

19   *Chiddushei Aggados, Bava Kama* 15b. The *Maharsha* (on *Shabbos* 63a) even prohibits owning a harmless dog, since not everyone will realize that it is not dangerous and poor people will avoid coming near the home. The *Ha'Ohr Hayashar* (*Yalkut Biurim* , *Shabbos* 63, p. 104) also prohibits owning a dog, even if it is tied up, since he believes that this, too, will discourage poor people from coming to one's home. The *Avos Harosh* (*Avos D'Rabbi Nassan*, ch. 7) similarly says that one should not have any type of guard dog—dangerous or not—based on the Mishnah in *Avos* (1:5) that says one's home should be open to poor people, and having any type of dog would discourage them from coming.

Rav Zilberstein explains that the *Maharsha* is not prohibiting own-ing a dangerous dog so that robbers don't get injured. The concern is that the dog will harm poor people or anyone else who comes to the house, all of whom are permitted to be there, because the dog does not recognize them.[20] Therefore, according to the *Maharsha*, one would not be permitted to own a dangerous dog in order to protect oneself from robbers.

The *Shulchan Aruch* rules that it is only forbidden to have a danger-ous dog on one's property if it is not restrained,[21] and the *Rema* rules like the *Shulchan Aruch* in this regard.[22] Additionally, the *S'ma* rules that if the dog is vicious, even though there is no concern that it might bite people, it still needs to be tied up if it will bark and frighten them.[23]

On the other hand, the *Shulchan Aruch* rules[24] that in a Jewish city

---

20   Rav Zilberstein finds further support from the *Talmud Yerushalmi*. The *Yerushalmi* (*Terumos* 8:3, as explained by the *P'nei Moshe*) relates that a person once invited a rabbi to eat at his house, and when the rabbi sat down at the table, the host seated his dog next to the rabbi. The rabbi responded in shock, "Did you invite me here to disgrace me?" The host responded that this was not at all his intention. Rather, he was trying to honor the dog. There had been a group of kidnappers who had recently come to the city, and when one of them tried to snatch his own wife, his dog protected her by severely injuring the would-be abductor. Thus, Rav Zilberstein notes that we should be careful with owning dogs. He maintains that had the case involved a friend of the host, unfamiliar to the dog, rather than a kidnapper, the dog would have likewise injured him; since it is a dog and doesn't know the difference between dangerous and safe people. One could argue on this point by Rav Zilberstein, though, that the dog only attacked the abductor in response to him abducting its master's wife, whom it was trying to protect.

21   *Shulchan Aruch, Choshen Mishpat* 409:3.

22   *Rema*, ibid.

23   *S'ma, Choshen Mishpat* 409:5. The *Rambam* (*Hilchos Nizkei Mammon* 5:9) prohibits owning any type of dog, dangerous or not, unless it is tied up. The *Chazon Yechezkel* (*Bava Kama* 8:5) explains the logic of the *Rambam*. According to the *Rambam*, it is Biblically prohibited to own a dangerous dog, based on the Gemara in *Bava Kama* 15b. It is also prohibited to own a harmless dog, such as one whose teeth have been removed, since people may not realize that it lacks teeth and will be scared nonetheless, which could have disastrous results (see *Shabbos* 63b). Rav Yaakov Emden (*She'eilas Yaavetz*, vol. 1, §17) explains that most *poskim* don't differentiate between dangerous or not, and prohibit owning any dog, since all types of dogs are really dan-gerous. The *Yerei'im* (§210), however, clearly states that it is only prohibited to own a dangerous dog, and the *Tur* (*Choshen Mishpat* 89:3) and the *Tosafos Yom Tov* (*Bava Kama* 7:6) agree. The *Hagahos Maimoniyos* (*Hilchos Rotzei'ach* 11:4) explicitly permits a harmless dog as well. Rav Yaakov Emden, though, says that even according to the *Yerei'im*, it is only permitted to own one dog at a time, based on the Gemara in *Bava Kama* 80a (cited in *Yalkut Biurim, Shabbos*, p. 104).

24   *Choshen Mishpat* 409:3.

that borders a non-Jewish city, it is permitted to have a dangerous dog since it is needed for protection.[25] Based on this ruling, Rav Shlomo Aviner, the Rosh Yeshivah of Yeshivat Ateret Kohanim, rules that it is permissible to have a guard dog to protect one's home.[26] However, Rav Aviner cautions, one must ensure it neither frightens people nor disturbs them at night. It should also be kept tied up and only be untied at night, when providing protection.[27]

Rav Menashe Klein, the Ungvarer Rav, discusses the plausibility of owning a dangerous dog without restraining it if one posts a sign warning people about it.[28] Rav Klein concludes that it would still be prohibited.[29] His proof is that the Gemara says a person could be excommunicated for having a dangerous, unrestrained dog until he removes the dangerous dog from his property,[30] implying that the only option is removal, and nothing else—not even a warning sign—would help.[31]

---

25 See *Aleinu Leshabei'ach* (*Shemos*, pp. 187–88) for a story about a guard dog in Eretz Yisrael that stopped a donkey from entering a Jewish community, and upon examination the donkey was found to be loaded with explosives.

26 *On the Air with Rav Aviner* (J Levine/Millennium, 2009), pp. 187–88.

27 Rabbi Avrohom Ehrman, *The Laws of Interpersonal Relationships: Practical Applications in Business, Home and Society* (ArtScroll/Mesorah, 2002), p. 331, based on *Shulchan Aruch, Choshen Mishpat* 409:3.

28 *Mishneh Halachos*, vol. 5, §297. The *Rambam* (*Hilchos Nizkei Mammon* 5:9) and *Shulchan Aruch* (*Choshen Mishpat* 409:3) permit owning a dog only if it is chained up, based on the Gemara in *Bava Kama* 83a. On a related topic, the following question was posed to Rav Asher Weiss on the Tvunah website ("Setting Trap to Kill an Intruder," http://en.tvunah.org): "When leaving one's home for a long time, is one allowed, according to Halacha, to put a trap in his safe where he keeps his money, potentially killing or maiming the intruder?" Rav Weiss wrote a response in Hebrew; this is the abbreviated English version: "One can put protective measures around his house and property to keep away and even scare intruders, such as a watchdog. This way, one is warned to stay away, and if he enters, he is hurting himself. This is similar to a minefield placed at the border with warning signs telling people of the danger. However, one cannot put a death trap in a place that will cause a common thief to be killed, because he is unaware of the danger at hand." Rav Moshe Feinstein permitted leaving traps to catch thieves, provided that a warning sign was posted outside the house (*Reshumei Aharon*, vol. 1, p. 91).

29 However, Rav Klein says that placing a warning sign would be a sufficient precaution for other dangerous objects one might have in his home, such as a fuse box or poisons.

30 *Bava Kama* 15b.

31 This conclusion seems to be supported by the *Rambam* in *Hilchos Rotzei'ach* 11:4, as pointed out in *Peninei Halachah, Bava Kama*, vol. 1, p. 13.

The Gemara states that one reason it is prohibited to own a dangerous dog is because it is tantamount to throwing away one's fear of Hashem.[32] The *Ben Yehoyada* explains that the Gemara means one shouldn't own a guard dog, as that will lead him to be dependent on it for security, instead of relying on Hashem for protection.

Although this idea is not binding according to halachah, as there are permissible ways to own even a dangerous dog for protection (such as keeping it restrained), one should remember this point about fear of Heaven when considering purchasing a guard dog or any other means of protection.

One final question on the subject of guard dogs: Is it permitted to have a "Beware of Dog" sign if one does not actually own a dog?

Rav Zilberstein was once asked this very question.[33] A man wanted to know if it was permitted for him to have a sign with a picture of a ferocious-looking dog that read, "Warning: Dogs on Property Will Bite," though he did not really own a dog.

Rav Zilberstein responded that the *Rambam* says a person should not say one thing outwardly and really believe something else in his heart,[34] and therefore, it is always prohibited to mislead people. Furthermore, the *Tosefta* says there are seven types of thieves—the first being one who misleads others.[35]

However, Rav Zilberstein didn't think this case is a violation of misleading people. The examples brought by Chazal of misleading people are where one person pretends to be interested in helping or befriending another when he knows that the would-be recipient is unable to accept his kindness; he's just acting as a friend so that he can take advantage of the recipient's good nature and interest in repaying the kind overture. However, in our case, the person posting the "Beware of Dog" sign is not interested in benefiting from another's kindness; his only interest is in preventing any damage from potential robbers.[36]

---

32   *Shabbos* 63a, as explained by the *Ben Yehoyada*, cited in the *Mesivta* edition of *Shas*.
33   See *Upiryo Matok, parashas Kedoshim*, p. 315.
34   *Hilchos Dei'os* 2:6.
35   *Tosefta, Bava Kama* 7:3.
36   At first glance, Rav Zilberstein's explanation seems difficult to comprehend, since there

Furthermore, Rav Zilberstein maintained that posting such a sign doesn't seem to be a violation of the prohibition of lying either. This is based on the Gemara in *Yevamos* that states that if one finds a container that says its contents are *terumah*, one can assume that the food is *chullin* (i.e., not *terumah*). This is because we assume the owner wrote "*terumah*" only so that people who are not permitted to eat *terumah* would stay away from his food, thinking it was forbidden to them.[37] Thus, the Gemara indicates that to protect one's property, he does not have to be concerned about lying.

Additionally, there was a recent incident in Israel where someone wanted to send his parents in America a package of matzah. The individual was concerned that the couriers would break the matzah, so he wrote on the package, "Fragile: Glass." When Rav Yosef Shalom Elyashiv, *zt"l*, was asked if it was acceptable to write this, he responded that it was indeed permissible.[38]

Rav Zilberstein concluded that although it is permitted to hang a "Beware of Dog" sign when one doesn't have a dog, the best thing to do is hang a sign that states, "Dog That Bites," without stating explicitly that there is one on the premises.

SUMMARY

A homeowner is exempt from paying damages to a trespasser injured by his pet. It is a matter of dispute whether a worker seeking payment is considered a trespasser or not. It is also a matter of dispute whether a trespasser who injured a pet while defending himself is

---

are other examples given by Chazal of the prohibition of misleading people that are more similar to putting up the "Beware of Dog" sign. The *Shulchan Aruch* (*Choshen Mishpat* 228:6), for example, includes the case of misleading people by selling merchandise that is damaged without notifying the buyer of the damage. Based on these similar examples, it would seem that it is forbidden to put up the "Beware of Dog" sign. However, it appears that Rav Zilberstein means that the examples that Chazal give for the prohibition of misleading people are all where one is seeking to take advantage of another person, but in the case of the "Beware of Dog" sign, one is merely seeking to protect himself from others.

37   *Yevamos* 115b. Only *Kohanim* are permitted to eat *terumah*.

38   *Upiryo Matok*, *parashas Kedoshim*, p. 315. See *Teshuvos Vehanhagos* (2:523), where Rav Moshe Sternbuch rules that when flying with a *Sefer Torah*, it is permitted to write on the bag "Fragile" so that the airline handles the *Sefer Torah* carefully.

liable or not. It seems that a worker who is permitted by law to enter another person's property is not considered a trespasser. Additionally, according to the *Maharsha*, it is prohibited to own a guard dog in the first place. However, if the dog is restrained or only unrestrained at night, the *poskim* permit it.

CHASSID GOES UNDERCOVER

IN THE NEWS

The illicit drug market is nothing novel, but fighting it requires some out-of-the-box thinking. That is what led the Ramle-Lod police department to appoint a Chassid as an undercover agent to snag drug dealers.

Shlomo Treitel, a Sanzer Chassid and *kollel yungerman* from Netanya, was chosen to be the man. When he wasn't learning in *kollel*, he served as a community police officer, making him the right man for the job. But before taking on this mission, he approached his Rebbe, Rav Tzvi Elimelech Halberstam, for approval. The Rebbe met with the police chiefs to learn more about the operation and then blessed them with success. As Treitel remarked, his Rebbe said that "drugs are a problem for the whole of society and that it was an important task to take on."[1] That is how Operation Ketoret Hasamim was launched.

The long and short of the story is that Treitel played his role as a small-time drug dealer and purchased hard and soft drugs "for his students in yeshivah," as his story went, sometimes wearing recording devices under his Chassidic garb. After thirty meetings with the drug dealers and spending $14,000, he succeeded in implicating fifteen of them, leading to their arrests and putting them behind bars.

Let's try to understand the rationale behind the Sanzer Rebbe's ruling: Is one allowed to misrepresent himself this way to catch a

---

1   Yair Alpert, "Sanzer Chossid Goes Undercover To Aid Drug Sting" (Aug. 13, 2009), www.matzav.com.

crook—do the ends justify the means? In addition, was it permitted for the Chassid to act as an undercover agent, thereby endangering his life, in order to catch the drug dealers for the police?

A TORAH PERSPECTIVE

In order to analyze the case above, let's look at Rav Yitzchak Zilberstein's ruling on a similar incident. Another Chareidi Jew was asked by the police to serve as their undercover agent, in a Tel Aviv suburb, to catch drug dealers operating in the area. The police provided him with a large supply of money to impress the drug dealers, and when they were all gathered in one room, the undercover agent was to press a button signaling the police to enter and bust the drug dealers. A religious Jew was chosen because he was less likely to be suspected of having any connection to the police.

The religious Jew acquiesced to the police's request, and the sting operation was a success, catching many of the drug dealers. Afterward, the man asked Rav Zilberstein if what he did was permitted, since, after all, he was being dishonest by presenting himself as a drug dealer. Rav Zilberstein answered that there was no problem at all of dishonesty. On the contrary, he explained, what the agent did was a big mitzvah, since he was preventing the drug dealers from harming the community.[2]

Rav Zilberstein brought halachic support for such behavior from *Sefer Melachim*,[3] where the story of King Yeihu is told. In the beginning, he was a very righteous king who wanted to eliminate all of the worshippers of the idol Baal. King Yeihu remarked, "Achav worshipped Baal a little; Yeihu will worship him much more." He said this in order to pretend he was an idol worshipper himself, thus tricking the worshippers of Baal to gather together to support him, whereupon he would be able to kill them all. Although he was deceiving them, Hashem praised him for what he did. Therefore, concludes Rav Zilberstein, what this undercover agent did in order to catch the drug dealers was also permissible.

---

2   See *Chashukei Chemed*, Sanhedrin 102a. See also *Aleinu Leshabei'ach, Parshas Vayishlach*, p. 435, for slightly different details of the story.

3   *Melachim II* 10:18.

However, a statement from the Gemara tells us that this issue is not so clear-cut. The Gemara asks what caused Yeihu to eventually veer from the Torah later in his life, as the *pasuk* says, "Yeihu did not follow the ways of Hashem,"[4] referring to the fact that he permitted the worship of the golden calves previously established by Yaravam. Abaye answers that it was because *"b'ris kerusah lisfasayim*—a covenant was made with the lips."[5] In other words, since Yeihu had said that he would worship Baal, even though he was not sincere and only said it for the sake of Hashem, his own words had an effect on himself and ultimately caused him to sin against Hashem.[6] Thus, according to Abaye, an undercover

---

4   *Melachim II* 10:31.

5   *Sanhedrin* 102a.

6   The Gemara in *Mo'ed Katan* 18a says the source for this is Avraham at *Har Hamoriah*, when he was on his way to perform *Akeidas Yitzchak*. He said to his attendants, "Stay here with the donkey, and the lad and I will go there and bow down, and [then] we will return to you" (*Bereishis* 22:5). Avraham's words were effective, and both he and Yitzchak returned from the *Akeidah*. This constituted a "covenant made with the lips"; he said he would return and he did.

The *Ben Yehoyada* (cited in *Mesivta Shas, Bava Kama* 30, *Yalkut Biurim*, p. 167) writes that when the Gemara in *Bava Kama* mentions the importance of *milei d'nizikin* (literally, "matters of damages"), it refers to the idea that what we say (*milei* can also mean "words"), even unintentionally, can cause damage, based on this principle of *b'ris kerusah lisfasayim*.

The *sefer Kav Hayashar* (ch. 1, cited by Rav Gershon Eisenberger in *Otzar Hayedios*, p. 448) records the story of a woman who was sitting with her friends discussing how they would all have to give an accounting for everything they had done in their lifetimes. This woman joked that when she faced her ultimate judgment, she would pretend to be a mute who can't answer when asked. Shortly thereafter, this woman, in fact, became a mute and remained that way until the day she died.

Similarly, Rav Yitzchak Zilberstein tells the following story: "When the city of Petach Tikva was founded, a young *bachur* was present when the city's founders were planning the local cemetery, and he said jokingly, 'I don't mind being the first person in the settlement to die.' He died that same week and was the first person buried in the Petach Tikva cemetery. This story is actually inscribed on his tombstone" (*Aleinu Leshabei'ach, parashas Mattos*, p. 504). See also *Aleinu Leshabei'ach, parashas Ki Savo*, p. 367.

Finally, the Netziv (*Haamek Davar, Bereishis* 44:15) notes that Yosef remarked to his brothers, "Don't you know that a man like me practices divination?" instead of directly stating, "I practice divination," because this practice is prohibited. He therefore implied it and let the brothers assume that was how he knew they took his goblet.

The Netziv explains that Yosef was concerned about the impact his words would have on himself, even though he didn't mean them seriously. Our words can also have an effect on others, as the *Sefer Hachinuch* (§231) points out—see the chapter entitled "Kareem and the Power of a Curse" below. See also *Or Hachaim* (*Bereishis* 46:4), where he explains that even

agent should be careful with the statements he makes, or they might have a negative effect on him in the future.[7]

Rava, however, disagrees with Abaye, and says that Yeihu eventually sinned not because his words caused him to do so, but rather because he mistakenly thought that a prophet had approved of what Yaravam instituted.

The *Chida* says that Rava agrees with Abaye's principle that what one says has an effect on the person. However, that is only when it is said sincerely—when what he says is what he truly believes and not when he is only trying to fool people.[8] Therefore, concludes Rav Zilberstein, in the cases of Yeihu and the undercover agent, where they made disingenuous statements, they did not have to worry about their words having a negative effect in the future.[9]

---

though Yaakov Avinu mentioned a number of times that Yosef was dead, Yosef tells him not to be concerned that it would have an effect on him and cause him to die prematurely. The *Or Hachaim* points out that generally one should be concerned about such statements, based on the *pasuk*, "Like an error that came forth from the ruler" (*Koheles* 10:5), similar to the concept of *b'ris kerusah lisfasayim*.

For many more examples of *b'ris kerusah lisfasayim*, see *Upiryo Matok, parashas Shemos*, pp. 344–47. See also *Maharsha, Berachos* 19a, regarding the difference between the above-cited concept and the concept of *"al tiftach peh laSatan*—do not open your mouth to the Satan." See also *Nazir* 57b.

7   Rav Nachman of Breslov says that we should take Abaye's opinion seriously. He cites the Gemara and says, "Don't let a word of wickedness leave your lips. Do not say that you will commit a sin or do something wicked, even though you may not be serious and you may have no intention of carrying out your words. The words themselves can do great damage and later compel you to fulfill them, even if they were uttered as a joke" (*Sichos Haran* §237, cited by Rabbi Aryeh Kaplan in *The Light Beyond: Adventures in Hassidic Thought* [Moznaim, 1981], p. 302). Rav Shlomo Zalman Auerbach did not allow a religious man to act undercover in Arab countries as part of an espionage mission, out of fear that assassinations he would carry out would have a detrimental effect on his religious life after the missions were over (Rabbi Hanoch Teller, *And from Jerusalem, His Word* [New York City Publishing, 1990], pp. 141–43).

8   The *Chiddushei Halev* (*parashas Shelach*, pp. 90–91) says in the name of Rav Avraham Trop that Kalev is praised for not letting his speech, which at first seemed to be in agreement with the *meraglim* (spies), affect what he really believed in his heart. Kalev said things that made it seem like he agreed with the *meraglim* so that the people would listen to him, but in truth he rejected their beliefs and didn't let what he said affect him.

9   For a similar statement made by Rava, see *Nedarim* 62b, where he says that a Torah scholar is permitted to lie and say he is the servant of the priests of fire worship in order to avoid paying a certain tax. The commentaries explain that it is permissible to make such a declaration,

While the undercover Orthodox Jews were permitted to engage in such activities and make statements that a Jew would not usually make,[10] under normal circumstances we must be extremely careful about what we say and keeping our word, as stated explicitly in the *Rambam*.[11]

Also, Rav Gedalia Schorr[12] cites the midrash which says that when Yaakov was on his way to receive the *berachos* from his father Yitzchak, Yaakov prayed that he should be saved from uttering a falsehood. Even though Yaakov needed to use trickery in order for his father to bless him, he still prayed that the apparent dishonesty shouldn't become second nature to him. Therefore, even when one is lying in order to catch drug dealers, perhaps he should issue a prayer beforehand that the lying doesn't desensitize him.

Another issue with working undercover is the possible danger involved. The Torah commands us to avoid hazardous situations.[13] Rav Zilberstein, though, didn't mention this as a concern. Perhaps this is because the level of danger in the case was minimal, and Rav Moshe Feinstein maintains that a person is permitted to be involved in a profession that carries a minimal amount of risk.[14]

---

since it is clear that he doesn't actually mean what he is saying, and he is only saying it to avoid paying the tax which he was really exempt from. See *Otzar Piskei Avodah Zarah* (p. 94) for a comprehensive discussion of this Gemara and if it is permitted to lie by saying that one is a gentile.

10 A similar idea where the ends justify the means is found in a comment by the *Me'am Lo'ez* on the *pasuk*, "The ways of the wicked are an abomination to Hashem; He loves the one who pursues righteousness" (*Mishlei* 15:9). He explains that although the ways of the wicked are an abomination, if they are utilized with the intention of accomplishing good deeds, then those acts are desired before Hashem. He cites a story in the Gemara (*Taanis* 22a) to back up this point. The Gemara says that there was a man who wore black shoes (unlike the Jewish custom of the time—*Rashi*) and didn't put tzitzis on his clothes, but was nonetheless deserving of great reward in the next world. The man's secret righteousness was that he was a prison guard and made sure to separate the men from the women and always made sure to try to keep the gentile male inmates from getting too close to the female Jewish inmates. The reason he didn't wear tzitzis was because he circulated around non-Jews often, and he didn't want them to know he was Jewish, so that if they were plotting evil decrees against the Jews, he could quickly inform the rabbis, who would then be able to pray to Hashem to abrogate them.

11 *Hilchos Dei'os* 2:6.

12 *Or Gedalyahu, parashas Toldos*, p. 88.

13 *Devarim* 4:15.

14 *Igros Moshe, Choshen Mishpat*, vol. 1, §104. Rav Moshe was asked if it is permitted to be a

One final point: It is important that we be mindful of the Mishnah that cautions us to distance ourselves as much as possible from associating with bad people.[15] Merely spending time with criminals could have a negative effect on a person. However, if one is doing it for the sake of Hashem, He will certainly mitigate the harmful effects.

SUMMARY

It is permissible for an undercover agent to present himself as a drug dealer and make disingenuous statements without concern that they will have a negative impact on him in the future. Additionally, there is no problem with placing himself in danger, because it is permitted to undertake a certain level of risk in order to make a living.

---

professional football player. In addition, the *Noda B'Yehudah* (*Yoreh Dei'ah* §10) ruled it was permitted to be a hunter, despite the danger, if that was one's profession (cited in *Chashukei Chemed*, *Bava Kama*, p. 508).

15   *Avos* 1:7. See *Anaf Eitz Avos*, p. 28, by Rav Ovadiah Yosef, for more on this idea.

DONATING YEARS OF YOUR LIFE

IN THE NEWS

We have all heard of donating money to the poor and praying for the speedy recovery of the sick. But did you ever hear of donating your life to the sick?

That is exactly what happened when Rav Ovadiah Yosef, *zt"l*, was seriously ill. According to a Ynet report, a man by the name of Aharon not only donated a year of his life to Rav Ovadiah, but he also undertook a "fundraising" campaign to solicit others to donate at least two minutes of their lives, which would collectively amount to a significant amount of time.

Was Rav Ovadiah pleased with Aharon's campaign? We don't know. But the article claims that when Rav Yosef Shalom Elyashiv was seriously ill, this very same Aharon donated some of his life to Rav Elyashiv. When he told Rav Ovadiah about his donation, Rav Ovadiah was pleased with him.[1]

---

[1] Kobi Nachshoni, *"Yozmah Chareidit: Tormim chaim laRav Ovadiah"* (Sept. 24, 2013), www.ynet.co.il.

"About ten years before he passed away, Rav Elyashiv was very ill and underwent a surgery that had a very high prospect of failure. With Hashem's help, the surgery was successful and Rav Elyashiv recovered completely. Rav Chaim commented by citing a *Midrash* (*Devarim Rabbah* 9:1): "Rabbi Shimon ben Chalafta met the Angel of Death. He asked, 'When is my time up?' The Angel of Death answered: 'I have no power over you and your colleagues, for Hashem constantly adds time to your lives, as it says (*Mishlei* 10:27), 'The fear of Hashem will increase days." Rav Chaim elaborated, 'A *tzaddik* may seem very old and sick; however, Hashem deals with him in an extraordinary manner. Even when it seems that a *tzaddik's*

Rabbi Yissocher Frand said in a *shiur* on this subject that it used to happen often in Europe.[2] If a person was very sick, other people would give a year or a few months of their lives to that person. There was a case in Radin where the Rosh Yeshivah, Rav Naftali Trop, was deathly sick and other students went around collecting years from other students; each student donated a few months or a year. Then they went to the Chafetz Chaim and asked him how much he would donate. The Chafetz Chaim thought and thought, and finally said he would donate one minute.

Rabbi Frand explains that this was not because he was cheap, but because he understood what you could do with one minute.[3]

Rabbi Joseph Telushkin relates a similar incident about the first Lubavitcher Rebbe, the *Baal Hatanya*:

> *Devorah Leah, daughter of the Alter Rebbe, died at age twenty-six. It is widely accepted in Chabad that she took upon herself such a fate so as to spare her father, then sick, from a premature death. The Sefer ha-Toldot Admur ha-Zaken (the biography of the Alter Rebbe) relates that on the eve of Rosh Hashanah, just after the afternoon Mincha service, she entered the small synagogue where her family prayed and found other members of her family, along with her father's closest disciples, in the presence of the Torah scrolls: "I call all of you to witness that I, Devorah Leah, daughter of Sterna, hereby pledge upon the holy Torah scrolls—in full and complete awareness of my actions, and with the most solemn and binding vows—to take the place of my father, Rabbi Shneur Zalman ben Rivka, so that he may live and not die."*

---

life is over, Hashem may add to his days as a reward for his righteousness.'" (Rabbi Dovid Hollander and Rabbi Avraham Yeshayahu Kanievsky, *Rav Chaim Kanievsky Haggadah* (ArtScroll/Mesorah, 2014), p. 100).

2   *Commuter's Chavrusah Series 21*, parashas Toldos, "Accepting Someone Else's Curse." See *Mesoras Moshe*, vol. 2, p. 469, where Rav Moshe Feinstein notes that the notion of giving away years of one's life to another is found in Kabbalah. He also mentions an incident where people were told to donate a day of their lives to a child who was very ill.

3   See *Chashukei Chemed, Kiddushin*, p. 403, for another incident involving the Chafetz Chaim and the idea of donating years of one's life to another.

This act was done without her father's knowledge, and later that evening, when he tried to offer her the customary New Year's blessing, she cut him off before he could finish. She then offered him the traditional blessing, "Father, be inscribed and sealed for a good year," and then added, "Say nothing more, Father," thereby stopping him from completing his blessing to her. On the second day of Rosh Hashanah, Devorah Leah took ill and she died a day later, on the third of Tishrei 5553 (1792). Her dying wish, it is said, was that her father personally educate her son, a young child not yet three. The Alter Rebbe promised to do so, and declared, "Your son Menachem is a comfort to me [the name Menachem means "one who comforts"]; he will be a comfort to you and all of Israel." This son, Menachem Mendel, grew up to be the Third Rebbe, and the forebearer and namesake of the seventh Rebbe.[4]

Where does the idea of giving away years of one's life to someone else in need come from? And is it permitted?

A TORAH PERSPECTIVE

The most famous source actually comes from David Hamelech. The midrash says that David Hamelech was supposed to die at birth, but seventy years were suddenly added to his life.[5] The most famous explanation for where these years came from is that Adam Harishon gave them to him, and instead of living to the age of 1000, he died at 930,[6] since he gave away seventy years to David.[7]

---

4   Joseph Telushkin, *Rebbe: The Life and Teachings of Menachem M. Schneerson, the Most Influencial Rabbi in Modern History* (Harper Wave, 2014), p. 213.

5   *Bamidbar Rabbah* 14:11; *Yalkut Shimoni, Bereishis* §41. See Rabbi Avrohom Chaim Feuer, *Tehillim* (ArtScroll/Mesorah, 1996), vol. 1, p. 885, n. 1, that the *pasuk* indicates that David had hoped that he would live for more than seventy years.

6   *Bereishis* 5:5.

7   The midrash says that when Adam turned 930, he regretted the commitment he had made to give up years of his life. See Rabbi Yissocher Frand's article "Adam Regrets His Gift to Dovid" (www.torah.org) for a beautiful explanation of this midrash, and *Chashukei Chemed, Kiddushin*, p. 406. The Arizal says that David was a reincarnation of Adam, whose life mission was to fix Adam's sin; that is why Adam gave David years of his life. See *Sefer Halikutim, parashas Haazinu*, cited in *Shevilei Pinchas, parashas Balak*, p. 341.

However, there are other opinions as to where David's seventy years came from. The *Kedushas Levi* cites the *Zohar*,[8] which says that it was the *Avos* who donated part of their lives to make up the seventy years that David lived. Avraham gave five years, Yaakov twenty-eight years, and Yosef thirty-seven years. (Avraham lived five years less than Yitzchak, Yaakov lived twenty-eight years less than Avraham, and Yosef lived thirty-seven years less than Yaakov.)[9]

Another source for this idea of transferring years of one's life is in the Gemara.[10] The Gemara says that when Rav Yosef read the *pasuk*, "There are those who are removed [from the world] without judgment,"[11] he cried. Rav Yosef understood the *pasuk* to mean that people can die before their designated time and not because they sinned. The Gemara asks, "Is it really true that people leave the world before their time?" To which the Gemara answers, "Yes." The Gemara then brings a proof from Rav Bibi, the son of Abaye, whom the *Malach Hamaves* (Angel of Death) formerly accompanied.

> *The Malach Hamaves said to his messenger, "Go bring me [i.e., kill] Miriam, the one who braids hair," but the messenger made a mistake and brought Miriam, the one who raises children. The Malach Hamaves said to his messenger, "I was speaking about Miriam, the one who braids hair."*
>
> *The messenger asked, "Should I return her soul to her [i.e., restore her to life]?"*

---

8   *Vayishlach* 168a.

9   *Kedushas Levi, Likutim.* The *Chida*, in his *sefer Midbar Kedeimos*, p. 33 (cited in *Otzar Hayedios* [Eisenberger], p. 138), also quotes the *Zohar* that says that the *Avos* contributed years of their lives to David Hamelech. The *Chida* asks why this was necessary when Adam Harishon already gave years of his life to David. He answers that after Adam sinned, the years he gave to David were no longer effective. See *Chashukei Chemed, Kiddushin*, p. 404. The *Chanukas HaTorah* makes a similar calculation. He credits Yaakov for giving thirty-three years of his life (Yaakov lived thirty-three years less than Yitzchak) and Yosef for giving thirty-seven years (Yosef lived thirty-seven years less than Yaakov). See *Torah Ladaas*, vol. 1, *parashas Vayechi*, p. 205.

10   *Chagigah* 4b–5a.

11   *Mishlei* 13:23.

To which the Malach Hamaves said, "No, once you have already brought her, she will remain here." But the Malach Hamaves asked the messenger, "How were you able to take her soul in the first place?"

The angel replied, "She was stoking the fire and left the spit on her leg, and it singed her there. Since she was near death, I was able to take her."

Rav Bibi, who witnessed this whole discussion, said to the Malach Hamaves, "Do you really have permission to take people before their designated time?"

The Malach Hamaves responded, "The pasuk says, 'There are those who are removed [from the world] without judgment,' meaning that people are taken from the world before their time, even though they didn't sin."

Rav Bibi asked, "But what happens to the years that were taken away from the person who died before his designated time?"

The Malach Hamaves answered that if there is a talmid chacham who has been maavir al middosav (forgoes insults), they are given to him.[12]

In the Gemara, too, we find the concept of transferring years of one's life to someone else. However, the Gemara does not say that any individual can volunteer to give up years of his own life to another; it just says that the *Malach Hamaves* can do it. Rabbi Frand, though, cites sources for the idea that one can accept upon himself someone else's suffering, which may indicate that one could also give years of one's own life to another.

We find, for example, that Rivkah advised her son, Yaakov, to impersonate his brother, Esav, in order to receive the *berachos* from his father, Yitzchak. However, Yaakov was afraid that Yitzchak would

---

12   See *Mesivta Shas, Chagigah* 5a, *Yalkut Biurim*, p. 34, for an explanation as to why they are given to a *talmid chacham*, and specifically one who is *maavir al middosav*. See Rabbeinu Chananel on *Chagigah* 5a, who says that some suggest that the entire incident with Rav Bibi was a dream.

discover his plot and would then curse him. Rivkah assured Yaakov that he had nothing to worry about—she promised that if Yitzchak cursed him, the curse would fall upon her instead.[13] There are different ways to understand what this means. The *Seforno*[14] understands it the simple way, that Rivkah was actually prepared to accept the curse upon herself, and he brings proof for this idea from Shlomo Hamelech, as cited in the Gemara.[15]

Before David Hamelech's death, he spoke to his heir, Shlomo, about seeing to it that all of his enemies would be justly punished. For example, Yoav, David's general, had murdered Avner ben Ner (Avner was originally Shaul's general, but later supported David). David had initially cursed Yoav and his family,[16] but he also later told Shlomo to kill Yoav[17] because he was unable to do so himself.[18]

The Gemara comments that Yoav told Shlomo that he couldn't have it both ways; either Shlomo could kill him and take upon himself David's curses or let Yoav live with David's curses. This is because if Yoav was killed, that would serve as his punishment and he would no longer be deserving of David's curse, which would then befall David's descendants.[19] Shlomo ultimately had Yoav killed, which meant that Shlomo accepted upon himself David's curses.[20] Indeed, the Gemara says that David's curses fell upon David's descendants.

The *Seforno* notes that we learn the idea of accepting another's curse upon oneself from this incident and that this is what Rivkah was prepared to do when she accepted any curse that might befall Yaakov.

Rabbi Yehudah HeChassid writes of a person who approached a man who was deathly ill and, as a joke, offered to take his illness from him

---

13   *Bereishis* 27:13.
14   On *Bereishis* 27:13.
15   *Sanhedrin* 48b.
16   *Shmuel II* 3:29.
17   *Melachim I* 2:5–6. Yoav killed David's son Avshalom as well, which also angered David (*Sotah* 10b).
18   *Shmuel II* 3:38–39.
19   There is a principle found in the Gemara that a curse made in vain falls upon the one who made it (*Maharal, Chiddushei Aggados, Sanhedrin* 48b).
20   *Rashi, Sanhedrin* 48b.

for money. The sick person agreed, and the other man immediately contracted the illness and died.[21]

We see from these sources that not only is accepting the curse of another upon oneself effective, but also that one can take someone else's illness.[22] (However, this might not be recommended.)

Furthermore, the Gemara in *Kiddushin*[23] writes that after a parent dies, whenever the child mentions the parent during the first year, he should say, "*Hareini kapparas mishkavo*," which *Rashi* explains to mean that one accepts upon himself in this world the punishments that the parent is supposed to receive in the next world.[24] This would appear to support the idea that one can accept another's suffering upon himself.

However, the Gemara in *Kiddushin* also says that when honoring one's parents, all necessary expenses come out of the parents' pocket. How does this fit in with the previous halachah that states that a child should accept upon himself his parents' punishment, which is the greatest possible "expense" imaginable?

Rav Betzalel Stern, the *rav* of Melbourne, Australia, was asked this question, and he answered by citing Rav Moshe Feinstein, who said that saying, "*Hareini kapparas mishkavo*" doesn't mean that the child actually accepts the punishment instead of the parent. It is just a way of showing reverence for the parent by demonstrating that one would be willing to suffer for the parent.[25]

---

21   *Sefer Chassidim* §445.

22   See *Shu"t Minchas Asher*, vol. 2, p. 213, where Rav Asher Weiss discusses different proofs that people bring to prove that one can accept the punishments of another, but he rejects them all. Rav Chaim Kanievsky, however, cautions people not to say they will accept the suffering of another person on themselves, since such a remark may have a negative effect on the person accepting the suffering (*Upiryo Matok, Shemos*, p. 346).

23   *Kiddushin* 31b. See also *Beis Yosef, Orach Chaim* §284.

24   Rav Moshe Sternbuch points out, however, that most people don't say this (*Teshuvos Vehanhagos*, vol. 2, §447). See *Pesakim Uteshuvos* (§240, p. 66) for more on this.

25   *Betzeil Hachochmah*, vol. 6, §20; see *Igros Moshe, Yoreh Dei'ah*, vol. 5, §26. Rav Stern cites an additional proof that one can accept upon himself someone else's punishment from the Gemara (*Shabbos* 89b). The Gemara states, based on a *pasuk*, that in the future Hashem will come to Avraham and say, "Your children sinned against Me," and Avraham will say, "They should be killed." Then Hashem will turn to Yaakov, and Yaakov will say that they have to be punished. Then Hashem will turn to Yitzchak, and Yitzchak will ask, "Are they mine and not

Rav Stern, however, disagrees with Rav Moshe and holds that the child is really accepting upon himself his parent's punishment. According to Rav Stern, how do we reconcile these two halachos: If a child is not obligated to pay out of his pocket in order to honor his parents, why is he supposed to accept upon himself their punishment?

Rav Stern explains that when the Gemara says that the expenses come from the parents' pocket, that is only when they are alive; after they pass away, the child is obligated to pay for their honor, even by accepting their suffering.

Finally, the biography of Rav Moshe Feinstein shares the following beautiful anecdote, which highlights the merit of offering to sacrifice oneself for another:

> *After Reb Moshe took ill in 5738 (1978), he received a letter from a ben Torah who wrote that he was donating one year of his life in the hope that in this merit Reb Moshe's life would be extended. Reb Moshe responded, "I was tremendously moved by your letter, which I received during the days of my difficult illness, regarding the sacrifice of which you wrote. However, know, my precious one, you will not lose even a moment of life; on the contrary, in the merit of your mesirus nefesh to donate a year for my sake, Hashem Yisbarach will grant you many years of good health in which to toil in Torah..."[26]*

The Chafetz Chaim used to say that there are people who live their lives as if they will live forever. They pay no attention to the fact that one day they will meet their Creator. The reason for this is that they attach themselves so much to this world that when they see others die, they pay no attention to it, as if it has nothing to do with them. When that person gets to the next world, he will not feel at ease there, since he never spent

---

Your children?" Yitzchak will then say, "I will take half, and Hashem, You are responsible for the other half." We see from this piece of *aggadeta*, says Rav Stern, that Yitzchak accepted Bnei Yisrael's punishment, again proving the concept that one can accept someone else's punishment upon himself.

26   Rabbi Shimon Finkelman, *Reb Moshe: The Life and Ideals of HaGaon Rabbi Moshe Feinstein* (ArtScroll/Mesorah, 2012), p. 477.

time in this world thinking about or preparing himself for the eternal world.[27] The Chafetz Chaim, though, did internalize the importance of using every minute of his life to prepare for *Olam Haba*, and that may be why he only sacrificed one minute of his life in *Olam Hazeh*.

SUMMARY

Regardless of whether one can or should give away years of his life to someone in need, an important message emerges from this entire discussion. Those who offer to give away years of their lives exemplify the idea that our lives on earth are only temporary, and we should make the most of the time we have.

---

27 *Taam Vadaas, parashas Behar*, p. 159. See also *Upiryo Matok, parashas Emor*, for a tale about a rich man who saved his money to buy a pill that would give him immortality.

DO NOT HATE

IN THE NEWS

In January of 2016, *The Jerusalem Post* published an article entitled "LeBron James Becomes Israeli Public's Newest Enemy after Blatt Firing."[1] The reporter claimed that millions of Israelis went from being fans of the Cleveland Cavaliers to hating both the team and its main player, LeBron James, who is credited with firing Blatt.

David Blatt is an American-Israeli former basketball player who became a highly successful basketball coach. Prior to the 2014–2015 season, he was the Cavaliers' head coach and led the team to the NBA finals. The following season, he again led the Cavs to the top of the league standings, but was suddenly fired. LeBron James was blamed for his dismissal. The news of his firing was the main topic of discussion in the Israeli media that day, overshadowing major news items, such as Middle East violence. To show how furious Israelis were, an Israeli sports journalist even wrote that LeBron James was "the most hated person in Israel" at that time.[2]

Hatred can evolve into two people not speaking to each other. In May of 2016, Richard Kasich, the younger brother of the then presidential candidate John Kasich, revealed that John had not spoken to him for nearly twenty years because of a disagreement over the inheritance of

---

1   Allon Sinai, "LeBron James Becomes Israeli Public's Newest Enemy after Blatt Firing" (Jan. 24, 2016), www.jpost.com.

2   Joe Vardon, "Israelis going too far in backlash toward LeBron James over David Blatt firing" (Jan. 26, 2016), www.cleveland.com.

their parents' estate. Richard said that his brother swore he would never have anything to do with him again.[3]

In Ohr Somayach's question-and-answer book, *Question Market*,[4] someone wrote the following: "Dear Rabbi, I have a next-door neighbor who causes me great discomfort. The smoke coming into my yard when he burns his leaves and the volume of music he plays when I am trying to take an afternoon nap are examples of his inconsiderate behavior. Rather than get into a quarrel with him, I have just stopped talking to him. Is this the proper approach?"

Is this the proper approach? What does the Torah say about two people stopping to speak with each other due to hatred?

A TORAH PERSPECTIVE

The Torah states, *"Lo sisna es achicha bilvavecha*—You shall not hate your brother in your heart."[5] What are the parameters of this prohibition? How much anger or resentment qualifies as the hatred forbidden in this *pasuk*?[6]

Chazal mention three indicators that a person has reached the level of hatred that violates the prohibition of *lo sisna*. The first is hating someone so much that one will not speak to him for at least three

---

3   "John Kasich's Younger Brother Claims The Candidate Didn't Speak To Him For Almost Two Decades After Inheritance Feud" (May 3, 2016), www.matzav.com.

4   Rabbi Avraham Zuroff, *Question Market* (Targum, 2008), p. 176.

5   *Vayikra* 19:17.

6   This prohibition is connected to a number of others, including not bearing a grudge and not taking revenge (see the Chafetz Chaim's *sefer Ahavas Yisrael*, ch. 2). See Rabbi Daniel Z. Feldman's *The Right and the Good: Halakhah and Human Relations* (Yashar, 2005), p. 169, for additional sources on this topic.

   There seems to be a debate among the Rishonim when a person violates this prohibition. The *Rambam* (*Sefer Hamitzvos, Lo Saaseh* §302; *Hilchos Dei'os* 10:5) says this prohibition is violated only if the hatred stays in one's heart; once he has informed the other person about his hatred, he is no longer violating the prohibition of hating another Jew, but rather the prohibitions of bearing a grudge and taking revenge (see *Minchas Asher, parashas Kedoshim* §42, where Rav Asher Weiss provides a comprehensive explanation of this opinion of the *Rambam*). The *Ramban* (*parashas Kedoshim*) disagrees and says a person violates this prohibition whether the hatred is hidden or revealed. The *Me'iri* (*Yoma* 75a) says this prohibition is violated when a person stops doing good for another because of his hatred toward him. Rav Asher Weiss (loc. cit.) says the *Me'iri* implies that the hatred itself is not a violation, and he brings a proof for the *Me'iri's* novel understanding of this prohibition.

days.[7] This indicator assumes that the person comes in contact with the person on a daily basis, yet ignores him nonetheless. If the encounters were, for example, once a week, then the indicator would be met if he ignored the person for three weeks.[8]

This sign is an indicator that one has reached the prohibited level of hating another. However, one may still violate *lo sisna* while maintaining dialogue with the other person.[9] For example, if a person hates his boss intensely, but hides it so that he won't be fired, he has still violated this prohibition, even though he is still "speaking" to his boss, because if he weren't his boss, he wouldn't be speaking to him.[10]

A person is permitted, however, to disinvest in relationships, not out of hatred but out of other considerations, such as time or convenience.[11] But sometimes breaking relationships, even if it doesn't violate *lo sisna*, may violate other prohibitions, like not taking revenge and not bearing a grudge.[12]

The second indicator that is mentioned by Chazal is if one seeks ways to harm the other person.[13] Again, this is just an indicator, and if a person doesn't seek to harm another out of fear of being arrested or retaliated against, but would otherwise do so, he has reached the level of hatred of another Jew which is prohibited by the Torah.[14]

The third indicator is when a person rejoices when the other person suffers.[15] Here, too, even if the other person doesn't actually suffer,

---

7   *Sanhedrin* 27b, cited in *Lerei'acha Kamocha*, p. 19, and *Ahavas Yisrael*, ch. 2. See *Yalkut Biurim, Sanhedrin* 27b, p. 63, for the source that not speaking to another for three days is considered as hating him. It is based on the *pasuk*, "And he didn't hate him in the past" (*Devarim* 19:4). Here, the past is understood to mean for at least three days.
8   *Lerei'acha Kamocha*, p. 19, n. 5.
9   Ibid., p. 20, n. 8, citing the *Shu"t Maharil Diskin* §20, *Emek HaNetziv* (*Bamidbar*, vol. 2, p. 324), and the Chafetz Chaim in *Ahavas Yisrael*, ch. 2.
10   *Lerei'acha Kamocha*, p. 21.
11   Ibid., n. 10, citing Rabbeinu Yonah in *Shaarei Teshuvah* 3:215, and *Yad Ketanah, Hilchos Dei'os* 9:23.
12   *Lerei'acha Kamocha*, p. 22, n. 11.
13   Ibid., p. 23, based on *Bamidbar* 35:33.
14   Ibid., p. 24, n. 20.
15   Ibid., p. 25, n. 21, and p. 26, based on *Nedarim* 40a; *Shu"t Maharil* §197; Rabbeinu Yonah on *Mishlei* 11:10; *Rambam, Hilchos Aveilus* 1:10; and many more sources.

but deep down he knows that if the "enemy" would suffer he would be happy about it, this also violates the prohibition of hating another.

The Chafetz Chaim points out that if friends get into a disagreement and come to hate each other to the point that they won't speak to one another for at least three days, they violate this prohibition.[16] This is the case even if each person would help the other if he were in trouble. The hypothetical situation does not undo the prohibited hatred they have for one another.

However, it seems that the prohibition not to hate another person doesn't apply to non-Jews, as the *pasuk* forbids hating "*achicha*," your brother, and a non-Jew is not considered "*achicha*."[17] Nevertheless, as long as the non-Jews in question are good people, one should not hate them. This would appear to be appropriate based on the midrash that points out that if one speaks *lashon hara* about non-Jews, he will eventually come to speak *lashon hara* about Jews.[18] Similarly, one could claim that if a person hates non-Jews, even though it is technically permissible, he will come to easily hate Jews, and therefore one should not even hate non-Jews.

If the person is a *rasha*, then it is permissible to hate him.[19] Some point out that it is not only permissible to hate *resha'im*, but it is even a mitzvah.[20] The Chafetz Chaim, however, writes that the opposite is true—it is a mitzvah to love people, even if they are *resha'im*.[21] He explains that when the Gemara says one should hate *resha'im*, it refers

---

16   *Ahavas Yisrael*, ch. 2, cited in *Lerei'acha Kamocha*, p. 28, n. 24.

17   *Lerei'acha Kamocha*, p. 31, based on *Pesachim* 113b.

18   *Devarim Rabbah* 6:9. When approached by Jews who felt uneasy about their sadness over the assassination of President Kennedy, Rav Yaakov Kamenetsky related that the Alter of Slabodka didn't harbor hatred for an anti-Semitic priest so as not to come to hate Jews as well. His point was that if the Alter went out of his way to avoid hatred and preserve his sensitivity, it certainly is acceptable for Jews to grieve over the loss of Kennedy's life. (Yonason Rosenblum, *Reb Yaakov: The Life and Times of HaGaon Rabbi Yaakov Kamenetsky* [ArtScroll/Mesorah, 1993], p. 182).

19   *Lerei'acha Kamocha*, p. 48. See also *Shu"t Minchas Asher*, vol. 1, §64.

20   *Lerei'acha Kamocha*, p. 49.

21   *Ahavas Chessed* (toward the end of the book, subparagraph §28). See also *Meshech Chochmah*, *Devarim* 22:4, which says that after *chet ha'eigel*, it is no longer permitted to hate *resha'im* (generally speaking).

to those who continue their evil ways despite being rebuked. Since nowadays we are unable to give proper rebuke,[22] this Gemara doesn't apply, and the mitzvah to love them remains.

Generally speaking, instead of harboring hatred for another human being, we are required to confront him and ask him why he behaved the way he did, as the *pasuk* says, "You shall not hate your brother in your heart; you must surely rebuke your neighbor."[23] This way, the person will have a chance to explain himself. He might respond that he was unaware that he offended his fellow Jew, or he may actually apologize. The *Rambam*[24] says it is the way of the wicked to harbor hatred in their hearts and remain quiet about it, as the *pasuk* says about Avshalom, "He did not speak with Amnon neither good nor bad, for Avshalom hated Amnon."[25]

Unlike other sins, which are momentary, the sin of hating another Jew is constantly violated as long as one feels hatred in his heart for another. The Chafetz Chaim points out that hating another Jew is a very serious matter,[26] since it will most likely lead to the violation of many other sins, such as *machlokes* (causing strife), *lashon hara, onaas devarim* (insulting others), and embarrassing others in public.

Additionally, we should try to make sure that we don't cause others to hate us. Rav Shlomo Zalman Auerbach ruled that although in general it is prohibited to give food to one who will not recite a blessing, as this is a violation of *lifnei iveir*, if one knows that by not offering him food, the person will come to hate him (which is often the case), he should give the person food.[27] This is because not reciting a blessing before eating is a Rabbinic prohibition, whereas hating another Jew is a Biblical prohibition. By serving the person food, one is saving him from a greater sin and therefore not violating *lifnei iveir*.

---

22   However, the Chafetz Chaim does mention the mitzvah to rebuke nowadays in his *Mishnah Berurah* 608:3 and 608:5.

23   *Vayikra* 19:17.

24   *Hilchos Dei'os* 6:6.

25   *Shmuel II* 13:22.

26   See *Vehaarev Na*, vol. 3, *parashas Kedoshim*, p. 282, where Rav Yitzchak Zilberstein says that one should hire the person who fired you, since you will be overcoming your *yetzer hara* to dislike him.

27   *Minchas Shlomo*, vol. 1, §35:1, cited in *Minchas Asher, parashas Kedoshim* §42, p. 275.

Lastly, we should bear in mind the Gemara's statement that teaches that it was because of hatred of our fellow Jews that the Second Temple was destroyed.[28] The Chafetz Chaim warns that as long as we continue our hatred toward others, our long exile will likewise continue.[29]

SUMMARY

It is prohibited to hate another Jew. Some indicators that a person has reached the prohibited level of hating another Jew include not speaking to him for three days, seeking to harm him, and rejoicing in his suffering.

---

28 *Yoma* 9a.
29 *Ahavas Yisrael*, ch. 2, and see there, ch. 3, for advice on how to not come to hate others.

HOW TO CATCH A THIEF

IN THE NEWS

The following incident, witnessed by Steven Fong of San Francisco, was discussed in "The Ethicist" column of *The New York Times Magazine*.[1] Two drivers left their vehicles, started yelling at each other, and eventually drove away together in one of their cars. The remaining car was left as a test to see if passersby would steal it.

Fong wrote that he viewed a similar incident on the television show *Bait Car*. Feeling it was his duty to prevent anyone from attempting to steal the car and get caught by the police, Fong called out, "Bait car, bait car." But later, when retelling his story to others, he was criticized for protecting thieves from being arrested. So he submitted his quandary to "The Ethicist," whose verdict was that the bait game is an accepted method for catching criminals and is not considered entrapment. The police are only "presenting the opportunity" to commit a crime and not forcing anyone to do it.

While under secular law the police may have a special dispensation to use a bait car for the sake of bettering society, does such a dispensation exist in halachah?[2] Similarly, are individuals permitted to use the "bait car" method by leaving out money to test if employees are honest or have been stealing from them?[3]

---

1   Chuck Klosterman, The Ethicist, "So You Think You Can Steal?" (June 20, 2014), www.nytimes.com.

2   Regarding an interesting question about the permissibility of searching a suspect's property, see Rabbi Daniel Mann, *Living the Halachic Process: Questions and Answers for the Modern Jew* (Devora Publishing, 2007), vol. 2, p. 269.

3   For a story regarding a cleaning lady in the *frum* community who was caught on camera

A TORAH PERSPECTIVE

The *Ben Ish Chai*, Rav Yosef Chaim of Baghdad, was asked this question, and he ruled that it is forbidden to plant money in order to tempt one's employee and test the person's level of honesty.[4] His ruling is based on the prohibition of *"Lifnei iveir lo sitein michshol"* (whose literal meaning is that "you should not place a stumbling block in front of a blind man"),[5] which Chazal explain to mean that one should not cause or facilitate others to sin.[6] This is true even when it's not certain that the person will actually sin.[7]

The *Ben Ish Chai* brings support from the Gemara, which relates a story told by Rebbi's maidservant.[8] She witnessed a father hitting his adult son and exclaimed that he should be excommunicated since he violated *lifnei iveir*—that is, he was setting up his son to sin, as it was very likely the adult son would retaliate by hitting his father, which the Torah forbids.[9] The *Ben Ish Chai* says that we see from this that even leading someone to sin, without being certain that he will sin, and regardless of whether he actually ends up doing the sin, is a violation of *lifnei iveir* and is prohibited. Therefore, one would not be allowed to tempt his maid to sin in order to test her honesty, even if the maid doesn't end up taking the money.[10]

---

stealing from her employer, see: "Video: Far Rockaway Shomrim (RCSP) Help Catch Cleaning Lady Stealing Jewelry from Multiple Homes" (Oct. 2, 2014), www.theyeshivaworld.com. See *Chashukei Chemed, Bava Metzia* 76a, regarding a homeowner who suspected his cleaning lady of stealing, verified it with a lie-detector test, and then fired her, only to discover later that the maid was not the thief. Rav Yitzchak Zilberstein discusses what the proper response is in such a case and when one can fire a cleaning lady out of suspicion that she is stealing.

4   *Torah Lishmah* §407. (Rav Ovadiah Yosef writes in *Yabia Omer, Orach Chaim*, vol. 9, §96, that he does not believe this *sefer* was written by the *Ben Ish Chai*, but most assume it is.)

5   *Vayikra* 19:14.

6   *Nedarim* 62b. The *Minchas Chinuch* (§232) and *Chasam Sofer* (*Choshen Mishpat* §185) hold that this prohibition also applies to causing gentiles to sin.

7   *Pischei Choshen*, vol. 5, p. 4.

8   *Mo'ed Katan* 17a.

9   The *Ritva* (*Mo'ed Katan* 17a) says that the term *adult* is not meant to be taken literally; it can even refer to a child below the age of bar mitzvah. The Gemara merely means the age that a child may retaliate with words or actions in a prohibited manner.

10   The *Ben Ish Chai* cites additional reasons why one cannot set someone up for the possibility that he may steal.

However, the Acharonim[11] argue whether *lifnei iveir* is violated the moment a person does something that can cause someone to sin, even if the sin is not committed, or if it is only violated when the person does the sin. Some Acharonim agree with the *Ben Ish Chai*'s opinion that, yes, *lifnei iveir* is violated whether or not the sin was committed. Others hold that *lifnei iveir* is violated only when the other person actually commits the sin. In that case, the Gemara means that the excommunication was only issued after the maid saw that the son actually retaliated against his father.

According to the latter opinion, in our bait case, one would only violate *lifnei iveir* if the worker actually stole the money and violated the prohibition of stealing. These opinions, however, may agree that it's still not proper (or even *assur*) to leave out the bait money, since there is a chance that *lifnei iveir* will be violated.

However, there may be a simple loophole to allow testing one's employee in this manner—by declaring the money ownerless. If the employer relinquishes his ownership of the bait money, he can't be held responsible for causing anyone to sin by stealing, since it's not his money.

The Gemara relates a story about Rav Huna, who wanted to test his son to see if he had a bad temper.[12] Rav Huna ripped his own garment, one that his son would potentially inherit, and then waited to see whether his son would protest or not.

The Gemara asks how Rav Huna could do that. If his son did get upset and disrespected his father, then Rav Huna would have violated *lifnei iveir* by causing his son to sin.[13] The Gemara answers that Rav Huna was *mochel* his honor. Even if his son was to disrespect him, it wouldn't be a sin since Rav Huna pardoned his son in advance for any disrespect he might demonstrate against him.

---

11   Cited in *Mesivta Shas*, *Mo'ed Katan* 17a.
12   *Kiddushin* 32a.
13   This Gemara seems to takes the position that *lifnei iveir* is not violated unless the other person actually commits the sin.

Rav Yitzchak Zilberstein writes that it would seem from this story about Rav Huna that if a person relinquishes his ownership of the bait money in advance, it should be permitted to tempt him. This is because even if the worker takes the money, it wouldn't be stealing since it's now ownerless.[14]

However, Rav Zilberstein writes that this suggestion poses another problem.[15] Elsewhere, the Gemara states that if a person intends to sin and thinks that he is sinning, even if in reality he did not sin, he is nevertheless considered to have sinned.[16] This is learned from the *pasuk* that says that a woman who drinks wine when she thinks it is forbidden to her, due to a vow she made, requires atonement even if it was permitted to her at that moment.[17] Likewise, it wouldn't be permitted to leave the bait money even if one relinquished ownership, because one would still violate *lifnei iveir*; one is causing the worker to think he is sinning, which, as stated, is in itself a sin.[18]

Rav Zilberstein concludes that he isn't sure what the halachah would be in this case. He entertains an additional doubt. One may only violate *lifnei iveir* by giving a forbidden object to someone, as in the cases mentioned in the Gemara of giving wine to a *nazir* or giving someone *eiver min hachai* (a limb from a live animal).[19] But in our case, one is just leaving money out in the open and not directly giving anything *assur* to the employees.

The *Seridei Aish*, Rav Yechiel Yaakov Weinberg, felt that it should be permitted to test one's employees.[20] First of all, he says, all Jewish

---

14 *Torasecha Shaashu'ai* §40.

15 Ibid.

16 *Kiddushin* 81b. An example of this principle is found in the Gemara there (*Kiddushin* ad loc.) that relates a story of Rabbi Chiya bar Ashi, who thought he was having relations with a harlot, but in reality it was his wife. Since he intended to sin, he was guilty of violating the Torah. Note, though, that Rav Moshe Feinstein (*Igros Moshe, Yoreh Dei'ah*, vol. 2, §6) rules that a person who violates this level of sin is not *pasul* (invalid) as a witness in Jewish matters (court cases, *kiddushin*, etc.).

17 *Bamidbar* 30:13.

18 See *Or Hachaim* (Bereishis 50:19–20) and *K'li Chemdah* (parashas Vayechi §3), cited in *Tzefunos Haparshah* (pp. 380–81). See also *Upiryo Matok* (Shemos, p. 354) for more on this.

19 *Avodah Zarah* 6b.

20 *Seridei Aish*, vol. 1, §57.

people are presumed to be honest, and, therefore, one does not have to worry that the worker will steal. Second, the *Ritva* says that it is not a violation of *lifnei iveir* to give another person something with a permitted use, even if he is concerned the man will use it in a prohibited manner, because there remains the possibility that he will use it properly. As a proof, he cites the Gemara that says that one can give money to a non-Jewish or ignorant Jewish (*am haaretz*) worker and not be concerned he will buy a forbidden item with it.[21]

Rav Zilberstein thought, then, that perhaps one should reject this proof from the Gemara that one can give money to a non-Jewish or ignorant Jewish worker because the cases are not comparable. In that case, the money he gives to his employee is completely permissible, and he would not assume it will be used to sin. However, in our case, the entire purpose of placing the bait is to try to tempt the worker to see whether he will steal the money.[22]

On the other hand, Rav Chaim David HaLevi, former chief rabbi of Tel Aviv-Yafo, writes that it is permitted to leave out money to test a worker's level of honesty.[23] Rav Eliezer Melamed, author of *Peninei Halachah*, agrees, provided that the test isn't anything out of the ordinary that the worker would not face in his daily routine. For example, if a homeowner often leaves a maid alone in the house, then leaving some money out to test her honesty isn't challenging her beyond what

---

21   *Avodah Zarah* 63a.

22   *Torasecha Shaashu'ai* §40. Rav Zilberstein analyzes a case where an employer discovered that one of his workers was stealing from him, but nevertheless wanted to keep him, since he brought in a lot of business. The question is, by retaining the employee, the employer was enabling him to steal, which could in itself be considered *lifnei iveir*. Even if the employer relinquished ownership of whatever the employee stole, he was still enabling him to intend to steal, which is a sin in its own right. Rav Zilberstein in *Chashukei Chemed* (*Bava Metzia*, p. 44) seems to permit it, yet in *Vehaarev Na* (vol. 2, p. 412) he forbids it. Like Rav Zilberstein, Rav Yisroel Belsky is also unsure if testing the worker or cleaning lady is a violation of *lifnei iveir* (Rabbi Yair Hoffman, *Misguiding the Perplexed: The Laws of Lifnei Iver* [Israel Bookshop, 2004], p. 154).

23   *Aseih Lecha Rav*, vol. 7, §71, p. 100, cited by Rav Eliezer Melamed in *Peninei Halachah* (toward the end of *Hilchos Geneivah*). Rav Moshe Feinstein rules in *Igros Moshe* (*Yoreh Dei'ah*, vol. 3, §90) that there is no issue with *lifnei iveir* to leave out money knowing it may be stolen. However, he isn't discussing a case of planting money.

she faces throughout the course of her work. If she wanted to steal anything from the house, she could do so, since people don't take a daily inventory of items in their house. Moreover, Rav Melamed notes that if a maid is caught stealing, it may deter her from stealing in the future, which makes placing the bait a mitzvah. This is in line with the generally accepted rule that *lifnei iveir* is not violated if one is doing something for the other person's overall benefit.[24]

In the aforementioned Gemara about Rav Huna and his son, the *Ritva* and *Tosafos* disagree about why it was permitted for Rav Huna to test his son in this way. They both ask: How could Rav Huna test his son this way? He might have caused his son to think he was sinning, which is in itself a sin.

Tosafos explains that Rav Huna actually informed his son in advance that he was going to forgo his honor.[25] The *Ritva* argues that informing his son would have defeated the purpose of the test. Thus, the *Ritva* understands that the *issur* of *lifnei iveir* has a unique leniency because of its very general, wide-ranging nature and doesn't apply in a case where one is training his son to behave properly.[26]

Based on this, *Tosafos* would rule that testing a worker is forbidden because he wasn't informed about it in advance, while the *Ritva* would say it is permitted.

Practically speaking, Rav Tzvi Spitz, in his *Mishpetei HaTorah*,[27] rules that since *lifnei iveir* is an *issur d'Oraisa*, and there is a disagreement whether testing an employee falls under that category, one should be stringent in this matter. He concludes that one can only test someone if he has reason to suspect that he is already stealing or being dishonest. His proof is from *Maseches Derech Eretz Rabbah*.[28]

---

24   *Tzefunos Haparshah*, p. 380, citing the Chafetz Chaim, seems to agree.

25   *Tosafos, Kiddushin* 32a, s.v. *"demachal."*

26   See *Birkei Yosef, Yoreh Dei'ah* 240:13, which deals with a similar question: Granted, Rav Huna avoided the issue of *lifnei iveir* with regard to his son violating *kibbud av* (as the Rishonim explained), but there is also the issue of causing his son to get angry, which Chazal consider a terrible *middah*, tantamount to idolatry (*Zohar*, vol. 3, p. 179a).

27   Vol. 1, §78.

28   Ch. 5.

The *Beraisa* in *Maseches Derech Eretz* says that Rabbi Yehoshua arranged for a guest to stay in his attic, then proceeded to remove the ladder in the middle of the night because he suspected his guest of being dishonest. Not realizing the ladder had been taken away, the robber fell to the floor and was found in the morning with the possessions he was trying to steal.

Rav Spitz cites this *Beraisa* as proof that *lifnei iveir* is permitted in order to catch a thief. Thus, he explains that this case of Rabbi Yehoshua falls under the literal definition of *lifnei iveir* ("don't cause someone to stumble"), which was permitted in order to catch a thief. However, a case that falls under the other definitions, such as not causing someone to sin, would also be permitted if one already suspects the employee of theft, according to Rav Spitz.

SUMMARY

The *Ben Ish Chai* forbids testing one's cleaning lady because of *lifnei iveir*. Rav Zilberstein is unsure if it is in fact prohibited, since one is not actually giving her a forbidden item. Furthermore, Rav Chaim David HaLevi permits it, while Rav Melamed permits it only under certain circumstances. Similarly, Rav Spitz only permits it if one is already suspicious of the person.

INTERMARRIAGE INTERVENTION

IN THE NEWS

According to a March 2013 Ynet article,[1] spending weekends in Eilat has become a "real tradition" for mixed Israeli-Arab couples. The alarming figure of thirty thousand represents the approximate number of Jewish women currently living together with Arab men in the State of Israel.[2]

On many weekends, Rav Shalom Cohen, the *rav* of Eilat, has been approached by these Jewish women to help arrange a conversion for their Arab boyfriends. In response to these requests, Rav Cohen attempts to dissuade them from going through with their plans of marrying these gentiles. He noted that he has been successful in preventing around fifty such intermarriages.

A halachic issue that arises in some of these cases is whether it is permitted to drive to the Eilat checkpoint on Shabbos to stop these women from continuing to live with their Arab partners. Life-and-death issues warrant the violation of Shabbos; what about preventing intermarriage?

---

1   Kobi Nachshoni, "Rabbis: Stopping Assimilation Overrides Shabbos" (March 4, 2013), www.ynetnews.com.

2   In 2014, the Central Bureau of Statistics in Israel released a list of the most popular names given to babies that year. Yad L'Achim, an organization that fights against intermarriages, analyzed the statistics and discovered to their dismay that at least forty-five Jewish children were named Muhammad. The organization explained this is due to the large number of Jewish women who are led and ultimately trapped into marriages with Muslims. "The fact is that Jewish mothers are registering their babies with Muslim names, and dozens of Jewish women are converting to Islam" ("45 Jewish Mohammeds in Israel?" [Jan. 4, 2016], www.israelnationalnews.com).

The article cited the opinions of Rav Shlomo Aviner, Rosh Yeshivah of Yeshivat Ateret Kohanim, and Rav David Batzri, a renowned *mekubal* (Kabbalist), both of whom agreed that it was indeed permitted to desecrate Shabbos to prevent these women from intermarrying. Rav Aviner based his opinion on the classic leniency of *pikuach nefesh* in its literal sense—a risk that this union may ultimately lead to the woman's death, as is sometimes the case. Rav Batzri, though, ruled that even without concern for her mortal life, there are grounds to permit violating Shabbos in order to prevent the woman from assimilation, which essentially constitutes spiritual annihilation.[3]

At first glance, the ruling of Rav Batzri seems extreme, but is it? Are there any halachic precedents permitting one to violate Shabbos in order to save another from spiritual danger? If so, what is the rationale behind it? What are the parameters for these leniencies?

A TORAH PERSPECTIVE

As a rule, one is permitted, and even obligated, to violate all mitzvos of the Torah (except for the three cardinal sins) in order to save someone else's life. This principle is known as *pikuach nefesh*.[4]

Does this apply when an individual acted with negligence and endangered his own life (such as in attempted suicide)? Is one permitted to violate Shabbos, for example, in order to save his life? Rav Moshe Feinstein ruled that it is indeed permitted to override Shabbos to save his life.[5]

---

3   See the chapter entitled "The Magen David" below for Rav Zilberstein's story about a Jewish mother who had her son tattooed with a Magen David on his hand so that he would never forget he was Jewish and not marry a gentile.

4   *Sanhedrin* 74a.

5   *Igros Moshe, Orach Chaim*, vol. 1, §127, and *Yoreh Dei'ah*, vol. 2, §174, cited in *Halachos of Refuah on Shabbos*, by Rabbi Yisroel Pinchos Bodner (Feldheim, 2007), p. 75. See also *Headlines: Halachic Debates of Current Events* (OU Press, 2014), p. 33; *Torah Ladaas*, vol. 1, *parashas Ki Sisa*, pp. 381–86; and see *Torah Ladaas*, vols. 4–5, *parashas Ki Sisa*, pp. 246–49, regarding violating Shabbos to save a gentile whose life is in danger. If the victim resists being helped (for example, because of his concern about desecrating Shabbos), it is permitted to treat him against his will (*Mishnah Berurah* 328:6; Rabbi Yisroel Pinchos Bodner, *Halachos of Refuah on Shabbos* [Feldheim, 2007], p. 76).

What is the halachah if the other person's life is not in physical danger, but his spiritual well-being is in jeopardy—is one permitted to violate Shabbos (or any other mitzvah) to save him from sinning?

The Gemara establishes a principle that one may not sin for the purpose of preventing someone else from sinning. *Rashi* explains the Gemara to mean that one may not commit a "minor" sin even to save someone from committing a "major" sin.[6]

Tosafos mentions a number of limitations to this rule.[7] One of them is if the other person sinned without negligence; he didn't voluntarily place himself in that situation. In such a case, it would be permitted to violate a prohibition in order to save the person from sinning. If he had sinned intentionally, then he must pay for the consequences of his actions, and no one may violate an *issur* to save him from his transgression.[8]

---

6   *Shabbos* 4a and *Rashi* there, s.v. *"vechi."* The case the Gemara is discussing is where someone placed bread in an oven on Shabbos and will violate the Biblical prohibition of baking on Shabbos as soon as the bread reaches the stage of being sufficiently baked. The question the Gemara deals with is whether someone else may remove the bread before it is baked, violating the Rabbinic prohibition of removing bread from an oven in order to save the other person from violating the Biblical sin (which is more severe). The Gemara responds that a person should not commit a "small" sin even to save someone from a "greater" sin. See *Mesivta Shas, Shabbos* 4a, *Yalkut Biurim*, for more on this topic. The *K'sav Sofer* (*Orach Chaim* §62) says that sometimes we do say one should sin to stop another from a greater sin, based on the principle of *"Kol Yisrael areivim zeh bazeh*—all Jews are responsible for each other" (*Shevuos* 39a) and are held accountable for the mitzvos and *aveiros* that others commit (see *Rosh Hashanah* 29a regarding the relevant concept of *"yatza motzi"*). See *Mesivta Shas, Sotah* 37b, *Yalkut Biurim*, p. 177, for a nice summary of the topic of *arvus*. The *Avnei Nezer* (*Yoreh Dei'ah* §15) writes that if a person is negligent, there is no obligation of *arvus* to ensure that he doesn't sin or miss fulfilling a mitzvah (See *Masa Behar*, pp. 181–82). See *Shaar Hatziyun* (655:5) who seems to say that there is *arvus* even when the person was negligent with regard to the performance of a mitzvah.

7   *Tosafos, Shabbos* 4a, s.v. *"vechi."*

8   *Tosafos* brings a number of proofs for this idea. One of them is a Gemara in *Eiruvin* 103b that says one should commit an *issur d'Rabbanan* to save someone from an *issur d'Oraisa*. The case of the Gemara is a *Kohen* who has a wart on his body, thereby invalidating him to serve in the Temple. It is Biblically prohibited for him to remove the wart himself on Shabbos, but for someone else it would only be prohibited Rabbinically. The Gemara says someone else should do it for him. According to *Tosafos*, this is permitted because the person wasn't negligent; it's not his fault he has a wart. See *Kitzur Shulchan Aruch, She'arim Metzuyanim Behalachah* edition, p. 111 (§18), where it says that although generally it is prohibited to speak in the middle of *Shemoneh Esreh*, one is permitted to do so in

Another exception cited by *Tosafos* is for the sake of a *mitzvah rabbah*, a great mitzvah. For example, even though it is forbidden to free one's *eved Canaani* (gentile slave),[9] the Gemara says that one may free a slave who is half-free and half-slave (because he owns the slave with a partner and only one of them had freed the slave, giving the slave the status of only half-free) in order to allow him to perform the *mitzvah rabbah* of having children. Since he is only half-free, he is obligated to marry but isn't allowed to marry a free woman or a slave. By freeing the part of him that is half-slave, though it is prohibited, one allows

---

between *berachos* in order to remind people to say relevant insertions to the *tefillah*. Here, too, they didn't put themselves in this position on purpose, so this, too, is an example of when it is permitted to sin to save someone else from sinning, and it may even be a mitzvah for the public. See also *Mishnah Berurah* 90:84 for another example where, under certain circumstances, it's permitted to violate an *issur d'Rabbanan* (speaking in the middle of *Shemoneh Esreh*) to save others from violating an *issur d'Oraisa*, such as praying in front of waste (see *Vehaarev Na*, vol. 3, *parashas Eikev*, pp. 420–21). See also *Mishnah Berurah* 58:5.

Should one postpone a *bris milah* that is meant to take place on Shabbos for a newborn baby out of concern that some of the guests will violate Shabbos by driving to the *bris*? Rav Shlomo Aviner says one can postpone it (*On the Air with Rav Aviner* [J Levine/Millennium, 2009], p. 57), but the *Tzitz Eliezer* (vol. 6, §3) disagrees and rules that one should not postpone the *bris*. See *Teshuvos Vehanhagos*, vol. 6, §200, where Rav Moshe Sternbuch writes that if the parents are religious, they shouldn't delay the *bris milah*, even though it will lead to *chillul Shabbos* among their irreligious relatives. See *Yom Shabbason*, vol. 2, for more on this issue. See *Lehoros Nassan* (vol. 8, §96), which mentions this concept in connection to the *chiddush* of the *Taz*, who says that a *chassan* during *sheva berachos* should not go to shul so that he doesn't cause the *tzibbur* to omit *Tachanun*. See *Teshuvos Vehanhagos*, vol. 4, §152, regarding whether a son should eat on Yom Kippur in order to convince his very sick father that it's not Yom Kippur and that he, too, should eat.

Rav Shmuel Wosner (*Shevet HaLevi*, vol. 6, §36) permits those involved in *kiruv* to travel to secular kibbutzim in order to inspire them to become religious, even if traveling there causes them to miss *tefillah betzibbur*. See also *Chashukei Chemed*, *Berachos* 7b, about missing *Maariv* on *Motza'ei Shabbos* to help someone start his car, and see *Chashukei Chemed*, *Sanhedrin* 24b, about gambling with irreligious Jews on Shabbos in order to save them from violating the Biblical prohibition of driving on Shabbos. See also *Chashukei Chemed*, *Megillah* 3b, regarding spending money to stop someone from sinning, and *Chashukei Chemed*, *Megillah* 3b, *Gittin* 17a, regarding whether missing the opportunity to do a mitzvah to stop someone from sinning is also in the category of "don't sin to save someone else from sinning."

9 The Torah says, "*Le'olam bahem taavodu*—you should work them forever" (*Vayikra* 25:46). Chazal learn from here that freeing an *eved Canaani* is a *bittul aseih*, negation of a positive commandment (i.e., he is not fulfilling the mitzvah to work his slave forever).

the man the opportunity to fulfill his obligation to marry.[10] This is an example where sinning for a greater cause is allowed.[11]

Along these lines, the *Rashba* was asked if it is permissible to violate an *issur d'Oraisa* in order to save one's child from being forcibly taken to join another religion and renounce her faith.[12] The *Rashba* was inclined to rule that it would be prohibited to do so, based on the above-cited statement from the Gemara that one cannot even commit a minor (Rabbinic) sin to save someone from a greater sin (Torah mandated). Also, the *Rashba* rejects the second argument of *Tosafos* (that one may sin to help another perform a *mitzvah rabbah*), because he claims the prohibition against freeing an *eved Canaani* applies only to freeing full-slaves, not half-slaves, and therefore *Tosafos*'s proof is without basis.[13]

The *Beis Yosef* argues with the position of the *Rashba* and follows *Tosafos*'s first argument that if the other person did not intentionally disregard a prohibition and was not negligent, it is permitted to save him from violating it.[14] In this case, since the girl did not choose to sin—she was taken away from her family to reject her faith—it is permitted to violate even an *issur d'Oraisa* to save her from the very severe prohibitions involved in renouncing her faith for another religion.[15] Additionally, *Tosafos* said that it is permitted to sin to facilitate

---

10 See *Gittin* 41b.

11 Another exception cited by *Tosafos* is for the sake of a mitzvah for the public. His example is the Gemara in *Berachos* 47b that says that Rabbi Eliezer freed his slave in order to enable the public to fulfill the Biblical mitzvah of having a *minyan* (quorum of ten men) for the reading of *parashas Zachor*. The *Rambam* (*Hilchos Avadim* 9:6) says this is permitted even for a Rabbinic mitzvah.

12 *Shu"t HaRashba*, vol. 7, §267.

13 *Rashba*, *Shabbos* 4a, s.v. "*ha d'amrinan vechi.*"

14 *Beis Yosef*, *Orach Chaim* §306; see also *Shulchan Aruch*, *Orach Chaim* 306:14. The *Minchas Chinuch* 239:4 rules that just as there is an obligation to save someone from physical danger, there is an obligation to save him from spiritual danger as well. The *Maharshdam* (*Yoreh Dei'ah* §204) rules that, at times, one even has to spend money to stop others from sinning. However, see *Rema*, *Yoreh Dei'ah* 334:48, who seems to argue. See *Peninei Halachah*, *Kerisos* 3a, for more on this topic.

15 See *Shu"t Minchas Asher*, vol. 1, §22 and §23, where Rav Asher Weiss discusses the dispute between the *Rashba* and the *Beis Yosef* as it applies to the question of whether Hatzolah members who arrive at an emergency on Shabbos should commit an *issur d'Rabbanan* (such as radioing to other members that the emergency is under control and they shouldn't come)

someone to keep a great mitzvah, and there is no greater mitzvah than retaining one's faith and keeping all the mitzvos.[16]

Similarly, the *Mishnah Berurah* says that if a person is forcibly being taken to join another religion and will never be able to keep the Torah, one is permitted to violate Shabbos—even *melachos d'Oraisa*—to save him.[17] Violating Shabbos once, even though it is a great sin in its own right, is considered a minor sin in comparison to the sin of leaving Judaism, which the other person will be forced to commit if he is not saved.[18] However, if the person voluntarily chooses to embrace another religion, then the parents may not violate an *issur d'Oraisa* to stop him (since one exception to the rule was where the person does it without negligence, and here the violation is intentional), but they may violate an *issur d'Rabbanan* to save him.[19]

---

so that others don't violate an *issur d'Oraisa*. Rav Weiss states that they should radio the other Hatzolah members not to drive on Shabbos. Rav Yitzchak Zilberstein (*Toras Hayoledes* 21:1) says that on Shabbos, Hatzolah drivers should not radio other drivers to stop driving when they are not needed. See *Teshuvos Vehanhagos*, vol. 2, §207, and *She'eiris Yosef*, vol. 3, §43, for more on this topic. See also *Masa Behar*, p. 368.

16   See *Igros Moshe, Orach Chaim*, vol. 1, §116, for an explanation of the dispute between *Tosafos* and the *Rashba*.

17   *Mishnah Berurah* 306:57.

18   The *Mishnah Berurah* (254:40) rules that it is prohibited to commit a sin to prevent someone else from committing a greater sin, regardless of whether he sinned intentionally or not, if he was negligent. The *Shaar Hatziyun* (254:40) cites *Tosafos* who says that even sinning *beshogeg* (unintentionally) is considered negligent in this case, since the person should have been more careful. See *Teshuvos Vehanhagos*, vol. 4, p. 434, where Rav Moshe Sternbuch records that Rav Chaim Soloveitchik himself would violate Shabbos to save Jewish children from being drafted into the Russian army out of concern that the army would cause them to abandon Judaism. See *Vehaarev Na*, vol. 3, p. 181, and see *Torasecha Shaashu'ai*, p. 240, for an interesting discussion on whether one may violate Shabbos to save one's young child who is a convert to Judaism from being forced into living a life of a different religion. Perhaps it is forbidden in this case, because if the child rejects his conversion when he becomes an adult, which he is entitled to do, then retroactively it will be determined that Shabbos was violated for no reason.

19   *Mishnah Berurah* 306:56. This is based on *Tosafos*'s statement that one may violate a prohibition to enable another to perform a great mitzvah. In the case of an *issur d'Rabbanan*, one can rely on the exceptions mentioned in *Tosafos*, such as a *mitzvah rabbah*, like this case where one may be successful in returning Jews to their people and religion (*Shaar Hatziyun* 306:46). Rav Moshe Sternbuch (*Teshuvos Vehanhagos*, vol. 2, §207) says this leniency is limited to cases of saving Jews from abandoning their religion. Rav Moshe Avraham Avidan (*Masa Behar*, p. 369) says that even when it is permissible to commit a sin to save another from a greater sin,

The Gemara says that a child who was abducted and raised among gentiles—a *tinok shenishbah*—is not considered an intentional sinner.[20] There is a debate among the contemporary *poskim* on whether today's secular Jews who are raised in unobservant environments are also considered inadvertent sinners.

Rav Yaakov Ettlinger, the *rav* of Altona, Prussia, in the mid-nineteenth century, wrote in his responsa, *Binyan Tzion*, that they are considered like a *tinok shenishbah*.[21] He argued that the majority of the Jewish community, already in his time, was no longer observant, and the secular Jews are not considered to be rebelling against the Torah—they are just following the path in which they were raised. Rav Ovadiah Yosef agrees with the *Binyan Tzion* that irreligious Jews today are considered inadvertent sinners, since they grew up in an environment where most Jews were not religious.[22]

Rav Asher Weiss, citing the *Chazon Ish*,[23] also believes that most secular Jews have the status of a *tinok shenishbah*.[24] Rav Binyomin Zilber, himself a *talmid* of the *Chazon Ish*, says the logic to consider secular Jews as *tinokos shenishbu* is only in locations where they are not exposed to religious life.[25] However, in Israel, where they are often exposed to authentic Torah and mitzvos, their rejection of religion is considered

---

it is only on occasion, not as a policy or on a regular basis. However, see *Chashukei Chemed*, *Shabbos* 4a, where Rav Yitzchak Zilberstein says that it would not be permissible to violate the *issur d'Rabbanan* of disarming an alarm (that is, even doing it with a *shinui*, in an unusual way) to prevent irreligious Jews from violating Shabbos by phoning the police.

20 *Shabbos* 68b.

21 *Teshuvos Binyan Tzion Hachadashos* §23. Rav Hershel Schachter told me (on *parashas Vayigash* 2015) that we would consider them like a *tinok shenishbah* if they grew up in a secular environment.

22 *Yabia Omer*, vol. 1, p. 197.

23 *Yoreh Dei'ah* 2:28.

24 *Shu"t Minchas Asher*, vol. 1, §10, p. 41. See, however, the letters of the *Chazon Ish* (*Orchos Rabbeinu*, vol. 1, p. 226, cited in *Pesakim Uteshuvos*, §251, p. 391), who limits the applicability of *tinok shenishbah*. See also *Teshuvos Vehanhagos*, vol. 6, §90, where he cites the *Chazon Ish* (*Yoreh Dei'ah* 1:6, 2:28) as applying the concept of *tinok shenishbah* to those who were not educated in Torah and mitzvos, even if they were exposed to or knew about them.

25 *Az Nidbaru*, vol. 9, §55, cited in *Genuzos Haparshah*, p. 473. Rav Moshe Sternbuch (*Teshuvos Vehanhagos*, vol. 4, §32) says that Russians Jews who immigrated to Israel and know nothing about Judaism are certainly in the category of *tinokos shenishbu*.

one of rebellion, and they are not in the category of *tinokos shenishbu*. In general, Rav Moshe Feinstein and Rav Shlomo Zalman Auerbach[26] did not consider contemporary irreligious Jews as *tinokos shenishbu*.[27] However, Rav Moshe, elsewhere,[28] seems to accept the idea of *tinok shenishbah* in our times.

SUMMARY

Based on the opinions who rule that secular Jews are considered *tinokos shenishbu*,[29] it might be permissible to sin in order to save those who freely join other religions, since they don't really understand what Judaism is about, and because perhaps they are not considered to have intentionally and negligently disregarded their religion. Saving them is also considered a *mitzvah rabbah*, because we enable them to lead lives full of Torah and mitzvos.

This may also be the case where women fall prey to Arab men. They, too, are perhaps not considered negligent and may be saved by others, even at the expense of violating Shabbos in order to help them live as Jews. However, the Gemara says that *tinokos shenishbu* have to bring a *korban*. That, says Rav Moshe, means that they cannot be considered *ones*, implying they may be *shogeg* and negligent. This would seem to limit the type of *chillul Shabbos* that one could do on behalf of their spiritual danger.[30]

---

26   *Halichos Shlomo: Moadei Hashana Nissan-Av*, *Seder Leil Pesach*, siman 69, footnote 134.

27   *Igros Moshe*, *Even Ha'ezer*, vol. 1, §82:11. Rav Moshe doesn't consider irreligious Jews as *tinokos shenishbu* since they are exposed to Torah and mitzvos. We can infer that if there is an unobservant Jew who was not exposed to a religious lifestyle, he is considered a *tinok shenishbah*. See *Igros Moshe*, *Orach Chaim*, vol. 1, §23 and §33, where Rav Moshe says that nowadays, public Shabbos desecrators can count toward a *minyan*. See *Shu"t Takanas Hashavim*, p. 24. See also *Kovetz Mevakshei Torah*, vol. 15, p. 245, and *Teshuvos Vehanhagos*, vol. 2, §460, who says that irreligious Jews today have the status of *tinokos shenishbu*, unless they were educated properly and nevertheless rejected it.

28   *Igros Moshe*, *Orach Chaim*, vol. 4, §91:6.

29   See *Masa Behar* (p. 368), where Rav Avidan discusses whether a soldier can radio the army rabbi on Shabbos to ask him to overturn an officer's order entailing *chillul Shabbos*. Rav Avidan differentiates between soldiers who are in the category of *tinok shenishbah*, who are not considered negligent, and other irreligious soldiers who are. Therefore, he permits violating the *issur* of radioing the army rabbi to stop the *tinok shenishbah* soldiers from violating Shabbos, but forbids it if all the other soldiers are negligent and should have known to refuse such orders on their own. See *Teshuvos Vehanhagos*, vol. 2, §207, for a similar distinction.

30   *Igros Moshe*, *Orach Chaim*, vol. 5, §13:9.

INTERRUPTING SHEMONEH ESREH FOR A MISSILE

IN THE NEWS

The Iron Dome missile defense system has proven to be one of the most effective ways for the IDF to stop the assault of missiles from Gaza. Located near the border of Gaza and major population centers, the Iron Dome is designed to intercept missiles being shot into Israel. The overwhelming success of the system in preventing missiles from landing in and damaging populated areas has led to an interesting halachic discussion.

As a rule, when one is davening *Shemoneh Esreh* (the silent *Amidah* prayer), one is not permitted to interrupt his *tefillah*.[1] In recent years, the question arose: What should one do if the siren warning of a missile attack goes off while one is davening *Shemoneh Esreh*—should he interrupt his *tefillah* and run to the closest bomb shelter?

According to a Ynet news story,[2] Rav Yosef Sheinin, the Ashkenazic chief rabbi of Ashdod, ruled that if one is in a place that has the protection of the Iron Dome, one is not permitted to interrupt his *Shemoneh Esreh* and run to a bomb shelter when the sirens go off. Rav Sheinin explained that since the Iron Dome has been so accurate in stopping the missiles, one does not have to be concerned about being struck by a missile and should therefore not interrupt his *Shemoneh Esreh*.

---

1   *Shulchan Aruch, Orach Chaim* 104:1.
2   Kobi Nachshoni, *"Rav Ha'ir Ashdod: Azakah batefillah? Lo lazuz"* (March 18, 2012), www.ynet.co.il.

Rav Sheinin bases his *p'sak* on the Gemara's statement that if a snake is wrapped around a person's heel, he should not interrupt his *Shemoneh Esreh*.[3] However, if a scorpion is wrapped around his heel, he should interrupt his *tefillah* and distance himself from the scorpion. The difference is that with a snake, the danger is minimal, since if one remains calm, the snake will probably not bite him.[4] But a scorpion's nature is to bite regardless of whether a person stays calm, and therefore the danger is significant, and it's permitted to interrupt *Shemoneh Esreh* to deal with the situation. Rav Sheinin concludes that in areas that have an Iron Dome, the danger has been downgraded from the level of a "scorpion" to the level of a "snake," and one cannot interrupt his *Shemoneh Esreh* to respond when a siren rings, including walking to a bomb shelter.

This ruling may seem a bit surprising. Is there a halachic basis to permit running to a bomb shelter in the middle of *Shemoneh Esreh*?

A TORAH PERSPECTIVE

Indeed, Rav Shlomo Aviner ruled that if someone is in the middle of *Shemoneh Esreh* when he hears the siren of an incoming missile, he should run to the nearest bomb shelter and finish his *Shemoneh Esreh* there.[5] He permits this even in the event that there is an Iron Dome

---

3   *Berachos* 33a.

4   But if you see that the snake is agitated and may attack, you are permitted to move (*Shulchan Aruch*, *Orach Chaim* 104:3). Also, Rav Elyashiv says that today, most people are not accustomed to being around snakes; therefore, if one is davening and a snake appears next to him, he is permitted to walk away since it would be a complete distraction to his concentration (*shiurim* on *Berachos* 30b, cited in the Dirshu edition of the *Mishnah Berurah*, vol. 1, p. 264). The *Piskei Teshuvos* (104:3) also says that nowadays if one sees a snake, or any dangerous animal, one should move away and alert others to avoid any danger.

5   *On the Air with Rav Aviner* (J Levine/Millennium, 2009), p. 246.
       The following story occurred during the First Gulf War (January 17 to February 28, 1991):

> One Friday night in the middle of the war, we were davening in Rav [Moshe] Sternbuch's minyan when the urgent wail of the air-raid sirens was suddenly heard throughout the city. We were close to finishing the silent Shemone Esrei of Ma'ariv. The men were panicky, unsure whether or not they should run out in the middle of davening to take shelter in their sealed rooms. Every eye in the shul turned to Rav Sternbuch for guidance. By this time, everyone in the minyan had concluded Shemone Esrei. Rav Sternbuch didn't hesitate for a moment. He

system.[6] This is because walking without speaking is not considered an interruption, as long as it is for a legitimate need.[7]

Rav Aviner brings other, more common, examples where it is permitted to stop in the middle of *Shemoneh Esreh* to deal with an important matter. For instance, if a child is disturbing your concentration during *Shemoneh Esreh*, you can stop davening, walk to another place, and continue there.[8] Also, if you are davening from memory, and it is Rosh Chodesh, you can walk to the shelf and take a *siddur* to say *Yaaleh Veyavo*.[9] Similarly, Rav Chaim Kanievsky ruled[10] that if one is davening on a bus

---

gave a clop on the bima and told the chazzan to proceed with the davening, thus demonstrating a praiseworthy dose of emuna and bitachon, not only for himself but for the entire kehila as well. Subsequently, during the Gaza conflict in the summer of 2014, for the first time in Israel's history, there were missiles that landed on the outskirts of Jerusalem. In an eerie sense of déjà vu, the air-raid siren once again went off in the middle of Friday-night davening, just as it had 23 years earlier. As before, every eye in the shul turned to see how Rav Sternbuch would handle the emergency situation. The rav ignored the siren and kept on davening, calmly and with assurance. Everyone in the shul realized that Rav Sternbuch had no intention of running anywhere. He felt perfectly secure in his shul. Immediately, everyone calmed down and the davening concluded without overwhelming feelings of angst. After davening, I [Rabbi Yehoshua Liff] approached the rav and asked, "Does the rav hold that since we're currently in shul, there is no reason to be afraid? And if that is the case, what happens when we're at home and the sirens go off? Should we be afraid then?" Rav Sternbuch explained that he personally believed that the danger level did not approach that of pikuach nefesh, danger to life, and people did not have to run into their safe rooms. However, if a person is afraid, he should certainly go into his shelter. But what does this all mean? Should a person be afraid or not? No, he replied. A person should not be afraid. A person should have emuna and bitachon in the Ribbono Shel Olam and trust He knows what He's doing and that there is nothing to worry about. Again, this is only if a person isn't afraid. But anyone who feels fear and is worried about the sirens and the missiles should take the necessary precautions. (Nachman Seltzer, At His Rebbi's Side [ArtScroll/ Mesorah, 2017], pp. 368–70)

See the biography of Rav Eliyahu Lopian (Rabbi David J. Schlossberg, *Reb Elyah: The Life and Accomplishments of Rabbi Elyah Lopian* [ArtScroll/Mesorah, 1999], p. 68), regarding his eagerness to run to bomb shelters for safety.

6   Aviner, Rav Shlomo, "הפסק בתפילת שמונה עשרה": שיעורי הרב שלמה אבינר, shlomo-aviner.net.
7   *Rema in Shulchan Aruch* 104:3; *Mishnah Berurah* 104:10.
8   *Mishnah Berurah* 104:1
9   *Mishnah Berurah* 96:7; 104:2.
10 *Ishei Yisrael* 83:43.

and the bus reaches his stop while he is in the middle of *Shemoneh Esreh*, he may stop davening, get off the bus, and then finish *Shemoneh Esreh*.[11]

Rabbi Aryeh Lebowitz mentions a related case.[12] One Yom Kippur, in a shul in Queens, New York, during *Chazaras Hashatz* (the repetition of the *Amidah*) of *Shacharis*, the congregants heard "the chandelier rattling. People looked up and saw a squirrel running around the chandelier. When the squirrel fell down to the floor, everyone panicked. Even the chazzan ran for the exit door." Chaos reigned in the shul, and no one knew what to do. In the end, an announcement was made that everyone should vacate the premises until the squirrel was taken care of. The rabbi maintained that no matter where someone was up to in the davening, he should go outside so they could get the squirrel out of the shul, and then they would continue the davening. Was it permissible for the chazzan, and those still in the middle of *Shemoneh Esreh*, to interrupt their davening and walk outside?

Rabbi Lebowitz explains the issue by quoting the *Beis Yosef*.[13] The *Beis Yosef* cites *Rabbeinu Yonah*, who says that when the Gemara forbids interrupting *Shemoneh Esreh* on account of a snake, it means that one should not speak, but one can walk away from the reptile and continue davening in a new location. Thus, walking away from something that is bothering a person is not considered an interruption.

Likewise, the *Biur Halachah* and the *Mishnah Berurah* say that if there is a "*tzorech gadol*," a great need, then walking away in the middle of *Shemoneh Esreh* is not called an interruption, and it is permitted to do so.[14] The *Piskei Teshuvos* simiarly rules that if a cat or bird enters the

---

11 It would appear from the *Shulchan Aruch* (*Orach Chaim* 104:5) that this *p'sak* of Rav Chaim applies to a brief interruption in one's *Shemoneh Esreh*, for, the *Shulchan Aruch* (*Orach Chaim* 104:5) says that if one takes an extended break in between stopping and reaching the other place to finish *Shemoneh Esreh* (longer than the amount of time it takes to say the entire *Shemoneh Esreh*), one must restart *Shemoneh Esreh* from the beginning. If it's only a short break, then one continues from where he left off. At that point, if one is able, it is best to return to the location where he started reciting *Shemoneh Esreh* (*Piskei Teshuvos* 104:1).

12 Rabbi Aryeh Lebowitz, "From the Rabbi's Desk—The Squirrel That Stole Yom Kippur" (Oct. 15, 2015), www.yutorah.org.

13 *Orach Chaim* 104:3.

14 *Biur Halachah* 104:3, s.v. "*lo yafsik*"; *Mishnah Berurah* 104:10. Elsewhere the *Mishnah Berurah*

shul and distracts people from *Shemoneh Esreh*, they can go to a different room and continue davening there.[15]

Along these lines, on April 18, 2008, *The New York Times* ran a story about a Jewish passenger who was ejected from a plane prior to takeoff because he would not sit down.[16] The flight attendants repeatedly asked him to return to his seat, but the man was in the middle of praying and didn't respond to their request. By the time the man returned to his seat, a customer service agent had already been called in, and he ejected him from the plane.[17] A yeshivah student interviewed in the article covering the story supported the man's decision by quoting the Talmud that states that one may not interrupt the *Amidah* even if a snake is wrapped around one's leg, unless one's life is in danger.

However, according to the halachah, one *is* permitted to walk during *Shemoneh Esreh* and return to his seat, since that would be considered a legitimate need.[18] Furthermore, a number of *Gedolim* hold that one should daven at his seat on a plane, even when saying *Shemoneh Esreh*, and even if he has the opportunity to join a *minyan* in the back of the plane, so as not to disturb others on the plane.[19]

    (128:28) cites an opinion that a *Kohen* cannot interrupt his *Shemoneh Esreh* in order to walk over to where the other *Kohanim* are performing the *Birkas Kohanim* (Priestly Blessing).

15   *Piskei Teshuvos* 104:3, n. 55.

16   Ken Belson, "Praying Passenger Ejected From Jet for Failing to Return to His Seat" (April 18, 2008), www.nytimes.com.

17   See also *Vehaarev Na*, vol. 2, *parashas Ki Savo*, for a similar incident of a Jew who was praying with his *tefillin* on, causing angst among the other passengers. The stewardess asked him what they were, and the man refused to respond since he was in the middle of *Shemoneh Esreh*, prompting the plane to make an emergency landing. Rav Zilberstein says that although the *Shulchan Aruch* (*Orach Chaim* 104:1) says not to interrupt in the middle of *Shemoneh Esreh* even to respond to a king, and the *Mishnah Berurah* (104:2) adds that this applies even if one will lose money, because of the danger involved in making an emergency landing and the resulting contempt for Jews that may ensue, the man should have written down on a paper what he was doing and what the *tefillin* were.

18   See n. 22.

19   The *Gedolim* who give this ruling are Rav Shlomo Zalman Auerbach (*Halichos Shlomo*, p. 95), Rav Moshe Feinstein (*Igros Moshe, Orach Chaim*, vol. 4, §20), Rav Ovadiah Yosef (*Halachic Guide for the Passengers of El Al* 9:1), and Rav Shlomo Wahrman (*She'eiris Yosef*, vol. 7, §3). Rav Chaim Pinchas Scheinberg, zt"l, however, feels that one should pray with a *minyan* on a plane, provided one doesn't disturb other passengers (*Torat HaRav Aviner*, Short & Sweet—Text Message Q&A #321, www.ravaviner.com). Rav Elyashiv (*Vayishma Moshe*,

One final question about interrupting *Shemoneh Esreh*:

Rav Zilberstein relates the following incident:[20] A man was in the middle of praying *Shemoneh Esreh* when he realized that he had not inserted money into the parking meter. As a result, he was having difficulty concentrating on the *Amidah*, because his mind kept wandering back to the parking meter. He looked up and saw, through the window, two policemen writing a ticket for the car next to his. He put two and two together and understood that he was going to get a ticket next. He wondered if he was permitted to leave in the middle of *Shemoneh Esreh* and put money into the meter to avoid receiving the large parking fine.

Since the *Shulchan Aruch* says that one may not interrupt his *Shemoneh Esreh* even if a king speaks to him,[21] it would seem that it is not permitted to go put money in the meter unless there is a danger to his life. The *Mishnah Berurah* also writes that one may not interrupt his *Shemoneh Esreh* even to avoid a monetary loss.[22]

However, as mentioned earlier, some *poskim* say that as long as one doesn't speak or completely take his mind off his *Shemoneh Esreh*, then, for a great need, it is permitted to walk away in the middle of the prayer.[23] Therefore, it would seem to be permitted for the man to quickly walk and pay the meter, and then return to finish his *Shemoneh Esreh*. After all, the *Mishnah Berurah* says that one can calm a child down in the middle of saying the *Amidah* because it is distracting to his concentration,[24] and thinking about a possible parking fine is also very distracting.[25] Therefore, the *Piskei Teshuvos* rules that a person in the

---

vol. 4, pp. 23–24) believes that on an airplane it is preferable to pray while standing with less *kavanah*, than while sitting with more *kavanah*.

20   *Vehaarev Na*, vol. 1, p. 327.

21   *Shulchan Aruch, Orach Chaim* 104:1.

22   *Mishnah Berurah* 104:2. The *Kaf Hachaim* (*Orach Chaim* 104:6) says that although the *Rema* (*Orach Chaim* 656:1) rules that a person is not obligated to spend more than one-fifth of his assets to perform a *mitzvas aseih*, in this case, it would seem that one would be required to suffer a loss even greater than a fifth in order to not interrupt his *Shemoneh Esreh*. Since he has already begun to speak to Hashem, it is a disgrace to interrupt his prayer in order to prevent a financial loss.

23   *Mishnah Berurah* 104:10.

24   *Mishnah Berurah* 104:1. *Shaarei Teshuvah* 104:15 permits this only without speaking.

25   The *poskim* bring other examples of permitted activities in order to remove serious

middle of *Shemoneh Esreh* may, without speaking, go to his car, pay the meter, and then return to his *Shemoneh Esreh*.[26]

However, Rav Yitzchak Zilberstein disagrees with this *p'sak* and rules that one absolutely may not interrupt his *Shemoneh Esreh* to pay the parking meter, and someone who would leave shul in the middle of his *Shemoneh Esreh* for such a reason is fulfilling the *pasuk*, "He has scorned the word of Hashem and violated His commandment,"[27] because he is showing a severe lack of respect toward Hashem (especially since he put himself in this situation).[28] Rav Zilberstein asks: Would he do that if he were speaking to a human king? Rather, he should overcome the distraction to his concentration and ignore the monetary loss.[29]

SUMMARY

Thus, when there is an Iron Dome, according to Rav Sheinin, one should not interrupt his *Shemoneh Esreh* to find a bomb shelter if a missile siren rings out. Rav Aviner, though, maintains that it is permitted to move to a shelter, as this too would be included in moving for a legitimate need, which the *Mishnah Berurah* permits.

---

distractions while one is in the middle of saying *Shemoneh Esreh* (see *Tefillah Kehilchasah* 12:86). However, walking in the middle of *Shemoneh Esreh* for a mitzvah is generally not permitted (*Shulchan Aruch, Orach Chaim* 104:7; *Piskei Teshuvos*, p. 791).

26   *Piskei Teshuvos* 104:1.
27   *Bamidbar* 15:31.
28   *Vehaarev Na*, vol. 1, p. 327.
29   Rav Zilberstein cites the Gemara in *Sukkah* 25b as support for this idea.

JEWISH-GENTILE MUSIC

IN THE NEWS

In August of 2015, the Israeli website Kikar HaShabbat reported that many fans of Chassidic singer Levy Falkowitz were upset by his new song "*Achakeh Lo.*"[1] It appears that Falkowitz used the tune from American rock singer Amii Stewart's hit single "Working Late Tonight," which was released in 1983. Lipa Schmeltzer, himself a famous Jewish singer and entertainer, came to Falkowitz's defense and said that Chassidic Rebbes, including the Baal Shem Tov, taught that taking non-Jewish music and applying it to Jewish songs elevates them.

Also, in the summer of 2014, when the IDF was fighting a war in Gaza to protect Israel from enemy rockets, Hamas released a song called "*T'kof, Taaseh Biguim,*" which was meant to instill fear in the hearts and minds of Israelis. The music video went viral in Israel, with many parodies produced. Rav Shlomo Aviner ruled that it is prohibited to listen to the song, even to make parodies of it. Rav Aviner explained that in addition to the words and tune of a song, the composer's spirit can have an impact on the person listening to the music; therefore, the composer should be someone with good character. Clearly, Hamas is excluded.[2]

There are a number of examples of non-Jewish songs that have made their way into the world of Jewish music. Chabad Chassidim sing "Napoleon's March" at the conclusion of the *Ne'ilah* services on Yom

---

1   Yisrael Cohen, "*Se'arah BeSatmar: Niggun Chassidi nechshaf ke'giyur' lelahit shel zimras goyah*" (Aug. 4, 2015), www.kikar.co.il.

2   Yonatan Orich, "*Harav Aviner: Assur lishmo'a 'T'kof, Taaseh Biguim'*" (Aug. 28, 2014), www. nrg.co.il.

Kippur, before sounding the *shofar*. The song represents the victory of the Jewish People over the Satan and that our prayers have been accepted. The Alter Rebbe of Chabad considered it a song of victory.[3]

Similarly, Mordechai Ben David used the tune of the West German entry in the 1979 Eurovision Song Contest, "Dschinghis Khan," for his song "*Yidden*," and the whole archive of Shlock Rock music comes from secular tunes. Yosi Piamenta related that when composing his song "*Mitzvah Goreret Mitzvah*" (which means, one commandment leads to another, from *Pirkei Avos* 4:2), he was concerned that it may not be permitted to use a rock tune. However, a rabbi he asked said, "Permitted? It would be a mitzvah!" The apparent rationale was that it would spread the message that doing mitzvos is a good thing.[4]

Following the trend, on November 3, 2014, Arutz Sheva reported about a viral video of a Chassidic singer from the UK, Chaim Shlomo Mayes, rapping a song called "*Bas Kol*" (Talmudic term for "Heavenly voice") to the tune of Fifth Harmony's hip-hop track "Worth It."[5] Also, in 2019, "*Adama v'Shamayim*" became a popular song played at weddings, though the words are rooted in *avodah zarah* (specifically, an earth-worshipping pagan cult). And finally, there was a Jewish a cappella group that recently turned a Christmas song into a Chanukah song.

Can one use secular tunes for Jewish songs and prayer?

A TORAH PERSPECTIVE

Rav Hershel Schachter said that a person gives over part of his soul, his *neshamah*, into the songs he sings.[6] So when a person listens to a song, he is tapping into the soul of the composer. It is therefore crucial that the music he is listening to comes from a holy source.

Rav Yaakov Hillel supports this idea.[7] Rav Hillel notes that when the Jewish People were looking for a musician to play music for King

---

3   "Napoleons March," www.chabad.org.

4   Rabbi Jack Abramowitz, "Can Orthodox Jews Listen to Secular Music?" (Oct. 29, 2015), www.jewinthecity.com.

5   "Watch: The hassidic rap that went viral" (Nov. 3, 2015), www.israelnationalnews.com.

6   Rabbi Aryeh Lebowitz, "Ten Minute Halacha—Listening to Secular Music" (April 17, 2013), www.yutorah.org.

7   *Vayashav Hayam*, p. 148, cited in *Umekarev Beyamin*, vol. 2, p. 46.

Shaul, they found a musician (David) who was a Godly person.[8] Again, this was because the type of person who composes the music is significant when it comes to the impact it will have on the listener.

Additionally, Rav Ovadiah Yosef was asked if it is permitted to use non-Jewish love songs as the tunes for *Kaddish* or *Kedushah*.[9] Rav Ovadiah began by citing the *Sefer Chassidim*, which says one shouldn't sing non-Jewish songs and that our voices were given to us to praise Hashem, not for sinning.[10] He added, though, that the concern is only for singing non-Jewish love songs (or other inappropriate songs) with the actual words, but using the tune alone is permitted when praying. Rav Ovadiah finds support for this in the *Rif*,[11] who says that a *sheliach tzibbur* (cantor) who sings non-Jewish songs, even outside of shul, should be removed from his position, as the *pasuk* says, "She raised her voice against Me; therefore I hated her."[12] The *Rema* codifies this ruling of the *Rif*.[13] Rav Ovadiah points out that these sources imply that just using non-Jewish tunes in prayer, without singing the actual songs, would not be forbidden. Nevertheless, Rav Ovadiah rules that one should be strict and not use tunes that are used for idolatrous services, like Christmas carols.[14]

---

8   *Shmuel I* 16:18.

9   See *Yechaveh Daat*, vol. 2, §5.

10   *Sefer Chassidim* §768.

11   *Shu"t HaRif* §281.

12   *Yirmiyah* 12:8.

13   *Rema, Orach Chaim* 53:25. The *Shulchan Aruch Harav* (*Orach Chaim* §32) says that the *sheliach tzibbur* is disqualified only if he uses these tunes during the services, not if he sings them at other times. The *Levush* (ibid. §25) says that a person is disqualified from being a *sheliach tzibbur* if he sings non-Jewish songs at any time, since this will contaminate his body and soul, and it is very likely that during prayer he will be thinking about these songs, negatively affecting his own prayer.

14   Rav Ovadiah (*Yabia Omer, Orach Chaim*, vol. 6, §7) says that one shouldn't sing tunes used for *avodah zarah*, although he quotes some authorities who say that it is appropriate to use them for *kedushah* (holiness) and thereby uplift them. Rav Moshe (*Igros Moshe, Yoreh Dei'ah*, vol. 2, §56 and §111) says it is prohibited to listen to songs used by Christians in their services, and even listening to them on the radio is not permitted. The *Mishnah Berurah* (53:82) specifies that it is only forbidden to use non-Jewish tunes that were used in idolatrous services, though the *Mishnah Berurah* may agree that *singing* inappropriate non-Jewish songs at any time will disqualify a *sheliach tzibbur*. Using tunes from idol worship, though, will only disqualify him if used during davening (the *Tzitz Eliezer* mentions this distinction).

Rav Ovadiah notes that there were many great Jewish scholars who composed praises to Hashem using non-Jewish tunes,[15] and these songs of praise have become accepted by many Jewish congregations in the Friday night davening. Rav Ovadiah notes the importance of serving and praying to Hashem with joy and says that if the non-Jewish tunes help us achieve this, then it is praiseworthy and that was the basis for using them in the first place.[16]

Rav Ovadiah, though, is concerned that if we use non-Jewish tunes in our prayer, they will remind people of the original inappropriate lyrics. But, he says, it is certainly fine to use non-Jewish tunes that have long been accepted and whose non-Jewish origin has mostly been forgotten.

More stringently, the *Tzitz Eliezer* was very much opposed to using non-Jewish tunes in davening.[17] He compared it to Nadav and Avihu's bringing a foreign fire to the Altar, a fire that Hashem didn't command them to bring (they were subsequently killed by a Heavenly fire).[18] It is a disgrace, he said, to corrupt our souls and the holy words of the Jewish prayer with the impurity of these tunes, and they will cause one to go after his *yetzer hara*. He added that those great scholars who used them were probably unaware of their origin.

The *Shevet HaLevi* agrees with the *Tzitz Eliezer* and explains that this is the simple understanding of the *Rema* (i.e., that even just using

---

15   Rav Yaakov Hillel doesn't believe that great *tzaddikim* used songs from nonkosher sources for davening, and he holds that no one is allowed to listen to them, even in order to use them for *tefillah*. But with regard to those songs that became part of our *mesorah* and that everyone sings in davening, it seems that we have already sanctified them and therefore they are now permitted (*Umekarev Beyamin*, vol. 2, p. 45). Rabbi Ari Enkin writes in his *Halichot V'halachot: Halachic Insights and Responsa* (Mosaica, 2016), p. 259: "Rabbi Israel Moshe Hazzan writes that the great rabbis of Smyrna, under the leadership of Rabbi Abraham HaKohen Arias, went to a local Greek Orthodox church to listen to their melodies and adapted them for *Kaddish* and *Kedushah*! Rav Ovadiah Yosef did the same at a mosque in Cairo."

16   Rav Ovadiah Yosef enjoyed reminiscing about his childhood, when he and his friends would sing songs of praise to Hashem on Shabbos before prayer from 2 a.m. to 7 a.m. Rav Ovadiah noted that many of the songs utilized gentile melodies. (Yehuda Azoulay, *Maran: The Life and Scholarship of Hacham Ovadia Yosef* [Israel Bookshop, 2014], p. 73).

17   *Tzitz Eliezer*, vol. 13, §12.

18   *Vayikra* 10:1.

the tunes of non-Jewish songs is forbidden during prayer), unlike the way Rav Ovadiah understood the *Rema*.[19] With regard to the popular song, "*Adama v'Shamayim*," Rav Hershel Schachter ruled that songs that certainly come from *avodah zarah* are *assur* based on *chukas akum* and, therefore, one is prohibited from singing it.[20]

Music has such a great impact on a person that it is important not just for the *sheliach tzibbur* to be careful, but also for every Jew to try to listen to Jewish music and musicians that are in line with the messages and values of the Torah.[21] Certainly, non-Jewish songs that will be recognized throughout the shul and will lead to levity or mockery are inappropriate.

SUMMARY

Rav Ovadiah Yosef permits using secular tunes in prayer and in singing, as long as they don't have any connection to idolatry. He adds that it is best if people do not know the origins of the tune when it is used. The *Tzitz Eliezer* and *Shevet HaLevi*, however, rule that one should not use non-Jewish tunes in prayer.

---

19 *Shevet HaLevi*, vol. 9, §19.

20 "Ten Minute Halacha—*Adama v'Shamayim* and *Avoda Zara*?" (April 15, 2019) www.yutorah.org.

21 Rav Moshe Meir Weiss once said that he heard from Rabbi Shlomo Carlebach that the reason his music became so popular is because he never listened to secular music.

KAREEM AND THE POWER OF A CURSE

IN THE NEWS

Rabbi Abba Yaakov Liff, *zt"l*, was one of the original students of Rav Yaakov Yitzchak Ruderman, *zt"l*, at Yeshivas Ner Israel in Baltimore. His son, Rabbi Yehoshua Liff, published a *sefer* called *Birkas Abba Yaakov* in honor of his father's memory. The *sefer* contains numerous anecdotes, including the following story:[1]

Rabbi Abba Yaakov Liff was once returning to Baltimore from Milwaukee, where he had undergone an operation. On the plane, he was accompanied by the famous basketball player, Kareem Abdul-Jabbar, though Rabbi Liff did not know who he was.

While unpacking from the trip, Rabbi Liff realized that he and Kareem had mistakenly switched boxes; Rabbi Liff had brought home Kareem's electronics. The airline confirmed this when he called, so Rabbi Liff returned the electronics but never heard back about his missing *sefarim* boxes.

A little while later, an irreligious Jew, named Walter Levine, called Rabbi Liff to inform him that he had found his *sefarim* (identified by his name and address in them) tossed on the side of the road between Baltimore and Washington. The details pointed to Kareem having thrown them out of his car when he noticed the mistake.

---

1   Page 50, n. 37. As told in "Of Curses, Seforim & Kareem Abdul-Jabaar!" (April 27, 2011), rabbimichaelgreen.com. This story is also told in Rabbi Yehoshua Liff's book, *At His Rebbi's Side* (ArtScroll/Mesorah, 2017), pp. 14–16.

Rabbi Liff, who was very disturbed by what had happened to his precious *sefarim*, said that the hand of whoever was responsible for the disrespectful handling of the *sefarim* should be punished.

Shortly after this, an opponent collided with Kareem during an NBA game and hurt him. In reaction, he hit the hoop's support stanchion and broke his hand, causing him to miss a significant amount of games that season. That season was the first time in his career that his team missed the playoffs. Rabbi Yehoshua Liff understood that the reason Kareem injured his eye and hand was because of the way he had mistreated his father's holy books.

Rabbi Berel Wein, a famous historian, author, and lecturer, was once asked about the purported "Kennedy curse," an explanation for the numerous tragedies that befell the Kennedy family.[2] Some say that Joseph Kennedy was cursed by a Jew (there are several versions of the story, which include different accounts of who this Jew was and why he cursed him). Rabbi Wein responded that the Kennedy curse is a legend that was made up after John F. Kennedy ran for president. He added that Jews don't curse people.

In another sports-related news story, *The New York Times* published an article in 2016 detailing how some people believe that NBA star Kevin Durant's playoff failures are due to a curse placed on him by a Bay Area rapper.[3]

Is a person ever allowed to curse someone? Do curses have an effect?

A TORAH PERSPECTIVE

The Torah says, "Do not curse the deaf,"[4] and one who violates this prohibition incurs lashes.[5] *Rashi* and the *Sefer Hachinuch* explain that

---

2   Rabbi Berel Wein, "Ask the Rabbi: The Kennedy Family" (16 Cheshvan 5763), www.yeshiva.co.

3   Jonah Engel Bromwich, "Outplayed? Perhaps. But Some See Rapper's Hex Behind Thunder's Downfall" (June 1, 2016), www.nytimes.com.

4   *Vayikra* 19:14.

5   The *Shulchan Aruch* points out (*Choshen Mishpat* §27) that one only receives lashes if he cursed a person using one of the Names of Hashem. Therefore, to say "God damn you" may be considered a Biblical violation of cursing someone else, because God is considered a Name of Hashem according to some *poskim*. The *Rambam* (*Hilchos Sanhedrin* 26:3) explicitly says that the Biblical prohibition is violated not only using the Name of Hashem in *lashon hakodesh*, but in any language. Interestingly, with regard to the prohibition of erasing a Name

the example of a deaf person is merely that—an example—and the prohibition applies to cursing anyone.[6]

What is the reason that it is wrong to curse someone? The *Sefer Hachinuch* explains that even though we don't appreciate the harm and damage that a curse can cause someone, it does have a negative effect, and people are still afraid of being cursed. So, since the Torah forbids us from actively causing damage to others, we must also avoid something that they perceive as damaging, such as cursing them.[7]

---

of Hashem, some *poskim* say it does not include His Name written in a foreign language (*Shach, Yoreh Dei'ah* 179:11; *Rambam, Hilchos Yesodei HaTorah* 6:5). (Based on this halachah, Rav Shlomo Zalman Auerbach [*Halichos Shlomo, Tefillah,* ch. 20, n. 33] ruled that it is permitted to bring a dollar bill into a bathroom, even though the word "God" is written on it, because one doesn't have to treat this written word with respect.) The *Kitzur Shulchan Aruch* (6:3), though, writes that any cursing of another, even without using a Name of Hashem, is prohibited. An example would be, "May so-and-so not be blessed to Hashem," or any other statement of negative wishes.

6   *Rashi, Vayikra* 19:14; *Sefer Hachinuch* §231. See also *Torah Temimah,* cited in *Torah Ladaas* (vols. 4–5, *parashas Kedoshim*), who explains the Torah means that one cannot curse a deaf person, prince, or anyone in between. The *Shulchan Aruch* (*Choshen Mishpat* §27) says that the prohibition is to curse any Jew, while the *Shaar Mishpat* (to *Shulchan Aruch, Choshen Mishpat* §27) explains, based on the Gemara in *Makkos* 8b, that it is only forbidden to curse someone who acts properly. The *Minchas Chinuch* (§231) seems to say that it is also Rabbinically prohibited to curse a gentile, while the *Rambam* (*Hilchos Sanhedrin* 26:1) seems to indicate that the prohibition applies only to cursing another Jew.

Interesting to note is that there are additional prohibitions against cursing found in the Torah. For example, it is forbidden to curse Hashem, a judge, or a king (*Shemos* 22:27). It is also forbidden to curse one's parent (*Vayikra* 20:9). The *Rambam* (*Sefer Hamitzvos, Lavin* §317, and *Hilchos Sanhedrin,* ch. 26) explains the need for additional mentions of the same prohibition.

7   See *Rashi* on *Bereishis* 31:32, where he writes, citing the midrash, that Yaakov's curse caused Rachel to die on the road. See also *Megillah* 15a, where Avimelech's curse against Sarah caused Yitzchak's blindness, and see *Megillah* 28a. See *Bava Basra* 22a where Rav Nachman thought that it was his words that caused Rav Ada to die. And see *Mo'ed Katan* 18a and *Bava Metzia* 68a, where the Gemara says a curse uttered by a righteous man is carried out even if it was said unintentionally; similarly, see *Menachos* 68b, and see *Rashi* on *Sanhedrin* 49a, which says that if someone curses a person for no reason, the curse will ultimately affect the one who issued the curse (see *Upiryo Matok, parashas Kedoshim,* pp. 318–19). In addition, the Gemara (*Shevuos* 36b) points out that if a person curses himself, he has violated the mitzvah of protecting oneself from danger (*Devarim* 4:15); this is recorded in the *S'ma* (*Choshen Mishpat* §27). Rav Moshe Feinstein (*Igros Moshe, Orach Chaim,* vol. 3, §78, p. 390) counts this as a separate prohibition from that of cursing another; see also *Rambam, Hilchos Sanhedrin* 26:3. Similarly, see *Igros Moshe* (loc. cit.) where Rav Moshe says that one may permit another to curse him, but that a person may never curse himself. The reason is that cursing another

Additionally, says the *Chinuch*, Hashem planted within every Jew a holy soul that has the ability to effect changes through speech. The *pasuk* says that Hashem blew into Adam a "living soul,"[8] and Onkelos explains this to mean that he made him a "speaking being." Speech is the work of the soul, and the more one perfects his soul, the more effective and powerful his speech is. Thus, the *Chinuch* notes that curses righteous people issue do occur. It seems that curses others issue also have a chance of taking effect.

The *Rambam*, though, says the reason for the prohibition against cursing others is so that the one cursing doesn't become habituated in negative character traits, like anger and revenge.[9] According to the *Rambam*, then, the concern is not that one's curse actually has an effect.[10] Rav Moshe Feinstein agrees with the *Rambam* that a person cannot harm someone else with his curse. It can't be, Rav Moshe argues, that Hashem would listen to him and harm someone else when he himself has violated the prohibition of cursing another. Rather, says Rav Moshe, cursing someone else is prohibited because of the shame and embarrassment his words have caused.[11]

---

person doesn't actually take effect, and the person being cursed gave his permission, so he isn't concerned with the disgrace of being cursed. However, if one curses himself, and Hashem allows the curse to take effect, one is harming himself, which is prohibited. Rav Elyashiv said if someone is cursed for no reason, he has nothing to fear; the curse will turn to blessing (*Mishnas Ish*, p. 253).

8   *Bereishis* 2:7.

9   *Sefer Hamitzvos, Lavin* §317.

10   See *Sefer Hachinuch* §231. The *Rambam*, in *Hilchos Teshuvah* 2:9, also says that if one curses another, he must ask him for forgiveness. Rav Yitzchak Zilberstein (*Chashukei Chemed, Rosh Hashanah*, p. 217) says, based on the *Sefer Hachinuch* (§231), that one only has to ask forgiveness from someone if he cursed him in his presence, since, otherwise, the *Rambam* believes that curses don't actually harm people. See Rabbi Daniel Z. Feldman's *False Facts and True Rumors: Lashon HaRa in Contemporary Culture*, p. 242, n. 38, for a different understanding of the *Rambam* than that of the *Sefer Hachinuch*. For another explanation for why it's prohibited to curse others, see *Or Hachaim* (*Bamidbar* 23:8), cited in *Me'iros Einayim*, p. 627.

11   *Igros Moshe, Orach Chaim*, vol. 3, §78, p. 390. See also *The Rav Thinking Aloud on the Parsha: Sefer Bamidbar*, by David Holzer (Jerusalem: Laor Ltd.), pp. 188–92. See, however, *Teshuvos Vehanhagos*, vol. 3, §353, where Rav Moshe Sternbuch assumes that curses have a real effect and ponders whether one can revoke a curse right after making it, or whether the damage has already been done.

Rav Yonasan Eibeshitz also maintains that curses don't work.[12] He cites the Gemara, which teaches that curses cannot harm people.[13] Therefore, he says, the reason it is prohibited to curse people is because it is in violation of the mitzvah of *"Ve'ahavta lerei'acha kamocha*—Love your fellow Jew like yourself."[14]

Additionally, even if a person curses someone behind his back, the subject will probably find out about it, leading to strife between the two, and this runs counter to Hashem's wish that we have peace between us.

According to the *Sefer Hachinuch*, who maintains that curses can cause harm, can the injured party hold the one who curses responsible? The *Halachos Ketanos* actually examines the responsibility of someone who used the Name of Hashem or magic to kill someone. He writes that just as a person who killed someone with an arrow is responsible for the death he caused, so too, if a person killed someone with words, he is responsible for the death. Obviously, it is extremely difficult to convict someone in court for killing through a curse, but he will be held responsible by Hashem in the Heavenly court.[15]

The *Yehudah Yaaleh* agrees with the *Halachos Ketanos* and rules that if a person kills someone using a Divine Name, he is guilty of murder,[16] and he brings a proof from the Torah. The Torah says that if a person hits someone so hard that he dies, then the striker is punished and killed as well.[17] The Torah also says that when Moshe saw an Egyptian hitting his fellow Jew, Moshe struck and killed the Egyptian.[18] The midrash says that Moshe didn't actually strike the Egyptian but rather

---

12   *Urim Vetumim* 27:4.

13   *Makkos* 11a, citing *Mishlei* 26:2. However, the Gemara there clearly implies that if the person being cursed has sinned, then the curse can take effect. Rav Eibeshitz doesn't seem to address this.

14   *Vayikra* 19:18. A person should also not even give the impression that he is cursing someone. The *Mateh Moshe* says that is why, when saying *Kiddush Levanah*, after one mentions, *"Tipol aleihem eimasah vafachad*—Let fall upon them fear and terror," we say, *"Shalom aleichem"* to people: to make it clear we were not cursing them (*Chashukei Chemed, Nedarim*, p. 114).

15   *Halachos Ketanos*, vol. 2, §98. See also Rabbi Gil Student, "Superheroes in Jewish Thought and Law II" (June 9, 2015), www.torahmusings.com.

16   *Orach Chaim* §199.

17   *Shemos* 21:12.

18   Ibid. 2:12.

used the Divine Name to neutralize him.[19] We find, then, an equation between physically killing someone and spiritually killing someone using the Divine Name.[20]

On the other hand, Rav Yaakov Yisrael Kanievsky, *zt"l*, the Steipler Gaon, says that one is not considered to have harmed someone else with a prayer or a curse because it was not guaranteed to harm him, and only takes effect with Hashem's agreement, since Hashem (the Heavenly court) simply listened to the request.[21] However, killing someone in a more definite way, for example, by using sorcery (if one knew he would be able to harm the person), would be considered one's own action, and the sorcerer would be guilty of harming a fellow man.[22]

---

19 *Midrash Tanchuma, Shemos* §10, cited in *Rashi, Shemos* 2:14.

20 However, the way Rav Yitzchak Zev Soloveitchik, the Brisker Rav, explains the episode of Moshe and the Egyptian, there would be no proof for the opinion of the *Halachos Ketanos* that killing with the Divine Name is considered murder (*Chiddushei HaGriz, Shemos* 2:12, p. 191). The Brisker Rav asks: On what grounds did Moshe allow himself to kill the Egyptian? He answers that it was because the Egyptian had struck a Jew the day before (*Shemos* 2:11), and the Gemara says that Bnei Noach (gentiles) are *chayav misah* (deserving of capital punishment) for striking a Jew (*Sanhedrin* 58b). This halachah is codified by the *Rambam*, who says that a gentile who strikes a Jew—even if it is not fatal—is deserving of death by the hands of Heaven, but is not punishable by a Jewish court (*Hilchos Melachim* 10:6 and *Kesef Mishneh* there; see also *Maharsha, Sanhedrin* 58b, and see *Chiddushei HaRan, Sanhedrin* 58b, who disagrees with the *Rambam*). That is why, explains the Brisker Rav, Moshe killed the Egyptian using the Name of Hashem and not through physical force, because the use of a Divine Name to kill is like death by the hands of Heaven, which is exactly what the Egyptian deserved.

21 *Kehillos Yaakov, Bava Kama* §45. The Steipler explains that when the Gemara speaks of sages being upset with others, looking at them, and causing them to be punished or killed, it is not considered that they harmed or killed the person. It is, rather, like they issued a *p'sak* that these people deserved to be punished, and Hashem agreed to their *p'sak* and punished them. There are also instances where it seems that sages actually cursed people, but these cases are not to be taken literally, since it is prohibited to curse others. Rather, since these great rabbis determined that individuals should be punished for their actions, when they "cursed" those individuals, it is considered like they prayed to Hashem to punish them, and Hashem acquiesced and punished them.

Alternatively, a *talmid chacham* is actually permitted to curse sinners; just as a *talmid chacham* may excommunicate such individuals for the sake of his honor, which is equivalent to the honor of Hashem, he can also curse them when it is necessary. For an alternative explanation of what the Gemara means that a Torah sage caused another to die by merely gazing at him, see *Or Hachaim, Bereishis* 27:23, and *Shemos* 23:23.

22 Rav Aharon HaKohen of Lunil writes, in his *Orchos Chaim* (vol. 2, p. 14), that the practice in

Is it permitted to curse a *rasha*? The *Minchas Chinuch*[23] explains that although the Gemara says that if one curses a *rasha* he is *patur* (exempt from lashes),[24] it is still prohibited to do so, as the word *patur* is used throughout the Talmud to mean *"patur aval assur"*—meaning it is still forbidden Rabbinically to curse an evil person.[25] The *Chazon Ish* says that if a person intentionally sins and deserves to be excommunicated for what he did, it is permitted to curse him.[26]

---

his locale was to invite all of one's enemies to his child's *bris* so they would come to bless the father instead of cursing him (*Upiryo Matok, parashas Vayigash*, p. 460). (The practice not to invite people to a *bris* is beyond the scope of this note.)

23   Mitzvah §231. Rav Yitzchak Zilberstein says that the Steipler was asked: Just as he blesses so many people, why doesn't he curse the terrorists? To which he answered that it is the way of a Jew to bless and not curse others (*Lechanech Besimchah*, p. 286).

24   *Sanhedrin* 85a.

25   The *Minchas Chinuch* also says there that if one uses Hashem's Name to curse an evil person, then he has still violated the Biblical prohibition of using Hashem's Name in vain. See *Torah Ladaas* (vols. 4–5, *parashas Kedoshim*) for a discussion of the question the *Minchas Chinuch* asks regarding Elisha the prophet based on this premise. However, see *Sanhedrin* 105b, where we learn from a story about Rabbi Yehoshua that a righteous person should not punish. This teaches us not to curse any Jew, even a heretic. Similarly, the Gemara (*Sanhedrin* 99a) says that Rabbi Abba was careful not to curse the heretics. He spoke in the third person and cited a *pasuk* that indicates bad things are in store for them, but did not actually curse them.

26   *Chazon Ish, Sanhedrin* 20:10, cited in *Peninei Halachah, Mo'ed Katan* 16; *Chazon Ish, Yoreh Dei'ah* §205, cited in *Chashukei Chemed, Nedarim*, p. 274. See *Bava Basra* 4a, where the Gemara says that it is permitted to curse someone who doesn't keep the Torah and mitzvos. Rav Chaim David HaLevi, former chief rabbi of Tel Aviv-Yafo (*Aseih Lecha Rav*, vol. 3, §54), explains that the prohibition to curse applies only when the reason they are not keeping the Torah and mitzvos is not legitimate. (So, for example, if a person doesn't know better, or they are mentally ill, it is not permissible to curse him.) But the rabbis in the Gemara had very good reasons to curse those they did. However, Rav HaLevi says that since it is difficult to know when one is permitted to curse and when not, one should not do so at all. He also notes that the *poskim* didn't codify the leniency of cursing sinners. Rav Menashe Klein writes (*Mishneh Halachos, Orach Chaim*, vol. 6, §27) that one should not curse wicked people, but rather pray for them to repent.

Also, the Gemara cites a number of places that Abaye would curse those who were not careful about certain halachos. See *Hapardes* (§74, vol. 1 [Sept. 1999]) for reasons it was permissible for him to do so.

See the Gemara in *Avodah Zarah* 4b, where it says that Rabbi Yehoshua ben Levi was going to curse a heretic who was purposefully provoking him, but he fell asleep and took it as a sign not to curse the person. See also *Sotah* 46b. See, however, *Chagigah* 3b where one rabbi cursed a student who brazenly pointed out that the main yeshivah ruled a certain way with regard to the laws of *shemitah*, contrary to his *rebbi*'s ruling. He cursed the student, but then subsequently blessed him.

Rabbi Yissacher Frand quotes a story that Rabbi Yisroel Reisman once told about the Ridvaz (the *rav* of Slutzk, later in Chicago, and afterward in Tzfas):

> *The Ridvaz was the rabbi of a shul, and, for whatever reasons, his congregants did not like him. In fact, some of them hired a dayan (judge) to answer their questions instead of the Ridvaz. A sign was even put up saying that now one could receive unbiased answers to their questions. Upon seeing how he was being treated, that Shabbos the Ridvaz opened up the Aron Kodesh in the shul and remarked that if he was a baker or someone else, he would not be treated this way. The Ridvaz felt his mistreatment was due to the fact that he was a rabbi who represents the Torah, and he felt it was a big disgrace to the honor one must have for the Torah and Torah scholars. The Ridvaz then cursed everyone in the shul that they should die within a year. The Ridvaz closed the Aron Kodesh and sat down.*
>
> *Rav Isser Zalman Meltzer asked the Ridvaz what happens if those that were cursed don't die within a year? That will be a chillul Hashem, and people will make a mockery of the Torah and rabbis. The Ridvaz responded that it wouldn't take a year. "Give it five months, and they will all be dead." And, in fact, that is what happened. The entire group of people died a short while after.*[27]

Rabbi Frand says that we learn from here the power of speech and the power of a curse from a very righteous person.[28]

See also *Aseih Lecha Rav* (vol. 3, §54) for an explanation of how *rabbanim* could curse other *rabbanim*. Rav Chaim David HaLevi (3:54) explains that the curses of the righteous take effect based on the *pasuk* "[tzaddikim] decree and Hashem fulfills it" (*Iyov* 22:28, cited in *Shabbos* 59b). Rav Chaim David also disagrees with the *Sefer Hachinuch's* understanding of the *Rambam* and says that the *Rambam* may also agree that curses take effect.

27   *The Commuter's Chavrusa Series* audio lecture, "Accepting Someone Else's Curse."

28   Here is another interesting story in a similar vein: "During the first years after the Communist revolution in Russia, Leon Trotsky, a Jew by birth, rose to the very top level of leadership and power. Success smiled upon him and observant Jews became the victims of ever harsher persecution... At the behest of the Chafetz Chaim, a number of Jews were summoned in

Dr. Shnayer Leiman tells the following anecdote about Rav Yaakov Emden and the power of a curse:[29]

> *Rav Yaakov Emden was fond of noting that anyone he cursed during the controversy between him and Rav Yonasan Eibeshitz, even in passing, was struck down either immediately or a short time after.*
>
> *Rav Emden writes in Eidus L'Yaakov that there was a young couple in Altona whose home was a popular meeting place every Shabbos for the forces of Rav Eibeshitz. They had a wine cellar, and people came every Shabbos to drink. One Shabbos, followers of Rav Emden joined the crowd. The followers of Rav Eibeshitz drank in honor of their rebbi, the chief rabbi. The two followers of Rav Emden immediately drank a lechaim in honor of Rav Emden, and added in their lechaim that the wife's children and pregnant child all grow up to be like Rav Emden. The wife who heard this berachah immediately had the two children thrown out of her home and shouted at them that "sooner than my children grow up to be like Rav Emden, may my children die and may my fetus die." The moment the two children were thrown out of the house, the young son of this woman fell down the stairs and died. The funeral took place the next day, Sunday. Shortly after, the woman suffered a miscarriage, paying dearly for her verbal attack on Rav Emden's honor.*
>
> *Rav Emden gives us the names of this couple and the names of their children, and he published it in his sefer while all survivors were still alive in Altona.*

---

secret to the local synagogue and were admonished not to utter a word. They lit candles, took a *Sefer Torah* from the Aron Hakodesh, blew a shofar and, in that awe-filled assembly, placed a *cherem* upon Leib Trotsky and cursed him with all the terrible curses recorded in the Torah. From then onwards Trotsky's fortunes began to decline. He was expelled from the ruling cabinet and forced to flee from Russia. Finally, an assassin felled him in far-off Mexico City" (Aharon Sorasky, *Reb Elchonon: The Life and Ideals of Rabbi Elchonon Bunim Wasserman of Baranovich* [ArtScroll/Mesorah, 1982], p. 58).

29   Dr. Shnayer Leiman, "The Meshumad" (Nov. 19, 1990), www.yutorah.org.

SUMMARY

According to the *Sefer Hachinuch*, a person's curse can indeed harm another. The *Rambam*, on the other hand, disagrees, and explains that the reason for the prohibition against cursing is that it will lead to developing negative character traits. Finally, the *Minchas Chinuch* writes that it is even prohibited to curse a wicked person. The *Chazon Ish*, however, permits it.

KILLING INSECTS

IN THE NEWS

A group of fourth graders were visiting the governor of New Jersey, Chris Christie, when they noticed a spider on the governor's desk. They pointed to it, and the governor came to the rescue. He crushed the spider and then wiped it off his hand onto his trousers. He then remarked, "That's also one of the fun parts of being governor. Any bugs on your desk, you're allowed to kill them and not get in trouble."

Ingrid Newkirk, president of People for the Ethical Treatment of Animals (PETA), disagreed. Newkirk said the governor missed an opportunity to teach the youngsters the truth about spiders. "Some people put the spider outside," she said, "but spiders are often scary to people, and that can prevent them from pondering their worth." The article goes on to report that in 2009, PETA sent President Barack Obama a "humane fly catcher" (a device that catches insects and allows their safe release back into nature) after the president publicly swatted and killed a fly in middle of a televised interview. Vice President for policy of PETA, Bruce Friedrich, commented then, "We support compassion for even the smallest animals."[1]

Although these news stories may sound a bit petty, it's worthwhile to investigate whether or not halachah permits killing insects. And if halachah does forbid it as a rule, are there any specific circumstances when it would be permitted?

---

1   Claudine Zap, "New Jersey Gov. Chris Christie squashes spider; PETA not pleased" (May 6, 2013), www.yahoo.com.

A TORAH PERSPECTIVE

There is, indeed, a prohibition against being cruel or causing pain to animals and insects, referred to as *tzaar baalei chaim*. Many halachic authorities understand this to be a Biblical prohibition,[2] which seems to be the indication of the Gemara as well.[3]

As for insects, Rav Moshe Feinstein says that there is no prohibition against killing flies that are a nuisance to someone or will ruin his food.[4]

---

2   There are many mitzvos in the Torah that prohibit cruelty toward animals. This clearly shows that Hashem doesn't want us to be cruel or cause pain to animals. Rav Asher Weiss (*Minchas Asher*, *parashas Ki Savo* §51, p. 356) cites many of these mitzvos, eleven in total, such as the obligation to help unload a heavy burden from someone's animal (*Shemos* 23:5) and the prohibition against muzzling one's ox while it works so that it can graze comfortably (*Devarim* 25:4). Rav Weiss says that there is no explicit *pasuk* that says causing pain to animals is *assur*, but it's clear that it is *assur* since it is the "*ratzon Hashem*," the will of God, not to cause pain or be cruel to animals. A number of Acharonim point to the *pasuk* "God is merciful on all His creations" (*Tehillim* 145:9) as a source for *tzaar baalei chaim*, since we are obligated to emulate God and have mercy on His creations as well (see *Sotah* 14a; *Rambam*, *Hilchos Dei'os* 1:5–6).
In *Yechaveh Daat* (vol. 5, §65), Rav Ovadiah Yosef cites some opinions that say the *Rambam* understands that this is an *issur d'Oraisa*, but many more opinions understand that the *Rambam* holds it is an *issur d'Rabbanan*. Rav Yaakov Kamenetsky says in *Emes L'Yaakov* (*Bamidbar* 22:32) that the *Rambam* holds that *tzaar baalei chaim* is a *d'Oraisa* only with regard to inflicting pain on an animal; however, helping an animal in pain is only required *mi'd'Rabbanan*.

3   *Bava Metzia* 32–33.

4   *Igros Moshe*, *Choshen Mishpat*, vol. 2, §47. Rav Avigdor Miller (*Q&A 2: Thursday Nights with Rabbi Avigdor Miller*, vol. 2, p. 30) says that you can kill bugs that come into your house, but you should not kill them if they are outside. Some say there is no *tzaar baalei chaim* when you're killing an animal or insect, only when you are hurting them while they are alive (*Noda BiYehudah*, vol. 2, *Yoreh Dei'ah* §10). Rav Moshe seems to be saying, however, that there is *tzaar baalei chaim* when killing an animal unless there is a legitimate human need, which overrides it. The *Shaar Hatziyun* (167:26) says one should not kill insects that are on one's table since a table is compared to the *Shulchan* in the *Beis Hamikdash*, which brought a person atonement (i.e., life). Rav Yitzchak Zilberstein adds that if there is a need to kill an insect (for example, so it doesn't get into your food) and there is nowhere else to kill it except on one's table, it seems to be permissible, since there is a legitimate need.
Rav Chaim Kanievsky brought a proof that this is correct from an incident in *Sefer Melachim I* 2:28–34. Yoav fled from Shlomo and took refuge on top of the *Mizbei'ach*. Although killing someone on the *Mizbei'ach* is not respectful to its holiness, since Yoav refused to leave, Shlomo ordered Benayahu to kill Yoav where he was. We see from here that when it is necessary, one may kill even in a place that is not appropriate (*Vehaarev Na*, vol. 2, p. 223). See also *Chashukei Chemed*, *Shabbos*, pp. 378–79, regarding reciting the *berachah* of *hatov vehameitiv* (said upon purchasing new utensils) upon buying an electric flyswatter. Since its purpose is to kill insects, perhaps it is not appropriate to recite this *berachah* over it.

Since his intention is for the benefit of human beings, it is not a violation of *tzaar baalei chaim*.[5]

Nevertheless, Rav Moshe says that one should not kill the insect with one's hand, but rather use a flytrap instead. He brings support for his *p'sak* from the case of the *ir hanidachas*—a city whose majority worships idols. The Torah commands us to kill every single member of this city by sword, and afterward Hashem promises to grant the executioners compassion.[6] Why does the Torah promise a measure of compassion for the executioners? Because killing naturally desensitizes a person and can ruin his character, even when it is sanctioned. Therefore, when Hashem commands us to kill all the inhabitants of the *ir hanidachas*, He adds that He will make sure we won't lose our sensitivity and compassion toward others in the process.[7]

5　The benefit must, however, be a legitimate need (see *Rema, Even Ha'ezer* 5:14). For example, Rav Shlomo Aviner (*On the Air with Rav Aviner* [J Levine/Millennium, 2009], pp. 180–81) says that you shouldn't go fishing just for fun if you don't plan on eating the fish you catch. Since both the worms (if alive) and fish suffer, this constitutes *tzaar baalei chaim* and shouldn't be done just for the pleasure of fishing. Rav Moshe Sternbuch seems to disagree with this ruling of Rav Aviner (*Teshuvos Vehanhagos* 7:176). As a rule, Rav Moshe (*Igros Moshe, Even Ha'ezer*, vol. 4, §92) gives the following guideline: the benefit has to be something that people would normally do, and the purpose can't be to benefit from the cruelty itself. Therefore, you can't torture animals to entertain spectators, even if you will make money from it.

Along these lines, Rav Ovadiah Yosef (*Yechaveh Daat*, vol. 3, §66) says that it is forbidden to attend bullfighting, because it is abetting sinners ("*mesayei'a lidvar aveirah*"). In addition, Rav Ovadiah says one should not watch bullfighting where the bull is treated cruelly, because viewing cruel behavior can lead to actual cruel behavior. This would apply even to watching a video of it.

What about animal experimentation? The *Tzitz Eliezer* (vol. 14, §68) permits animal experimentation, provided one doesn't harm the animals unnecessarily (he recommends using anesthesia, but doesn't believe it is required). Rav Chaim Pinchas Scheinberg ruled that one is permitted to put animals to sleep in order to kill them, since there is no pain involved. However, he says, based on Kabbalah, there is a tradition not to put an end to any life (see Rabbi Avraham Zuroff, *Question Market* [Targum, 2008], pp. 50–51). Once an ant was walking on one of Rav Scheinberg's *talleisim*. Instead of removing it with a tissue, he had someone bring him a cup and told the person to knock it into the cup and set the ant free in the garden outside of the building (Rabbi Yechiel Spero, *Rav Scheinberg: Warmth and Wisdom Cloaked in Humility* [ArtScroll/Mesorah, 2013], p. 323). See also *Shevet HaLevi* (vol. 2, §7), cited in *Upiryo Matok* (*parashas Shemos*, pp. 46–47), which prohibits starving older chickens for a number of days (aside for providing them with water) so that they will continue laying eggs.

6　*Devarim* 13:13–18.

7　See *Or Hachaim* on *Devarim* 13:18.

Based on this principle, Rav Moshe says that when a person kills an insect that is bothering him and no mitzvah is involved, he needs to be careful that this act of killing doesn't have any negative influence on himself. Therefore, it is better to kill the insect indirectly with traps or with one's shoe.

Rav Moshe Sternbuch writes that there is no concern at all with killing flies if they are bothering you. He says that though the Arizal refused to even kill flies, that was not because of *tzaar baalei chaim*; it was because all living beings have a purpose and he didn't want to destroy any creature's purpose in this world.[8]

On this subject, Rav Chaim Friedlander writes:

> At each and every second, God, by virtue of His will, causes the entire Creation to exist, from the smallest creature to the biggest. So when we see a little fly alive and fluttering around, we should meditate and think to ourselves that right now God is granting it life and the ability to move.[9]

In addition, Rav Shlomo Zalman Auerbach points out that there is no concern for *tzaar baalei chaim* when nature is running its course. Therefore, you don't have to stop a bigger fish from eating a smaller one. And even those opinions that permit one to handle *muktzeh* objects to prevent *tzaar baalei chaim* would not permit it in this case, as there is no issue of *tzaar baalei chaim* between animals.[10]

It's interesting to note that in Rav Moshe Feinstein's biography, a number of stories are told about how insects never seemed to approach him:[11]

> *Rebbetzin Feinstein told her son, Reb Reuven, that in Russia, on a summer day, Reb Moshe would sit under a tree writing*

---

8   *Teshuvos Vehanhagos*, vol. 2, §726.

9   *Sifsei Chaim, Emunah Vehashgachah*, vol. 1, p. 15.

10   *Shemiras Shabbos Kehilchasah* 27:58, n. 179. See Rabbi Ari Enkin's *Halichot V'halachot: Halachic Insights and Responsa* (Mosaica, 2016), vol. 8, p. 237, on whether *tzaar baalei chaim* applies to fish. See also *Upiryo Matok, parashas Shemos*, pp. 49–50, regarding whether one should intervene in order to save animals from being attacked by other animals.

11   Rabbi Shimon Finkelman, *Reb Moshe: The Life and Ideals of HaGaon Rabbi Moshe Feinstein* (ArtScroll/Mesorah, 2012), pp. 164–65.

his chiddushim. All around him, people were swatting the flying creatures that were attacking them, but none came near Reb Moshe.

In their early years in America, Reb Moshe and his family would vacation in Toledo, Ohio, at the home of his brother-in-law, Rabbi Nechemiah Katz. The first time Rabbi Katz found Reb Moshe learning in the backyard, he was surprised. That summer, the mosquitoes were everywhere, and it seemed impossible to immerse oneself in learning while swatting the insects at the same time. After observing Reb Moshe for a couple of minutes, Rabbi Katz realized that there were no mosquitoes in his vicinity. It was as if an invisible net surrounded him, preventing the insects from coming near.

Years later, in the Catskill Mountains, a talmid was sitting with Reb Moshe on his porch, and both were served cups of tea. The talmid could not drink his tea, because some of the gnats swarming around him had landed in his cup. But none were found in Reb Moshe's cup.[12]

When Rabbi Yisroel Belsky observed a similar [phenomenon], he asked Reb Moshe about it.[13] *Reb Moshe smiled and replied with the verse, "When Hashem favors a man's ways, even his enemies will make peace with him."*[14] *In one interpretation, the midrash defines "enemies" as insects.*[15]

---

12 See *Aleinu Leshabei'ach* (*parashas Bechukosai*, pp. 531–32) for more interesting mosquito stories, including one with a fascinating message involving former President Richard Nixon.

13 Rav Belsky commented that one could prove the existence of God from the fact that insects didn't approach Rav Moshe, which was an open miracle.

14 *Mishlei* 16:7.

15 *Pesikta D'Rav Kahana* 11:9. Along the same lines, Rabbi Shimon Finkelman wrote: "In *Sefer Melachim II* (2:9), the Shunamis woman referred to Elisha Hanavi as a 'man of God.' One reason for this, says the Gemara, is that she noticed that a fly never went near his table (*Berachos* 10b)." See *Reb Moshe: The Life and Ideals of HaGaon Rabbi Moshe Feinstein* (ArtScroll/Mesorah, 2012), p. 165.

SUMMARY

It is prohibited to cause pain to animals. Nevertheless, Rav Moshe Feinstein permits killing insects when there is a need to do so, but he advises against killing them with one's actual hand.

LASHON HARA— ABOUT YOURSELF

IN THE NEWS

On March 12, 2015, President Barack Obama made a guest appearance on a television comedy show.[1] In one segment of the show, called "Mean Tweets," the president read mean Twitter comments written about him (only in America!). One such comment was, "Is there any way we could fly Obama to some golf course halfway around the world and just leave him there?" Obama, an avid golfer, responded, "I think that's a great idea." After reading aloud his share of Mean Tweets, the president told the show's host, "You should see what the Senate says about me."

In the world of sports, Charles Barkley, named one of the greatest basketball players of all time, said in a TV commercial, "I'm not paid to be a role model. I'm paid to wreak havoc on the basketball court." Another famous basketball player, Karl Malone, responded to that remark by saying, "Charles...I don't think it's your decision to make. We don't choose to be 'role models,' we are chosen. Our only choice is whether to be a good role model or a bad one."[2]

Although Obama didn't seem to be embarrassed by the statements he read, this episode raises the question of whether Jewish law permits making derogatory statements about oneself. Could it be that

---

1   "President Obama Reads Mean Tweets on 'Jimmy Kimmel'" (March 12, 2015), www.variety. com.

2   "I'm Not a Role Model" (June 27, 1993), www.newsweek.com.

deriding oneself, even for the sake of good humor, is considered *lashon hara*?

As Jews, is it up to us to decide whether to be a good role model or have a good reputation, or not? May Jews choose to ruin their reputations by ridiculing themselves?

A TORAH PERSPECTIVE

There is a famous story told about the Chafetz Chaim.[3] He was once traveling by train to Radin, and the person next to him, unaware of his identity, mentioned that he was on his way to go see the great, holy *tzaddik*, the Chafetz Chaim. The Chafetz Chaim responded that the rabbi he was speaking about was not so great. The man was so furious at the disrespect shown to such a great person that he rebuked him for his words. Later, the Chafetz Chaim remarked that he learned from this encounter that one is not permitted to speak *lashon hara* even about himself and that he deserved that admonishment.

Rav Yosef Shalom Elyashiv, however, is reported as commenting on the above story of the Chafetz Chaim as follows:[4] There is no prohibition against making derogatory statements about oneself. Had there been an *issur*, the Chafetz Chaim never would have made bad comments about himself in the first place, because he of course thoroughly knew the halachah. But in order to alleviate the person's embarrassment when he realized that he had rebuked the venerable Chafetz Chaim, he said that it was wrong for him to make those comments about himself. So really it is permissible for a person to say what he wants about himself.[5]

---

3   Cited by Rabbi Daniel Z. Feldman, *False Facts and True Rumors* (Maggid, 2015), p. 224, and Rav Hershel Schachter, *Nefesh Harav*, p. 150.

4   Cited in the *Torah Tavlin parashah* sheet, *parashas Metzora* 5774.

5   The Chafetz Chaim himself seems to indicate that there is no prohibition against speaking *lashon hara* about oneself (*Hilchos Lashon Hara* 1:9 and 7:6). However, the Lubavitcher Rebbe wrote in a letter (*Igros Kodesh*, vol. 6, §1546) that just as it is forbidden to speak *lashon hara* about any Jew, it is logical that it is similarly forbidden to speak *lashon hara* about yourself. Rav Elyashiv adds that it is prohibited for others to speak *lashon hara* about a person, even if he speaks disparagingly about himself (*Vayishma Moshe*, vol. 1, p. 417).

Rav Shlomo Aviner seems to agree with this approach. Rav Aviner was asked for the source that it is forbidden for a person to speak *lashon hara* about himself, and he responded, "There is no such halachah. It is a personal decision based on the circumstances."[6]

Rav Hershel Schachter strongly disagrees. He quotes Rabbi Joseph B. Soloveitchik,[7] who comments on this story saying the Chafetz Chaim's conclusion is obvious. The Rav explains that the prohibition to speak *lashon hara* about oneself falls under the halachah of *maris ayin*, which teaches that a person may not squander his reputation if and whenever he wants to.

The prohibition of *maris ayin* is sourced in the *pasuk*, "And you shall be innocent before Hashem and the Jewish People."[8] Here, Rabbi Soloveitchik notes that a person must be careful not to do that which might make people suspect him of doing an *aveirah*. This is the concept of *maris ayin* found throughout the Gemara.[9] Thus, having a good reputation is important, and no Jew may ruin his own, saying, "What do I care what people think of me?" In contrast, we must always be careful to act appropriately.[10]

---

6   *Short and Sweet: Text Message Responsa from Ha-Rav Shlomo Aviner Shlit"a* (American Friends of Yeshivat Ateret Yerushalayim, 2012), p. 356.

7   In *Nefesh Harav*, p. 150.

8   *Bamidbar* 32:22.

9   The Gemara in *Yoma* 38a provides an example of *maris ayin*. *Beis Avtinas* (the family of Avtinas) was responsible for preparing the *ketores* (incense) in the Beis Hamikdash. The rabbis praised them because the women in their family would not wear perfume at their weddings, and if one of their men married a woman from another town, it was on the condition that she would not wear perfume. In this way, they would not be suspected of using the *ketores* from the Beis Hamikdash for their own benefit. The Mishnah in *Shekalim* (3:2) says that *Kohanim* were not permitted to have hems in their garments when entering the *lishkah* (Temple treasury chamber) to take out coins, so they should not be suspected of pocketing some of the money. Similarly, the Gemara in *Beitzah* (9a) says that it is prohibited on Shabbos to hang up wet laundry to dry, lest people suspect a person of laundering it on Shabbos.

10   Rav Yosef Engel (*Gilyonei HaShas, Shabbos* 23) says that we see from this *pasuk* that being innocent in others' eyes and making sure people don't suspect us of doing wrong is a *mitzvah d'Oraisa*. Rav Moshe Feinstein (*Igros Moshe, Orach Chaim*, vol. 2, §40) explains that the *issur* involves a situation of *maris ayin* where Chazal were concerned that others would learn from one's behavior and commit an *issur* themselves. However, even if people won't learn from you and commit an *issur*, there is still a concern that they will think you are doing an *issur*

Rav Pinchas Zevichi bases the importance of maintaining a good reputation on the Gemara that prohibits injuring oneself[11] and concludes that this prohibition includes embarrassing oneself as well.[12]

The *Chasam Sofer* states that it is very difficult not to violate the mitzvah to "be innocent before others."[13] He explains that the tribes of Gad and Reuven were sent into exile before the other tribes because they didn't fulfill this mitzvah. Before the conquest of the land, the other tribes resented them, claiming it was unfair that they would remain on the other side of the Jordan and receive more land. Gad and Reuven were obligated to speak up to defend their name when this happened, explaining why their behavior was justified. Since they did not, they were exiled before the other tribes.[14]

---

and misjudge you, which is considered *chashad*, and also prohibited. Rav Moshe notes that the prohibition of *chashad* is based on the *pasuk* quoted above, "You shall be innocent before Hashem." Like Rav Moshe, Rav Feivel Cohen (*Badei Hashulchan, Hilchos Tzedakah*, p. 99) says *chashad* is *d'Oraisa*.

11 *Bava Kama* 91b. See also *Shulchan Aruch, Choshen Mishpat* 420:31, and *Rambam, Hilchos Chovel Umazik* 5:1.

12 Rav Zevichi, *Ateres Paz*, part 1, vol. 3, *Choshen Mishpat* §7, n. 2. See also *Torah Ladaas*, vol. 1, *parashas Noach*. Although the *Shulchan Aruch* (*Choshen Mishpat* 420:31) only seems to mention that it is prohibited to harm oneself, the *Shulchan Aruch Harav* (*Hilchos Nizkei Guf Venefesh* §4) says people are also not permitted to embarrass themselves. Rav Yaakov Blau (*Pischei Choshen, Hilchos Nezikin* 2:2) writes that it is prohibited to embarrass oneself. However, there is an opinion in the Gemara (*Bava Kama* 91) that holds that while it is prohibited to injure oneself, it is permitted to embarrass oneself.

Rav Moshe Feinstein is quoted in *Mesoras Moshe* (vol.1, *Inyanim Shonim* §11) as prohibiting speaking *lashon hara* about oneself and about one who has granted others permission to speak *lashon hara* about him. See *False Facts and True Rumors*, p. 224. But see *Igros Moshe* (*Orach Chaim*, vol. 3, §78), where Rav Moshe says one can permit others to curse oneself. His reasoning is that it is prohibited to curse another person because it is a disgrace to the person being cursed, but in this case, he is forgoing his own honor, which is allowed. It seems from this that a person can allow others to disgrace him. Note the distinction: Rav Moshe seems to permit allowing others to embarrass you, but prohibits allowing others to speak *lashon hara* about you.

13 *Likutei Shut Chasam Sofer* §59 cited in *Torah Ladaas*, second series, *parashas Mattos*. He says this is one of the reasons it says, "There is no righteous person on earth that does [only] good and [never] sins" (*Koheles* 7:20).

14 The Gemara in *Berachos* 31b says that if you are accused of something, you must inform the accuser that you are doing the right thing. This is learned from Chanah, where Eli mistakenly accused her of being drunk in the Beis Hamikdash when, in fact, she was praying. The *Arugas Habosem* (*Orach Chaim* §17) says that in the case of Gad and Reuven, they did something

To the modern mind, this concept is difficult to accept. We tend to think, "Why can't I do what I want with my own reputation? Why should I care what people think?" But, says Rabbi Joseph B. Soloveitchik, this way of thinking is tainted. If your reputation is ruined, it means a "human personality is desecrated"—if we allow people to disrespect us, we are desecrating ourselves, and no one has the right to let that happen.[15]

Commenting on this concept in the *parashah*, Rabbi J. J. Schacter points out[16] that the *meraglim*, the twelve spies that Moshe sent to scout the Land of Israel, committed a subtle yet serious sin: besides speaking badly about Hashem and Eretz Yisrael—they put themselves down too. They said, "We will not be able to do it. We won't be able to conquer them."[17] Through this statement, they spoke *lashon hara* about themselves and didn't appreciate their own strength and ability to conquer the land that was promised to them. Kalev, though, offers us inspiration in this area. He declared, "*Aloh naaleh*—We can go up."[18] We must believe in our own capabilities and utilize our talents to the best of our abilities.

SUMMARY

According to Rabbi Soloveitchik, one is not permitted to speak *lashon hara* about himself, since he is prohibited from sullying his reputation. According to Rav Elyashiv, there is no prohibition against speaking *lashon hara* about oneself.

---

questionable that caused others to suspect them. The mitzvah of "You shall be innocent" teaches us that in such a case one must explain what he is doing. In the case of Chanah, though, she did nothing questionable, yet Eli still thought she was doing something wrong. Thus, we learn from Chanah that one must explain his actions even in such a case.

15   David Holzer, *The Rav Thinking Aloud on the Parsha: Sefer Bamidbar* (Jerusalem: Laor Ltd.), *parashas Chukas*; see also *Nefesh Harav*, p. 15.

16   Rabbi Dr. Jacob J. Schacter, "What was the sin of the spies?" (May 3, 2003), www.yutorah.org.

17   See *Bamidbar* 13:31.

18   *Bamidbar* 13:30.

MODERN-DAY SLAVERY

IN THE NEWS

Mike Merrill is no ordinary guy. Hailing from Portland, Oregon, he is a publicly traded person with a signature song, a logo, and 320 shareholders.

Back in 2008, Mike decided to sell shares of himself, allowing his shareholders to make his life decisions for him. They decided he should change from being registered as a Democrat to a Republican, and he did. He requested permission to wear Brooks Brothers shirts, and they granted it. When he went out on a date, he was required to file a report to his shareholders, who luckily decided he could continue seeing this lady for another six months.

Interviewed on NBC's *Today Show* and by the *Atlantic* magazine, Mike received plenty of publicity, which was surely good for his stock value. When asked if he would avoid doing something nutty if his shareholders told him to do so, he responded, "If I did do that, I imagine my stock would plummet."[1]

If a Jew were to do this today, what would the Torah say?

A TORAH PERSPECTIVE

In *parashas Behar*, the Torah teaches, "For the Children of Israel are slaves to Me; they are My servants, whom I took out of the land of

---

1   Amy Langfield, "Selling Yourself: Publicly Traded Portland Man Lets Shareholders Run His Life" (March 28, 2013), www.cnbc.com.

Egypt..."[2] Commenting on this *pasuk*, the *Sifra* explains that Hashem is saying, "My deed of ownership takes precedence over any other."[3]

Commenting on the *pasuk*, "For they are My servants,"[4] the *Seforno* writes that even after a person sells himself into servitude (and thereby violates this *pasuk*[5]), he is still the servant of Hashem and, therefore, may not relinquish himself as an absolute slave. Hence, Jews are forbidden to sell themseleves permanently, since they are servants of God.

Under very specific circumstances, however, Jews may sell themesleves. The Torah writes that if a person becomes absolutely impoverished, he is permitted to sell himself as an *eved Ivri*, a Jewish slave.[6] In fact, the Torah gives explicit permission for this scenario; otherwise it would have been prohibited, because, as the midrash stated above, we are slaves to Hashem and do not have ownership of ourselves.[7] Even though the Torah does allow a Jew to sell himself in this case, all Jewish slaves are released in the *Yovel* (Jubilee) year.[8]

Since *Yovel* is not practiced today, the mitzvah of *eved Ivri*—the ability to sell oneself as a slave when impoverished, or to be sold by *beis din* (rabbinical court)—no longer applies.[9] Nevertheless, the message of the

---

2   *Vayikra* 25:55.

3   According to another interpretation in the midrash, the *pasuk* means that a Jew is not to be sold on an auction block. This is counted as Mitzvah §345 in *Sefer Hachinuch*: a Jew should not be sold as a slave in the same manner as a non-Jew, by being auctioned off in public. Rabbi Binyamin Tabory ("Parashat Miketz: Is It Permissible to Sell Oneself as an Eved Ivri?," www.etzion.org.il) points out that according to this view, a Jew can sell himself as a slave (*eved Ivri*) in a dignified manner.

4   *Vayikra* 25:42.

5   See *Tosafos, Bava Metzia* 10a.

6   *Vayikra* 25:39. See *Shemos* 22:2 for the halachos of when *beis din* can sell a Jew as a slave.

7   See *Rambam, Hilchos Avadim* 1:1. See also *Lehoros Nassan*, vol. 3, §118, which points out that the *Rambam* cites the *pasuk*, "When your brother will become impoverished and sold to you" (*Vayikra* 25:39), not the *pesukim*, "For they are My servants" (*Vayikra* 25:42, 55). See *Rambam, Hilchos Avadim* 1:3, which says that a Jew is only permitted to be sold to other Jews, and see *Chut Shani, Milei D'nezikin*, p. 322.

8   *Vayikra* 25:10; *Sefer Hachinuch*, Mitzvah §331.

9   *Rambam, Hilchos Avadim* 1:10; *Chut Shani, Milei D'nezikin*, p. 325. The *Ritva* (*Kiddushin* 28a, 69a), however, says that one may sell himself today as a slave and have the status of *eved Ivri*, but he would not have the *dinim* of an *eved Ivri*—that is, he would not be released in the *Yovel* year or be permitted to marry a *shifchah Canaanis* (non-Jewish slave woman) like a classic *eved Ivri*. The *Rashba* (*Teshuvos HaRashba*, vol. 2, §72) argues and says that, today,

eved Ivri is still relevant today. Rav Leibele Eiger says that in all of one's endeavors he must make sure that he does not enslave himself to anyone but Hashem.[10] Even if a person finds himself in a situation where he is "enslaved," he must realize that he can mentally release himself from that state, just as the *eved Ivri* was released from his state of slavery.[11]

In the case of Mike Merrill, he didn't actually sell himself as a slave. Presumably, he can opt out of his obligations to his shareholders. Nevertheless, such conduct prevents one from internalizing that he is a slave only to Hashem.

When the Torah speaks about selling oneself as a slave, it is meant as a last resort for someone with extreme financial hardship. The institution of *eved Ivri*, according to Rav Shimshon Raphael Hirsch, is only meant to rehabilitate a person. Rav Hirsch writes, "When the slave completes his period of service, he goes out with savings he has accumulated during his service, and he attempts to earn an independent living."[12]

---

one cannot be sold as an *eved Ivri* at all. *Rashi* (*Bava Metzia* 60b, s.v. *"zivnan"*) writes that since the destruction of the Beis Hamikdash, it is prohibited to own an *eved Ivri*. Rav Moshe Feinstein (*Igros Moshe, Choshen Mishpat*, vol. 3, §18) seems to follow the *Rambam's* and *Rashba's* opinion.

10   *Toras Emes, parashas Mishpatim,* p. 110.

11   Rav says in *Bava Kama* 116b that an employee may break an employment agreement, even in the middle of the day, and pay for any losses he caused the employer because of the concept that Jews can only be permanently indentured to Hashem. This is codified by the *Shulchan Aruch* (*Choshen Mishpat* 333:3), citing the *pasuk*, "For they are My servants" (*Vayikra* 25:55). The *Rema* (*Choshen Mishpat* 333:3), as explained by the *Shach* (ibid. 333:17), says that based on this ruling, a *rebbi* or any employee should not sign a contract for more than three years. See *Chut Shani, Milei D'nezikin,* p. 325, where it says that according to the *Chasam Sofer* (*Shu"t Chasam Sofer, Choshen Mishpat* §172) and *Tosafos*, a rabbi of a shul cannot obligate himself to his shul in an agreement that does not permit him to back out of it, irrespective of the three-year limit. But the *Pischei Choshen* (*Hilchos Sechirus* 7:1) writes that the maximum of three years was only said with regard to employees who not only worked for their employers, but also ate their meals and slept on their employers' premises. Since this type of employment resembles slavery, the limit of three years was given. However, in today's world, since the conditions of employment are much more accommodating to the employee, he may commit to work for more than three years. The *Shach* (*Choshen Mishpat* 333:16) says that someone who is impoverished and has no source of income would be permitted to sell himself as a slave today and would certainly be permitted to employ himself for more than three years. See Rabbi Ari Enkin's essay "Quitting a Job" in *Halichot V'halachot: Halachic Insights and Responsa* (Mosaica, 2016), pp. 189–90.

12   *The Hirsch Chumash, Sefer Vayikra* (Feldheim, 2008), p. 927, translated by Rabbi Daniel Haberman.

In that case, selling shares of oneself should be avoided at all costs. Auctioning off parts of the ownership of oneself is submitting oneself to the control of others, reminiscent of slavery. The more extreme form of selling oneself (i.e., as an *eved Ivri*) was never meant to replace earning a living. As the *Rambam* says, when the Torah permits an impoverished person to sell himself as a slave, it is only after he finds himself without any possessions.[13] This is because it detracts from a person's ability to be a full-time *eved Hashem*.

Another concern with selling shares of oneself is that one is debasing himself in doing so. One of the halachos of owning an *eved Ivri* is that the owner is not permitted to force him to do degrading work.[14] This is a true concern in the case of Mike Merrill, whether or not he takes pride in his succesful business venture.[15]

In support of this idea, Rav Moshe cites the Gemara in *Kiddushin* that disqualifies someone from giving testimony if he eats in the marketplace, an act considered to be degrading and that signifies a lack of self-respect and proper moral behavior.[16] Similarly, since the shareholders make many of Mike's life decisions, and Mike is prepared to do even "nutty things," this would go against a Jew's responsibility not to degrade himself.[17]

---

13 *Hilchos Avadim* 1:1.

14 *Rambam, Hilchos Avadim* 1:7. This is the meaning of the *pasuk* that says that one should not subjugate his Jewish slave through hard work (*Vayikra* 25:43). See *Teshuvos Vehanhagos* (vol. 5, §394), where it says that this prohibition may apply today in that we shouldn't force anyone to do something he doesn't want to do.

15 Along these lines, in discussing the halachic issues involved in using hypnotism for therapeutic purposes, Rav Moshe Feinstein writes (*Igros Moshe, Yoreh Dei'ah*, vol. 3, §44) that while a person is hypnotized, he is tremendously disgraced. Degrading oneself in order to be healed, says Rav Moshe, is acceptable, but under normal circumstances it would be frowned upon. Rav Moshe writes that making a fool of oneself would be considered an act that has *reicha d'issura* ("a smell of prohibition")—not something strictly prohibited, but certainly not the way a Jew should behave.

16 This halachah is codified in the *Shulchan Aruch* (*Choshen Mishpat* 34:18), where the *S'ma* explains the rationale: We are concerned that someone who isn't particular about his own dignity may not mind the embarrassment that ensues if people discover that he gave a false testimony. See *My Uncle the Netziv: Rabbi Baruch HaLevi Epstein Recalls His Illustrious Uncle, R' Naftali Zvi Yehudah Berlin, and the Panorama of His Life* (ArtScroll/Mesorah, 1988), by Rabbi Baruch HaLevi Epstein, pp. 195–97, where the Netziv discusses this halachah from the *Shulchan Aruch* while mentioning the importance of self-respect.

17 See Rav Hershel Schachter, *Nefesh Harav*, p. 233. This is different from, for example,

If this were the only concern, then it might be technically permitted for a Jew to do what Mike did, since the *Rambam* maintains that a poor *talmid chacham* should be involved even in a degrading profession rather than relying on the public for financial support.[18] However, the *Aruch Hashulchan* says that a *talmid chacham* should not engage in an occupation that will denigrate his reputation as a *talmid chacham*.[19] It would, therefore, seem that the *Aruch Hashulchan* would forbid a *talmid chacham* from selling himself as an *eved Ivri*, since it would disparage the honor of the Torah.[20]

With regard to other people, Rav Yitzchak Zilberstein cites the *Chazon Ish*, who was unsure whether a person would be required to do degrading work in order to earn a living.[21] Similarly, the *Ezer Mikodesh* discusses whether hiring oneself out to work for others, like a slave, is considered more painful and degrading than any other job. Therefore, he does not write that one must do so.[22]

SUMMARY

Selling stock in oneself is contrary to the ideals and values of the Torah and what it means to be a servant of Hashem. In all that we do, we must position ourselves to be able to be the best servants of Hashem—and no one else—that we can be.

Chassidim going to their Rebbe for advice on almost all day-to-day issues, since they are going to hear what Hashem wants them to do and not what the Rebbe personally wants. The Lubavitcher Rebbe once said, "If you give over your will, you become a robot. God doesn't want that" (Joseph Telushkin, *Rebbe: The Life and Teachings of Menachem M. Schneerson, the Most Influencial Rabbi in Modern History* [Harper Wave, 2014] , p. 208; see also pp. 25 and 100).

18   *Hilchos Matenos Aniyim* 10:18.

19   *Aruch Hashulchan, Yoreh Dei'ah* 255:1.

20   See *Pesakim Uteshuvos, Hilchos Tzedakah* §255, p. 435, that today Torah scholars should not perform demeaning work since it will most likely cause a *chillul Hashem*.

21   *Chashukei Chemed, Pesachim*, pp. 593–94. See *Chut Shani, Milei D'nezikin*, p. 252, which cites the *Chazon Ish* saying that with regard to paying back a loan, a person would not have to hire himself out; however, in order to perform all other mitzvos, a person would have to do so.

22   *Ezer Mikodesh, Even Ha'ezer* §70.

Rabbi Soloveitchik once said, "If God is the King of honor, then the commandment 'And you shall walk in His ways'[23] suggests that man, too, must display honor."[24]

23 *Devarim* 28:9.

24 Debra and Robert Kasirer, *Rosh Hashanah Machzor: With Commentary Adapted from the Teachings of Rabbi Joseph B. Soloveitchik* (K'hal, 2007), p. 81.

OLAM HABA FOR GENTILES

IN THE NEWS

In February of 2016, the Jewish Telegraphic Agency ran a story entitled "With 75% Non-Jewish Students, Utah's Jewish School Seeks to Universalize Judaism."[1] The McGillis School in Salt Lake City, Utah, is a unique K–8 school where three-quarters of the students are not Jewish, 90 percent of the staff is not, and the entire administration is not either, yet the school is teeming with Jewish wisdom and culture.

On Friday afternoons, third- to fifth-graders gather to light Shabbos candles, recite *kiddush* over grape juice, and make *hamotzi* on challah bread, mimicking the mitzvos performed by Jews for Shabbos. *Mezuzos* are present on every door in the school, and the walls are decorated with Hebrew artwork and Israeli landscapes. Posters hang all around the school demonstrating many of the Jewish themes that the school values, such as tzedakah, *gemillus chassadim* (kind deeds), *derech eretz* (having respect for all), *limud lishmah* (learning for the sake of learning), and *kehillah* (community). Liz Paige, the school's ethics and culture teacher, said, "We are trying to teach Jewish values broadly... We're not proselytizing here. We're teaching Torah as literature, philosophy, ethics—but not religion."

Keeping mitzvos in the gentile world is more widespread than one would imagine. Six-time NBA all-star Amar'e Stoudemire, who is not Jewish, has kept some mitzvos over the years, including wearing a *tallis*

---

1   Uriel Heilman, "With 75% non-Jewish students, Utah's Jewish school seeks to universalize Judaism" (Feb. 29, 2016), www.jta.org.

and *kippah* at his wedding[2] and having a sukkah built on his penthouse apartment in New York City.[3] Another celebrity who likes to keep mitzvos is Marla Maples, Donald Trump's second wife. Although she's not Jewish, she says she keeps Shabbos and eats kosher.[4]

The preoccupation with mitzvos at this unique school and by gentiles around the world raises a very basic question: According to the Torah, do non-Jews receive reward for the mitzvos they keep?

A TORAH PERSPECTIVE

All gentiles are obligated to keep seven mitzvos, known as the *Sheva Mitzvos Bnei Noach*.[5] The *Rambam* says that gentiles are rewarded in the next world for keeping the *Sheva Mitzvos* they are obligated to keep.[6] However, says Rav Moshe Feinstein, gentiles who perform mitzvos that a Jew is commanded to keep do not receive reward for doing so.[7] Although the *Rambam* seems to say, in his *Peirush HaMishnayos*,

---

2   "All-Star 'Jewish' Amare Stoudemire Headed for Jerusalem" (Feb. 8, 2016), www.hidabroot.com.

3   Litton, Steven and Jonathan. "The Co-Owners of Litton Sukka, Based in Lawrence, NY." Interview by Rachel Bachrach. *Mishpacha*, Sept. 20, 2018.

4   Ron Kampeas, "Donald Trump's Ex-Wife Marla Maples is Christian—But Keeps Kosher and Shabbat" (Sept. 22, 2016), www.forward.com.

5   *Sanhedrin* 56b. The Gemara in *Sanhedrin* 58b says that the list of *Sheva Mitzvos* includes what gentiles are obligated to keep passively, but there are additional mitzvos that they actively have to fulfill. Interestingly, the Gemara in *Chullin* (92a) says that gentiles had originally accepted upon themselves thirty mitzvos, which are connected to the *Sheva Mitzvos*, but kept only three of them. The *Sefer Hachinuch* (Mitzvah §416) writes that the *Sheva Mitzvos* are merely categories, and gentiles are obligated to observe more than just seven mitzvos.

6   *Hilchos Melachim* 8:11; *Hilchos Teshuvah* 3:5. The *Rambam* in *Hilchos Melachim* 8:10 writes (based on *Sanhedrin* 105a) that Hashem commanded Moshe to force all the non-Jews to accept the *Sheva Mitzvos*, while the *Ramban* (*Makkos* 9a) says that even without this acceptance, the non-Jews are still obligated to keep them. However, he says, with acceptance, they are rewarded like those who are commanded to keep the mitzvos. See *Bava Kama* 38a; *Haamek Davar, Vayikra* 26:3, and *Mesivta Shas, Bava Kama, Yalkut Biurim*, pp. 268–69. See also *Hegyonei Haparshah, parashas Lech Lecha*, p. 81, for more on this. The *Rambam* writes (*Hilchos Issurei Bi'ah* 14:4) that *Olam Haba* is only for Jews, yet, elsewhere (*Hilchos Teshuvah* 3:6)—as noted—he writes that righteous gentiles do merit *Olam Haba*. Rav Aharon David Goldberg (*Shiras David, Yamim Nora'im*, p. 146) elucidates by explaining that although righteous gentiles merit *Olam Haba*, their portion is not comparable to that which Jews will receive.

7   *Igros Moshe, Yoreh Dei'ah*, vol. 2, §7. As the *Or Hachaim* points out (on *Shemos* 19:5), non-Jews do not receive reward for performing mitzvos that they are not commanded in.

that gentiles who perform our mitzvos do receive some reward,[8] Rav Moshe maintains that this refers only to a few mitzvos, such as tzedakah and *korbanos* (sacrificial offerings); regarding those mitzvos, the Torah mentions that gentiles were rewarded for doing them (for example, Balak brought *korbanos*; Nevuchadnetzar gave tzedakah[9]). Mitzvos such as Shabbos, kashrus, tallis and tefillin, and *shaatnez*, to name a few, are not relevant to gentiles at all, as they did not receive the Torah like the Jewish People did, and so they are not rewarded for keeping them.[10]

However, we find that the *Rambam* writes that if a gentile wants to keep mitzvos in order to receive reward, we don't stop him from doing so.[11] Rav Moshe qualifies this statement by saying that although we won't stop him from performing any of the mitzvos, he still won't receive reward for keeping them, even if this is the reason he is doing them.[12] Rav Moshe says this is clearly the intent of the *Rambam*, since if he held that gentiles do receive reward for keeping mitzvos, it would be *obvious* that we shouldn't stop them since Hashem wants them to do so and will even reward them. Rav Moshe adds that, nonetheless, gentiles may only keep mitzvos occasionally, not with any regularity.[13]

Rav Asher Weiss disagrees with Rav Moshe's understanding of the *Rambam*.[14] He learns that what the *Rambam* is saying is that gentiles

---

8   *Peirush HaMishnayos, Terumos* 3:9. Additionally, the *pasuk* says, "Praiseworthy are those who keep My ways" (*Mishlei* 8:32), and in its commentary to this *pasuk*, the *Me'am Lo'ez* explains that the *pasuk* also refers to non-Jews who learn Torah.

9   See *Yalkut Biurim, Bava Basra* 10b, p. 160, for a nice summary of the opinions that hold that gentiles are obligated to give charity.

10   Rav Elyashiv ruled that a gentile cannot wear tefillin even during the last few months before his conversion (*Mishnas Ish*, p. 25).

11   *Hilchos Melachim* 10:10. However, in 10:9, the *Rambam* says it is prohibited for gentiles to keep Shabbos (*Sanhedrin* 58b) or learn Torah (ibid. 59a); the parameters of these prohibitions are beyond the scope of this article. See *Igros Moshe, Even Ha'ezer*, vol. 5, §43, p. 249, regarding the parameters of the prohibition of a non-Jew who keeps Shabbos.

12   *Igros Moshe, Yoreh Dei'ah*, vol. 2, §7.

13   It would seem from the *Rambam* that it is prohibited for a gentile to keep any of the mitzvos while believing he is actually obligated to do so; see *Hilchos Melachim* 10:9, as explained in *Igros Moshe, Yoreh Dei'ah*, vol. 2, §7, and *Orach Chaim*, vol. 2, §24.

14   *Minchas Asher, parashas Vayigash* §43, p. 288. See there for a number of possible sources for his understanding of the *Rambam*.

who perform mitzvos do receive reward for them, provided that they perform them with the understanding that they are not obligated to do so.[15]

Rav Moshe explains that the reason gentiles don't receive reward for keeping mitzvos they are not obligated to fulfill is because a person needs *kedushas Yisrael* in order to keep the mitzvos. We acknowledge this in the text of the *berachos* we say before performing mitzvos: "*Asher kideshanu bemitzvosav vetzivanu*—Who sanctified us through His mitzvos and commanded us."[16] Even women, who are not obligated in time-bound mitzvos (*mitzvos aseih shehazeman gerama*), if they choose to keep them, recite a blessing beforehand, since they also have *kedushah*.[17] But gentiles, says Rav Moshe, do not have the same *kedushah* as the Jewish People and therefore have no connection to mitzvos and will not receive any reward for keeping them.[18]

---

15   Based on the *Rambam, Hilchos Melachim* 10:9. The *Rambam* seems to say that non-Jews are obligated in the prohibition of *bal tosif*—not to add new mitzvos (*Devarim* 13:1; *Rambam, Sefer Hamitzvos, Lavin* §313; *Sefer Hachinuch* §454). This point is made by Rav Hershel Schachter (Rabbi Hershel Schachter, "Highlights of Sheva Mitzvos Bnei Noach" [May 25, 2016], www.yutorah.org). Rav Schachter also cites a *Tosafos Rid* (brought by the *Chemdas Yisrael*), which seems to argue that non-Jews are not prohibited from keeping more than their seven mitzvos.

16   See *Hegyonei Halachah*, vol. 3, pp. 199–200, where Rav Yitzchak Mirsky explains that there is a significant difference between the obligation of a gentile to keep the *Sheva Mitzvos* and a Jew's obligation to keep the 613 commandments. This difference, says Rav Mirsky, explains the Gemara in *Sanhedrin* 74b, which records that Jews are obligated to die "*al kiddush Hashem*." See also *Toras Bnei Yissaschar* (*parashas Naso*, pp. 223–24), where the *Bnei Yissaschar* differentiates between mitzvos performed by Bnei Noach and by Jews and says that Jews perform mitzvos with all their details, not trying to get out of them. See also *Likutei Shevilei Pinchas, parashas Chukas*.

    See also *Imrei Baruch, parashas Chukas* §1, who cites Rav Hershel Schachter (*Eretz Hatzvi* §12), who makes the following differentiation between non-Jews and Jews who keep mitzvos: when a non-Jew does a mitzvah, his body does not become intrinsically holy from its observance, whereas a Jew's body does. The Gemara (*Bava Basra* 10b) differentiates between the Jews' and gentiles' approach to tzedakah; see *Shefa Chaim, parashas Balak*, p. 409, for a distinction between Jews and gentiles in this regard. See *Zahav Mishva* (*parashas Noach*, p. 8) for the difference between theft for Jews and non-Jews. See also *Pachad Yitzchak, Igros Umichtavim*, p. 50, and *Pachad Yitzchak, Chanukah* §9, for the difference between the seven mitzvos of Bnei Noach and the 613 mitzvos of Bnei Yisrael.

17   This is the Ashkenazic custom, based on *Tosafos* in *Kiddushin* 31a, s.v. "*delo*."

18   *Igros Moshe, Yoreh Dei'ah*, vol. 5, §10.

Rav Moshe adds that for certain mitzvos, such as honoring one's parents, gentiles would receive reward, since they are mitzvos that stem from our obligations toward others based on their *tzelem Elokim* (Godly image), regardless of their *kedushah*.[19] This is also why non-Jews are rewarded for giving charity, according to Rav Moshe. Addtionally, Bnei Noach who pray will receive reward for doing so, based on the *pasuk*, "*Ki veisi beis tefillah yikarei lechol haamim*—For My house shall be called a house of prayer for all peoples,"[20] even though they are not commanded to pray.[21] However, Rav Moshe adds, praying in a time of distress and great need is a mitzvah even for Bnei Noach, as it is rooted in the basic belief that Hashem controls everything that happens to us, a belief that even Bnei Noach are obligated in.[22]

Moreover, Rav Yaakov Kamenetsky explains that all of mankind is created in the image of God, and all are beloved to Him. However, the Jewish People have accepted upon themselves to keep Torah and mitzvos, and therefore they have an even closer connection to Hashem. This connection is open to all of mankind by opting to become part of the Jewish People through conversion and keeping the mitzvos. Any gentile can join the ranks of the Jewish People by converting and even rise to become one of our leaders, as Shemayah and Avtalyon did in their time.[23]

---

19   According to Rav Chaim Kanievsky, gentiles are not obligated in *kibbud av va'eim* but receive reward for doing so (*Derech Sichah*, p. 290).

20   *Yeshayah* 56:7.

21   See *Mishneh Halachos* 13:8, which questions whether there is a concept of prayer for gentiles and if their prayers are even answered; see also *Peninei Halachah, Bava Kama* 3b. The Brisker Rav says that although there is a concept of *tefillah* for gentiles, they don't have the concept of *tefillah betzibbur* or the Yud-Gimmel Middos (*Shiras David*, p. 42). See also *Pesichos Ha'igros, Orach Chaim*, vol. 2, §25 for more about the opinions that disagree with Rav Moshe.

22   See *Teshuvah Mei'ahavah*, p. 112, regarding whether non-Jews are obligated in the mitzvah of fearing and loving Hashem. Rav Moshe Sternbuch discusses whether gentiles are required to believe in *hashgachah p'ratis*—that Hashem supervises everything that occurs in the world—and writes that they would certainly have to if they saw miracles, as Pharaoh did (*Taam Vadaas, parashas Bo*, p. 53). Rav Yaakov Kamenetsky writes that non-Jews are also commanded to believe in one God, but only Jews have to believe in the creation of the world *ex nihilo* (*Emes L'Yaakov, parashas Noach*, p. 70).

23   *Emes L'Yaakov, Pirkei Avos*, pp. 38–40. Rav Yaakov said this in response to those who say the Jewish People are racists for proclaiming that they are the chosen people. Since our elevated

SUMMARY

Gentiles will receive reward for keeping the *Sheva Mitzvos Bnei Noach*. According to Rav Moshe Feinstein, they will not receive reward for any additional mitzvos they keep, though there are a few exceptions. However, Rav Asher Weiss understands the *Rambam* to mean that gentiles will receive reward for all additional mitzvos they keep.

---

status and close relationship with God is due to our keeping extra mitzvos, which anyone can accept upon themselves as well, it is obviously not a racist belief. For further elaboration, see also *Emes L'Yaakov, parashas Noach*, p. 75.

OLAM HABA FOR SALE

IN THE NEWS

The Jewish daily *Forward* reported that a New Jersey man posted on eBay his share in *Olam Haba*.[1] Although bidding only started at ninety-nine cents, within hours, it rose to $100,000. In the end, eBay removed the listing due to regulations requiring objects for sale to be concrete.

In September of 2015, a religious Jew in Israel put up signs advertising that he was willing to purchase people's sins if they would pay him the right price. The person said he was doing this to save people from suffering unnecessarily in the next world.[2]

More recently, Dovid Lichtenstein, of the popular Headlines radio program, related that he once approached Michael Steinhardt (the founder of Birthright Israel) and offered to buy his share in the World to Come. He did this in response to Mr. Steinhardt telling him that he didn't believe in *Olam Haba*. Mr. Steinhardt agreed, and Mr. Lichtenstein, on the spot, wrote him a check for $100,000.[3]

Several questions need to be addressed here. First, does selling one's *Olam Haba* indicate some sort of regret for the mitzvos? If so, what is the status of someone who regrets having performed a mitzvah? Next, can a person actually sell his reward in *Olam Haba*? Finally, can someone be paid to take the sins of another?

---

1   Debra Nussbaum Cohen, "eBay Kills 100K Bid for Jewish Spot in Heaven" (May 28, 2013), www.forward.com.

2   "Sell Your Sins" (Sept. 20, 2015), www.lifeinisrael.blogspot.com.

3   "Vegetarians in Halacha—Does a vegan restaurant need a hashgacha?" (Dec. 2, 2017), www.podcast.headlinesbook.com.

A TORAH PERSPECTIVE

Regarding regret, the Gemara says that someone who regrets performing a mitzvah is considered as if he never performed that mitzvah.[4] The *Rambam* records this idea in *Hilchos Teshuvah*, where he writes, "Whoever regrets the mitzvos that he did and laments their reward, and says in his heart, 'What did I gain by doing them? If only I never did them!' he loses all of them, and they [the Heavenly court] don't mention any merit for him in *Olam Haba…*"[5]

Rabbi Eli Mansour writes that this statement of the *Rambam* explains a difficult section in the evening *tefillah*: "*Vehaser Satan milfaneinu umei'achareinu*," which literally means, "Remove the Satan from before us and from behind us." We ask God not only to protect us from the Satan "before us," namely, the evil inclination that wants to stop us from fulfilling mitzvos, but also from the Satan "behind us," that causes us to regret having done mitzvos.[6]

Rabbi Mansour gives the following example: If a person receives a parking ticket while davening in shul, and he then regrets coming to shul, he loses the "credit" for the mitzvah of davening in shul.[7]

Rav Avigdor Miller offers another example.[8] He explains that when a person is approached by a collector, he should not respond, "I gave so much money last week." That, says Rav Miller, is regret for having given

---

4   *Kiddushin* 40b. The *Kehillos Yitzchak* (cited in *Imrei Baruch, parashas Chayei Sarah*, p. 106) explains that the reason is based on the principle of *teshuvah*. Just as *teshuvah* (i.e., regret for one's sins) uproots the sin that was committed as if it had never happened (see *Yoma* 86b), so too, regret for a mitzvah uproots the mitzvah as if it hadn't been committed.

5   *Hilchos Teshuvah* 3:3. Rav Chaim Kanievsky points out that one can infer from this statement of the *Rambam* that if the person only regrets having performed the mitzvah, but not the reward that comes with it, he still retains some part of the reward for the mitzvah (*Shuvi Nafshi*, a commentary by Rabbi Hillel Kuperman on the *Rambam's Hilchos Teshuvah*, p. 72). See also *The Torah Commentary of Rabbi Shlomo Carlebach* (Urim, 2012), p. 157, citing Reb Yissachar Dov, who explains that when Hashem came to visit Avraham on the third day after his *bris milah*, when the pain was the greatest, Avraham still didn't regret performing the mitzvah. In the merit of his devotion, Hashem gave Avraham, and all of his descendants, added strength to resist the temptation to regret performing a mitzvah.

6   "The Scale of Misvot and Sins," www.dailyhalacha.com.

7   See *Kehillos Yitzchak*, cited in *Imrei Baruch, parashas Chayei Sarah*, p. 106, where another example is given.

8   *Q&A 2: Thursday Nights with Rabbi Avigdor Miller*, p. 131.

the tzedakah. If a person does a mitzvah, regrets it, and then wants to repent and get his credit back, can he? No, says Rav Miller. "The mitzvah is lost forever."

In terms of selling one's *Olam Haba*, the Gemara in *Sotah* asks, "What does the verse mean by 'He will scorn him to the extreme'?"[9] The Gemara answers that this statement refers to the brothers Hillel and Shavna. Rav Dimi explained that Hillel learned Torah, and that Shavna would be involved in business. One day Shavna said to Hillel, "Let us combine our assets and divide them." At this point, a Heavenly voice emerged saying, "Should a man give all the wealth of his house for love, he will scorn him to the extreme."[10] The commentators understand this Gemara to mean that once the learning has been done, its reward can no longer be given to anyone else. Therefore, in our case, once *Olam Haba* has been earned, it certainly cannot be given to anyone else.[11]

Based on the above Gemara, the *Beis Yosef* says that if you are unable to learn Torah yourself, you can have someone learn for you.[12] The *Rema* explains that you can stipulate in advance that you will support those who are learning, and in return you will receive part of their reward. However, the stipulation must be made before the learning is done.[13]

This type of agreement is generally known as a "Yissachar-Zevulun arrangement."[14] Zevulun in the Chumash engaged in business and

---

9   *Shir Hashirim* 8:7.
10   *Sotah* 21a.
11   Rav Chaim Kanievsky, in *She'eilos Rav*, p. 88, clearly says a person cannot sell his *Olam Haba*.
12   *Beis Yosef*, *Yoreh Dei'ah* 246:1.
13   See *Shulchan Aruch* 246:1 and *Shach* and *Biur HaGra* there.
14   See *Bereishis* 49:13–15 and *Devarim* 33:18. See also *Shu"t Minchas Asher*, vol. 2, p. 214, where Rav Asher Weiss discusses whether it is ideal to enter such an arrangement. Rav Moshe Feinstein (*Igros Moshe*, *Yoreh Dei'ah*, vol. 4, §37:8) writes that for this arrangement to be valid, the financier ("Zevulun") must have a great appreciation for Torah learning and is not exempt from the obligation to learn Torah during the time he is not occupied with his business (cited by Ari Wasserman, *Making It Work* [Feldheim, 2016], pp. 154–55; see there for a comprehensive discussion of this topic). See *Igros Moshe*, *Yoreh Dei'ah*, vol. 4, §37:3, where Rav Moshe Feinstein writes that the impetus for the Yissachar-Zevulun partnership was so that people would be able to learn the entire Torah, which, historically, most working people have been unable to accomplish, even during the times of the *Neviim*.

supported his brother Yissachar, who would study Torah. In return, Zevulun would have an equal share in Yissachar's Torah learning.[15]

The Netziv writes about a man who had a reputation of being very righteous, who sold a portion of his reward in *Olam Haba* to a wealthy man for a large sum of money. The rich man later found out that the person wasn't as righteous as he had thought and wanted to invalidate the sale and retrieve his money. The Netziv goes on to say that the sale was invalid in the first place, since the reward for mitzvos is in the next world and is not subject to being sold. This is what the Talmud calls a "*davar shelo ba la'olam*," an asset the seller doesn't have in his possession. Therefore, the Netziv ruled that the seller was required to return the money to the rich man.[16]

If this is the case, how may one ever enter into a Yissachar-Zevulun arrangement? How can a person sell the reward for the learning he does if it's something that he does not yet possess?

The *Maharit Algazi*, who served as the *Rishon Letzion* at the end of the eighteenth century, writes that this arrangement is not a sale, but a partnership.[17] The *Shulchan Aruch* says that although one cannot sell something that he doesn't yet have in his possession, in a partnership all parties may stipulate that they will split future profits, even though they are not yet in possession of them.[18] Similarly, in the Yissachar-Zevulun arrangement, Yissachar is not selling his reward for learning Torah; Yissachar and Zevulun are becoming partners in Yissachar's Torah in exchange for a portion of Zevulun's earnings.[19]

---

15   In *Shu"t Minchas Asher*, vol. 2, pp. 210, 212–14, Rav Asher Weiss discusses whether the concept of a Yissachar-Zevulun partnership applies to all mitzvos or only to learning Torah. He concludes that it is only for Torah learning.

16   *Meishiv Davar*, vol. 3, §14.

17   *Kuntres Mechiras Olam Haba*, p. 28.

18   *Shulchan Aruch, Choshen Mishpat* 176:3.

19   This is the opinion of Rav Moshe Feinstein as well (*Igros Moshe, Yoreh Dei'ah*, vol. 4, §37, cited in *Shu"t Minchas Asher*, vol. 2, p. 210)—that it is like any other monetary partnership and is not connected to the mitzvah of tzedakah. Therefore, says Rav Moshe, the general rules of priority that are in effect with the mitzvah of tzedakah (such as the obligation to give first to one's relatives, then to one's community, and so on) do not apply to the partnership of Yissachar and Zevulun. Furthermore, Rav Moshe says that this agreement must be an equal partnership in which the reward for the Torah learning and profits from the business are

Rav Shlomo Kluger, the famous nineteenth-century Rav of Brody, explains this partnership slightly differently. He writes that, in this arrangement, the one who is supporting the learner is actually considered as if he learned the Torah, too (and is not purchasing the Torah or reward), since he is the one who is enabling the other to learn.[20] Along these lines, the *Sefer Hafla'ah* says that supporters of Torah do not diminish any of the reward that those learning Torah receive. Rather, both the supporter and the learner receive a complete share. This is because the learner is not selling his reward to the supporter; rather, the supporter receives reward since it is as if he learned the Torah as well. The *Sefer Hafla'ah* gives the *mashal* of the flame of a candle to elucidate this concept. A candle can provide fire to other candles without losing any of its own light. So too, there is plenty of reward for both Yissachar and Zevulun.[21]

Rav Shlomo Kluger adds that a person can't sell his *Olam Haba* or reward for mitzvos to someone else.[22] His rationale is that the reward

---

divided evenly, and one therefore can't use *maaser* money for this arrangement. Similarly, Rav David Sperber says that if the Zevulun doesn't keep his side of the deal, the Yissachar can take him to *beis din* (*Afrakasta D'Anya*, vol. 1, §57, cited by Ari Wasserman in *Making It Work* [Feldheim, 2016], p. 159). However, see *Shu"t Minchas Asher*, vol. 2, pp. 209–10 and p. 212, for other approaches on how to understand the Yissachar-Zevulun relationship.

20   See *Shu"t Minchas Asher*, vol. 2, p. 210, for an interesting understanding of the Yissachar-Zevulun arrangement. Rav Weiss says there that the arrangement does not take effect if the Yissachar is otherwise able to support himself on his own.

21   *Haflaah*, introduction to *Maseches Kesubos* §43. See, however, *Shu"t Minchas Asher*, vol. 2, pp. 211–12, for other opinions on this matter. For example, the *Meshech Chochmah* (*Bereishis* 49:15) argues that the Yissachar does lose some of his reward. Rav Moshe Feinstein says this, too, and therefore concludes that both the Zevulun and the Yissachar split both the reward for the Torah learning and the profits made by the supporter. If the profits far exceed the needs of one Yissachar, they can be used to support others in Torah learning (*Igros Moshe, Yoreh Dei'ah*, vol. 4, §37:6). See *Making It Work* (Feldheim, 2016), by Ari Wasserman, p. 157, for two other approaches. Rav Asher Weiss himself says (*Shu"t Minchas Asher*, vol. 2, pp. 211–12) that both the Yissachar and the Zevulun will receive the full reward. Rav Moshe Feinstein (*Mesoras Moshe*, vol. 1, p. 499) explains that the concept of learning for the merit of someone else does not mean that the reward goes to the deceased, but rather to the one who learned the Torah. However, the deceased still receives merit for being the cause of the extra learning. He explains that there is no such concept as selling or transferring the reward of a mitzvah to someone else.

22   *Tuv Taam Vadaas*, vol. 1, §117.

Hashem bestows on us for keeping mitzvos is a *chessed*, as the *pasuk* says, "It is a *chessed* that Hashem repays man according to his deeds."[23] Therefore, it is possible that Hashem only wants to do the *chessed* with the person who is deserving of it and not another. However, in the Yissachar-Zevulun arrangement, since the Zevulun is enabling the Yissachar to learn Torah, it is as if Zevulun learned the Torah as well and deserves the reward.

Another issue with the idea of "selling" one's *Olam Haba* is found in the *sefer Aish Das*, which cites the *Maharit*. The *Maharit* says that if a person attempts to sell his *Olam Haba*, he is degrading the importance of *Olam Haba* and therefore loses the share he had. As a result, nothing is actually being sold, since his portion is already lost. Similarly, Chazal say that one of the sins of Esav was that he degraded the value of the *bechorah* (birthright) by selling it to Yaakov.[24]

The Netziv comments on the distorted approach of passing over the spiritual pleasures of *Olam Haba* for the physical pleasures of this world.[25] We find in the Torah that Hashem was upset with such an attitude. The Jews who left Egypt were living a very spiritual lifestyle and felt the presence of Hashem daily. Nevertheless, when they complained about not having enough physical pleasures and demanded meat, Hashem rebuked them by saying, "You have despised Hashem who is among you,"[26] and Hashem punished them for this. Therefore, the Netziv says, such an attitude of choosing physical pleasure over spiritual pleasure is punishable by Heaven in our day as well.[27]

There is a beautiful story told in the biography of Rav Moshe Twersky, *Hy"d*, about the seriousness we should have with regard to *Olam Haba*:

> *Someone close to Rav Twersky once took care of a certain financial matter on his behalf. The transaction involved a potential*

---

23   *Tehillim* 62:13.
24   *Kuntres Mechiras Olam Haba*, p. 47. Rabbi Akiva Eiger (*Yoreh Dei'ah* §246) references this *Aish Das*.
25   *Meishiv Davar*, vol. 3, §14.
26   *Bamidbar* 11:20.
27   *Kuntres Mechiras Olam Haba*, pp. 52–53.

for incurring interest charges, but seeing that most people
rely on the general heter iska associated with such things, the
individual executed the transaction without a second thought.
When Rav Twersky found out about this, though, he was terri-
bly distraught. The tears streaming down his face, coupled with
his heartrending expression that he was worried this would
make him lose his entire Olam Haba, made it immediately
clear how very seriously he regarded the matter.[28]

With regard to the final question—can a person sell his sins—Rav
Chaim Sofer, a student of the *Chasam Sofer*, writes about a case of a rich
man who paid a poor man to accept his sins.[29] Rav Chaim rules that
such a sale is completely invalid for a number of reasons. One of the
reasons is based on the Gemara's statement that a person doesn't die or
suffer without committing a sin, as the *pasuk* says, "The soul who sins
will die,"[30] meaning that punishments are not transferrable (because
only the one who committed the sins will die, not someone who "purchased" them).[31]

The *Mishneh Halachos*,[32] however, cites an incident that occurred
with the *Maharsha*. A person agreed to take upon himself the punishment of a terrible sin committed by another in exchange for a large sum
of money, and the punishment was believed to have been transferred.[33]
Nevertheless, the *Mishneh Halachos* rejects the possibility of selling
one's sins to another.

---

28   Rabbi Yehoshua Berman, *A Malach in Our Midst: The Legacy of a Treasured Rebbi, Harav*
Mosheh Twersky (Feldheim, 2016), pp. 342–43.

29   *Machaneh Chaim, Choshen Mishpat*, vol. 2, §20. The *Be'er Moshe* (vol. 4, §87) says that under
no circumstance may a person sell his sins to someone else. See *Shu"t Minchas Asher*, vol. 2,
p. 213, where Rav Asher Weiss argues that there is no validity to selling one's sins to another.
Rav Weiss discusses different proofs that some bring to prove that one can accept the punishments of another, but he rejects them all.

30   *Yechezkel* 18:20.

31   *Shabbos* 55a.

32   Vol. 5, §174, cited in *Otzar Hayedios* (Rav Yechiel Michel Stern), vol. 1, p. 352.

33   See *Shu"t Minchas Asher*, vol. 2, p. 212, regarding this *Maharsha* and opinions that accept and
reject it. See there also for the interesting practice of great, pious Jews who would agree to
share their reward for mitzvos and Torah learning.

SUMMARY

If one regrets performing a mitzvah, it is considered as if he didn't perform it, and he loses the merit of that mitzvah. Moreover, according to the Netziv, people are unable to sell their *Olam Haba* since they are not in possession of it. Rav Shlomo Kluger agrees, but he maintains that it is because Hashem may only want to reward the one who actually performed the mitzvah, not the one who bought its merit. Finally, while the *Maharsha* may disagree, Rav Chaim Sofer rules that paying another person to accept one's sins is not a valid sale.

PAYING A RANSOM

IN THE NEWS

On December 21, 2015, Yeshiva World News ran a story entitled "Father and Son Abducted on Their Way to Shul in Venezuela on Shabbos."[1] What transpired was that a father and son were walking to shul on Shabbos morning when they were kidnapped by armed men. The kidnappers contacted members of the family, demanding they pay a ransom in exchange for their safe return. Working through a negotiator, the two were quickly released.

According to the article, kidnappings are not uncommon in Venezuela. In recent years, many Israelis have become afraid to travel there due to fear of being kidnapped.

In January of 2016, Iran captured four US hostages, whom they subsequently released. The day following their release, $400 million in cash was sent to Iran. Commenting in August of that year about the payment, President Obama rejected claims that the money was paid in order to release the sailors. The payment, the president said, was the settlement of a legal dispute between the two countries. "We do not pay ransom for hostages," Obama said.[2]

---

1   "Father and Son Abducted on their Way to Shul in Venezuela on Shabbos" (Dec. 21. 2015), www.theyeshivaworld.com.

2   Alex Johnson, "'We Do Not Pay Ransom,' Obama Declares, Calling Criticism of Iran Deal Illogical" (Aug. 4, 2016), www.nbcnews.com.

In June of 2015, *The New York Times* ran an article outlining President Obama's change in policy for cases of kidnapped US citizens.[3] Longstanding US policy was never to negotiate with the kidnappers nor pay ransoms. Not only that, but the federal government had also warned family members of the victims of kidnapping that if they paid ransom to the abductors, they would face prosecution.

Obama's new policy was intended to abolish the threat to the abducted person's family. He also planned on appointing an FBI point man to coordinate any negotiation with kidnappers. The details of the plan were not made clear, but lawmakers worked hard to change a policy that all believed was unsuccessful in freeing American citizens in captivity and insensitive to the feelings of the kidnapped.

Kidnapping has, perhaps, become more common recently, but it's not a new phenomenon. How does the halachah guide us when faced with a ransom situation?

A TORAH PERSPECTIVE

The *Rambam* says that there is no greater mitzvah than redeeming captives, and one who ignores the plight of a captive has violated a number of prohibitions, while one who is involved in their redemption has fulfilled a number of commandments.[4]

To explore the halachos of such a situation, the Gemara says that one should not redeem captives for a sum greater than their value,[5] "because of *tikun olam*." The Gemara presents two interpretations as to

---

3   Julie Hirschfeld Davis, "Obama Ordering Changes in U.S. Hostage Policies" (June 23, 2015), www.nytimes.com.

4   *Hilchos Matenos Aniyim* 8:10. Rav Yisrael Salanter was once collecting money to redeem a Jewish captive, and several members of a certain congregation were not interested in helping. He declared that, as a result of this community's apathy toward a fellow Jew's plight, it was prohibited to pray in their shul. How could someone pray alongside Jews who do not feel the pain of others? (*Aleinu Leshabei'ach, Shemos*, p. 59)

5   *Gittin* 45a. The *Pischei Teshuvah* (*Yoreh Dei'ah* 252:5) brings two opinions regarding what this means—either more than they are worth in the slave market, or more than most people are ransomed for. See *Pesakim Uteshuvos* (§252, p. 406), where it is explained that, today, when it is not common for slaves to be sold in the marketplace, one's value is determined either by the going rate for what gentiles will typically pay to redeem captives, or by the wealth and prominence of the captive.

what *tikun olam* means. The first is that it will cause a tremendous financial strain on the community if it were compelled to redeem captives for an exorbitant amount of money.[6] The other interpretation is that it would lead to more kidnappings.

Rashi presents a practical difference between these two explanations—a case where the family of the captive is wealthy and willing to spend any amount necessary to redeem the captive.[7] According to the first explanation, in this case it would be permitted to spend whatever it takes to redeem the captive, since there are no financial ramifications for the community. But according to the second explanation, it would be prohibited, since it would also incentivize more kidnappings.

The *Rambam* and *Shulchan Aruch* rule according to the Gemara's second explanation that it is prohibited to redeem hostages for more than their value because that would encourage more kidnappings in the community.[8] The *Shach* understands the *Shulchan Aruch* to mean that it is prohibited in all cases, and even relatives may not redeem captives for more than their value.[9] The *Bach*, however, rules that they may spend more than the captive's value to redeem him if they have the means, accepting the first explanation in the Gemara above.[10]

There is another possible scenario: that the hostage himself is able to produce the ransom money. Would he, then, be permitted to pay an exorbitant price to free himself?

---

6   The Abarbanel ransomed 120 Jews taken captive by Afonso V of Portugal in North Africa in 1471. "He took pride in the fact that the money was collected solely by the Jews of Spain, without their having to turn for help to the Jews of other lands" (Julian G. Jacobs, *Judaism Looks at Modern Issues* [Aviva Press, 1993], p. 106).

7   *Gittin* 45a.

8   *Hilchos Matenos Aniyim* 8:12; *Shulchan Aruch, Yoreh Dei'ah* 252:4.

9   *Shach, Yoreh Dei'ah* 252:4.

10   Cited in *Shach, Yoreh Dei'ah* 252:4. The Vilna Gaon (*Biur HaGra, Yoreh Dei'ah* 252:6) says that the debate regarding the reasons an exorbitant ransom is prohibited in the Gemara in *Gittin* is not resolved, but in *Kesubos* 52a, the Gemara indicates that the reason is so that it doesn't incentivize more kidnappings, which is how the *Shulchan Aruch* rules. The Radvaz (*Shu"t Radvaz*, vol. 1, §40), cited in *Pesakim Uteshuvos* (p. 407), says that today we may redeem captives for more than their value.

The *Shulchan Aruch* rules that he may redeem himself for any amount of money.[11] *Tosafos* adds that one's wife is like oneself (*ishto kegufo*), so a man can also redeem his wife for any amount of money.[12]

The Gemara records an incident where Rabbi Yehoshua ben Chananiah redeemed a child for much more than his value.[13] *Tosafos* offers two explanations for why this was permitted.[14] The first is that the child's life was in danger and, in a case of danger, the rule not to redeem for more than the captive's value doesn't apply. The second explanation is that Rabbi Yehoshua knew that the boy was a child prodigy and would become a great Torah scholar one day, and, in that case, it is permissible to redeem a captive for more than his value.[15]

---

11   *Shulchan Aruch, Yoreh Dei'ah* 252:4. It would seem that this is permitted, either because redeeming oneself is not considered a strain on the community, or because it is an exception to
the other reason that we shouldn't incentivize future kidnappings. (Rabbi Jonathan Ziring,
"Pidyon Shevuyim in General and of Ishto" [December 16, 2014], www.yutorah.org)

12   *Tosafos, Kesubos* 52a, s.v. "*vehayu*."

13   *Gittin* 58a.

14   Ibid.

15   In a more recent example, in 1970, Rav Yitzchak Hutner was on a plane that was hijacked,
and his students wanted to pay millions of dollars for his release, based on the halachah
that a great Torah scholar can be redeemed for more than his value. However, Rav Yaakov
Kamenetsky opposed the idea. Rav Yaakov argued that this halachah doesn't apply
during wartime, and Israel was, and still is, at war with the Arab nations (*Be'ikvei Hatzon*,
pp. 206–7). In any case, The State Department didn't permit negotiating with the terrorists
(see *Mishpacha* magazine for more on the Rav Hutner hijacking story: Dov Bin-Nun and
Rachel Ginsberg, "He Swallowed My Papers to Save Me" [Sept. 14, 2011], www.mishpacha.
com). In a behind-the-scenes article about Rav Hutner's hijacking episode, Rav Shlomo
Aviner wrote the following: "Rav Yitzchak Hutner—former Rosh Yeshivah of Rabbi Chaim
Berlin in New York, and author of *Pachad Yitzchak*—once visited our Rabbi Ha-Rav Tzvi
Yehudah [Kook] in Israel. Our Rabbi asked him which airline he was flying. Rav Hutner
mentioned the name of a foreign airline. Our Rabbi pressed him, 'You need to fly El Al.'
Rav Hutner responded that terrorists were beginning to hijack planes and he was therefore
concerned about flying an Israeli airline. Our Rabbi stood firm, but Rav Hutner did not
change his flight. In the end, the plane on which Rav Hutner flew was hijacked to Jordan"
(*Iturei Kohanim* §176; "Redeeming Captives in Exchange for Releasing Terrorists," www.
ravaviner.com; see also *Aleinu Leshabei'ach, parashas Bechukosai*, p. 492, for an interesting
story regarding Rav Moshe Feinstein and the Rav Hutner hijacking).
After Rav Hutner was released from captivity, Rav Gifter said, "Until now we said *Tehillim* for
his release. Now we must say it to thank Hashem for saving him." Rav Gifter's message was
that many people say *Tehillim* during a crisis, but really it must be said afterward as well, to
thank Hashem for His salvation (Rabbi Yechiel Spero, *Rav Gifter: The Vision, Fire, and Impact*

The *Shulchan Aruch* cites the second explanation in *Tosafos*, that it is permitted to redeem a Torah scholar or a budding scholar for more than his value.[16] The *Pischei Teshuvah* records a debate among Rabbinic authorities whether to accept the first or second explanation of *Tosafos*.[17]

Rav Yitzchak Zilberstein cites his father-in-law, Rav Yosef Shalom Elyashiv, who says that when one is unsure of the halachah regarding a Rabbinic law, he should disregard the Rabbinic law and just follow the Torah law on the matter.[18] Based on this, Rav Zilberstein seems to be suggesting that we leave aside the debate on whether it is Rabbinically permitted to redeem someone for more than his value if his life is in danger, and follow Torah law that requires one to save another whose life is in danger.[19]

The *S'dei Chemed* writes that even according to the second answer in *Tosafos*, the halachah is that we would redeem someone in danger for more than his value, and *Tosafos* simply meant that if one's life was *not* in danger, we would redeem him for more than his value only if he

---

of an American-born Gadol [ArtScroll/Mesorah, 2011], p. 184). It's interesting to note how *Gedolim* responded to Rav Hutner's captivity. The Steipler and his son learned the *sefarim* that Rav Hutner wrote as a merit for his release (*Hesafrim*, p. 223).

During the entire time that Rav Yechezkel Abramsky was imprisoned by the Bolsheviks, the Chafetz Chaim would recite eight chapters of *Tehillim* a day for his release (Aharon Sorasky, *Reb Elchonon: The Life and Ideals of Rabbi Elchonon Bunim Wasserman of Baranovich* [ArtScroll/Mesorah, 1982], p. 54, n. 10).

16   *Shulchan Aruch*, *Yoreh Dei'ah* 252:4. It would seem that redeeming a scholar for more than his value is either not considered a strain on the community, as the advantage of having the scholar is a great benefit to the community, or that it won't lead to more scholars being captured. The second possibility is contradicted by the famous case of the Maharam MiRottenberg (1220–1293), a great scholar who refused to be ransomed from prison so as not to cause a precedent for the future. The *Yam Shel Shlomo* (*Gittin* 4:66) notes that the Maharam was correct in this decision, because, after that incident, kidnapping Torah scholars became less prevalent in his community. Some argue that the Maharam did want to be released and it was the emperor who refused to release him, despite being offered a large ransom by the Jewish community. See "The Tower of Ensisheim Revisited" (July 30, 2008), www.bdld.info.

17   *Pischei Teshuvah*, *Yoreh Dei'ah* 252:4.

18   *Medical Halachic Responsa* (Maimonides Research Institute, 2013), pp. 246–48.

19   *Vayikra* 19:16. See *Chashukei Chemed*, *Kiddushin*, p. 415, where Rav Zilberstein discusses an interesting question: Is a prominent person permitted to endanger his life by negotiating with the captors of a man being held in the African jungle?

was a Torah scholar or prodigy.[20] Therefore, based on this, it would be permitted to redeem someone whose life is in danger, even if it is for much more than his value.[21]

Rav Ovadiah Yosef writes about the Entebbe hostage crisis, where the captors demanded the release of terrorists in exchange for the hostages.[22] He says that it was permitted to redeem the hostages for more than their value, and that one could spend whatever was needed to redeem the captives. Rav Ovadiah explains that, after all, it was only a *takanah* (Rabbinic enactment) that one cannot spend more than a captive's value to redeem him, and, when lives are in danger, it is not clear if it is prohibited to spend more than the captives' value, so we can follow what was done before this *takanah*, where surely they paid more than the captives' value to redeem them. This is counter to the simple understanding of the *Shulchan Aruch*, which rules that even if the captives' lives are in danger, one may not spend more than their value to redeem them.

In contrast, Rav Shlomo Aviner was asked: Is it permissible to release terrorists in exchange for a captured soldier?[23] He responded that, based on the *Shulchan Aruch*'s ruling, we don't redeem captives for more than their worth since it will cause more kidnappings. He added that it

---

20   *S'dei Chemed*, vol. 1, §1:129, cited by Rav Zilberstein, *Medical Halachic Responsa* (Maimonides Research Institute, 2013), pp. 246–48.

21   Rav Yitzchak Zilberstein, in his *Medical Halachic Responsa* (Maimonides Research Institute, 2013), p. 247, analyzes the differences between the two answers in *Tosafos*, apparently with a different understanding than that of the *S'dei Chemed* cited above. He writes that according to the first answer, the certain rescue takes precedence over the doubtful rescue of many other lives, and therefore we should rescue the captive whose life is presently in danger, even though it is possible that it may cause a large-scale danger to the Jewish community in the future. According to the second answer, it is prohibited to save someone's life by putting the community in danger. Rav Zilberstein then discusses whether this understanding of the two answers of *Tosafos* can be used to answer the following question: A terrorist entered a settlement, wounded the guard, and killed several Jews, *Rachmana litzlan*. If a physician had been there and either could have saved the guard's life or chased after the terrorist to try to kill him in order to stop him from causing more harm, what would the physician have been required to do?

22   *Torah Shebe'al Peh*, vol. 19, p. 37. See also *Yabia Omer*, *Choshen Mishpat*, vol. 10, §6, where Rav Ovadiah discusses the Entebbe operation.

23   "Redeeming Captives in Exchange for Releasing Terrorists," www.ravaviner.com.

would similarly be prohibited to swap a captive soldier for a terrorist, since that would also lead to more kidnappings. Rav Aviner notes the discussions of the *Tosafos* and *Pischei Teshuvah* on redeeming captives in danger, but doesn't seem to consider them a factor.[24]

SUMMARY

According to the *Shulchan Aruch*, one may not redeem a captive for more than his value. However, the *Bach* rules that relatives may redeem a person for more than his value, if they have the means. In terms of a person redeeming himself, the *Shulchan Aruch* rules that one may spend the amount required to do so.

There is a debate regarding how much one may spend to redeem a captive that is in danger. Rav Zilberstein writes that, due to the doubt, one may redeem a captive whose life is in danger for any amount necessary.

---

24   In 1985, Israel released 1,150 terrorists from prison in exchange for a number of captured Israeli soldiers. Rav Shlomo Goren stated that the Israeli government's decision was against halachah and cited the arguments that Rav Aviner mentioned. However, Rav Chaim David HaLevi (*Aseih Lecha Rav*, vol. 7, §53) disagreed with Rav Goren and said that the rulings of the Gemara were not applicable to the current situation. Israel was fighting against hostile countries and had to protect the morale of the army, unlike the cases of the Gemara, where lone robbers would take people captive (Marc D. Angel and Hayyim Angel, *Rav Haim David Halevy* [Urim, 2006], pp. 109–11).

RAISING WHAT?

IN THE NEWS

The night before Israel's declaration of independence, while the pioneers discussed important issues facing the new state, oddly enough, they discussed whether it should be permitted to raise pigs in the country as well.[1] The Jewish Telegraph Agency archive contains a story from July 25, 1962, entitled "Knesset Bans Pig-Raising in Israel; Farmers Get Year to Sell Stock."[2] The article reported that the Knesset approved a private member's bill by a vote of 42 to 15 to ban "raising, keeping, or slaughtering" pigs in Israel. The law contains a few exceptions. It permits raising pigs in Nazareth and "six other places which have large Christian populations," as well as keeping them for "scientific purposes or for display in zoos." Anyone caught in violation of this ban faces a fine equivalent to $333 and the "renting of premises for a pigsty carries a fine" equivalent to $166.50.

The ban on raising pigs in Israel still stands today, although some farmers have made use of "legal loopholes" in order to get around it. In 2015, the *Times of Israel* reported that "Kibbutz Lahav in the northern Negev raises pigs legally as part of their research center" and sells surplus pigs for consumer consumption.[3]

According to the Torah, why would raising and selling pigs be worse than selling any other nonkosher animal?

---

1   Jeffrey Yoskowitz, "Israel's Pork Problem" (Aug. 8, 2012), www.slate.com.
2   "Knesset Bans Pig-Raisng in Israel; Farmers Get Year to Sell Stock" (July 25, 1962), www.jta.com.
3   Lee Gancman, "Swine carcasses strewn on Rishon Lezion street" (Dec. 14, 2015), www.timesofisrael.com.

A TORAH PERSPECTIVE

The Gemara in *Sotah* discusses how two rival factions of Chashmona'im kings battled each other for control of the kingdom of the Jewish People.[4] Aristobulus was inside Jerusalem, and Hyrcanus laid siege on the city. Every day, Aristobulus's group would lower gold coins down the wall, outside the city, to purchase two lambs for the daily communal sacrifice. The Gemara records that one day an old man advised Hyrcanus's group that as long as those inside Jerusalem continued to offer the daily sacrifice, it could be impossible to conquer them. So, instead of sending lambs, they sent a pig. As the pig was being raised over the wall, it stuck its hooves into the wall, and the entire Eretz Yisrael shook. Immediately, the Sages cursed anyone who raised pigs.[5]

The Mishnah says that it is prohibited to do business with forbidden foods,[6] and the Gemara adds that one cannot benefit at all from the proceeds of selling nonkosher animals.[7] The Gemara's statement is based on the *pasuk*, "They shall be an abomination to you,"[8] which is understood to mean that it is prohibited to eat nonkosher food and do business with it.[9]

Based on this, *Tosafos* in *Pesachim* asks why it was necessary for the Sages to forbid us to raise pigs.[10] After all, we see that there is a preexisting Biblical prohibition to own nonkosher animals.[11]

---

4   *Sotah* 49b.

5   See *Moreh Nevuchim*, ch. 48, regarding the harmful effects of consuming pig meat, as well as the negative effect it would have on the cleanliness of our streets, had they been permitted to be eaten, since pigs are filthy creatures that wallow in the mud and spread their filth everywhere.

6   *Sheviis* 7:3; see *Shulchan Aruch, Yoreh Dei'ah* 117:1.

7   *Pesachim* 23a.

8   *Vayikra* 11:11.

9   *Aruch Hashulchan, Yoreh Dei'ah* 117:2.

10   *Tosafos, Pesachim* 23a, s.v. *"amar."*

11   *Tosafos* clearly assumes that not only may one not eat or sell certain nonkosher animals, but that it would be prohibited to simply own them as well. The *Terumas Hadeshen* (§200) says the prohibition against owning them is Rabbinic, and the *pasuk Tosafos* cites is an *asmachta*, a support from the Torah for the Rabbinic enactment. The *Noda BiYehudah* (*Mahadura Tinyana, Yoreh Dei'ah* §62) writes that *Tosafos* believes it is a Rabbinic prohibition, based on what it says in *Bava Kama* 82b (see *Yalkut Biurim, Sotah*, p. 303). The *Mishneh Lamelech* (*Hilchos Maachalos Assuros* 8:18) proves that the *Rambam* holds it is a Biblical prohibition. Rav Ovadiah Yosef (*Yabia Omer, Yoreh Dei'ah*, vol. 8, §13) also believes it is a Biblical

The *Me'iri* answers that the curse, which was specifically against rais-ing pigs, was made in addition to the prohibition against owning non-kosher animals.[12] *Tosafos* answers that it is permitted to own nonkosher animals, such as horses and donkeys, that are not raised in order to sell as food, but are to be used for other purposes,[13] but the Gemara in *Sotah* is coming to teach us that it is prohibited to own pigs for any reason.[14]

The *Rashba* disagrees with the entire premise of *Tosafos* and holds that the prohibition to do business with nonkosher animals is only *mi'd'Rabbanan*.[15] He explains that the reason for the Rabbinic prohibi-tion against trading nonkosher food is so that one does not come to accidentally eat the food himself.[16]

The *Shulchan Aruch* codifies the Gemara in *Sotah* and states that one may neither raise pigs for any reason nor sell them.[17] The *S'ma* cites another halachah in the *Shulchan Aruch*[18] that says that anything that it is Biblically forbidden to eat, and is normally raised to be eaten, may not be sold, even if it is permitted to personally benefit from it (for example, by feeding it to a pet).[19] However, one may engage in trade for nonkosher animals (except pigs) that are likely not used for food,[20] or that are only Rabbinically prohibited.[21]

---

prohibition. Rav Moshe Sternbuch (*Teshuvos Vehanhagos*, vol. 1, §797) explains that most *poskim* say it is Biblically prohibited.

12 *Me'iri*, *Bava Kama* 79b.

13 *Tosafos*, *Bava Kama* 82b, s.v. *"lo."*

14 The *Rashba* (*Shu"t HaRashba*, vol. 3, §223) says it is prohibited to raise any nonkosher animal that is fit for consumption, for any reason, so that you won't come to eat it yourself. Horses and donkeys were not commonly eaten, so that is why a Jew is permitted to sell them.

15 However, the *Taz* (*Yoreh Dei'ah* 117:1) writes that even the *Rashba* agrees that the prohibiton is *mi'd'Oraisa*.

16 *Shu"t HaRashba*, vol. 3, §223; *Taz*, *Yoreh Dei'ah* 117:1.

17 *Shulchan Aruch*, *Choshen Mishpat* 409:2.

18 *Yoreh Dei'ah* §117.

19 *S'ma* 409:4. There are certain foods, such as mixtures of milk and meat, that are not only Biblically prohibited to eat, but are also Biblically prohibited to benefit from, such as feeding them to your dog. However, most other nonkosher foods, although they cannot be eaten, may be fed to one's pet (*Igros Moshe*, *Yoreh Dei'ah*, vol. 2, §37; *Shevet HaLevi*, vol. 6, §114), though they still may not be sold.

20 *Shach*, *Yoreh Dei'ah*, 117:1.

21 *Shulchan Aruch*, *Yoreh Dei'ah* 117. Rav Moshe Feinstein (*Igros Moshe*, *Even Ha'ezer*, vol. 1, §7) says that one may own stock in a nonkosher food company, but should not be involved in the

SUMMARY

It is prohibited to do business with prohibited foods. One may not even benefit from the proceeds of such a sale. One may not raise or sell pigs for any reason. However, one may sell animals that are not commonly eaten, even if they are not kosher.

---

decision-making of that company. See also *Teshuvos Vehanhagos* (vol. 1, §797), which permits this as well, since there is no concern you may come to eat the prohibited foods, and they may not even be considered yours. However, one should not operate a vending machine with nonkosher food (*Rivevos Ephraim*, vol. 3, §252). See *Teshuvos Vehanhagos* (vol. 2, §393–94) regarding purchasing nonkosher food for one's worker.

In the event that one receives nonkosher food, though, he may sell it (*Hagahos Rabbi Akiva Eiger, Yoreh Dei'ah* 117). For more on this topic, see *Shu"t Hashulchani: Halachic Insights and Responsa*, by Rabbi Ari Enkin, vol. 5, pp. 148–49. See also *Chashukei Chemed, Bava Kama*, p. 432, where Rav Yitzchak Zilberstein says that it would be permitted to raise pigs in Israel in order to use them for heart valve replacement for people with heart conditions, and one need not be concerned about the Rabbinical curse in that case. But if possible, it is preferable to arrange for a gentile to own the pigs. See also *Yam Shel Shlomo, Bava Kama* §9, cited in *Mesivta Shas*, vol. 2, *Yalkut Biurim*, p. 2.

REMOVING TATTOOS

IN THE NEWS

In a CNN article entitled "Suffering from 'Tattoo Regret,'" Dr. Anthony Youn, a plastic surgeon in Metro Detroit, recounts how he once met with a man to discuss renovating his house. He writes, "I noticed a teardrop tattoo at the top of his left cheek. Prior to hiring him, I searched online for what this design signified. My mouth dropped when I found out. A teardrop tattoo can mean he murdered someone. So I hired someone else."

"According to the American Society for Aesthetic Plastic Surgery, the number of people undergoing laser tattoo removal increased 43 percent from 2011 to 2012." Laser treatment is the most popular and successful way to remove a tattoo. "Most tattoos require three to four treatments to remove, and the costs can range from several hundred to several thousand dollars, depending on the size and location of the tattoo."

A *Wall Street Journal* article quoted a January 2012 Harris Interactive poll which reported that 21 percent of adults in the US have one tattoo or more, and 22 percent of eighteen- to twenty-four-year-olds have at least one.[1] Dr. Youn issues a warning to potential tattoo getters: "Ask yourself: Do you really want a permanent reminder of what may be a temporary feeling?"[2]

A *baal teshuvah* (penitent Jew) once posed the following question to his rabbi: "Before I became observant, I got a tattoo of Snoopy on

---

[1]   Liz Rappaport, "A Tattoo Is Forever—Except When You Don't Want It" (June 3, 2015), www.wsj.com.

[2]   Dr. Anthony Youn, "Suffering from 'tattoo regret'" (April 8, 2013), www.edition.cnn.com.

my arm. It doesn't really bother me, except for occasions such as going swimming or to the *mikveh* where other *frum* people can see it. I occasionally consider having it removed, but I understand that it would be as wrong to have it removed as it was to have it put on in the first place, since in both cases you're damaging your body. Is this correct?"

What does the Torah say regarding tattoos? And if a Jew received a tattoo and it is prohibited, is he required to get it removed?

A TORAH PERSPECTIVE

The Torah says in *parashas Kedoshim*, "And you shall not place a tattoo on yourselves; I am God."[3] As interpreted by Chazal, the Torah is prohibiting both applying a tattoo and allowing a tattoo to be applied to one's body.[4] Rabbi Chaim Jachter points out that immediately after the Torah states the prohibition of tattoos, it says, "I am Hashem," as if to remind us that our bodies don't belong to us[5]—they are on loan from Hashem, given to us only to serve Him.[6]

---

3   *Vayikra* 19:28.

4   See *Tosefta, Makkos* 3:9, and *Minchas Chinuch* 253:4. See also *Rambam, Hilchos Avodas Kochavim* 12:11. Rabbi Chaim Jachter says the *Shulchan Aruch* in *Yoreh Dei'ah* 180:2 may imply that only applying a tattoo is an *issur d'Oraisa*, but receiving the tattoo is an *issur d'Rabbanan* (see *Gray Matter: Exploring Contemporary Halachic Issues*, vol. 3 [Kol Torah Publications, 2008], p. 75). On the other hand, Rabbi Dr. Ari Zivotofsky quotes the *Nishmas Avraham* (vol. 5, §67–68), which permits a doctor to make a permanent mark on the skin to identify the area where surgery will be performed. Rabbi Zivotofsky also debunks the myth that a Jew with a tattoo can't be buried in a Jewish cemetery (Rabbi Dr. Ari Zivotofsky, "Tzarich Iyun: Jews with Tattoos," www.ou.org).

5   *Gray Matter*, vol. 3, p. 78. See *Shu"t Minchas Asher*, vol. 1, §122, where Rav Asher Weiss discusses whether the sale of one's organs is valid, since we do not have ownership over our bodies. See also *Igros Moshe, Yoreh Dei'ah*, vol. 4, §59, p. 290, where Rav Moshe Feinstein explains that we do not have ownership over our bodies, and see *Rambam, Hilchos Rotzei'ach* 1:4, and *Radvaz, Hilchos Sanhedrin* 18:6, which cite the *pasuk*, "All of the souls are Mine" (*Yechezkel* 18:4), also implying that our bodies don't belong to us.

6   The *Sefer Hachinuch* (Mitzvah §253) says that the Torah wants us to stay away from the practices of idolaters who would tattoo themselves in submission to their idol. See *Gray Matter*, pp. 73–74, on whether tattooing for non-idolatrous purposes is a Biblical prohibition or not, and see pp. 70–71 on whether one must write letters in order for the prohibition to be violated. The rationale behind this is that some Rishonim (*Rambam, Hilchos Avodas Kochavim* 12:11; *Tur, Yoreh Dei'ah* 180; and *Sefer Hachinuch* §253) explain that the reason the Torah prohibited tattoos was because idol worshippers would tattoo the names of their gods on their bodies. Hence, the prohibition only applies to writing words. Rav Moshe Feinstein (*Mesoras Moshe*, vol. 2, pp. 199–201) and Rav Yosef Shalom Elyashiv (*Vayishma Moshe*, vol. 1,

Removing tattoos is a common procedure today, either done through creams, laser surgery, or plastic surgery. The question, then, is whether one is required to remove a tattoo from one's body.[7]

It seems that the *Rambam* and *Shulchan Aruch* rule that it is not prohibited to leave a tattoo on one's body because neither mentions such a halachah. However, Rabbi Jachter points out that the *Rambam* and *Shulchan Aruch* may not have discussed it simply because it may not have been possible to remove a tattoo in their times.[8]

Dayan Yitzchak Yaakov Weiss, the late *av beis din* of the Eidah Chareidis, discusses a case where someone had an inappropriate tattoo on his arm (from before he became observant) on the place where he should place his *tefillin*. Rav Weiss advised him to remove the tattoo, but he didn't go so far as to say that he was required to do so because of the prohibition against having a tattoo.[9]

Rav Elyashiv says that removing a tattoo is the proper thing to do—that it's proper to remove something that is against the will of Hashem.[10] A proof that is brought to support Rav Elyashiv's position comes from the *Minchas Chinuch*.[11] The *Rambam* rules that if someone erases incorrect or unnecessary writing, he has violated the *melachah* of *mocheik*, the prohibition against erasing on Shabbos, even though he didn't erase it in order to write something new. This is because

---

pp. 261–62) both hold this way. However, the *Minchas Chinuch* (253:3) and Rav Nassan Gestetner (*Lehoros Nassan*, vol. 10, §64) argue, in the name of the *Rambam*, that tattoos are Biblically prohibited even without letters.

7   See *Lehoros Nassan* (vol. 8, §72), which says that although it's generally forbidden to wound oneself, it is permitted to remove tattoos if it is done in order to repent for the sin committed when getting the initial tattoo. Alternatively, it may be permitted based on the ruling of Rav Moshe Feinstein (*Igros Moshe, Choshen Mishpat*, vol. 2, §66), who explains that the prohibition to wound oneself applies only if it is done in a destructive or demeaning manner, which is not the case when removing a tattoo, because it is beneficial to the person.

8   *Gray Matter*, vol. 3, p. 76.

9   *Minchas Yitzchak*, vol. 3, §11. Rav Chaim Kanievsky ruled that a *baal teshuvah* is not obligated to remove a tattoo of a cross. See *Maalos Rivkah*, cited in *Short and Sweet: Text Message Responsa from Ha-Rav Shlomo Aviner Shlit"a* (American Friends of Yeshivat Ateret Yerushalayim, 2012), p. 190.

10   See *Chashukei Chemed, Pesachim*, p. 427, where Rav Elyashiv is cited.

11   Mitzvah 32, end of *Meleches Mocheik*.

the very act of erasing was in itself a constructive act.[12] The *Minchas Chinuch* adds that if a Jew has a tattoo, and he erases it on Shabbos, he has violated the *melachah* of *mocheik* according to the *Rambam*. Even though he didn't erase the tattoo in order to write something in its place, the very existence of the tattoo is improper, and therefore by removing it, a constructive act has been committed. Rav Elyashiv's very idea in this ruling of the *Minchas Chinuch*—that it is not proper to keep a tattoo on one's body—suggests that one should make an effort to have it removed.[13]

In regard to the Holocaust, Rav Ephraim Oshry, renowned author of *Responsa from the Holocaust*, believed strongly that survivors should not remove the tattoos that the Nazis, *yimach shemam*, put on them.[14] He writes that the tattoos should be viewed as badges of honor.[15] Thus, in this case, Rav Oshry held that there is no obligation to remove a tattoo.

Rav Meir Amsel, however, disagreed with Rav Oshry. He maintained that one should not discourage those who wanted to remove the tattoos. Removing the tattoo would help eradicate the memories of the Nazis, restore a relative degree of dignity to a survivor, and ease the constant pain that seeing the tattoo caused the survivor.[16]

Along the lines of Rav Oshry's view, when the Nazis were transporting Jews to the gas chambers, a passenger jumped out of a moving train, injuring his hand. The person was thankful to Hashem that he was able to escape and survive the Holocaust, but his hand was slightly deformed. Whenever he looked at his hand, he recalled the great miracle Hashem did for him in helping him escape the Nazis. He didn't

---

12 *Hilchos Shabbos* 11:9. See *Biur Halachah* 340:3, s.v. "*hamocheik*." *Rashi* (*Shabbos* 75b, s.v. "*machak*") rules that the *melachah* of *mocheik* applies only where one erases in order to write.

13 See *Chashukei Chemed, Pesachim*, p. 427. See also the chapter entitled "The Magen David" below for Rav Zilberstein's story about a Jewish mother who had her son tattooed with a Magen David on his hand, so that he would never forget he was Jewish and marry a gentile.

14 *Mimaamakim*, vol. 4, §22; see also vol. 1, §27, and see the English edition, *Responsa from the Holocaust* (Judaica Press, 2001), pp. 193–95.

15 Rav Moshe Feinstein once said about a Holocaust survivor, "She has numbers on her arm… She is holier than I am" (Rabbi Shimon Finkelman, *Reb Moshe: The Life and Ideals of HaGaon Rabbi Moshe Feinstein* [ArtScroll/Mesorah, 2012], p. 267).

16 *Oraisa*, vol. 22, "*Acharei Hashoah*."

know whether he should undergo surgery to fix his hand; he wondered if he should leave it so that he would always remember the miracle that Hashem did for him.[17]

To answer this question, Rav Yitzchak Zilberstein cites the *Ramban*, who asks why Moshe didn't pray to Hashem to have his speech impediment cured.[18] The *Ramban* answers by quoting the midrash, which says that since his speech impediment was the result of a miracle that Hashem did for him, he didn't want to forget it, and that is why he didn't pray to have it removed.[19] Therefore, Rav Zilberstein said, if the deformity on the person's hand was the result of a miracle that Hashem did for him, and through it he recalls the kindness Hashem did for him, then it is proper not to remove it (provided that it doesn't interfere with his ability to learn Torah and do mitzvos).[20]

---

17   See *Chashukei Chemed, Gittin* 20b, regarding someone who got a tattoo of the Name of Hashem on his leg. On one hand, he had a problem entering a bathroom and *mikveh* because of the presence of the Name of Hashem, but on the other hand he couldn't remove the tattoo since it might be included in the prohibition against erasing a Name of Hashem. Rav Asher Weiss discusses three different possibilities for removing tattoos with the Name of Hashem. One of them is to have it removed through a laser, which would be considered indirectly removing it. The fact that a gentile would do it would help too ("*Kesoves Kaaka Shel Shem Kadosh*," www.tvuna.org). See also *Bamareh Habazak*, vol. 5, §78, for more on this. The *Bamareh Habazak* also says that, strictly speaking, one doesn't have to remove the tattoo if it's in the image of *avodah zarah*, but one should cover it before entering shul and he adds that it's praiseworthy to remove it.

18   *Ramban, Shemos* 4:10.

19   The midrash (*Shemos Rabbah* 1:26) says that when Pharaoh's daughter brought baby Moshe to the palace, Pharaoh kissed him and Moshe grabbed the crown off his head. Some of Pharaoh's officers said that was a bad sign, and Moshe should be killed. Yisro was there and said that Moshe was just a baby; he didn't know what he was doing. He suggested that Pharaoh test the child by placing in front of him hot coal and gold to see which one he'd choose. If he reached for the coal, that would show he didn't know what he was doing. If he reached for the gold, it meant he did have the ability to reason and should be killed. The coals and gold were brought out, and Moshe was about to reach for the gold when the angel Gavriel pushed his hand to take the coal. Moshe placed the burning coal in his mouth, in pain, and that left him with his speech impediment. See *Rabbeinu Bachya* (*Shemos* 4:10) for a different reason as to why he didn't pray to be healed.

20   *Vehaarev Na*, vol. 3, p. 123; see also *Aleinu Leshabei'ach, parashas Lech Lecha*, p. 172. Should a soldier avoid surgery so that he can remember his wounds and the miracle that Hashem did for him? See *Chashukei Chemed, Nedarim*, p. 458. See also *Chashukei Chemed, Kiddushin* 49a, where Rav Zilberstein responds to a certain community that wanted to leave part of a shul damaged in order to remember the great miracle Hashem did for them when they were

Rabbi Eliezer Silver was also asked about removing the tattooed numbers from the arms of Jews after the Holocaust. He agreed that they shouldn't remove them, but for a different reason—because through the numbers they are fulfilling the mitzvah of *zechiras Amalek* (recalling what Amalek did to the Jews).[21]

SUMMARY

It is permitted to remove a tattoo because it is a constructive act, which would not count as wounding oneself. Although one is not obligated to remove a tattoo, it seems that it is proper to do so. Rav Ephraim Oshry encouraged Holocaust survivors to keep the numbers tattooed on their forearms, while Rav Meir Amsel disagreed.

---

saved from a missile that hit the shul. Rav Zilberstein ruled that they should repair the shul and not leave part of it damaged because it's more important that the shul look respectable.

21   *Chashukei Chemed, Kesubos* 26b.

RENEGING ON A PLEDGE

IN THE NEWS

In February of 2016, Arutz Sheva ran a story entitled "Large Donation Canceled after Palestinian Event."[1]

The story began when Milbank, a well-established international law firm, pledged a million dollars toward student conferences at Harvard Law School. However, after Justice for Palestine, a student group, used $500 from the fund to purchase pizza during a "pro-Palestinian" discussion in the fall of 2015, Milbank withdrew its pledge.

Milbank representatives did not respond to requests for comment on the report, but Harvard officials were quoted as saying that the law firm wanted to avoid creating any feeling it took "a stance on any political issue."

Is it permissible, according to halachah, to withdraw a pledge to a law school because one doesn't approve of an event that took place after the pledge was made?

A TORAH PERSPECTIVE

When addressing the importance of keeping one's word, it's essential to remember that honesty is a hallmark of the Jewish code of ethics, as it is stressed in the *pasuk*, "The remnant of Israel will not commit corruption nor speak falsehood, and a deceitful tongue will not be found in their mouth..."[2]

---

1   Raphael Poch, "Large Donation Canceled after Palestinian Event" (Feb. 21, 2016), www.israelnationalnews.com.
2   *Tzefaniah* 3:13.

With regard to the halachah, the *Shulchan Aruch* rules that a pledge to tzedakah is treated as a *neder* (vow) and is legally binding.[3] However, a verbal commitment to make a purchase without consummating the acquisition is not legally binding, and a person who reneges on his commitment is only considered a *mechusar amanah*, a person who doesn't keep his word, not someone who violated a *neder*.[4] However, such an action is still not proper in the eyes of Chazal.[5]

The *Rambam*, *Shulchan Aruch*, and *Rema* rule that a person who promises another a gift and doesn't keep his word is also considered *mechusar amanah*.[6] The *Rambam*, though, says that this is only if he promised a small gift, since the other person reasonably expected him to give what he promised, but not when he promised an expensive present.[7] However, Rav Betzalel Stern, the *av beis din* of Melbourne, Australia, says that if the person who promised a very large gift is very wealthy, the prospective recipient has every reason to believe that he will keep his word. If he backs out of this promise, even though he cannot be forced to give the gift, his refusal would deem him a *mechusar amanah*.[8]

---

3   *Shulchan Aruch, Yoreh Dei'ah* 257:3.

4   *Rema, Choshen Mishpat* 204:11, based on *Bava Metzia* 48a. See *Shu"t Minchas Asher*, vol. 2, §112, for limitations of this principle.

5   The Gemara in *Bava Metzia* 44a (codified in *Shulchan Aruch, Choshen Mishpat* 204:4) says that someone who retracts a verbal agreement accompanied by payment is subject to *beis din* pronouncing on him the curse of *Mi Shepara*—"He who took retribution from the generation of the Flood and the Tower of Bavel will take retribution against one who doesn't keep his word." The *Darchei Moshe* (*Choshen Mishpat* 204:2) explains that violating *mechusar amanah* means one is not following the ways of the Jewish People. Some say that if one signals for a taxi to pick him up, he may not ride in a different taxi that arrives sooner. See Rabbi Avraham Zuroff, *Question Market* (Targum, 2008), p. 199. Another example of *mechusar amanah* is if a parent makes a verbal agreement to enroll a child in a playgroup and subsequently changes his mind. Some are lenient and permit one to back out of an agreement due to significant unexpected circumstances that arose after the commitment. (See Rabbi Baruch Meir Levin, *Playgroups in Halacha* [CreateSpace, 2013], ch. 2, for more on this.)

6   *Hilchos Mechirah* 7:9, based on *Bava Metzia* 49a; *Shulchan Aruch, Choshen Mishpat* 204:8; *Rema, Shulchan Aruch* 204:11.

7   The *Beis Yosef* (*Yoreh Dei'ah* 264) cites the Maharam MiRottenberg who rules that if a father asks a *mohel* to perform a *bris*, he may not then ask a different *mohel* to do it instead. The reasoning is that this offer is considered like offering a small gift, where one is obligated to keep his word.

8   *Betzeil Hachochmah*, vol. 5, §158.

It would seem, then, that Milbank's reneging on its pledge, even though it was a very large one, would deem it *mechusar amanah*, since Harvard Law School had every reason to expect Milbank to fulfill its promise.

However, Rav Asher Weiss explains that the notion of *mechusar amanah* means that one should act with righteousness toward others. But when the other party involved does not act the same way, and acts with deception or other inappropriate behavior, one would not have to fulfill his commitment.[9]

One could say this is true in the case of Harvard Law School. If the school permits pro-Palestinian groups to meet on campus—groups that support terror against Israel—perhaps Milbank does not have to fulfill its pledge, which would contribute to such inappropriate activities.

But what about the law firm's promise to donate to Harvard Law School from the perspective of their having made a *neder*, a vow? Assuming the owners of the firm are Jewish, of course, would they be obligated to keep their promise because of the halachos of *nedarim*?

The answer is that there are a few reasons it would be permitted for Milbank to back out and be absolved of its *neder* to Harvard. First of all, there is a concept of *nidrei shegagos*—oaths made under faulty assumptions; if the one making the promise had known the truth, he would not have made his promise to begin with. These *nidrei shegagos* are not binding.[10] In this case, since the law firm would not have made the pledge had it known that Harvard would permit such activities to be sponsored by their funds, the pledge is not binding.

Another reason the firm may retract its pledge is because the *Shulchan Aruch* says that a pledge is only considered a *neder* when it is made to a poor person, in fulfillment of the mitzvah of tzedakah.[11] In our case, the pledge was not made to a poor person. Even if one were to argue that committing to give money to an educational institution is a pledge to

---

9   *Shu"t Minchas Asher*, vol. 2, pp. 370–71.
10   *Shulchan Aruch, Yoreh Dei'ah* 232:6. See also *Rema, Yoreh Dei'ah* 258:2.
11   *Shulchan Aruch, Yoreh Dei'ah* 258:12.

do *chessed* or a mitzvah and would be treated like a *neder*,[12] Rav Shlomo Zalman Auerbach rules that one can be lenient and rely on the *hataras nedarim* (traditional annulment of all vows) performed on Erev Rosh Hashanah.[13] Rav Moshe Feinstein cautions, though, that in general one should not rely on the *hataras nedarim* of Erev Rosh Hashanah for reneging on pledges.[14]

Interestingly, Rav Moshe Sternbuch cites Rav Betzalel Stern who rules that it is permitted to publicly embarrass those who don't keep their word. Rav Sternbuch, however, rejects this ruling, maintaining that the prohibition of embarrassing another person is very severe.[15] Although Chazal are not pleased with someone who doesn't keep his word, he is not considered a *rasha*, and therefore it is forbidden to humiliate him in public. Also, says Rav Sternbuch, in today's day and age, publicly embarrassing people will not prevent them from reneging on their word. Therefore, he concludes that it is completely wrong to do so.

Regarding the gravity of making *nedarim* to begin with, the *Chazon Ish* related, before teaching *Maseches Nedarim*, that, strictly speaking, every commitment a person makes should be treated like a *neder*. However, Hashem knew that people would not be able to handle this, so He had mercy upon us and decided to only consider actual vows with severity.[16]

SUMMARY

One should honor his promise to give a gift if the recipient expects to receive it. Oaths made under faulty assumptions, however, are not binding. Furthermore, according to the *Shulchan Aruch*, a pledge is only considered a *neder* with regard to tzedakah. Some extend this to include

---

12   *Ran* and *Ritva, Nedarim* 8a.
13   *Minchas Shlomo*, vol. 1, §91:20.
14   *Mesoras Moshe*, vol. 2, p. 234. See also *Piskei Teshuvos*, vol. 6, p. 193.
15   *Teshuvos Vehanhagos*, vol. 2, §705. See also vol. 5, §374. See *Chashukei Chemed, Bava Kama*, p. 197, regarding the question of whether it is permissible to embarrass someone in public in order to stop him from talking during the Torah reading.
16   *Chut Shani, Rosh Hashanah-Yom Kippur-Sukkos*, p. 332. See *Chiddushei Haleiv, parashas Shelach*, p. 92, which cites *Rabbeinu Bachya* about the importance of keeping one's word. The *Radak* (on *Tehillim* 15:2) says a truly righteous person keeps even his mental commitments to do good.

all acts of *chessed* that one pledges to do. However, one may be lenient in this case and withdraw the pledge, relying on the *hataras nedarim* performed on Erev Rosh Hoshanah, since some do not consider pledges of *chessed* to be binding to begin with.

REVEALING YOUR SINS

IN THE NEWS

In February of 2014, CBS ran a news story about a new government initiative, called My Brother's Keeper, aimed to "unlock the full potential of young men and boys of color."[1]

The initiative was launched by President Obama himself in the East Room of the White House. In his address, Obama said, "I could see myself in these young men...I didn't have a dad in the house, and I was angry about it, even though I didn't necessarily realize it at the time. I made bad choices, I got high without thinking about the harm it would do, I didn't always take school as seriously as I should have...I grew up in an environment that was a little bit more forgiving. When I made a mistake, the consequences were a little less severe."

Shaar Press Publications published a fascinating book, entitled *Incredible!*, about the life of Rabbi Yossi Wallis, the CEO of Arachim. The book follows Rabbi Wallis through a wide variety of locations and challenges, including violent experiences as a New York street gang member and encounters with the Mafia.

In January of 2013, after years of rumors, Lance Armstrong admitted to Oprah Winfrey on television that he used performance-enhancing drugs throughout his Tour de France victories from 1999 to 2005.[2]

What is the Jewish approach to revealing one's past mistakes? Is it

---

1   Stephanie Condon, "Obama Launches 'My Brother's Keeper' initiative" (Feb. 27, 2014), www.cbsnews.com.

2   "Lance Armstrong Admits to Using Performance-Enhancing Drugs" (Jan. 17, 2013), www.npr.org.

permitted for leaders to reveal their past sins and mistakes in order to inspire others?

A TORAH PERSPECTIVE

The Gemara in *Pesachim* relates how Rabbi Akiva told his students that when he was an *am haaretz*, he hated Torah scholars and used to remark that he wished one would come near him so that he could bite him as if he were a donkey![3] This seems to suggest that a mentor, even a *talmid chacham*, can share mistakes from his past with his students in order to teach them a lesson.

In fact, Rav Eliyahu Eliezer Dessler, in his *sefer Michtav M'Eliyahu*, relates how he struggled to quit smoking and failed, but he waged war after war to stop. In the footnotes, his students added that he finally succeeded in quitting.[4]

The Chozeh of Lublin spoke freely of his weaknesses,[5] and Rabbi Yehudah Amital made the following observation:

> *There has been a tendency in recent years to idealize great rabbis, to the point of total disregard of their human feelings and weaknesses. The Torah presents the opposite approach: every person has a human side, which must not be denied. Even the prophets had doubts and difficulties. The Torah recognizes that man lives in this world, and it has no expectations that one behave as if he were living in an ideal and unreal universe.[6]*

It seems, though, that there are halachic conditions under which one may share past sins. The Gemara notes an apparent contradiction in the Torah in answer to the question of whether one may reveal his

---

3   *Pesachim* 49b.

4   *Michtav M'Eliyahu*, vol. 1, p. 79.

5   Michael Rosen, *The Quest for Authenticity: The Thought of Reb Simhah Bunim* (Urim, 2008), p. 32. However, even when it is permissible to share one's sins, a person is never permitted to be proud or boast about what he did. The *Rambam* writes (in *Hilchos Teshuvah* 2:2) that one must regret his sins.

6   Elyashiv Reichner, *By Faith Alone: The Story of Rabbi Yehuda Amital* (Koren, 2011), p. 367.

past sins or not and suggests two answers.[7] Rav says to only publicize sins that are already well known, and Rav Nachman says to only reveal sins committed against another person (*bein adam lachaveiro*) and not against God (*bein adam laMakom*).[8]

The *Rambam* follows the opinion of Rav Nachman, who only permits publicizing sins against people.[9] The *Mishnah Berurah* seems to follow Rav, and says that if the sin is not well known, one should not publicize it; if it is well known, it is permitted to publicize it.[10] However, Rabbi Daniel Travis believes the *Mishnah Berurah* is also concerned about the opinion of Rav Nachman.[11] Based on his understanding of the *Mishnah Berurah*, one may only publicize and admit to sins against people if they are also already public knowledge.

However, Rabbi Daniel Travis also cites Rav Shlomo Zalman Auerbach, who says that a *baal teshuvah* can discuss his former sinful behavior, including sins against God.[12] When the Gemara says not to disclose one's sins against God, Rav Shlomo Zalman says, it is because it would have a detrimental effect on people's *yiras Shamayim* (fear of God). However, that is not a concern today, when people are aware of *baalei teshuvah* and their previous lifestyles.

---

7   *Yoma* 86b.

8   According to Rav, if it is public knowledge, one should admit to the sin and suffer the embarrassment that will ensue as part of the *teshuvah* process. If the sin is not known, Rav holds that one should not publicize it, since that will minimize God's honor in this world (*Rashi, Yoma* 86b). According to Rav Nachman, one should only publicize sins committed against another person as a way of receiving forgiveness from the person he wronged. If the person he wronged refuses to forgive him, then he can publicize the sin so that others will implore the person to forgive him (*Rashi, Yoma* 86b). According to *Rashi*, it emerges that according to both Rav Nachman and Rav, sins committed against God that are not public knowledge should not be publicized (*Takanas Hashavim* §6, p. 47; see there for a comprehensive discussion of this topic).

9   *Hilchos Teshuvah* 2:5.

10   *Mishnah Berurah* 607:6, 9; *Shaar Hatziyun* 607:5.

11   *Shu"t Takanas Hashavim*, p. 47. He explains the *Mishnah Berurah* this way so that the *Mishnah Berurah* is not disagreeing with most of the Rishonim (*Rambam, Rif, Rosh*), who accept Rav Nachman's opinion. The *Lechem Mishneh* on *Hilchos Teshuvah* 2:5 notes that the *Raavad* also accepts both the opinions of Rav and Rav Nachman. See *Shu"t Takanas Hashavim* §6, pp. 46–47.

12   *Shu"t Takanas Hashavim*, p. 48.

Rav Moshe Sternbuch adds that it is beneficial for *baalei teshuvah* to discuss their once sinful past, since it encourages others to repent as well.[13] Some point out that it all depends on the context. It may not be appropriate to discuss sinful behavior with those who are already religious, since it may cause more harm than good.[14]

Rav Shlomo Zalman says this leniency doesn't apply to those who grew up Orthodox, left religion, and then returned. Aside from the issue of publicizing one's sins, there is also the harm and embarrassment such discussions will cause to their families.

On the other hand, Rav Moshe Feinstein writes that a person should never reveal his sins to others, unless there is a good reason.[15] For example, if a person wants to know what the halachah is in order to repent properly, he may tell his *rav* what he did wrong. Otherwise, a person should only confess to Hashem and no one else, because it is the ways of the gentiles to confess their sins to priests and then assume they are absolved from fully repenting.

In discussing the power of past experiences, the Rav, Rabbi Joseph B. Soloveitchik, said:

> *The kiruv movement is dominated by people who themselves are baalei teshuvah. Rather than cut themselves off from the past, they are able to build on it. Possibly, Rabbi Akiva's ignoble past is what enabled him to become a great leader, for the masses connected with him more than they could with those who lived in a segregated world. Thus, the past of a baal teshuvah can, indeed, be the source of his greatness.*[16]

---

13   *Teshuvos Vehanhagos*, vol. 2, §462.

14   See *Shu"t Takanas Hashavim*, pp. 48–49.

15   *Igros Moshe, Orach Chaim*, vol. 4, §118. It should be noted that Rav Moshe was not commenting on whether the halachah is like Rav or Rav Nachman. See Rav Shraga Neuberger's *Ayalah Sheluchah*, pp. 48–49, where he notes that it seems that according to Rav Kahana (*Sotah* 7b, *Berachos* 34b) one should not publicize his sins. He also points out that Rav Kahana does not limit this to sins against man or sins that are not already known to the public.

16   David Holzer, *The Rav Thinking Aloud on the Parsha: Sefer Bamidbar* (Jerusalem: Laor Ltd.), p. 65.

Rav Yitzchak Hutner, in one of his letters, agreed with this approach and wrote that it is a big mistake to focus on the *Gedolim* only after they are already mature and have reached a high spiritual level. He writes that it's better to focus on what they were like before they became *Gedolim* and on what they had to do to get there—the struggles and battles they went through.[17]

In the beginning of *parashas Shemini*, Hashem commands Aharon to complete the inauguration of the *Mishkan* with special *korbanos*. *Rashi* tells us, based on the *Sifra*, that Aharon was embarrassed to do this job, because he felt unworthy as a result of his involvement in the *chet ha'eigel* (sin of the golden calf). But Moshe encouraged him, nonetheless, and said, "Why are you embarrassed? That is what you were chosen for!"[18] This message—"That is what you were chosen for!"—doesn't sound right. Why didn't Moshe say, "Nevertheless, Hashem chose you!"

Rabbi Bernard Weinberger explains that what Moshe was telling Aharon was that it is precisely because he was embarrassed about being involved in the *chet ha'eigel* that he was chosen. In other words, by being a true *baal teshuvah*, Aharon would be the one who could inspire the Jewish nation to repent in turn.[19]

Rabbi Bernard Weinberger points out that Nadav and Avihu, Aharon's eldest sons, believed otherwise. They were waiting for the day when they would replace Aharon as the *Kohen Gadol* (high priest), because they felt that the nation needs leaders who are *tzaddikim gemurim* (absolutely righteous), not *baalei teshuvah*. Moshe, however, taught that this is not the correct path; the nation needs leaders who are *baalei teshuvah*. Thus, people will be inspired to be better Jews when they know that their own leaders also overcame adversity and repented for their own sins.

SUMMARY

The simple reading of the *Mishnah Berurah* indicates that one may only publicize and admit to sins that people already know about. Rabbi Travis understands the *Mishnah Berurah* to permit publicizing sins

---

17   *Pachad Yitzchak, Igros Umichtavim* §128.
18   See *Vayikra* 9:7.
19   *Shemen Hatov*, vol. 1, *parashas Shemini*.

against one's fellow that are well known, but not to permit revealing sins committed against Hashem. Rav Shlomo Zalman Auerbach permits a *baal teshuvah* to admit and discuss his sins against Hashem. Rav Sternbuch agrees due to the fact that such discussions can inspire others to repent as well. Similarly, Rav Dessler and the Chozeh shared their challenges in order to inspire others to improve as well.

RISKING YOUR LIFE
TO SAVE OTHERS

IN THE NEWS

In the wake of Hurricane Irene, in Spring Valley, NY, David Reichenberg found a father and son stuck in a fallen electrical wire that had electrocuted them. He ran to save them, but died in the process.

"He was lying on the floor and his clothes were on fire," a passerby said. "I thought it was a grass fire at first, but it was him." David Reichenberg died from an electrical fire while saving the lives of others.[1]

In Israel, Rabbi Nechemiah Lavi, *Hy"d*, was killed on Shabbos Chol Hamo'ed Sukkos (October 3, 2015), when he risked his life to save a victim from the hands of a Muslim terrorist. "He was celebrating the Third Meal of Shabbat with his wife and seven children in their rooftop sukkah above their Jerusalem Old City apartment...Suddenly they heard a woman screaming. Rabbi Lavi, an officer in the I.D.F. Reserves, grabbed his gun and ran downstairs to save her. The Arab terrorist, who had already murdered 22-year-old Aaron Benitah and seriously wounded his young wife Odel, killed Rabbi Lavi by repeatedly stabbing him in the chest and neck..." Odel, who was badly injured, managed to run to the police, who succeeded in neutralizing the terrorist.

That year, after Simchas Torah, there were *Hakafos Sheniyos* on Chagai Street, at the exact spot where he was murdered. Hundreds of

---

1   "Good Samaritan David Reichenberg Dies Trying To Save Father, Son From Flood Waters In Spring Valley" (Aug. 29, 2011), www.newyork.cbslocal.com.

people showed up, and the square has since been renamed Nechemiah and Aaron Square.[2]

A few days later, after a wave of terror attacks against innocent Jews throughout the country, another attack took place outside a Petach Tikva shopping mall. Renaddi Kasau endangered his life to save a twenty-five-year-old man who had been stabbed by a Muslim terrorist. Kasau succeeded in his rescue mission, and the terrorist was apprehended.[3]

In January of 2016, Hollywood star Jamie Foxx was in his Hidden Valley, California, home when he heard a loud crash outside. He rushed outside to find an overturned truck. Without delay, he pulled the driver out of the truck. Foxx told reporters, "As we pulled him out, within five seconds...the truck goes up [in flames]... I don't look at it as heroic. I just look at it as, you know, you just had to do something. And it all worked out."[4]

Finally, On March 30, 1981, John Hinkley Jr. fired at the then president, Ronald Reagan, as he left the Hilton Hotel in Washington, D.C. One bullet hit the president in the chest, nearly killing him. The president's wife, Nancy, later reflected that she regretted not being near the president at the moment he was shot "so that she could have taken the bullet for him." She said, "I usually stand at Ronnie's left side, and that's where he took the bullet."[5]

According to the Torah, what should a person do if he sees a fellow Jew in mortal danger—risk his life to save him or protect his own life by avoiding danger?

A TORAH PERSPECTIVE

The Gemara in *Sanhedrin* states that one is obligated to save someone who is drowning in a river or being dragged away by an animal.[6] This is

---

2   Sara Yoheved Rigler, "The Murder of a Hero" (Oct. 6, 2015), www.aish.com.

3   David Daoud, "Ethiopian-Israeli Subdues Palestinian Terrorist In Petah Tikva, Says: 'This is My Country; I Have No Where Else To Run'" (Oct. 9, 2015), www.algemeiner.com.

4   "Jamie Foxx Doesn't Consider Himself Heroic For Pulling Driver From Burning Truck" (Jan. 19, 2016), www.losangeles.cbslocal.com.

5   Paul Kengor, "The untold story of how Nancy Reagan would have taken a bullet for her husband" (Oct. 6, 2016), www.foxnews.com.

6   *Sanhedrin* 73a. The Gemara says that unlike the obligation to return someone's lost object, one is required, if necessary, to spend one's own money to save another person's life. The Chafetz Chaim (*Ahavas Chessed*, vol. 2, §20) rules that a bystander must spend all of his

based on the verse, "Do not stand [idly] by your friend's blood."[7] This ruling is codified by both the *Rambam* and the *Shulchan Aruch*.[8]

However, the Gemara in *Bava Metzia* describes a scenario where two people are traveling in the desert, and one of them has a container of water.[9] If they would share the water, they would both die of dehydration. If one of them would drink the water, he would manage to reach civilization and live, but the other would die. What should they do?

Ben Petura rules that they should split the water, rather than one person drinking it all and witnessing the other's death.[10] However, Rabbi Akiva argues that the person with the water should drink it himself. Rabbi Akiva cites the *pasuk*, "Your brother should live with you,"[11] to mean that one must first survive in order for his brother to live with him. Thus one's own life comes first—he is not obligated to sacrifice his own life in order to save another. The halachah seems to be in accordance with Rabbi Akiva,[12] that one doesn't have to—and may even be prohibited to—sacrifice his life for another.

---

money to save a life. Rav Yosef Shalom Elyashiv argues that a bystander does not have to give up more than a fifth of his wealth (*Nishmas Avraham, Choshen Mishpat* 426:1). See Rav Yitzchak Zilberstein, *Medical Halachic Responsa* (Maimonides Research Institute, 2013), p. 361, who cites the *Rosh* as saying that the rescuer is entitled to be reimbursed for the expenses he incurred in rescuing someone.

7   *Vayikra* 19:16.

8   *Rambam, Hilchos Rotzei'ach* 1:14; *Shulchan Aruch, Choshen Mishpat* 426:1

9   *Bava Metzia* 62a.

10   The Netziv (*Haamek She'eilah* 129:4) says Ben Petura agrees that one doesn't have to give up all his water if both will die. The point of contention, says the Netziv, is where he needs to give up some of his water, endangering his life, so that both can drink and live a little longer with the hope of finding more water. Ben Petura says that they should share the water in the hope that they both live long enough to find more water, but Rabbi Akiva argues that one doesn't have to endanger his life to save another. Rav Asher Weiss agrees with this explanation of the Netziv; see *Shu"t Minchas Asher*, vol. 1, §115, p. 395. Rav Yisrael Zev Gustman related that the question of Ben Petura and Rabbi Akiva came up daily in the Vilna Ghetto, and noted, "We acted according to Ben Petura" (David Page, *Rav Gustman: The Youngest Dayan of Vilna and Illustrious Rosh Yeshivah in New York and Yerushalayim* [ArtScroll/ Mesorah, 2017], pp. 104–5).

11   *Vayikra* 25:36.

12   The halachah is stated explicitly in *Igros Moshe, Yoreh Dei'ah*, vol. 1, §145. See also *Shu"t Minchas Asher*, vol. 1, §115.

What about *endangering* one's life to try to save another? Is one obligated, permitted, exempt from, or prohibited to put himself in potential danger in order to save another person's life?

The *Kesef Mishneh* quotes the *Hagahos Maimoniyos*, which says that one is obligated to endanger one's own life in order to save another from certain death.[13] The *Kesef Mishneh* supports this idea by explaining that the certain death of one person outweighs a possible risk to the life of another. This is based on the passage in the *Yerushalmi* that says, "Rav Imi was trapped in Safsifa. Rabbi Yochanan said, 'Let him prepare his shrouds.' Rabbi Shimon ben Lakish said, 'I will either kill or be killed; I will go and save him by force.'"[14] This story clearly indicates that Rabbi Shimon ben Lakish was prepared to endanger his own life to save someone else from certain danger.

However, this *Yerushalmi* is not cited as proof by the halachic authorities, such as the *Shulchan Aruch* and *Rema*. The *S'ma* says that the reason for this is because it was omitted by the *Rambam, Rosh,* and *Tur.*[15] Nevertheless, the *S'ma* seems to indicate that no one actually disagrees with the *Yerushalmi*, and the fact that the *Yerushalmi* wasn't codified is insignificant.[16] Therefore, according to the *S'ma*, one should risk his life to save another from certain danger.

Additionally, the *Chavos Ya'ir* accepts the *Yerushalmi* and says that one must risk his own life to save another.[17] He cites the Gemara in *Bava Metzia* about the desert travelers, mentioned above, as support and says that Rabbi Akiva only said that one should drink the water himself if splitting it will lead both of them to certain death. If both of them might live, then they must share the water.

---

13   *Hilchos Rotzei'ach* 1:14; see also *Beis Yosef, Choshen Mishpat* §426. Rabbi Michael Taubes points out that this comment of the *Hagahos Maimoniyos* appears in the back of the edition of *Mishneh Torah* published by Rabbi Shabse Frankel.

14   *Yerushalmi, Terumos* 8:4. The translation is from Rav Yaakov Navon, *Cross Roads: Halacha and the Modern World,* vol. 3 (Zomet Institute, 1987), "Risking Lives to Save Lives," p. 50.

15   *S'ma, Choshen Mishpat* 426:2.

16   Navon, *Cross Roads,* p. 50.

17   *Chavos Ya'ir* §146.

The *Pischei Teshuvah*,[18] however, cites the *Agudas Eizov*, which says that the reason for the omission of the *Yerushalmi* from the halachic codes is because the *Talmud Bavli* disagrees with this *Yerushalmi*, and the halachah is in accordance with the *Talmud Bavli*, not the *Yerushalmi*.[19] Therefore, he contends, one doesn't have to risk his life to save another.

The Maharam Schick says that the statement in the *Talmud Bavli* that holds that one doesn't have to risk his life for another is from the afore-mentioned Gemara in *Bava Metzia* about the desert travelers, and that was exactly the dispute between Rabbi Akiva and Ben Petura.[20] Rabbi Akiva held that one is not obligated to sacrifice, or even risk, his own life to save another, because one's own life takes precedence.[21] The *Bach* agrees with this approach, and states that the *Rambam* does as well.[22]

Along these lines, the *Radvaz* says that one is not obligated to give up one of his own limbs in order to save another. If one does give up a limb and, as a result, he endangers his own life, he is called a "pious fool." The *Radvaz* says that even a possible danger to one's own life takes precedence over certain danger to another.[23] Thus, clearly the *Radvaz* believes one should not endanger his own life to save another's life.

---

18   *Pischei Teshuvah, Choshen Mishpat* 426:2. Rav Ovadiah Yosef (*Yechaveh Daat*, vol. 3, §84) understands this opinion to mean that one should not endanger one's life to save another.

19   The source in the *Talmud Bavli* that argues with the *Yerushalmi* is in *Niddah* 61a with *Tosafos*. See also *Haamek She'eilah* (§38) and *Tzitz Eliezer* (vol. 9, §45:4 and vol. 10, §25:7), which cite *Sanhedrin* 73a as a proof that one must exert effort and money to save someone from danger, but one is not required to risk his own life to do so. However, Rav Shlomo Aviner (*On the Air with Rav Aviner* [J Levine/Millennium, 2009], p. 111) cites Rav Tzvi Yehudah Kook who held that people should endanger their lives to save others. After all, the Gemara in *Sanhedrin* 73b says that if one sees someone drowning in a river or being chased by bandits, he is commanded by the Torah, "Do not stand [idly] by your friend's blood," and must intervene to try and save the person. Clearly these are situations where one would be placing his own life in danger, and yet a person is still required to intervene.

20   *Shu"t Maharam Schick Yoreh Dei'ah* §155 , *Sefer Hamitzvos* §238; he clearly understands the Gemara differently than the *Chavos Ya'ir*. See *Yechaveh Daat*, vol. 3, §84, for a different source from the *Talmud Bavli*.

21   The *Or Hachaim* (*Rishon Letzion* §155) says that, according to Rabbi Akiva, one is not obli-gated to sacrifice his own life to save another, but he is permitted to do so. Rav Asher Weiss (*Shu"t Minchas Asher*, vol. 1, §115, p. 394) notes that this opinion is rejected by most *poskim*, and one is not allowed to sacrifice his own life to save another person's life.

22   *Bach, Choshen Mishpat* §426.

23   *Shu"t Radvaz*, vol. 3, §627, cited in *Pischei Teshuvah, Yoreh Dei'ah* 157:15.

Rav Ovadiah Yosef also says that most authorities believe that one may not endanger his own life in order to rescue someone else from certain danger.[24] Rav Moshe Feinstein, though, says that one is not obligated to endanger his life to save someone else, but he is permitted to do so if he wants to. If it is certain that the person risking his life will die, then it is prohibited.[25]

The *Mishnah Berurah*, based on the *Pischei Teshuvah* mentioned above, writes that one is not obligated to endanger his own life to save another.[26] It is not clear if, according to the *Mishnah Berurah*, it is prohibited to do so.

However, if the danger is minimal, one should definitely try to save the other person. In fact, the *Shevet HaLevi* says those opinions that forbid one to endanger his life to save another person would agree that if the danger is less than 50 percent, one must risk his life to save the other.[27]

Rav Shlomo Aviner was asked "if it is permissible, an obligation, or forbidden for a bodyguard of the prime minister to jump on him to be killed in his place." Rav Aviner responded that it is permissible for him to sacrifice his life in order to save the prime minister, based on the

---

24   *Yechaveh Daat*, vol. 3, §84. Among these authorities are the *Elyah Rabbah* 329:8, *Shulchan Aruch Harav* 329:8, *P'ri Megadim* in *Mishbetzos Zahav* 328:7, Netziv in *Haamek She'eilah* 147:4, and *Aruch Hashulchan, Orach Chaim* §426. See *Shu"t Minchas Asher*, vol. 3, §122, where he discusses a question asked by one of the survivors of the Har Nof Massacre. The person wanted to know if it was permissible for one of the victims to endanger his life by actively fighting with the terrorists, which ultimately allowed for a number of people to escape. Rav Weiss also discusses whether a doctor is obligated to endanger his own life by treating people who have the Ebola virus.

25   *Igros Moshe, Yoreh Dei'ah*, vol. 2, §174:4, p. 393. See *Shu"t Minchas Asher*, vol. 1, §115, p. 393, for similar and dissenting opinions. See *Shu"t Minchas Asher*, vol. 1, §115, p. 398. This is also the opinion of Rav Yosef Shalom Elyashiv, cited in *Chashukei Chemed, Kiddushin*, p. 412; see there for more on this topic.

26   *Mishnah Berurah* 329:19. Rav Yitzchak Zilberstein (*Chashukei Chemed, Kiddushin*, pp. 411–12) ponders the following question: If one endangers his life to save another, has he fulfilled a mitzvah in doing so, since he was not obligated to do it? Rav Zilberstein discusses the practical differences that result from saying he has fulfilled a mitzvah or not, and concludes that he has.

27   *Shevet HaLevi*, vol. 8, §87.

above-cited *Hagahos Maimoniyos* in the name of the *Yerushalmi*.[28] The application of this *Yerushalmi*, however, in this situation is difficult to understand, as the *Yerushalmi* only required one to endanger his life, not sacrifice it to save another.[29] This also seems to counter Rav Ovadiah Yosef's ruling, which prohibits one from endangering his life to save another, and against Rav Moshe's ruling, which permitted it only if one was not sacrificing his own life. Rav Yosef Shalom Elyashiv also only permits one to endanger, but not give up, his own life for another.[30]

We can understand the ruling of Rav Aviner, but for a different reason. Rav Yitzchak Zilberstein notes that a bodyguard would be permitted to sacrifice his life to protect someone like the prime minister, whose life many people depend on.[31] Rav Moshe Feinstein, however, only permits a person to sacrifice his life in order to save a significant part of the Jewish People, but prohibited it in order to save an individual Jew.[32]

Rav Aviner was also asked if it is permissible to give mouth-to-mouth resuscitation (assuming no barrier device is available), since perhaps the patient has a contagious disease. Rav Aviner said that

---

28   *Short and Sweet: Text Message Responsa from Ha-Rav Shlomo Aviner Shlit"a* (American Friends of Yeshivat Ateret Yerushalayim, 2012), p. 179. See *Chashukei Chemed, Bava Kama* 60b, for more interesting cases on this topic.

29   See Rabbi J. David Bleich, *Judaism and Healing: Halakhik Perspectives* (Ktav, 2002), p. 162.

30   See *Chashukei Chemed, Kiddushin*, p. 416, as explained by Rav Yitzchak Zilberstein. Rav Meir Simcha of Dvinsk writes that one is not obligated to risk his life in order to save a fellow Jew (*Meshech Chochmah, Shemos* 4:19 and *Or Samei'ach, Hilchos Rotzei'ach* 7:8).

31   *Vehaarev Na*, vol. 3, pp. 334–35; *Chashukei Chemed, Kiddushin*, p. 416. Rav Zilberstein's ruling that a bodyguard may sacrifice his life in this case is based on the Gemara in *Taanis* 18b and the *Sefer Chassidim* §698. Rav Asher Weiss (*Shu"t Minchas Asher*, vol. 3, §122, p. 414) also seems to agree with the ruling of Rav Aviner. Rav Weiss explains that the Gemara in *Taanis* may only be a proof that an individual whose life is already in danger and will die with the rest of the city may sacrifice his life to help save the city. Additionally, Rav Weiss writes that any person who holds a position that involves saving lives, such as a police officer, a firefighter, a rescue diver, and a government security agent, is required to sacrifice his life to save the public and sometimes even an individual. See *Vehaarev Na*, vol. 3, p. 335, n. 4, citing *Mishneh Halachos*, vol. 9, §171, where he relates that during the Holocaust the Nazis were searching the ghetto for Rav Aharon of Belz, and there was a holy Chassid who presented himself as the rebbe, letting the Nazis kill him instead of the real Rav Aharon.

32   *Igros Moshe, Yoreh Dei'ah*, vol. 2, §174:4. Rav Moshe supports this from the Gemara in *Taanis* 18b, as explained by *Rashi*, s.v. "*beludkiya*," who states that two brothers, Pappus and Lulianus, sacrificed their lives to save the Jewish community.

there is minimal risk involved, and therefore one should do it in order to save the person's life. This may be based on the *Shevet HaLevi* cited above, which says that, when the danger is low, one should try to save someone's life.

On the other hand, Rav Eliezer Waldenberg ruled that it is forbidden for a healthy person to donate his kidney to a person whose kidney is not functioning, since there are risks involved during and after the surgery, and there is a concern about the proper functioning of the remaining kidney.[33] This is in line with the sources cited above that forbid endangering oneself even to save someone from imminent danger.

Rav Ovadiah Yosef disagrees with Rav Waldenberg and believes (after consulting with medical experts) that there is only minimal risk involved in kidney donations and that one is also performing a great mitzvah, so it is permitted to donate a kidney while still alive.[34] Rav Ovadiah brings support from the *Radvaz*. While the *Radvaz* prohibits saving another if there is a possible danger involved, when the danger involved is very low, he permits it. Additionally, the Gemara in *Sanhedrin*, cited above,[35] requires one to save someone else from danger even if it would clearly pose a small danger to his own life.[36]

As mentioned above, Rav Moshe agrees that, while not obligated, one is permitted to endanger himself to save someone else, unless the danger to his life is definite; therefore, he allowed kidney donations.[37]

Regarding the cases of Rabbi Nechemiah Lavi and Renaddi Kasau, even according to those opinions that forbid one from endangering his

---

33   *Tzitz Eliezer*, vol. 10, §25:7, and vol. 13, §101.

34   *Yechaveh Daat*, vol. 3, §84. See also *Yabia Omer, Choshen Mishpat*, vol. 9, §12. See *Chashukei Chemed, Sanhedrin* 44b, on whether or not there is a general obligation to donate a kidney. Rav Zilberstein also discusses whether a person who injured someone else's kidney is obligated to donate his own kidney to save the injured person's life.

35   *Sanhedrin* 73a.

36   Rav Zilberstein (*Upiryo Matok, parashas Bechukosai*, pp. 465-66) cites the *Shevet HaLevi* (vol. 8, §87) mentioned above that says where the danger is minimal—less than 50 percent—one must try to save another from certain danger. Rav Zilberstein (*Vehaarev Na*, vol. 1, p. 311) also explains which measures should be taken in order to obtain forgiveness when failing to take the necessary measures to save someone from danger and as a result the person dies.

37   *Igros Moshe, Yoreh Dei'ah*, vol. 2, §174. See also *Igros Moshe, Choshen Mishpat*, vol. 1, §103, regarding the permissibility of blood donations.

life to save another, the cases of Rabbi Lavi and Kasau may be different. The *Minchas Chinuch* writes that although all mitzvos are pushed aside in the face of danger and one doesn't have to fulfill them,[38] fighting a war is different; the Torah permitted waging war, which means that one must endanger oneself to do so.[39] Rav Waldenberg says explicitly that in a war soldiers must endanger themselves to save others.[40]

According to this *Minchas Chinuch*, perhaps the battlefield is not limited to where IDF forces are fighting against their enemies, but is expanded to all areas where terrorists attempt to kill innocent Jews and strike fear in the hearts of the Jewish People.[41] Renaddi Kasau risked his life to stop a terrorist who was part of a wave of terror attacks against Israel. Rabbi Nechemiah Lavi, as well, was killed trying to save someone from a terrorist.[42]

Therefore, both of the heroic actions taken by Rabbi Lavi and Kasau seem to be justified by halachic sources.[43]

---

38   Except for three: the prohibitions of murder, idolatry, and certain forbidden relationships (*Sanhedrin* 74a–75a; *Yoma* 82a–82b; *Rambam, Hilchos Yesodei HaTorah* 5:2, 5).

39   *Minchas Chinuch* §425. Rav Shach wrote about Operation Entebbe and said that it was wrong for the IDF to endanger their lives on such a dangerous mission to save the lives of the captives (*Rivevos Ephraim*, vol. 8, p. 500). However, Rav Ovadiah Yosef (*Torah Shebe'al Peh*, vol. 19, p. 37) cites this *Minchas Chinuch* that explains that during wartime there will be casualties, and we have to do what is best for the Jewish People, despite the danger involved, and therefore Operation Entebbe was permitted. As an aside, Rav Moshe (*Igros Moshe, Yoreh Dei'ah*, vol. 4, §8) adds that Operation Entebbe was a completely open miracle performed by Hashem.

40   *Tzitz Eliezer*, vol. 12, §57.

41   Explaining why a Jerusalem rally against terror was canceled, Gush Etzion Regional Council Head, David Perl, said that "we have made the decision now, while the state of Israel is under a war—it's a real war, with our enemies from the inside—we have to come all together, to be together, and not make events that may show we are not with all the nation" (Yoni Kempinski, "Jerusalem Rally Against Terror Canceled Amid Flurry of Attacks" [Oct. 13, 2015], www.israelnationalnews.com).

42   In this case, it was unclear if he even saw the terrorist when he went to help the victims. See *Vehaarev Na*, vol. 3, p. 340, with regard to shooting innocent civilians being used as shields by terrorists during wartime.

43   Rabbi Shay Schachter quotes his father, Rav Hershel Schachter, as applying the *Minchas Chinuch* this way (Rabbi Shay Schachter, "Jewish Heroes Who Put Their Lives on the Line to Save Others" [Oct. 13, 2015], www.yutorah.org). See also *Chashukei Chemed, Kiddushin*, pp. 416–17, where Rav Zilberstein agrees with this, as does Rav Asher Weiss (*Shu"t Minchas Asher*, vol. 3, §122, p. 414).

SUMMARY

One is obligated to save another Jew whose life is in danger. The *S'ma* and *Chavos Ya'ir* maintain that one should even risk one's life to save another person's life. However, the *Maharam Shick*, the *Bach*, and *Pischei Teshuvah* disagree, stating that one need not do this. Moreover, Rav Ovadiah Yosef actually prohibits one from risking his life to save another's. Rav Moshe Feinstein only forbids it if a person is certain that he will die by attempting to save the other person. However, Rav Zilberstein stipulates that one would be permitted to risk and sacrifice his life to save a person that the Jewish People depend on. Finally, in situations of war, one is certainly permitted to risk his life to save and defend others.

SAND AND SNOW SCULPTURES

IN THE NEWS

A February 2015 UPI news story featured a fourteen-year-old girl named Jasmine Wilson from Warrick County, Indiana, who sculpts realistic human figures from ice and snow.

"'I didn't expect it to actually look like a human being,' Wilson told WTHR-TV of one of her sculptures, which bears a resemblance to Michelangelo's David. 'I thought it would look like a bunch of mashed-up snow.'"[1]

Another modern form of sculpting that has appeared in the news is sand sculpting. In 2013, the Eretz Israel Museum in Tel Aviv hosted an exhibit of dozens of sand sculptures created by the Dutch World Sculpting Academy and their Israeli associates. The exhibit included real-life figures of classic children's stories, such as *The Three Musketeers*, *Peter and the Wolf*, and *Alice in Wonderland*. There were also sculptures of Biblical personages: David and Goliath, King Solomon and the Queen of Sheba, Jonah and the whale, and more.[2]

Is it permitted to create three-dimensional figures of sand and snow?

A TORAH PERSPECTIVE

The Gemara[3] derives a number of laws from the *pasuk*, "*Lo saasun Iti elohei chesef veilohei zahav lo saasun lachem*—You shall not make

---

1   Ben Hooper, "Indiana teen turns snow into stunning sculptures" (Feb. 24, 2015), www.upi.com.
2   "Tales in Sand 2," www.eretzmuseum.org.il.
3   *Avodah Zarah* 42b–43b.

[images] with Me; gods of silver and gods of gold you shall not make for yourselves."[4] Rabbi Michoel Zylberman explains, "One may not produce images of the upper celestial sphere's inhabitants, namely, angels; the lower celestial sphere's inhabitants, including the sun, moon, stars, and signs of the zodiac; or of man."[5] In addition to the Torah prohibition against making these images, there is a Rabbinic prohibition against possessing them as well.[6]

With regard to producing images of the sun, moon, and stars, the *Shulchan Aruch* rules that both two- and three-dimensional images of these objects are prohibited.[7] The generally followed rule is that creating any image that represents the way people view these figures is prohibited. Therefore, one should not make a circle with emanating rays, even though the actual sun doesn't have rays coming out of it, since we generally identify this image with the sun.[8]

With regard to making an image of man, most *poskim* say, based on the *Shulchan Aruch*,[9] that only three-dimensional images are prohibited (sculptures), not two-dimensional ones (portraits).

---

4   *Shemos* 20:20.

5   Rabbi Michoel Zylberman, "The Laws of Forbidden Images" (Sept. 6, 2004), www.yutorah. org. The *Rambam* (*Sefer Hamitzvos, Lavin* §4) says the reason for this prohibition is so that one doesn't think they are idols. The *Sefer Hachinuch* (Mitzvah §39) also explains that the Torah wants us to stay away from idolatry. However, this prohibition stands regardless of whether the images will be used for idolatry or not.

6   See Rabbi Michoel Zylberman's article, n. 4, regarding the nature of this prohibition and if there are any leniencies.

7   *Shulchan Aruch, Yoreh Dei'ah* 141:4. See *Tosafos* 43b and *Rambam, Hilchos Avodah Zarah* 3:11. This is the opinion of the *Shach* (*Yoreh Dei'ah* 141:25), which is accepted by later *poskim*, while the *Taz* (*Yoreh Dei'ah* 141:13) permits two-dimensional pictures.

8   *Yad Ketanah*, cited in *Darchei Teshuvah* 141:46. See Rabbi Michoel Zylberman's article regarding drawing parts of the sun, moon, and stars. There Rabbi Zylberman also explains that there is a *machlokes* among the *poskim* whether it is permitted to draw pictures of the sun, moon, and stars for educational purposes. Rav Moshe Feinstein (*Igros Moshe, Orach Chaim*, vol. 5, §9:6) forbids it, and Rav Shmuel Wosner (*Shevet HaLevi*, vol. 7, §134:8) says there is room to be lenient based on the opinion of the *Shach* (*Nekudas Hakesef* on the *Taz* 141:13), who says that images of constellations in *machzorim* are not included in the prohibition of *lo saasun Iti*, since they are intended for educational purposes. Rav Hershel Schachter says this ruling of the *Shach* was never accepted as normative halachah. See there also regarding the permissibility of taking pictures of the sun, moon, and stars.

9   *Yoreh Dei'ah* 141:4.

There is a dispute whether one can sculpt a human head without a body (a bust) or make a full body with a head that has no features. The *Shulchan Aruch* permits this, while Rav Yaakov Emden forbids it.[10] Rav Hershel Schachter says we should follow Rav Yaakov Emden's ruling;[11] however, the *Shevet HaLevi* says most *poskim* disagree with Rav Emden.[12]

Is one permitted to visit a wax museum? Rav Moshe Sternbuch advises against visiting any wax museum, especially one in Eretz Yisrael, out of a serious concern for *chillul Hashem*.[13] Rav Yosef Shalom Elyashiv also advises not to visit a museum where the statues were made by Jews, because one shouldn't enjoy something that the Torah prohibits. In addition, the visit itself gives the impression that the visitor is supportive of this endeavor, when in reality these statues stand in violation of the Torah.[14] If it is indeed prohibited to create snow and sand sculptures, then Rav Elyashiv and Rav Sternbuch would also probably forbid going to museums where such sculptures were made by Jews.[15]

Rav Chaim David HaLevi, former chief rabbi of Tel Aviv-Yafo and the author of *Aseih Lecha Rav*, rules that it is permitted to go to a wax museum, even if it is owned by Jews, who are forbidden to own and make the wax sculptures.[16] His reasoning is that since the entire prohibition against making statues stems from the impression that one is worshipping them, in the case of a museum, where this concern is not relevant,

---

10   Ibid. 141:7; *Pischei Teshuvah* 141:10.
11   Cited in Rabbi Zylberman's article, p. 115, n. 18.
12   *Shevet HaLevi*, vol. 7, §134:2.
13   *Teshuvos Vehanhagos*, vol. 3, §263.
14   *Avnei Yashfeh*, vol. 1, §51.
15   The *Rambam* (*Hilchos Melachim* 9:2) says that the prohibition of worshipping idols, which is one of the *Sheva Mitzvos Bnei Noach* that gentiles are obligated to keep, includes making statues for the sake of beauty. However, Rav Moshe Feinstein doesn't seem to rule according to the *Rambam* (*Igros Moshe, Yoreh Dei'ah*, vol. 2, §54). Rav Moshe permitted the Jewish community in McKeesport, Pennsylvania, to contribute to a statue made in honor of President Kennedy after his assassination. Rav Moshe said it was permitted as long as they have in mind not to own the statue. Rav Yisroel Reisman points out that Rav Moshe seems to assume that gentiles are not prohibited to make statues. However, Rav Moshe does mention the opinion of the *Rambam* in his next *teshuvah* (*Igros Moshe, Yoreh Dei'ah*, vol. 2, §55).
16   *Aseih Lecha Rav: She'eilos Uteshuvos Bekitzur*, vol. 5, §72.

there is no issue at all. He does not seem to be worried that visiting the museum will cause a *chillul Hashem*.

Rav Herschel Schachter was asked if one violates the prohibition against creating images of the sun, moon, and stars by bringing them up on a computer monitor. Rav Schachter said that since the image is only temporary, the prohibition doesn't apply.[17] This is in accordance with the *Maharit*, who says that *lo saasun Iti* applies only to permanent images.[18]

According to this, perhaps it is not prohibited to make ice sculptures, which melt over time, as they may be considered only temporary statues.[19] I asked Rav Schachter[20] and Rav Mordechai Willig[21] if my leniency is correct, and they both agreed with me. Rav Nissim Karelitz ruled that it is forbidden to construct a human sculpture out of snow.[22]

What about sand sculptures? Are they also considered temporary? One sand sculptor says he uses "packed" sand, which resists crumbling even when no longer wet. "If a bird doesn't land on it," he said, "or someone doesn't run through it, and you don't get hard rain, the sculptures could, in theory, last for years. They don't fall down by themselves; they don't get dry and blow away."[23]

However, it could be that since sand sculptures are perceived to be only temporary, and since a number of things can happen that will knock them down, they have the same status as snow sculptures and are permitted. Rav Willig told me that it would be prohibited to make them.[24]

---

17   Cited in Rabbi Zylberman's article, p. 118; see n. 4 there.

18   *Maharit, Yoreh Dei'ah* §35.

19   With regard to *hilchos Shabbos* (laws of Shabbos), although some say making a snowball isn't considered a violation of the prohibition of *boneh*, building, almost all agree that building a snowman or snow sculpture is considered *boneh*, since it is meant to last for a few days, and it is therefore prohibited on Shabbos (see Rav Moshe Feinstein, cited in *Mesoras Moshe*, vol. 1, p. 68, and the Debrecener Rav in *Be'er Moshe*, vol. 6, §30).

20   In a conversation on Shabbos, *parashas Vayigash* 5775 (Dec. 19, 2015).

21   In a conversation on Shabbos, *parashas Tetzaveh* 5776 (Feb. 20, 2016).

22   *Kuntres B'lav D'lo Saasun Iti*, at the end of *Chut Shani Hilchos Pesach*, p. 230.

23   Andrew Abramson, "Sand sculptures offer a holiday trip around Old Florida right in Downtown West Palm Beach" (Dec. 15, 2011), www.palmbeachpost.com.

24   In a conversation on Shabbos, *parashas Tetzaveh* 5776 (Feb. 20, 2016).

SUMMARY

It is prohibited to make a three-dimensional statue of a person. For this reason, Rav Elyashiv and Rav Sternbuch prohibit visiting a wax museum in Eretz Yisrael since it is prohibited to make wax figures. However, Rav Chaim David HaLevi permits visiting the museum.

There is a dispute if it is permitted to construct a bust sculpture of a person.

While Rav Karelitz prohibits making an ice or snow sculpture, other *poskim* permit it because it will melt and is, therefore, considered temporary in nature. Sand sculptures, on the other hand, can last much longer and may be prohibited to make.

SEEKING BERACHOS FROM TZADDIKIM

IN THE NEWS

When a Jew is in a difficult situation—whether it is a matter of health, family, business, or whatever—many turn to *tzaddikim* for *berachos*. Before the risky air bombing of the Iraqi nuclear reactor in 1980, the Israeli pilots went to the Steipler Gaon, Rav Yaakov Yisrael Kanievsky, for a blessing. He told them, "Go in peace and return in peace," and, indeed, their mission was successful.[1]

Similarly, a student once asked Rav Ovadiah Yosef for a *berachah* and the following beautiful story ensued.

> *In 1991, Rav Ovadiah Yosef, zt"l, came to YU to give a shiur. There were 1,500 people waiting for "Maran" in the beis midrash to deliver his shiur. Right before he entered, as Rabbi Lamm was ushering him in, a student approached him and said in Hebrew, "My father is in Iran and can't get out. Please give him a berachah." Rav Ovadiah stopped dead in his tracks and said, "What? Your father is stuck in Iran and they won't let him out?" Rav Ovadiah started to cry. And cry. And cry. This went on for a number of minutes, even though he was already supposed to have entered the beis midrash to start the shiur. Finally, he blessed the boy's father with a long, intense berachah that he should have the good fortune to leave Iran...*

---

1   Rabbi Yirmiyahu Ullman, "Astonishing Blessing" (Jan. 3, 2015), www.ohr.edu.

> *Thirteen hours later [after a wait of three years!], his father re-*
> *ceived his papers allowing him to leave, and eventually arrived*
> *in the US and was reunited with his family.*
>
> *We see the love of Chacham Ovadiah for a fellow Jew he never*
> *met, and we also see the power of a berachah of a tzaddik.*[2]

But the definition of a "time of need" is relative. In 2014, prior to an NBA playoff game between the Oklahoma City Thunder and Los Angeles Clippers, Oklahoma City star Kevin Durant received blessings from three Rabbinic brothers—Rabbis Hertzel, Yossi, and Benjamin Illulian. Did their *berachos* have the desired effect? One can never know, but Durant did score thirty-nine points, leading his team to victory that day.[3]

Recently, a device has been placed in front of Rav Chaim Kanievsky's home in Bnei Brak, enabling people to submit names of people that are in need of prayer and blessing. The machine asks for the name and reason for the request, and the *rav* davens for them.[4]

It seems that some disagree with this quest for blessings, though. According to a report on Arutz Sheva,[5] Rabbi Yaakov Ariel, the chief rabbi of Ramat Gan, discourages the practice of visiting rabbis for a blessing to resolve difficult situations. Instead, he advises, they should turn to Hashem directly in prayer, preferably at the Kotel or *Me'aras Hamachpeilah*. Rabbi Ariel admits that there are some very spiritual people whose blessings have an effect, but such people are unknown to the public.

Is there a precedent in the Torah for this practice of receiving *berachos* from rabbis and *tzaddikim*? If so, are there any limitations? And how do these *berachos* work?

A TORAH PERSPECTIVE

The *Ramban* notes that when the Jewish People were being counted, they would come one by one before Moshe and Aharon, telling them

---

2   Ally Ehrman, "The Empathy of a Gadol" (Nov. 9, 2014), www.mevakeshlev.blogspot.co.il.

3   Shiryn Ghermezian, "Kevin Durant Received 'Triple Rabbi Blessing' Just Hours Before Powering Thunder To Game 6 Victory" (May 16, 2014), www.algemeiner.com.

4   "New 'Brachos Machine' at Home of Rav Chaim Kanievsky" (Jan. 21, 2016), www.matzav.com.

5   Maayana Miskin, "Rabbi Ariel: Don't Go to Rabbis for Blessings—Pray" (June 14, 2013), www.israelnationalnews.com.

their names. Knowing everyone's names was important, says the *Ramban*, since this enabled Moshe and Aharon to beseech mercy and blessing from Hashem for each person who came before them.[6]

The Gemara records that if a person has someone sick in his home, he should go to a *chacham*, a sage, who will daven for him.[7] Additionally, the *Nemukei Yosef* writes that the custom in France was that anyone whose relative was sick would go to the rabbi of the yeshivah in his community for a *berachah*.[8] Rav Asher Weiss explains that this means they would ask the rabbi to pray to Hashem to have mercy on their family (in addition to their own prayers).[9]

Rav Moshe Feinstein writes that over the years many people came to him for blessings regarding various issues (having children, *parnassah*, success in Torah learning) and for his prayers on their behalf.[10] This was one of the reasons Rav Moshe only visited Eretz Yisrael once in his lifetime:

> One reason he never returned there was that during his visit, he was able to receive only a fraction of the scores of petitioners who wanted to meet him. Reb Moshe did not want to be in a situation where he had to close his door to someone who needed him.[11]

---

6   *Ramban* on *Bamidbar* 1:45; see also *Ramban* on *Shemos* 18:15 and *Bereishis* 30:1.

7   *Bava Basra* 116a, codified by the *Rema* (*Shulchan Aruch, Yoreh Dei'ah* 335:10). The *Shevet HaLevi* (*Yoreh Dei'ah*, vol. 3, §163) cites the *Me'iri*, who understands the Gemara to mean that a person should go to a *chacham*, and the *chacham* will teach *him* the proper way to pray during his crisis. *Rashi* (*Bereishis* 21:17) cites the midrash, which teaches that if a sick person prays for himself, it is more effective than if others pray for him. Rav Moshe Sternbuch (*Taam Vadaas, parashas Vayeira*, p. 83) elaborates on this idea and explains the importance of praying for oneself and not relying solely on the prayers of the righteous. Rav Chaim Soloveitchik believed that it was permissible to send a telegram to a righteous person on Shabbos, requesting that he pray for a gravely ill person, since this was considered *safek pikuach nefesh* (possible risk of death), which overrides the prohibition of writing and delivering a letter on Shabbos (*Nefesh Harav*, p. 167).

8   Cited in *Minchas Asher, parashas Bamidbar*, p. 145.

9   *Minchas Asher, parashas Behaalosecha*.

10   *Igros Moshe, Yoreh Dei'ah*, vol. 4, §51.

11   Preface to *Igros Moshe*, vol. 8, cited by Rabbi Shimon Finkelman in *Reb Moshe: The Life and Ideals of HaGaon Rabbi Moshe Feinstein* (ArtScroll/Mesorah, 2012), p. 261.

He explains that anyone who is asked to pray for another should do so, since Hashem may listen to his prayers based on specific merits he possesses. Feeling someone else's pain and fulfilling the mitzvah to love every Jew are also highly meritorious and may help the prayer be accepted by Hashem.[12]

Rav Moshe asserts that a *chacham* certainly must pray when asked for help by someone in need, since the Gemara teaches us that a *chacham* has a much greater chance of having his *tefillos* answered. Rav Moshe adds that he doesn't consider himself the *chacham* the Gemara is speaking about, but since the people who approach him view him that way, he feels that he must help them.[13]

There is actually a specific protocol for giving *berachos*, which the *Sefer Ha'ikarim* describes.[14] The *tzaddik* giving the *berachah* is a pipeline between the source of the blessing (Hashem) and the blessing's recipient.[15] The *tzaddik* puts his hands on the person he wants to bless in order to prepare himself to bring down the blessing from above. The more preparation he has, the more effective the blessing will be. This is why, says the *Sefer Ha'ikarim*, Yaakov put his right hand over the head of Efraim before blessing him. Using the right hand was a greater act of preparation for the blessing, and Yaakov wanted Efraim to receive as much blessing as possible. When it came to Menashe, Yaakov used his left hand, which was a lower degree of preparation, but enough to bring blessing to Menashe as well.

The *Sefer Ha'ikarim* adds that just as davening to Hashem is supposed

---

12   *Igros Moshe, Yoreh Dei'ah*, vol. 4, §51.

13   In this *teshuvah*, Rav Moshe explains his practice of giving blessings, even though it is known that many *Gedolim* send people away, telling them they are not worthy of giving *berachos* and that they should go to someone else. See also Rabbi Shimon Finkelman, *Reb Moshe: The Life and Ideals of HaGaon Rabbi Moshe Feinstein* (ArtScroll/Mesorah, 2012), p. 455, and see Rabbi Chaim Dalfin, *Rav and Rebbe* (Jewish Enrichment Press, 2016), p. 50, which relates that in the mid-1940s the Rav, Rabbi Joseph B. Soloveitchik, was ill and went to Rav Menachem Mendel Schneerson (who later became the seventh Lubavitcher Rebbe) for a *berachah*. The Rav said, "Although I am a Litvak and he is not a Rebbe, nevertheless, he was my good friend and I knew his awe of God. He was a person who I truly felt was connected to God. Hence, if he blesses me, it will help. His blessings indeed were fulfilled..."

14   Part 4, ch. 19, cited in *Imrei Baruch, parashas Naso*, p. 50.

15   See *K'li Yakar, Bereishis* 12:2.

to motivate us to change ourselves into better people who will then merit Hashem's blessing, so too, when a *tzaddik* blesses people, it is supposed to inspire them to improve themselves to deserve Hashem's blessing.[16]

Rav Mordechai Neugroschel provides a different perspective on the concept of going to a *tzaddik* for a *berachah*.[17] He explains that when a person pours out his heart to Hashem and is in great need of blessing, the *tzaddik*, due to his great sensitivity, is pained as well. Since the *tzaddik* doesn't deserve this pain, Hashem will remove his pain by removing the troubles that the other person has.[18] Obviously, the *tzaddik* is not the source of the blessing; Hashem blesses the person for the *tzaddik*'s sake.

The Chafetz Chaim cites the idea of going to a *tzaddik* for a *berachah* to illustrate the beauty of how Jews respond to difficult situations. When a Jew is in trouble, he goes to a *tzaddik*, who prays to Hashem that he should be saved. The example of Balak, on the other hand, shows how other nations react in their times of need. When Balak was afraid of Bnei Yisrael attacking his country, he didn't ask Bilam for a *berachah*, rather he asked him to curse the Jews.[19]

Along the same lines, Rav Yisrael Salanter said that there are two ways a person can achieve greatness over another: either he can work on himself to become a better person and in that way become greater than others, or he can push other people down, embarrass them in front of others, and so forth. The first way is the way of *tzaddikim*.[20]

Although there is value in receiving a blessing from a great person in a time of need, a person must do whatever he can (physically and spiritually) to remedy his own situation as well. The Lubavitcher Rebbe

---

16   *Sefer Ha'ikarim* 4:16–18, cited by Rabbi Gil Student, "How Does a Tzadik's Blessing Work?" (Nov. 24, 2014), www.torahmusings.com.

17   *Sefer Vahasheivosa El Levavecha*, pp. 150–51.

18   This idea is similar to the Gemara's statement in *Berachos* 12b that says if a *talmid chacham* is sick, people should daven for him until they also feel sick due to the pain they feel for the *talmid chacham*. See also *Chashukei Chemed, Rosh Hashanah*, p. 224.

19   See also *Lechanech Besimchah*, p. 286, where Rav Chaim Kanievsky was asked why he doesn't curse the terrorists in the same way that he blesses so many people. Rav Kanievsky, in his response, made reference to this lesson of the Chafetz Chaim and answered that it is the way of a Jew to bless and not curse.

20   *Torah Ladaas, Tzamah Lecha Nafshi*, vol. 2, *parashas Balak*.

once told this to his Chassidim. He remarked, "In Chabad, the Rebbes have always demanded of Chassidim to take action personally, and not to rely on anyone else to do their work for them... Each of you, on your own, has to toil to transform [the darkness of impurity] and the passion of your own animal soul into great holiness."[21]

Rachel embodies a powerful example of this concept. The *Ramban* says that when Rachel realized that Yaakov wasn't praying for her, she turned to Hashem with heartfelt prayer. She realized that she had no one else to rely on except for Hashem, and ultimately she was answered.[22]

Additionally, we should take note and appreciate the blessings Hashem has already bestowed upon us. When Rav Shlomo Aviner was asked if it is worthwhile to travel to a righteous person for a blessing,[23] he answered that the *Birkas Kohanim* is more powerful, because it is a blessing that comes directly from Hashem. He added that Rav Aharon Leib Steinman, *zt"l*, was also perplexed by the distance people in Israel travel to receive a blessing when they receive one every day from Hashem during *Birkas Kohanim*.

Furthermore, Rav Aviner reminds us that the greatest factor in bringing blessing into our lives is our own effort.[24] *Teshuvah, tefillah*, and tzedakah done by a person in need can overturn any harsh decree.[25]

SUMMARY

The practice of going to *tzaddikim* for *berachos* dates back to the period of Moshe and Aharon. The Gemara recommends that a person should go to a *tzaddik* in a time of need so that the *tzaddik* can pray for him. The *Sefer Ha'ikarim* explains that the *tzaddik* is actually the pipeline for Hashem's blessings to the individual in need. However, it is crucial that the individual prays for himself as well and does not rely solely on the *tzaddik's berachah*.

---

21 Joseph Telushkin, *Rebbe: The Life and Teachings of Menachem M. Schneerson, the Most Influential Rabbi in Modern History* (Harper Wave, 2014), p. 479.

22 *Ramban, Bereishis* 30:1.

23 Torat HaRav Aviner, Short & Sweet—Text Message Q&A #301, www.ravaviner.com.

24 *Ner B'ishon Lailah*, p. 78.

25 *Bereishis Rabbah* 44:12, *Rosh Hashanah* 16a, and *Yamim Nora'im* prayers.

SELLING KOTEL STONES

IN THE NEWS

According to a February 2012 report on Arutz Sheva, a seller on eBay was offering real stones taken from the Kotel, claiming they would bring blessing.[1] Jews from around the world viewed this as disrespectful behavior and informed the rabbi of the Kotel, Rabbi Shmuel Rabinovitch. Rabbi Rabinovitch, in turn, wrote to eBay's owner, insisting that he stop the listings.

The rabbi expounded that using the stones was a grave sin, prohibited by the Torah,[2] and also violated Israel's "Antiquities Law." Additionally, the rabbi said the entire sale was a fraud since the Kotel stones will not impart blessing to anyone, and, in fact, possession of them may bring a curse since it is a sin to use them.

According to halachah, is it permissible to chisel off a piece of the Kotel wall and sell the stones?

---

1   Gil Ronen, "Kotel Rabbi to eBay: Stop Selling Kotel Stones" (Feb. 13, 2012), www.israelnationalnews.com. In the past, more than a hundred years ago, there were some who had the custom of coming to Israel and praying before the Western Wall, cutting off a piece of the Wall, and bringing it home, thinking it would provide protection for them; see *Peninei Halachah, Megillah*, p. 22.

2   See *Kitzur Shulchan Aruch, Orach Chaim* 13:4, citing *Rashi* to *Megillah* 29a, which says that during *galus Yechoniah* the Jews took stones from the Kotel and used them to build shuls in *galus*. In *Shu"t Chasam Sofer* (*Yoreh Dei'ah* §264), it is explained why this was permitted, but Rav Moshe Feinstein (*Igros Moshe, Yoreh Dei'ah*, vol. 4, §63) argues that the stones were not taken from the Beis Hamikdash, but from the Land of Israel; Rav Moshe elaborates why he believes it would not be permitted to take any stone from the Beis Hamikdash or its surrounding walls; see *Peninei Halachah, Megillah*, p. 22.

A TORAH PERSPECTIVE

There was once a very wealthy non-Jew who managed a number of successful hotels around the world. His wife became ill and the man heard of a mystical cure: to place a small stone from the Kotel under one's head while sleeping. The man contacted a Jewish friend in Eretz Yisrael and asked him to chisel off a small stone from the Kotel and send it to him.

The Jew went to the Kotel in the middle of the night, cut off a piece of stone from the Wall, and sent it to the non-Jew. The man gave it to his wife, thinking it would cure her, but it didn't, and she died. The Jew who chiseled off the stone suffered too. The Jewish man realized that what he had done was wrong, and he asked Rav Yitzchak Zilberstein what he should do to receive atonement.[3]

Rav Zilberstein said that removing stones from the Kotel involves three different sins.[4] First of all, the Torah says that it is prohibited to destroy the altars and places of worship for Hashem's service, namely, the Beis Hamikdash.[5] Based on this, the *Shulchan Aruch* says that it is prohibited to destroy anything from a *beis hakenesses* (synagogue) as well,[6] since a *beis hakenesses* is considered a miniature Beis Hamikdash.[7] Therefore, removing a stone from the Kotel is considered like destroying part of the shul, since the Kotel and the plaza in front of it are fixed places for prayer and have the status of a synagogue.

Second, it violates the prohibition of stealing. The *Rambam* writes that the walls of the Beis Hamikdash were built with communal funds and that the Kotel is one of these walls.[8]

---

3   *Vehaarev Na*, vol. 2, *parashas Re'eh*, p. 445.

4   Many wonder how they hung the huge stones up there in the first place. The midrash says that the winds and angels assisted them; see *Bamidbar Rabbah, parashas Naso* 14:3.

5   *Devarim* 12:3–4.

6   *Orach Chaim* 152:1.

7   *Megillah* 29a. Rav Moshe, in *Igros Moshe, Yoreh Dei'ah*, vol. 4, §63:13, makes the same point.

8   *Rambam, Hilchos Shekalim* 4:8. There is a discussion amongst the Acharonim if the Western Wall (what we call the Kotel) was part of the wall of the *Azarah*, the Temple Courtyard, and therefore part of the Beis Hamikdash, or part of the wall surrounding the *Har Habayis*, the wall surrounding the Temple, and therefore outside the Beis Hamikdash. The *Radvaz* (§691) says it was the wall of the *Azarah*, but the *Avnei Nezer* (*Yoreh Dei'ah* §450–51) says it was the

The third violation is the prohibition of using the Torah for healing purposes. The *Shulchan Aruch* says that if someone is sick, it is forbidden to read *pesukim* thinking that the words themselves will heal.[9] Reciting *Tehillim* as a prayer to Hashem in order to merit healing the sick is permitted, but reciting verses in the form of an incantation, thinking that the words will heal the sick person is not permitted. Similarly, the *Shulchan Aruch* also says that one cannot place a *Sefer Torah* over a sick person with the intention of healing him, since it is not permitted to use the Torah as a means of healing someone.[10] So too, says Rav Zilberstein, it would seem that it is prohibited to attempt to heal the sick with the stones of the Kotel.[11]

---

wall of *Har Habayis*. One practical difference is whether we may enter the area in front of the Wall (i.e., the Western Wall plaza) or not. If the Wall was actually part of the Beis Hamikdash, the laws of *tumah* and *taharah* (ritual purity) apply and one cannot be there if he is *tamei*.

The Mishnah (in *Maseches Keilim* 1:7–9) says that the restriction of entering the Beis Hamikdash while *tamei* parallels the restrictions of entering the encampments of the Jews when they traveled in the desert. In the desert there was the camp of Hashem, surrounded by the camp of the *Levi'im*, and further surrounded by the camp of the rest of the Jewish People. The *Azarah* parallels the camp of Hashem, *Har Habayis* parallels the camp of the *Levi'im*, and Yerushalayim parallels the camp of the Jewish People. A *metzora, zav, niddah,* and *yoledes* were barred from entering an encampment, each according to his or her level of *tumah*. All were prohibited from entering *Har Habayis*, the epitome of holiness on earth. The *Rambam* (*Hilchos Bi'as Hamikdash* 3:5–6) adds that a *baal keri* cannot enter *Har Habayis* either, but by going to the *mikveh*, he would be permitted to enter *Har Habayis* (but not the *Azarah*, since he is a *tevul yom*).

Today, we are all *tamei meis* with no possibility of purifying ourselves from it, which means that we cannot enter the *Azarah*, and the restriction was extended *mi'd'Rabbanan* to most of *Har Habayis* as well (see Rabbi Aryeh Lebowitz, "Ten Minute Halacha—Visiting Har Habayis" [July 20, 2016], www.yutorah.org). If a person hasn't gone to the *mikveh*, he is not permitted to be on top of *Har Habayis*, and if the Kotel is a wall of the *Beis Hamikdash*, he can't stand in front of the Kotel either. Rabbi Eliezer Yehudah Waldenberg (*Tzitz Eliezer*, vol. 10, §1), Rav Tzvi Pesach Frank (*Har Tzvi, Yoreh Dei'ah* §271), and Rav Yosef Shalom Elyashiv (*Kovetz Teshuvos*, vol. 3, §20), however, say the consensus is that the Kotel is not part of the *Azarah* but part of the wall surrounding *Har Habayis*. Therefore, when one stands in front of the Wall, it's not a problem to be there if he is *tamei*, since one is standing outside the Beis Hamikdash, and the laws of *tumah* and *taharah* don't apply there. See *Shu"t Minchas Asher*, vol. 1, §7.

9   *Shulchan Aruch, Yoreh Dei'ah* 179:8–9.

10   Ibid.

11   Rav Moshe (*Igros Moshe, Yoreh Dei'ah*, vol. 4, §63:12–13, cited in *Peninei Halachah, Nedarim*, vol. 1, p. 19, and *Kiddushin*, vol. 3, p. 23) says that according to the *Rambam*, the prohibition of *me'ilah* (misappropriating consecrated property) applies to the walls surrounding the Beis

Rav Zilberstein went on to say that his father-in-law, the renowned *posek* Rav Yosef Shalom Elyashiv, suggested the following steps be taken to achieve atonement for the serious sins that were committed. Rav Elyashiv said that the person should first return the stone that was taken from the Kotel and reattach it. Also, since this Jew desecrated the *kedushah* of the *Beis Hamikdash* and the place of worship of Hashem, he should tell others how he was punished in order to deter them from treating holy places without the proper respect.

And finally, Rav Elyashiv said he should help with the writing of a *Sefer Torah* for a place that doesn't have a kosher *Sefer Torah*, and also be involved in strengthening others to learn Torah. He cited the Gemara that says that Hordus killed many Torah scholars, and his *teshuvah* was to rebuild the Beis Hamikdash.[12] Therefore, this person's *teshuvah* is the reverse—since he destroyed part of the wall of the Beis Hamikdash, he should strengthen Torah learning among the Jewish People. [13]

In a related question, Rav Zilberstein analyzes whether it is permitted to remove the weeds from the Kotel stones.[14] The Gemara says that one should not remove overgrown grass from a *beis hakenesses* that was destroyed so that people would see the shul in its devastated state and feel the pain of the tragedy.[15] *Rashi* explains that the ultimate goal is so that people will see the devastation and pray to Hashem to rebuild it;[16] the *Shulchan Aruch* says that the goal is for people to see it and rebuild it themselves.[17]

Hamikdash, and therefore cutting off the stones of the Kotel would violate the prohibition of *me'ilah*. Since the *Rambam* says that the Kotel was one of the walls of the Beis Hamikdash, we can assume the Kotel is holy, and *me'ilah* applies to it. The midrash points out (*Bamidbar Rabbah* 11:2, *Eichah Rabbasi* 1:31) that the Western Wall will never be destroyed, because Hashem's presence dwells there forever. See *Shu"t Maharsham* (vol. 4, §66) where he discusses whether Hashem's *Shechinah* is still present at the Western Wall.

12 *Bava Basra* 3b–4a.

13 Rav Chaim Shmuelevitz used to say that the Kotel was *kodesh*, holy, but those who studied Torah were *kodesh kodashim*, holy of holies (*Taam Vadaas, Bamidbar*, p. 16).

14 *Chashukei Chemed, Megillah* 28a. Rav Zilberstein doesn't think the grass is *hekdesh*, but Rav Elyashiv thought it was (*Vayishma Moshe*, vol. 1, p. 191).

15 *Megillah* 28a.

16 *Rashi, Megillah* 28a.

17 *Shulchan Aruch, Orach Chaim* 151:10.

Although it is not in our hands to rebuild the Beis Hamikdash today, we can still pray to Hashem that He does. Therefore Rav Zilberstein said one would not be permitted to remove the grass from the Kotel, so that we are reminded of the destruction and continue to pray to Hashem that He rebuild the Beis Hamikdash.

SUMMARY

It is prohibited to remove stones from the Kotel wall, because it is prohibited to destroy any part of the Beis Hamikdash, and, by extension, any part of a shul. Removing part of the Kotel wall is also considered stealing, and therefore prohibited for a second reason. One who has taken a stone from the Kotel should return it and resolve to support Torah learning.

SHEVA MITZVOS CAMPAIGN IN EAST JERUSALEM

IN THE NEWS

In December of 2015, during a wave of Palestinian terror, Matzav reported a story entitled "Chabad to Visit East Jerusalem Arabs to Do *Kiruv*."[1] As amazing as it sounds, Boaz Kali, who ran the project, announced that they would be producing 100,000 billboards, each containing a picture of the Lubavitcher Rebbe, the word "Mashiach" in Arabic, and a call for world peace through the keeping of the *Sheva Mitzvos Bnei Noach* (the Seven Noahide Laws).[2]

Kali explained the intent of the campaign: "This is a religious war, so it requires a religious response, and the Seven Laws of Noah are the basis." Matzav reported that "one of the city's Arab sheikhs says he has no problem with the Chabad activity, as long as it is done in a pleasant manner, as the promoted mitzvos match Islamic customs, but in the current security situation he sees it as a bad idea."

Should we publicize and teach the *Sheva Mitzvos Bnei Noach* to gentiles?

---

1 "Chabad to Visit East Jerusalem's Arabs to Do Kiruv" (Dec. 6, 2015), www.matzav.com.
2 See *Sanhedrin* 56b for the source that gentiles are obligated to observe the *Sheva Mitzvos*. See *Avodas David, Sanhedrin*, pp. 359–60, regarding the reason why Bnei Noach are obligated to keep the *Sheva Mitzvos*. Although not included in the *Sheva Mitzvos*, the Klausenberger Rebbe writes that the harmful effects that nonkosher meat has on Jews also affects gentiles (*Divrei Yatziv, Orach Chaim*, §260, cited in *Upiryo Matok, parashas Noach*, p. 106). See also "Olam Haba for Gentiles" above for a discussion of whether gentiles receive eternal reward for fulfilling mitzvos.

A TORAH PERSPECTIVE

Rav Moshe Sternbuch offers a number of arguments against running such a campaign.[3] First, the moment we begin to teach the *Sheva Mitzvos* to members of idolatrous religions, such as Christianity, we run into a basic issue.[4] Aiding them in better serving God would be conveying a message that we believe they are acting correctly, but in reality, they are sinning with their idolatrous beliefs, such as attributing physicality to God.[5]

Another reason to prohibit teaching gentiles, even monotheistic ones, about the *Sheva Mitzvos* is based on a Gemara that states[6] that one reason Jews shouldn't accept tzedakah from gentiles is because the *pasuk* says, "When its harvest dries, they shall be broken."[7] *Rashi* explains that this means that the downfall of our enemies will occur when their merits are used up.[8] We shouldn't be aiding gentiles to achieve more merits, says Rav Sternbuch, which may only prolong our own exile.

Rav Sternbuch also argues that with idolatrous religions, such as Christianity, there is no value in teaching them the other six of the *Sheva Mitzvos* when they will definitely continue to violate the one against *avodah zarah*, idolatrous beliefs. In other words, the fulfillment of mitzvos is valuable only if one has the proper belief in the

---

3   *Teshuvos Vehanhagos*, vol. 3, §317. See also Rav Moshe Feinstein in *Mesoras Moshe*, vol. 1, pp. 504–5, who has similar views.

4   See *Yafeh Lev* (vol. 5, §246:9) and *Pe'as Hasadeh* (vol. 1, §102) on whether teaching the *Sheva Mitzvos* to non-Jews is included in the general prohibition against teaching Torah to non-Jews (cited in *Peninei Halachah*, vol. 2, *Bava Kama*, p. 18). Rav Moshe Feinstein (*Igros Moshe, Yoreh Dei'ah*, vol. 3, §89) and Rav Yosef Shalom Elyashiv (*Kovetz Teshuvos*, vol. 3, §142) ruled that it is permissible to teach the *Sheva Mitzvos* to non-Jews. Interestingly, Rav Yaakov Emden says that Paul (the student of Yeshu) intended to teach the non-Jews the *Sheva Mitzvos*, yet Paul was of the opinion that they were not obligated to reject belief in the Trinity (Rav Gershon Eisenberger, *Otzar Hayedios*, p. 633).

5   This argument is not relevant to the case of this Lubavitch group, though, since most *poskim* do not consider Islam to be idolatry.

6   *Bava Basra* 10b.

7   *Yeshayah* 27:11.

8   For a comprehensive discussion of this topic, see Dovid Lichtenstein, *Headlines: Halachic Debates on Current Events* (OU Press, 2014), p. 170.

Commander of those mitzvos. The Christians, however, do not have this belief system, since they attribute physicality to God and equate their bible with ours.[9]

Furthermore, Rav Sternbuch says that we have no obligation to correct gentiles' erroneous beliefs and set them on the right path, as we do for our fellow Jews.[10] Based on these reasons, Rav Sternbuch says our ancestors did not reach out and publicize the *Sheva Mitzvos* to the gentiles, so neither should we. Rather, we should simply be role models of integrity and righteousness for the rest of the world.

On the other hand, the *Rambam* writes that part of the mitzvah to love Hashem includes teaching others about God.[11] This is based on the accounts of Avraham, who, out of his great love for Hashem, desired to spread the recognition of God throughout the world.[12]

Based on this view, the Rav, Rabbi Joseph B. Soloveitchik, was asked if this means we should encourage others to convert to Judaism, as the *Rambam* seems to suggest.[13] The Rav answered that he believed

---

9 The *Rambam* (*Hilchos Melachim* 8:11) says that gentiles are not only obligated to keep the *Sheva Mitzvos*, but they also merit *Olam Haba* if they believe they were given the *Sheva Mitzvos* by Hashem through Moshe. He says this is not the case if they simply keep them because they believe it is the right thing to do. The *Chasam Sofer* (*Choshen Mishpat* §185) writes that when the Gemara in *Bava Kama* 38a says the non-Jews were released from having to keep the *Sheva Mitzvos*, it means they are obligated to keep them but are only rewarded like those who are not commanded yet keep mitzvos nonetheless, a lower level of reward. They lost the opportunity to receive the higher level of reward because they were lax in keeping the *Sheva Mitzvos*. The *Chasam Sofer* says that non-Jews are still obligated to keep the *Sheva Mitzvos* and that Jews are obligated to guide them in how to do so because we should guide them in serving Hashem; see *Peninei Halachah, Bava Kama*, vol. 2, p. 18.

10 See Rav Yitzchak Zilberstein, *Medical Halachic Responsa* (Maimonides Research Institute, 2013), pp. 71–73, regarding whether we are obligated to try to stop gentiles from sinning, and see *Bava Basra* 4a for a discussion on whether it is proper to guide gentiles to repent. The Baal Shem Tov is reported as saying that the concept of *arvus*, responsibility, applies to the Jewish People with regard to non-Jews keeping the *Sheva Mitzvos*, and therefore Jews are responsible for teaching gentiles about the *Sheva Mitzvos* (*Pardes Yosef, parashas Nitzavim*, p. 223).

11 *Sefer Hamitzvos, Mitzvos Aseih* §3.

12 Rav Shlomo Aviner was asked what the *Avos* studied in Yeshivas Shem and Ever. Rav Aviner responded, "*Sheva Mitzvot*, and general ethics. Rav Kanievsky said they learned about *Yirat Shamayim*." See *Short and Sweet: Text Message Responsa from Ha-Rav Shlomo Aviner Shlit"a* (American Friends of Yeshivat Ateret Yerushalayim, 2012), p. 218.

13 David Holzer, *The Rav Thinking Aloud* (Jerusalem: Laor Ltd., 2009), pp. 147–48.

Avraham was trying to encourage everyone to accept the *Sheva Mitzvos Bnei Noach* and was not trying to convert them to Judaism. The Rav said that would be the extent to which a Jew can proselytize.[14]

It would seem from this account of the Rav that, in theory, he would not oppose publicizing and teaching the *Sheva Mitzvos Bnei Noach* to gentiles, although this doesn't mean that he encouraged people to actually do this.

The Lubavitcher Rebbe, Rav Menachem Mendel Schneerson, was completely in favor of teaching the *Sheva Mitzvos* to gentiles, and that is the basis of the *Sheva Mitzvos* campaigns by Chabad today:[15]

> *Bringing non-Jews closer to God was not a goal that would have occurred to, let alone preoccupy, many Jewish leaders. Indeed, throughout the Jewish People's millennia-long history in exile, they generally did little to make known their religious teachings to the non-Jewish world... Therefore when the Rebbe launched his campaign in 1980 to bring knowledge of the Sheva Mitzvos Bnei Noach to the non-Jewish world, many Jews, particularly in the Orthodox world, were surprised and some were upset... The Rebbe's response was that his program did not represent a change in ideology but a recognition of the historical circumstances... He saw America as perhaps the first society in which there was hope of carrying out Judaism's universal mission: not to make the whole world Jewish but to bring the world, starting with the United States, to a full*

---

14   David Holzer (loc. cit.) points out that although the *Rambam* is cautious in accepting converts (in *Hilchos Issurei Bi'ah* 13:18, 14:1), that may be limited to converting gentiles to Judaism, not to teaching the *Sheva Mitzvos Bnei Noach*. The *Rambam* writes that Hashem commanded Moshe to force all non-Jews to accept the *Sheva Mitzvos* (*Hilchos Melachim* 8:10). In fact, the *Sefer Hachinuch* (Mitzvah §192) says that when we have the ability to force non-Jews to keep the *Sheva Mitzvos*, we must. Rav Moshe Sternbuch (*Teshuvos Vehanhagos*, vol. 4, §35) explains that when the *Rambam* talks about forcing non-Jews to accept the *Sheva Mitzvos*, this is only at a time when the halachah of *ger toshav* applies.

15   Rav Asher Weiss's website posted a ruling that it is a worthy act to inspire gentiles to keep the *Sheva Mitzvos*, as it is surely the desire of Hashem ("Bnei Noach," http://en.tvunah. org). See *Headlines: Halachic Debates of Current Events*, vol. 2, by Dovid Lichtenstein (OU Press, 2014), pp. 121–34, for more on the subject of promoting *Sheva Mitzvos* to gentiles.

awareness of One God, who demands human beings' moral behavior.[16]

SUMMARY

According to Rav Moshe Sternbuch, we should not teach the *Sheva Mitzvos* to gentiles. One reason he cites for this is because we are not trying to convert them, so if they continue serving idols but keep the other mitzvos of Bnei Noach, then we may give them the impression that it is acceptable to do so. Another reason is that it may give them extra merits and prolong our exile. On the other hand, the Lubavitcher Rebbe felt strongly that we should be teaching the *Sheva Mitzvos* to gentiles.

---

16   Joseph Telushkin, *Rebbe: The Life and Teachings of Menachem M. Schneerson, the Most Influential Rabbi in Modern History* (Harper Wave, 2014), pp. 158–59. For a comprehensive discussion on this topic, see Rabbi Michael J. Broyde, "The Obligation of Jews To Seek Observance of Noachide Laws by Gentiles: A Theoretical Review," www.jlaw.com.

STANDING UP TO BULLIES

IN THE NEWS

In May of 2016, *Associated Press News* published findings and recommendations to schools based on recent research on bullying.[1] The article cited a report released by the National Academies of Science, Engineering, and Medicine, which said that both bullies and their victims suffer long-term effects, such as anxiety and depression. According to an independent government consulting group, "zero-tolerance policies are ineffective in combating bullying," whereas teaching tolerance of others may have a greater impact.

Bullying isn't limited to school settings. Also in 2016, the then presidential hopeful Donald Trump was interviewed by *Fox News* and asked if he had ever been bullied, to which he responded that "he had not been, but bullying isn't solely a youth phenomenon. People are bullied when they are fifty-five...but you gotta get over it. Fight back, do whatever you have to."[2] Trump added that "he is a counterpuncher who goes after people when they go after him, only ten times harder."[3]

In 2015, ESPN reported a bullying story entitled "Rookie Watch: The Cruel Tutelage of the Wolves' Kevin Garnett." The article focused on mentorship in sports—to what degree older, experienced players are willing to groom younger ones. The focus of the article was Kevin

---

1   Jennifer C. Kerr, "Report: Bullying Is a Serious Public Health Problem" (May 10, 2016), www.apnews.com.

2   Nico Lang, "Donald Trump Has Message for Bullying Victims: 'Get Over It'" (May 18, 2016), www.advocate.com.

3   "Trump talks to Megyn Kelly about bullying" (May 16, 2016), www.seattletimes.com.

Garnett and his role in mentoring younger players throughout his career. The article highlighted how Garnett would actually bully other teammates.[4]

In the 2008–2009 season, when Garnett was playing for the Boston Celtics, he tried to mentor young Patrick O'Bryant. Garnett thought O'Bryant was too timid, so one day he decided to try to alter the young player's demeanor by rebuking and criticizing him. O'Bryant didn't show any reaction to Garnett's intimidation tactics. "From that day forward…Garnett would go out of his way to bully O'Bryant. Patrick would miss a shot, and he'd just torture him," testified teammate Leon Powe. Celtics coach Doc Rivers said, "Kevin destroyed him. It was mean-spirited." O'Bryant was traded just twenty-six games into his Celtics career and played only another twenty-four games in the NBA.

In 2014, Miami Dolphins offensive tackle Jonathan Martin left the team after being bullied by other Dolphins players. An investigation spearheaded by the NFL revealed that Martin was the subject of "vicious taunts" and threats to his family with racist motives. This story caught national attention and led to a broad debate on bullying.[5]

What does the Torah say about bullying?

A TORAH PERSPECTIVE

There is a Biblical prohibition of *onaas devarim*, causing pain to others with words.[6] This also means that one is not allowed to be oppressive in his behavior toward others.[7]

We find a case of *onaas devarim* in the Torah with regard to Midian. Hashem commanded the Jewish People to attack the nation of Midian for causing the Jewish People to sin.[8] The Torah singles out Pinchas by

---

4   Jackie MacMullan, "Rookie Watch: The Cruel Tutelage of the Wolves' Kevin Garnett" (Nov. 25, 2015), www.espn.com.

5   "Miami Dolphins trade away alleged bullying victim Jonathan Martin," (March 12, 2014), www.foxnews.com.

6   *Vayikra* 25:17; see *Bava Metzia* 58b. Rav Yitzchak Zilberstein (*Chashukei Chemed, Yevamos*, ch. 6, p. 426) found a case where one can violate *onaas devarim* even while being silent. See also *Atarah Lamelech*, pp. 118–19.

7   See *Aleinu Leshabei'ach, Devarim*, pp. 25–28, for the severity of mistreating others and the detrimental effect bullying has on others.

8   *Bamidbar* 31:2.

name as one of the soldiers in the war.[9] *Rashi* there explains that his involvement is highlighted to indicate that Pinchas went to take revenge against Midian for their involvement in the sale of Yosef, his ancestor.[10]

Rabbi Matis Blum explains why Pinchas was angered specifically by the actions of Midian when the nations of Yishmael and Mitzrayim were also involved in the sale of Yosef.[11] He quotes the *Taz*, who explains that it was specifically Midian who saw signs of greatness in Yosef and feared he would one day become a king. Therefore, they decided to denigrate him and sell him as a slave into Egypt, where the law stated that a slave can never be king, thus preventing him from becoming great.[12] The most destructive thing a person can do is to stop another from becoming great, stopping him from reaching his potential. That is why, says Rabbi Blum, Pinchas thought that Midian deserved a greater punishment than the other nations.[13]

Earlier in the Torah, the *pasuk* says that Kayin spoke to his brother, Hevel, and when they were in the field, he killed Hevel.[14] The commentators are perplexed by this mysterious discussion Kayin had with Hevel. What did he actually say?

Perhaps the idea is that in addition to actually killing Hevel physically, Kayin also killed Hevel verbally.[15] His comments caused Hevel to feel terrible about himself. He bullied and tormented Hevel, which the Torah teaches is actually like killing someone.

---

9   Ibid. 31:6.

10   The Torah says that the Midianites sold Yosef to Mitzrayim (*Bereishis* 37:36). *Rashi* (to *Bereishis* 37:28) writes that the brothers first sold him to Yishmaelim (as it says in *Bereishis* 37:28), and they sold him to Midianites, who sold him to Egypt.

11   *Torah Ladaas*, vols. 9–10, *parashas Mattos*.

12   *Divrei David, Bamidbar* 31:6. See *Or Hachaim, Bereishis* 37:28, where he similarly explains that the brothers' intention in selling Yosef was to prevent him from rising to greatness.

13   See *Aleinu Leshabei'ach, parashas Bechukosai*, pp. 486–89, for an interesting story cited in *Otzar Hamidrashim* about Rav Kahana and his son Selik, who nearly abandoned Torah learning because of what someone had said to him.

14   *Bereishis* 4:8.

15   Fascinatingly, the midrash (*Bereishis Rabbah* 22:17) relates a different account of these events: Hevel was actually stronger than Kayin, and when Kayin tried to attack him, he defended himself and overtook Kayin. Kayin persuaded Hevel to have mercy on him, which he did. Kayin then caught Hevel offguard and killed him.

While one should never take lightly the detrimental effects bullying can have on a person, some strong people have been able to overcome the challenge of being bullied by choosing how to react. The *Yalkut Shimoni* says that Yehoshua didn't start out as a child prodigy or *ben Torah* and that people would call him a fool, but because he served Moshe, he merited becoming his spiritual heir.[16] Yehoshua merited wisdom from his own efforts and did not let himself be destroyed when others called him a fool. Yehoshua serves as an inspiration to people to never stop learning and serving Hashem, even when others may ridicule them for it.

Similarly, the Baal Shem Tov taught that "when people ridicule you about your worship, whether it be with regard to prayer or other matters, do not respond. Do not reply even in a positive way, so that you will not be drawn into quarrels or into haughtiness, which causes one to forget the Creator, blessed be He. As our Sages said, 'Man's silence leads him to humility.'"[17]

However, Rav Asher Weiss cites the *Sefer Hachinuch*, which says that although it is prohibited to cause pain to others, even through speech, if someone else bullied you with hurtful words, it is permissible to respond by disgracing him in return.[18] The *Chinuch* proves this from the

---

16   *Yalkut Shimoni, Mishlei* §959, cited in *Aleinu Leshabei'ach, parashas Pinchas*, p. 459. The Gemara (*Sanhedrin* 107a) says that Hoshea bin Nun received the extra letter *yud* from Sarah's name, which had been Sarai, becoming Yehoshua, as the *pasuk* says, "Moshe called Hoshea the son of Nun, Yehoshua" (*Bamidbar* 13:16). Some explain (Rav David Silverberg, "Parashat Shelach," www.gush.net) that Moshe prayed to Hashem that Yehoshua should be imbued with the extra letter from Sarah's name in order that he could tap into her inner strengths (for a comprehensive discussion on this topic, see *Mesivta Shas, Sotah* 34b, *Yalkut Biurim*). Moshe knew that Yehoshua was reserved and not naturally assertive, and he worried that the spies would have a negative influence on him, leading him to also give a bad report about the Land of Israel. Moshe knew that Sarah was an assertive woman who stood up for what was right, as she was the one who demanded that Yishmael be sent away when she saw the danger he presented to Yitzchak. So Moshe prayed that Yehoshua would follow in Sarah's ways and have the courage to stand up to his fellow spies.

17   *Tzavaas HaRivash: The Testament of Rabbi Israel Baal Shem Tov* (Kehot, 1998), translated by Rabbi Jacob Immanuel Schochet, p. 31.

18   *Shu"t Minchas Asher*, vol. 2, §112, citing *Sefer Hachinuch*, Mitzvah §338. Based on this statement from the *Sefer Hachinuch*, Rav Weiss extrapolates that one doesn't have to honor a monetary agreement if the other side is taking advantage of him; one is permitted to stand

pasuk, "If a thief is discovered while tunneling [into a house], and he is struck and dies, he has no blood."[19] *Rashi* there explains that "he has no blood" means that it is not considered murder if the homeowner kills the intruder, since the intruder knows a person will protect his property with force, and so it can be assumed that he came with intent to kill the homeowner. The Gemara says we learn from this *pasuk* that if someone comes to kill you, you should kill him first.[20] So too, says the *Chinuch*, you don't have to tolerate someone else's verbal abuse; you can defend yourself.[21]

Yet the *Chinuch* does note that it is praiseworthy not to rely on the permissibility of responding to one's disgrace, lest one respond with too much anger.[22] As support, he cites the Gemara in *Shabbos*, which

---

up for his rights. Along these lines, Rav Shlomo Aviner was asked, "Is it permissible for a child who is being hit by another student at school to hit him back?" Rav Aviner's reply was "Yes, [according to] *Sefer Ha-Chinuch* (§338). But the school can establish a rule that one may not hit back and should instead turn to a teacher to deal with such situations. In this case, he must follow the rules." See *Short and Sweet: Text Message Responsa from Ha-Rav Shlomo Aviner Shlit"a* (American Friends of Yeshivat Ateret Yerushalayim, 2012), p. 301.

19   *Shemos* 22:1.

20   *Sanhedrin* 72a.

21   Rav Asher Weiss (*Shu"t Minchas Asher*, vol. 2, §112) cites the *Rema* in *Choshen Mishpat* 228:1 which, according to one opinion brought in the *S'ma* (*Choshen Mishpat* 228:4), says that if one is insulted by another person, he can ridicule the person back. However, the *S'ma* himself argues with this interpretation of the *Rema*. The *Rosh* (*Bava Kama* 3:13) says that if a person is attacked physically, he can retaliate immediately and would not be obligated to pay for any resulting damages, unless he retaliated more than was necessary. This is codified by the *Shulchan Aruch* (*Choshen Mishpat* 421:13). The *Rema* (*Choshen Mishpat* 421:13) says you can defend yourself if you are being verbally abused. See also *Lehoros Nassan* (vol. 3, §128), which says that if one feels his life is in danger, he can even fight back more than necessary. See Rabbi Daniel Z. Feldman's *The Right and the Good: Halakhah and Human Relations* (Yashar, 2005), ch. 11, for more on the subject of striking another person.

The Gemara in *Sanhedrin* 107a says that David's enemies would taunt him by asking, "What is the punishment for having relations with another man's wife?" To which David would respond, "Strangulation, but the person receives *Olam Haba*. Those that publicly embarrass others, however, do not." This is an early example of one standing up for himself and responding to his tormentors.

22   There are many sources throughout Chazal that speak of the importance of being *mevater*, giving in, and being *maavir al middosav*, overlooking the wrongs committed by others. See *Yoma* 75a; *Rosh Hashanah* 17b; *Pesachim* 113b; *Bava Kama* 93a; *Tomer Devorah* (English edition), p. 10; *Sichos Mussar*, p. 422; and *K'li Yakar*, *Shemos* 15:11. See also *Rambam*, *Hilchos*

praises people [23] "who suffer insult but do not insult, who hear their disgrace but do not reply…regarding them the verse says, 'But they who love Him [Hashem] shall be as the sun going forth in its might.'"[24]

May one pray to Hashem that He punish those who are bullying him?

The Gemara says that if someone is punished for wronging a fellow man, the one who was hurt does not enter the abode of Hashem.[25] The *Parashas Mordechai* says this is because we are supposed to emulate Hashem whose attribute is to overlook our sins; in the same way, we should strive to overlook the wrongdoings of others.[26]

However, the *Iyun Yaakov* says the Gemara's statement applies only where one actively tried to bring about the punishment of another—for example, he prayed that Hashem should punish the person.[27]

Dei'os 2:3; Rav Yaakov Meir Schechter, *Osaf Michtavim*, p. 119; Rav Chaim Kanievsky, *Orchos Yosher*, ch. 8; and Rav Shlomo Wolbe, *Alei Shur*, Second Gate, ch. 9.

23   *Shabbos* 88b.

24   *Shoftim* 5:31. The *Maharsha* (*Gittin* 36) explains the *pasuk* to mean that those who have these *middos* described by the Gemara are beloved by Hashem. See *Mesivta Shas, Shabbos* 88b, n. 20, for an alternative explanation, based on *Koheles Rabbah* 1:7. The *Tosafos HaRosh* (*Shabbos* 88b) explains, based on the Gemara in *Chullin* 60b, that those who are silent when disgraced won't be negatively affected, whereas their adversaries will be.

25   *Shabbos* 149b. See also *Bava Basra* 22a, where several *rabbanim* bemoaned the fact that they each felt Rav Ada bar Abba was punished on their account. Similarly, the Gemara in *Rosh Hashanah* 16b states that someone who asks Hashem to punish another person is punished first. *Rashi* there explains that the reason is because such a request causes the Heavenly court to determine if the person who made the request is worthy of having someone else punished on his account, thus bringing upon himself judgment in the Heavenly court. Nevertheless, see *Tehillim* 31:18, where David HaMelech did ask for his enemies to be punished.

26   See *Mesivta Shas, Shabbos* 149b, n. 26. See also *Chashukei Chemed, Rosh Hashanah*, pp. 521–22, on the importance of overlooking the wrongs others commit against us. However, with regard to a *tzaddik* who was wronged, the Gemara says (*Yoma* 22b) that although it is proper to be *maavir al middosav*, that is only where the person who wronged him apologized and tried to appease him. For everyone else, the idea of *maavir al middosav* seems to apply even if the person did not first try to appease him.

27   *Iyun Yaakov, Shabbos* 149b, s.v. "kol." The Gemara in *Rosh Hashanah* 16b says that if a person has been wronged, he shouldn't turn to Hashem to judge the matter. However, the *Rema* (*Choshen Mishpat* 422:1) brings an opinion based on the Gemara in *Bava Kama* 93a that if there is no *beis din* to adjudicate a monetary dispute, a person may bring his complaint to Hashem. See *Minchas Shmuel* (*parashas Chayei Sarah*, pp. 72–73) where he notes instances in the Torah where it is permitted to cry out to Hashem to stop one's oppressors. For example, the Torah discusses (*Shemos* 22:21–22) harassed widows and orphans who pray to Hashem to save them from their tormentors.

Addtionally, the *S'fas Emes* points out that if one is able to stop the other person from sinning against him but doesn't, the Gemara applies to him as well.[28]

The *Tzvi Kodesh* adds a caveat: If the person can withstand the wrongdoing of the evil person without having him punished, he should not wish his punishment on his account, but if the wicked person is persistent in causing pain to another, the victim is permitted to pray to Hashem that he be punished.[29]

In terms of witnessing others being bullied, standing up for them is the mark of a leader. The midrash says that Moshe was chosen as the leader of the Jewish People when he was leading a stray lamb back to his flock. Identifying that the source of the lamb's wayward behavior was due to thirst, Moshe picked up the lamb and carried it all the way back to the flock.[30] That is the definition of a leader—a person who shows compassion and care for even the weakest among the flock. It wasn't Moshe's great strength, his great mind, or anything else, but his personal caring for every one and every thing that made him a great leader.

Along these lines, we learn that Shmuel HaNavi was the one who wrote *Megillas Rus*.[31] The midrash asks why Shmuel felt the need to

---

28 *S'fas Emes, Shabbos* 149b, s.v. *"vedilma."* Based on this opinion of the *Iyun Yaakov* and *S'fas Emes*, when Mar Zutra, before going to sleep, would proclaim that he forgave all who had wronged him (see *Megillah* 28a)—this was *middas chassidus*, a pious act (*Mesivta Shas, Shabbos* 149b, p. 177). It seems that they, of course, agree that one should overlook the wrongdoings of others, as it is an explicit Gemara in *Rosh Hashanah* 17a (and *Yoma* 22b). However, if one doesn't, it doesn't preclude him from "entering Hashem's abode." Furthermore, they would agree one should forgive another who actually came asking for forgiveness, as codified by the *Shulchan Aruch* in *Orach Chaim* 606:1. However, the *Rosh Yosef* (cited in *Mesivta Shas, Shabbos* 149b, p. 177) explains that Mar Zutra forgiving all those who wronged him without being asked was not *middas chassidus* but required, as seen from the Gemara in *Shabbos* 149b. Rav Chaim Berlin said that "during that period when I was being persecuted, every night I said the words of Mar Zutra, 'I forgive all those who have caused me pain,' and therefore there is no reason to ask me for forgiveness, for from my side it has already been forgiven" (Rabbi Shimon Yosef Meller, *Reb Chaim Brisker* [Feldheim, 2016], vol. 1, p. 459).

29 *Tzvi Kodesh, Shabbos* 149b, cited in *Mesivta Shas, Shabbos* 149b, n. 25.

30 *Shemos Rabbah* 2:2.

31 *Bava Basra* 15a.

write this particular *megillah*.[32] Rabbi Yitzchak Mirsky cites those who say that it was in order to defend David's lineage and David's reputation.[33] We can learn from this that we, too, should stand up and help defend a person's character.

Rabbi Jonathan Sacks writes in his commentary on the Pesach Haggadah that we lost our freedom in Egypt so that we would forever cherish it and ensure that no one else loses theirs.[34] This certainly applies to standing up for those who are bullied.

SUMMARY

The prohibition of *onaas devarim* teaches that one may not cause emotional pain to another person. Therefore, bullying, taunting, and teasing a person are clearly forbidden, since they cause distress to the victim. According to the *Sefer Hachinuch*, while it is praiseworthy and proper to overlook insults from others, one is permitted to respond and defend oneself. This is certainly the case when the bullying is consistent and harming one's well-being. One should not pray that Hashem specifically punish the bully, unless the bully is persistent and overbearing. Lastly, we must all do our best to defend and help those who are bullied.

---

32   *Rus Rabbah* 2:15.

33   *Hegyonei Halachah*, vol. 3, p. 222. The Gemara says (*Chagigah* 5b) that Rav Idi was only able to go to the *beis midrash* one day a year. (*Rashi* says it was because he lived far from the *beis midrash*; the *Maharsha* says it was because he was traveling to earn a living.) Some of the *rabbanim* ridiculed him for it. However, Rabbi Yochanan defended him and expounded a *pasuk* that teaches that if one is only able to learn Torah one day a year and he does, it is like he learned the entire year. The Gemara is difficult to understand, since it says that Rav Idi wanted Hashem to answer him and end the pain the other *rabbanim* were causing him, and Rabbi Yochanan told him not to be upset with the *rabbanim* so they would not be punished on his account. How could Rav Idi have created a situation where others would be punished on his account when the Gemara in *Shabbos* 149b says that this prevents someone from coming close to Hashem? Perhaps the answer is that since Rav Idi wasn't directly asking for them to be punished, it would have been better to ask Hashem to save him from the distress caused by others.

34   *Rabbi Jonathan Sacks's Haggadah* (Continuum, 2007), pp. 163–66.

STEVE JOBS AND YOSSELE THE HOLY MISER

IN THE NEWS

Billionaire businessman Steve Jobs, best known as the CEO of Apple, was criticized throughout his life for not giving enough charity. In fact, a *New York Times* article claimed there was no public documentation of Jobs ever donating any amount of money to any charity.[1] Despite the criticism, Jobs made no attempt to clear his name and disprove the critics.

After his death in 2011, Jobs's wife told *The New York Times* that he had in fact donated millions to charities but was very quiet about it, to the point that he didn't even tell his biographer about his charitable donations. Jobs's wife explained, "We don't like attaching our names to things," so they donated quietly. Jobs's successor, Tim Cook, also came forward to defend Jobs and said that Jobs donated over $50 million to a California hospital.[2]

There is a similar story that Rabbi Shlomo Carlebach enjoyed telling about "Yossele the Holy Miser."[3] The story goes that Yossele was a very rich Jew from Cracow, who was known for being a miser. When

---

1   Andrew Ross Sorkin, "The Mystery of Steve Jobs's Public Giving" (Aug. 29, 2011), https:// dealbook.nytimes.com.

2   "Steve Jobs secretly gave millions to charity, publically criticised for not doing enough" (May 27, 2013), www.news.com.au.

3   See *Lamed Vav: A Collection of the Favorite Stories of Rabbi Shlomo Carlebach* (Israel Bookshop, 2004), p. 135, for a more detailed description of this story. See also Rav Yaakov Meir Schechter, *Osaf Michtavim*, p. 48, for similar stories.

poor people would come to his door for donations, he would ask them where they lived and how much they needed, but would then throw them out of his house without giving them a penny. When he died, no one paid any respect to him, and he was buried in a disgraceful manner. However, when the poor people of the city stopped receiving their weekly donations, they deduced that none other than Yossele himself had been the one who had secretly delivered money to their door every week. Thus, like Jobs, Yossele presented himself as a great miser, when he secretly donated a fortune of tzedakah to the poor.

More recently, Rabbi Aryeh Lebowitz was once asked the following question by a rabbi in South America. There is a very wealthy man, the owner of an international company worth millions, who has been extremely generous with donations. His contributions to charity far exceed *maaser*. However, he is extremely private about his donations, to the point that he doesn't permit organizations to put his name on any buildings or inform others of his financial assistance. Due to all the above, this very wealthy man appears exceedingly stingy to his community.

At one point, some of his community members held a board meeting for another institution in the community, and a member raised this man's name as a possible donor. Immediately, the other board members began disparaging him, saying that he is a miser and doesn't contribute any money to the causes in the Jewish community. They remarked that despite his being the most successful businessman in the community, he didn't have his name on any buildings, unlike most other wealthy families in the community. When the man heard about the meeting, he was greatly concerned about his reputation. He considered calling the institutions that he had donated to in the past and asking them to reveal his name and how greatly he has helped them. He wanted to know if this was advisable.[4]

Is it permitted to quietly give tzedakah but outwardly appear as a miser, causing people to suspect that you are not properly fulfilling the mitzvah of tzedakah?

---

4   Rabbi Aryeh Lebowitz, "From the Rabbi's Desk—Secret Philanthropist" (Sept. 15, 2016), www.yutorah.org.

A TORAH PERSPECTIVE

Rav Yitzchak Zilberstein discusses the story of Yossele the Holy Miser from a halachic perspective.[5] At first, Rav Zilberstein says, it seems obvious that it's not proper to act this way. The Mishnah teaches us,[6] "A person has to satisfy the scrutiny of human beings just as he has to satisfy the scrutiny of Hashem, as the *pasuk* says, 'You shall be innocent before Hashem and the Jewish People.'"[7] There is also a *pasuk* that says, "Find favor and good understanding in the eyes of God and man."[8]

However, the Gemara also records the statement of Rabbi Yosi, who wanted his lot to be among those who are accused of sinning, but in fact are truly innocent.[9] This implies that it is acceptable, if not ideal, to act in a way that casts doubt on one's integrity. However, the *Me'iri* rejects this possibility and says that a person must do his utmost to avoid being in a position where he will be suspected by others of wrongdoing,[10] as the Gemara says, "Stay away from unseemliness and anything resembling it."[11]

Rav Zilberstein explains that although Rabbi Yosi wanted to be suspected of doing wrong because that would bring him atonement for his real sins,[12] nevertheless, he didn't actively cause others to suspect him of wrongdoing. Rabbi Yosi was only praying that he suffer from suspicion without his doing anything to cause others to suspect him.[13]

Based on these sources, it seems clear that one may not actively cause others to think that he has done something wrong.

---

5   *Peninei Halachah, Chashukei Chemed, Pesachim,* pp. 28–30. See n. 6 there for an interesting story about the daughter of the *Noda BiYehudah,* whose husband, a great Torah scholar, told her to publicly humiliate him so that he wouldn't become arrogant from all the praise he received. The community was obviously very upset with her, but she never revealed why she humiliated him until after he died.

6   *Shekalim* 3:2.

7   *Bamidbar* 32:22. Rav Yosef Engel (*Gilyonei HaShas, Shabbos* 23) says that being innocent before others and making sure people don't suspect you is a *mitzvah d'Oraisa.*

8   *Mishlei* 3:4.

9   See *Shabbos* 118b.

10   *Me'iri, Shabbos* 118b.

11   *Chullin* 44b.

12   See *Ritva, Shabbos* 118b.

13   *Maharsha, Shabbos* 127b.

In spite of this, the *Talmud Yerushalmi* records that Rabbi Zechariah, the son-in-law of Rabbi Levi, had a bad reputation due to his taking charity when he clearly didn't need it. When Rabbi Zechariah passed away, those who investigated found in his personal ledger a record of all the money he had ever taken from charity, along with a record of his giving it all away to those who were really in need.[14]

Likewise, the *Sefer Chassidim* records an incident involving a Torah scholar who didn't need financial assistance, yet went around begging for money in order to give it to genuinely poor people.[15] The *Sefer Chassidim* says that it was permissible for the scholar to embarrass himself and collect tzedakah when people knew he didn't need it himself, in order to collect for the poor people to whom the townspeople would otherwise not have donated.

From these sources it would seem that a person may cause himself to be wrongly suspected of wrongdoing in order to give more charity to poor people. In that case, maybe Yossele, too, would have been permitted to cause others to suspect him of not giving charity in order to achieve the lofty level of giving tzedakah secretly,[16] saving himself from the honor and respect given to those who donate large sums of tzedakah.

However, Rav Zilberstein says that one could differentiate between the cases. In the instances of the *Yerushalmi* and *Sefer Chassidim*, the righteous men were embarrassing themselves so that more charity would be given to poor people. Otherwise, the rule that one must behave in a manner that does not cast suspicion on himself would have been in effect. However, in the case of Yossele the Holy Miser, all he accomplished was to give charity without any fanfare, but he didn't bring about any extra benefit to the poor people of Cracow—they received the same sums of money he would have given if he had given it openly.

---

14   *Shekalim* 5:4.

15   *Sefer Chassidim* §318.

16   See *Sotah* 5a and *Bava Basra* 10b, where the Gemara mentions the idea of giving tzedakah secretly. This is one of the highest levels in the *Rambam*'s eight levels of giving tzedakah (*Hilchos Matenos Aniyim* 10:7–14). The *Shulchan Aruch* (*Yoreh Dei'ah* 249:7) also says that giving tzedakah anonymously is one of the highest levels possible.

Ultimately, Rav Zilberstein points out that Yossele may have had grounds for his actions, since it was something that was eventually revealed to the world. Although during his lifetime people suspected him of being a miser, after he passed away, the record was made straight, rectifying the original impression.[17] Nevertheless, it seems that Rav Zilberstein does not recommend that people replicate the behavior of Yossele the Holy Miser, since a person's reputation may not be fully cleared posthumously.[18]

As far as the wealthy man in South America is concerned, Rav Hershel Schachter advised him to publicize that he gives a certain amount to tzedakah so that he doesn't appear stingy, without revealing the full extent of what he actually gives.

Furthermore, as we discussed in the chapter entitled *"Lashon Hara*—about Yourself," Rabbi Joseph B. Soloveitchik explains the *pasuk,* "Be innocent before Hashem and the Jewish People," to mean that having a good reputation is so important that one has no right to ruin his name. No one should say, "What do I care what people think of me?" and one should always be careful to act appropriately.[19]

---

17 Rav Yisrael Zev Gustman was rebuked for coming late to davening and morning *seder.* Only after he left the yeshivah did he explain that it was because of extra learning he was doing, and not because he was slacking off (David Page, *Rav Gustman: The Youngest Dayan of Vilna and Illustrious Rosh Yeshivah in New York and Yerushalayim* [ArtScroll/Mesorah, 2017], pp. 53–54). This suggests that you don't have to clear your name immediately but can do so at a later time.

18 For a slightly different response from Rav Zilberstein, see *Aleinu Leshabei'ach* (*parashas Metzora*, p. 188) where he discusses a similar story involving a wealthy miser in Yerushalayim. Rav Zilberstein said, "I am not even sure that a person is halachically permitted to humiliate himself and his entire family in this way. But I am sure that many bad decrees that could have come upon the people of Yerushalayim during Moshe the Miser's lifetime were annulled because of the extraordinary modesty that accompanied Moshe the Miser's acts of tzedakah and *chessed.*"

See *Igros Moshe, Yoreh Dei'ah,* vol. 3, §95, where Rav Moshe Feinstein permits institutions to share donor lists with other institutions so that they, too, can seek donations from these people. However, Rav Shlomo Aviner writes that if the donor doesn't want others to know about his donations, the one who revealed it may have violated the *pasuk,* "He who reveals secrets is a talebearer" (*Mishlei* 11:13). See Torat HaRav Aviner, Short & Sweet—Text Message Q&A #320, www.ravaviner.com.

19 David Holzer, *The Rav Thinking Aloud on the Parsha: Sefer Bamidbar* (Jerusalem: Laor Ltd.), *parashas Matos,* pp. 236–37; see also Rav Hershel Schachter, *Nefesh Harav,* p. 150.

According to this, even if one's name will be cleared at a later point, he may not be permitted to tarnish it.[20]

SUMMARY

A person may not cause others to suspect him of wrongdoing. Therefore, he should give enough tzedakah that he does not appear stingy or lax in this mitzvah. He may then give additional tzedakah anonymously.

---

20   The Gemara (*Sanhedrin* 11a) mentions a number of instances in which individuals falsely admitted to sinning or other improper behavior in order to save the actual sinners from public embarrassment. The *Maharsha* (ibid.) asks how they were permitted to make themselves out to be sinners, and responds that since the Gemara proves from examples in the Torah involving both Moshe and Yehoshua that it is permitted for a person to present himself as sinning to save others from embarrassment, we can apply it to all people in all generations. Perhaps this source can justify Yossele the Holy Miser, where he comes off as being stingy and doesn't give tzedakah publicly in order to save poor people the embarrassment of having to receive tzedakah publicly. Although Yossele most certainly embarrassed the collectors in the way he sent them away, perhaps he felt that a one-time embarrassment for each pauper who approached him was overall less embarrasing than the constant embarrassment they would have faced in returning frequently for the charity they needed.

SYNAGOGUE OR CYBER-SHUL?

IN THE NEWS

Back in 2011, the CNN Belief Blog published an interesting article on modern prayer practices, which raises questions for us as Jews.[1] It all started when the students at Liberty University had nowhere to conduct their church services. Their services were usually held in either the basketball arena on campus or in the sanctuary of Lynchburg's Thomas Road Baptist Church, but on this particular week, both were occupied. So Pastor Johnnie Moore and his congregation racked their brains to find a solution to their homeless dilemma, and a solution they found—conduct their service on Facebook.

After all, explains Moore, "Church and Facebook are places where we share in life together, learn about one another, encourage each other." Both Facebook and church are communities. Therefore, argues Moore, doing "church on Facebook...[is] intuitive." Additionally, says Moore, "Facebook can be a place where we encounter God and others. It can be a place where we teach and provide counsel, facilitate conversations, share experiences, and worship."

A simple Google search reveals that some Jewish temples (non-Orthodox) actually conduct virtual *minyanim*. Another modern reality is that some Orthodox Jews have started a program for those unable to daven in shul to connect to their synagogues at davening time through Skype.

---

1 Johnnie Moore, "My Faith: Why we're doing church on Facebook tonight" (Nov. 2, 2011), http://religions.blogs.cnn.com.

Recently, in September of 2017, Hurricane Irma hit Florida. Unable to leave their homes and go to shul, members of the Boca Raton Jewish community virtually joined a live *minyan* that took place in Atlanta, Georgia.[2]

What is the Torah response to this? May we or may we not, as Orthodox Jews, conduct a *minyan* on Facebook's live feature and virtual hookups?

A TORAH PERSPECTIVE

To begin with, there are two major problems with conducting prayer services on Facebook or having virtual *minyanim*. The Gemara tells us that it is extremely important to pray together in a *minyan*, and this is not facilitated through a cyber-*minyan*. The Gemara also says that prayers in a shul are much stronger and have a greater chance of being accepted than those outside a shul, and this facet is also absent in a cyber-shul.[3]

The *Rambam* stresses the importance of praying in shul with a congregation:

> *The prayer of a congregation is always heard, and even if there are sinners among them, Hashem does not despise the prayers of the group. Therefore, a person must join together with the congregation, and he should not pray alone as long as he can pray with the congregation. And a person should always get up early and stay up late to pray in a shul, because a person's prayers are not heard at all times except when he prays in a shul. And anyone who has a shul in his city and does not pray in it with the congregation is called a bad neighbor.[4]*

We can understand the value and importance of davening with a *minyan* from a *p'sak* of Rav Moshe Feinstein. He writes that one should

---

2   (Rabbi) Efrem Goldberg, Facebook post on Sep. 10, 2017.

3   *Berachos* 8a, cited in *Aruch Hashulchan, Orach Chaim* 90:13. The Gemara there says that one who consistently goes to shul during the day and night will merit a long life.

4   *Hilchos Tefillah* 8:1. This is cited by the *Shulchan Aruch* in *Orach Chaim* 90:11. See *Divrei HaRav*, pp. 148–49, for a beautiful explanation of this Gemara. Even when one cannot daven with a *minyan*, it's still valuable to daven with as many people as one can (*Minchas Asher, parashas Vayeira* §20, p. 127).

pray in a shul with a *minyan* even if he will have greater concentration when praying alone at home.[5]

Additionally, for a *minyan* to take place, says the *Shulchan Aruch*, it needs to be done in one room.[6] This is clearly not the case with Facebook, virtual *minyanim*, or viewing other members on a computer screen or via a television hookup.

---

5   *Igros Moshe, Orach Chaim*, vol. 3, §7. Rav Moshe (*Igros Moshe, Orach Chaim*, vol. 2, §27) was asked if a *talmid chacham* may stay up all night knowing that he would miss davening with a *minyan* in the morning. Rav Moshe responded that this is not permitted, since it is an obligation (*mi'd'Rabbanan*) to daven with a *minyan*. The *Emek Berachah* (pp. 7–8), however, writes that davening with a *minyan* is not an actual obligation; it is simply the ideal way to daven. Rav Hershel Schachter agrees with this opinion. Likewise, Rabbi Joseph B. Soloveitchik said that even if there is no obligation to pray with a *minyan*, if one does, he has fulfilled the *mitzvah min haTorah* of "*Venikdashti besoch Bnei Yisrael*" (*Vayikra* 22:32), sanctifying the name of God among Bnei Yisrael (Rabbi Aryeh Lebowitz, "Ten Minute Halacha—Minyan: Cake or Icing?" [March 8, 2010], www.yutorah.org). However, the *Ramban* (*Vayikra* 23:2) writes that praying with a *minyan* on Shabbos and Yom Tov is an obligation *min haTorah*. Shabbos and Yom Tov are called in the Torah "*mikra'ei kodesh*," which means a unique gathering of Jews; this, the *Ramban* explains, is done through *tefillah betzibbur* (praying with a *minyan*). See *Rashi* to Shabbos 24b, s.v. "*mishum*," where it states that during the Talmudic era some people did not daven *Maariv* with a *minyan* all week due to the danger involved in leaving the city at night to reach the shul, and only on Friday night did they do so. This leniency may have only been with regard to *Maariv* since there is an opinion that holds it is an optional prayer. Nevertheless, this *Rashi* is important for understanding the history of davening with a *minyan*.

6   *Shulchan Aruch, Orach Chaim* 55:13. Rabbi Joseph B. Soloveitchik said (*Mipeninei HaRav*, p. 46) that if there is an overflow crowd and people are standing outside the room where the *minyan* is taking place, they are still considered to be praying with a *minyan* and could answer *devarim shebikedushah* (*Barchu, Kedushah*, and *Kaddish*). Still, it is best to have at least ten people together in one room forming the *minyan*; see *Mishnah Berurah* 55:48, 50, 52, 60–62. Rav Ephraim Oshry was asked the following question during the Holocaust. "The young members would hide in the hideout built behind the ark in case of a sudden search, because the Germans, looking for strength and youth, rarely took the old and weak off to forced labor. I was asked by the younger members of the Tiferes Bachurim whether, when they had to hide in the middle of a prayer service and were unable to see the others who were praying inside the room, their prayers were considered prayer with the *minyan*, or were counted as private, individual prayer." Rav Oshry ruled "that since the boys could hear the others saying *Kaddish* and *Kedushah* while they waited in their hideout for the Germans to pass, they were fulfilling the obligation of praying in public. It is conceivable that if there were fewer than ten men in the *beis hamidrosh* itself, those in the hideout could not be included in the *minyan*. But as long as there were ten others, they were considered as having prayed with the *minyan* if they heard and could participate in what was going on in the *beis hamidrosh*" (*Responsa from the Holocaust*, Rabbi Ephraim Oshry [Judaica Press, 1989], pp. 93–94).

Although one cannot comprise a *minyan* through a cyber video hookup or Skype connection, Rav Herschel Schachter said in a *shiur* that one may answer *Amen* to *berachos* said in a bona fide *minyan*.[7] He also ruled that one could answer *devarim shebikedushah* (*Kaddish* and *Kedushah*) with such a hookup.[8] Rav Schachter even added that one could probably accomplish *tefillah betzibbur* this way, even if he was located in a different city from the one in which the broadcasted *minyan* was held. Nevertheless, as mentioned, this person would not count as one of the ten members of the *minyan*.

The *Tzitz Eliezer* rules that it is forbidden to answer *Amen* to *berachos* heard over the radio or telephone.[9] One of the reasons he mentions is that it is not considered as if you are hearing the actual voice of the one

---

7 Rav Hershel Schachter, "*Berachos* #11 7a–8a—Authentic Nevuah, Davening with a Live Feed, Yikanes Shnei Petachim, Shaarim Metzuyanim, Learning during Krias HaTorah" (Sept. 17, 2017), www.yutorah.org.

8 Rabbi Lebowitz ("Ten Minute Halacha—Virtual Minyanim" [April 7, 2014], www.yutorah.org) quotes Rav Hershel Schachter, who says that if you know which *berachos* the *minyan* is saying, you can answer *Amen* to them (based on the Gemara in *Sukkah* 51b). Also, *Rashi* (*Berachos* 47a) remarks that if one knows which *berachah* is being recited, he may answer *Amen* to that *berachah* even if he doesn't actually hear the *berachah*. Therefore, if you are watching the *minyan* live, you know exactly which *berachos* they are saying and you can answer *Amen*. Rabbi Lebowitz (*Mishnah Berurah, Shiur* §22) points out that Rav Schachter seems to think that what the *Mishnah Berurah* says in 55:20 about not having filth, waste, or idolatry between you and the *minyan* in order to be permitted to answer *devarim shebikedushah* is not a problem when listening through the phone or Skype since those things are not perceptible to you. See also *Igros Moshe, Orach Chaim*, vol. 4, §91:4, where Rav Moshe Feinstein says that if you hear a *berachah* over the telephone, you should answer *Amen*.

9 Vol. 20, §19. The *Tzitz Eliezer* rejects the Gemara in *Sukkah* 51b (cited in the previous note) as being a source to be lenient since *Tosafos* says (to *Sukkah* 52a) that the Gemara is not referring to a case where they were fulfilling a personal obligation, like prayer—it was used for the Torah reading. Rav Moshe Sternbuch (*Kuntress Teshuvos Vehanhagos, Purim*, p. 286) also refutes the proof from Alexandria and says that case was different since they were all in the same location. However, if one is standing in a different location from the *minyan*, he does not answer *Amen*, even if he listens to the *minyan* over a microphone or telephone, according to Rav Sternbuch. Rav Ovadiah Yosef (*Yechaveh Daat*, vol. 2, §68) seems to disagree. Rav Ovadiah says that you can answer *Amen* to *berachos* and *Kaddish* when listening to them on live radio; presumably, Rav Ovadiah would say the same when watching a live *minyan*. However, if there is a time delay between the radio or television and the "live" show, then it would seem that you cannot answer as if you were in the *minyan*, just as you can't answer when hearing a recording of a *berachah* or *tefillah* (*Umekarev Beyamin*, p. 26).

reciting the blessings. Presumably, this would be his opinion regarding a virtual hookup as well.

Rabbi Aryeh Lebowitz mentions in a Ten Minute Halacha *shiur* on this topic that watching a live *minyan* also fulfills the Gemara in *Berachos*[10] that states that if one cannot make it to shul (not because he is lazy), he should pray at the same time that the *minyan* in his town is praying.[11]

Another perspective that will shed light on this question is an explanation of the Rav regarding the significance of having separate seating between men and women during prayer. Rabbi Joseph B. Soloveitchik proclaimed that the whole concept of "family pews" is "in contradiction to the Jewish spirit of prayer."[12] He explained that

> *prayer means communion with the Master of the world, and therefore withdrawal from all and everything. During prayer man must feel alone, removed, isolated. He must then regard the Creator as his only Friend, from whom alone he can hope for support and consolation. "Behold as the eyes of servants look onto the hand of their masters, as the eyes of the maiden onto the hand of her mistress, so our eyes look onto the Lord our God, until He be gracious to us."[13]*

The point of separation between men and women (and having a *mechitzah*), then, is in order to create the atmosphere most conducive for praying and connecting to God. If, according to Rabbi Soloveitchik, the purpose of prayer is to be alone with God (although for men, as part

---

10 *Berachos* 7b–8a. When Rav Chaim Pinchas Scheinberg, Rosh Yeshivah of Torah Ore in Jerusalem, was unable to attend the *vasikin minyan* in person, he had a remote audio hookup to the *minyan* so he could follow along. Thus, he was fulfilling the idea of the Gemara in *Berachos* of praying at the same time as the *minyan* in your area. He held that you could also respond to the *devarim shebikedushah* said by the congregation (Ask the Rabbi, "Minyan via computers," www.ohr.edu).

11 Rabbi Aryeh Lebowitz, "Ten Minute Halacha—Virtual Minyanim" (April 7, 2014), www. yutorah.org.

12 Rabbi Joseph B. Soloveitchik, *Community, Covenant and Commitment: Selected Letters and Communications* (Ktav, 2005), pp. 134–35.

13 *Tehillim* 123:2.

of a *minyan*) and one must feel a sense of inadequacy and dependence on God in order to be able to pray properly, then none of this will be achieved if the prayer service is held on Facebook, while interacting with others during prayer. Prayer is a time to have a personal conversation with God alone. One must leave the comforts of the outside world behind in order to reach a state of mind like that of David HaMelech when he said, "Out of the depths have I called Thee, O Lord."[14] "Such a state of being will not be realized amid family pews," noted Rabbi Soloveitchik.[15] And one can add that such a state will not be realized amid Facebook or through virtual *minyanim*, either.

In the same vein, the *Shulchan Aruch* speaks about the importance of removing ourselves from the physicality of this world (*hispashtus ha-gashmiyus*) when standing before Hashem in the *Amidah*.[16] Rabbi Aryeh Kaplan explains that by being "totally divorced from the physical, one would be more ready to be in tune with the spiritual."[17] When it comes to praying, we need to remove all foreign thoughts from our minds and concentrate only on speaking to God. Prayer is a time to connect to God, not to human beings.

Similarly, Rav Hershel Schachter once explained why one should try to stand in the front of the synagogue as close to the *Aron Kodesh* as possible. He said the reason for this is to distance oneself from the outside world when praying, through limiting outside distractions.[18]

Rav Eliezer Waldenberg made related comments in a responsum he wrote to the question of whether one may answer *Amen* to blessings heard over the radio or telephone.[19] He explained that prayer is supposed to be an experience that comes from the depths of one's heart.

---

14   Ibid. 130:1.

15   Rabbi Joseph B. Soloveitchik, *Community, Covenant and Commitment: Selected Letters and Communications* (Ktav, 2005), pp. 134–35.

16   *Shulchan Aruch, Orach Chaim* 98:1.

17   *The Aryeh Kaplan Reader* (ArtScroll/Mesorah, 1986), p. 190.

18   I heard this in a *shiur* by Rav Schachter. Another reason that is given is that the *kedushah* of the shul emanates from the *Aron Kodesh*, and therefore it is beneficial to pray as close to it as possible.

19   *Tzitz Eliezer*, vol. 20, §19.

Prayer is called *"avodah shebalev,"* serving Hashem with our heart.[20] Listening to prayer over the telephone or radio is too passive, he says, to engender the *avodah shebalev* element, where we are supposed to be moved and passionate in praying to Hashem.

Additionally, Rav Waldenberg writes, a person must have a sense of seriousness when praying; he should feel that he is standing before Hashem and be focused only on that. When listening to prayers over the radio or the telephone, it is unlikely that one's sole focus is on the prayers.

Lastly, he says that it is not proper that the very same device (i.e., telephone or radio) that is used to listen to the news and mundane matters should be used to listen to Torah or prayer. Clearly, the issues brought up by the *Tzitz Eliezer* would apply to Facebook and virtual *minyanim*.

SUMMARY

A *minyan* cannot be formed using a cyber connection. If one is unable to attend a shul, the *poskim* debate which responses he can answer when listening to or viewing, via the Internet, a live *minyan* taking place in a shul.

---

20   *Sifri, parashas Eikev.*

THE APOCALYPSE

IN THE NEWS

Would you consider buying an underground home capable of withstanding a nuclear bomb? Even if you wouldn't, there are those who would.

Yahoo News reported that in April 2013, Robert Vicino purchased a giant underground cavern made of limestone.[1] The area is located in eastern Kansas and was prepared by the US Army as a storage facility over one hundred years ago. It is about 150 feet underground with room for up to 5,000 people and 150 recreational vehicles. Vicino hopes to rent parts of the cavern to prospective post-apocalyptic residents and name it Vivo's Survival Shelter and Resort.

"I've heard people say, 'I will just show up at the door,'" Vicino told the AP. "Our response is, 'Great, where is the door?' At our secret shelters, you don't know where to go, and your cash will be worthless at that time."

In March of 2017, CNN quoted Vicino, who reported that he already sold all the spaces in the shelter and added that "the compound itself will be equipped with all the comforts of a small town, including a community theater, classrooms, hydroponic gardens, a medical clinic, a spa and a gym."[2]

---

1   Eric Pfeiffer, "Giant caves once used by military now billed as best place to survive the apocalypse" (June 22, 2013), www.yahoo.com.
2   Elizabeth Stamp, "Billionaire bunkers: How the 1% are preparing for the apocalypse" (April 13, 2017), www.edition.cnn.com.

In the same news piece, Gary Lynch, general manager of Texas-based Rising S Company, disclosed that "2016 sales for their custom high-end underground bunkers grew 700% compared to 2015, while overall sales have grown 300% since the November US presidential election alone."[3]

Commenting on the apocalyptic phenomenon, California State University history professor Ken Rose said that some people are obsessed with this idea, but, in reality, the terror threats were much more serious during the Cold War than they are today.

In a March 13, 2015, article, *Washington Post* columnist Daniel W. Drezner quoted a YouGov poll that surveyed people's expectations for the end of time.[4] The poll showed some trends: "Republicans, as a group, said nuclear war and Judgment Day will be the most likely causes of the apocalypse. Democrats cited climate change, although they were more confident than Republicans that there won't be an apocalypse at all."

What is the Torah's approach to the mythical apocalypse? Do we believe that the world will really come to an end one day?

A TORAH PERSPECTIVE

The *Tanna D'vei Eliyahu Rabbah* states that the world will exist for six thousand years—two thousand years of emptiness, two thousand years of Torah, and two thousand years of the days of the "son of David" (i.e., Mashiach). Just as we keep the *shemittah* every seven years, so too, Hashem will make a *shemittah* for one year, which with regard to Hashem is a thousand years.[5]

The simple understanding of this midrash leads us to believe that there will indeed be an apocalypse of some sort after six thousand years.[6]

The *Rashbash* was asked our question—will the world be destroyed?—and he answered, based on this midrash, that the world will exist for six thousand years and then be destroyed for a thousand

---

3   Ibid.

4   Daniel W. Drezner, "Do experts and the public think differently about the apocalypse?" (March 13, 2015), www.washingtonpost.com.

5   *Tanna D'vei Eliyahu Rabbah*, ch. 2. The same idea is mentioned in the Gemara in *Rosh Hashanah* 31a, *Sanhedrin* 97a, and *Avodah Zarah* 9a.

6   We are currently in the year 5779, so the six thousand years will end in 221 years.

years.[7] The *Rashbash* is not alone; the *Ramban* also cites this midrash, as well as others, and explains it literally—that the world as we know it will come to an end after six thousand years.[8]

There are a number of *pesukim* that support this idea, such as the *pasuk* in *Yeshayah* that says, "Hashem alone will be glorified on that day."[9] The *pasuk* means that after the destruction of the world, Hashem will be all alone for a day, and one day for Hashem is the equivalent of a thousand years.[10]

The *Rambam*, however, disagrees.[11] He cites a number of *pesukim* that seem to indicate the everlasting nature of the world. For example, the *Rambam* quotes the *pasuk* in *Koheles* that says, "I knew that everything Hashem made will last forever; we cannot add to it nor detract from it..."[12] and the *pesukim* in *Tehillim* that state, "They shall praise Hashem, for He commanded and they were created. He set them up for eternity; He issued a decree that will not change."[13]

The *Rashbash*, in his responsum, writes that in truth this issue is not one of primary importance. He says that a Jew must believe that Hashem created the world from nothing, and one who does not believe

---

7   *Shu"t HaRashbash* §436. *Rashbash* is an acronym for "Rabbi Shlomo ben Shimon." He was the son of the *Tashbetz*, Rabbi Shimon ben Tzemach, and he lived from 1400 to 1467 in Algeria. The *Shach* and some Rishonim, such as *Rashi* (*Sanhedrin* 97a) and Rav Chasdai Crescas, understand that the world will not be permanently destroyed; it will only be destroyed for a thousand years (*Otzar Hayedios* [Rav Yechiel Michel Stern], vol. 2, p. 557). There is another opinion in the Gemara, that of Abaye, who says the world will be destroyed for two thousand years—the seventh and eighth millennia (*Sanhedrin* 97a; *Rosh Hashanah* 31a). "The *Yalkut Shimoni* (*Yeshayah* 447) teaches that this world is destined to be covered with water from which a new, perfect world will emerge. While the process of renewal takes place beneath the surface, Hashem will fashion eagles' wings for the righteous. Then they will fly over the water, i.e., they will soar to new spiritual heights" (*Tehillim*, Tanach Series [ArtScroll/ Mesorah, 1995], p. 1241).

8   *Kisvei HaRamban* (Mosad Harav Kook), vol. 1, pp. 159–60. See also *Raavad* on the *Rambam*, *Hilchos Teshuvah* 8:8.

9   *Yeshayah* 2:11.

10 See *Tehillim* 90:4 and *Rashi* to *Sanhedrin* 97a, s.v. "*trei.*" God is above time, but when man is told about God's day, it means a thousand years (*Yefeh To'ar*, cited in the ArtScroll Gemara, *Sanhedrin* 97a).

11 *Moreh Nevuchim* 2:28.

12 *Koheles* 3:14.

13 *Tehillim* 148:5–6.

this is denying a fundamental principle in Judaism.[14] However, with regard to believing that the world will be destroyed after six thousand years, the *Rashbash* writes that one who does not believe this is not considered a heretic, as long as he believes that Hashem could destroy the world if He so desired.

The *Rashbash* concludes with the *pesukim*, "The earth and heavens…will be destroyed, but You [Hashem] will exist."[15] The *Rashbash* states that these *pesukim* clearly demonstrate that the world will have an end.[16]

Rav Yosef Caro follows the opinion of the *Rashbash*, but he explains that the notion that after six thousand years the world will be "destroyed" for a thousand years doesn't mean that it will actually be destroyed; it just means that the world's existence will become very different from the way it is now.[17]

The *Ben Yehoyada* seems to agree with Rav Yosef Caro. He says that in the seventh millennium the world won't actually be destroyed, but rather we will be living a much more spiritual existence.[18] In this "new world" we will not be dependent on physical nourishment, but on a spiritual one, comparable to what the righteous people are experiencing now in *Gan Eden*.[19] Similarly, in one interpretation cited by the *Me'iri*,

---

14   Rabbi Gil Student, on his Torah Musings website, points out that the "standard editions of *Rambam*'s thirteen principles do not include Creation as a fundamental principle, although [Rabbi] Yosef Kafach includes it in his edition from *Rambam*'s handwritten manuscript."

15   *Tehillim* 102:26–28.

16   The *Rashbash* acknowledges that there are commentaries who explain these *pesukim* differently, but disagrees with them.

17   *Maggid Meisharim* (Rav Caro's conversations with an angel), *parashas Emor*, cited in *Otzar Hayedios* (Rav Yechiel Michel Stern), vol. 2, p. 557.

18   Cited in *Mesivta Shas, Rosh Hashanah* 31, *Yalkut Biurim*, p. 105. See *Sanhedrin* 92b, where it says that during this time righteous people will have wings like eagles to float above water.

19   There is a dispute between the *Rambam* and *Ramban* regarding where the soul goes after it leaves this world. The *Rambam* (*Hilchos Teshuvah* 8:2) says that after a person dies the soul goes straight to *Olam Haba* (the "World to Come" or "Future World") to receive its eternal reward in a completely spiritual world without a body. At one stage in time, Hashem will resurrect the dead, which is called *techiyas hameisim*, pulling the souls out of *Olam Haba* to live and die again. According to the *Ramban* (*Toras Haadam*, end of *Shaar Hagemul*) and many other opinions, *Olam Haba* is the world that will exist after *techiyas hameisim*,

he writes that the world won't actually be destroyed, but rather the *yetzer hara* will be destroyed.[20]

Another fundamental Jewish belief is that Mashiach, a descendant of David HaMelech, will come and redeem Klal Yisrael from their exile. The question is when he will come—before or after the destruction of the world. This is, in fact, a point of disagreement between the Rishonim. The *Yad Ramah* and *Rashi* say that the Messianic era will precede the destruction of the world, but according to one approach in the *Me'iri*, the world will be destroyed before the Messianic era.[21]

However, the *Rambam* writes that we won't know what will happen in the Messianic era until it comes, and, therefore, one should not spend time thinking about these matters or consider that they are essential, as they won't bring one to a greater fear or love of Hashem.[22] Furthermore, the Gemara states that one should not calculate when Mashiach will come, since if the date arrives and he doesn't come, a person might think that he will never come. Rather, a person should wait and anticipate his arrival.[23]

In conclusion, we should not dwell on determining if the world will actually be destroyed after six thousand years or whether Mashiach will come before this event. It is more productive to have *emunah* in Hashem and do as many mitzvos as we can until that time.

SUMMARY

According to the *Rashbash* and the *Ramban*, the world will come to an end after six thousand years. The *Rambam* disagrees, maintaining that the world will exist forever. Rav Yosef Caro offers a middle ground. He

---

which will include both body and soul, and the pleasure will be both physical and spiritual; those who merit living in *Olam Haba* will live forever. When a person dies, then, his soul temporarily goes to the *Olam Haneshamos* ("World of Souls" or "*Gan Eden*"), not to *Olam Haba*. For a comprehensive discussion on this topic, see Rabbi Aryeh Kaplan's *Immortality, Resurrection, and the Age of the Universe: A Kabbalistic View* (Ktav, 1993), pp. 29–42.

20   *Me'iri*, introduction to *Avos*.

21   *Yad Ramah, Sanhedrin* 97a; *Rashi, Sanhedrin* 92b; *Me'iri*, introduction to *Avos*.

22   *Hilchos Melachim* 12:2.

23   *Sanhedrin* 97b, cited in the *Rambam, Hilchos Melachim* 12:2. See the ArtScroll Gemara (*Sanhedrin* 97b, n. 29) for a summary regarding the idea that throughout the centuries many great sages have tried to calculate the arrival of Mashiach.

states that after six thousand years, the world will be different, but not destroyed. Similarly, the *Ben Yehoyada* and the *Me'iri* write that we will be living in a much more spiritual world after that time.

THE CELEBRATION OF SIN?

IN THE NEWS

In March of 2015, Facebook issued new community guidelines regarding what can and cannot be posted on its social media website.

> *Upsetting graphic pictures which "condemn or raise awareness" about terrorism, human rights abuses, or violence are acceptable, but when they're shared for "sadistic pleasure," they'll be removed. Similarly, posts containing hate speech, threats (to people or property), bullying, shaming, or those "celebrating any crimes committed" are also out.*

In addition, Facebook outlined rules for posting about terrorists and criminal organizations and outlawed the attempted purchase of drugs and other moral vices through the site.[1]

Similarly, a popular blog called Mevakesh Lev once posted, "A number of years ago a famous Jewish reggae star publicly announced that he was going off the *derech*. Now, another famous entertainer has announced that he is going off the *derech*. He will still keep some of the mitzvos, but others he will no longer keep…"[2]

Intentionally abandoning the mitzvos is serious enough. This severity is only compounded by a public announcement. Regardless of why Facebook has its rule against "celebrating any crimes committed," it is a reminder for all of us to take seriously the severity of celebrating our sins.

Is the celebration of sin also a sin?

---

1   Andy Boxall, "Facebook's New Rules" (March 16, 2015), www.digitaltrends.com.
2   Ally Ehrman, "Off the Derech" (July 12, 2015), www.mevakeshlev.blogspot.com.

A TORAH PERSPECTIVE

Someone once asked Rav Shlomo Aviner if he could attend a family *seudas hodaah* that was being held in honor of the millions of shekels they evaded in taxes to the Israeli government. Rav Aviner responded that of course he should not attend. "It is not a *seudat mitzva*, rather it is a *seudat aveira*, a *seudat chillul Hashem*."[3] The sin is not just that the person evaded paying taxes, but also that he was celebrating the fact that he had done so. The celebration of sin is also a sin, something that we must not take lightly.

The *Seforno* says regarding the *chet ha'eigel* that the dancing and singing that took place was much worse than the actual sin of making and worshipping the Golden Calf.[4] When Moshe heard from Hashem that the Jewish People had made the Golden Calf, he thought they would eventually come around and do *teshuvah* for their sin. But once he saw them rejoicing and celebrating what they had done, he knew they would never reach complete *teshuvah*, and that is when he broke the *Luchos* (Tablets).

Rav Yonasan Eibeshitz makes a similar comment.[5] He explains that normally when a person sins, he feels bad about what he did, and that itself diminishes the severity of the sin and is part of the *teshuvah* process. When Moshe saw the Jewish People reacting to the *chet ha'eigel*

---

3   "Interesting Psak: Seudat Gezel" (July 31, 2011), www.lifeinisrael.blogspost.com. The midrash says that after the brothers threw Yosef into the pit, "they sat down to eat a meal," and then they were going to bless Hashem. Yehudah noted the contradiction and said, "We are about to kill our brother and we bless God?" (Rabbi Eliyahu Eliezer Dessler, translated by Rabbi Aryeh Carmell, *Strive for Truth: Days of Awe*, part 4 [Feldheim, 2002], p. 91). Likewise, Rav Yerucham Levovitz of Mir would say, "If a person can commit a sin and immediately afterward find it possible to do a mitzvah without feeling any embarrassment at the contradiction, this shows how far he is from any level of sincerity" (ibid., p. 90). Indeed, the Gemara in *Nedarim* (20a) says that *bushah* (embarrassment) brings about *yiras chet*, the fear of sinning. A person who has a good amount of *bushah* won't come to sin quickly. The Gemara then says that someone who has no shame must not descend from the Jewish People who stood at *Har Sinai*. This is in consonance with the Gemara in *Yevamos* (79a) that says there are three defining characteristics of a Jew: mercy, embarrassment, and kindness.

4   *Seforno, Shemos* 32:19, 21. See there where he quotes the *pasuk*, "For [with] your evil, then you rejoice" (*Yirmiyah* 11:15).

5   Quoted in *Torah Ladaas*, vol. 1, *parashas Ki Sisa*, p. 365.

by rejoicing and dancing, he realized that they were not engaged in any sort of *teshuvah*, and his hopes for their doing *teshuvah* dimmed.

Similar to his comments on *chet ha'eigel*, the *Seforno* asks why the *pasuk* says, "*Nosei avon vafesha vechataah*—He forgives intentional sins, negligent sins, and unintentional sins."[6] The order seems to be backward: if Hashem forgives intentional sins, then of course He will forgive unintentional sins! The *Seforno* answers that *chataah* here is not referring to sins committed unintentionally;[7] rather it refers to the joy one has when committing the sin, which is worse than the *avon* and *pesha*, intentional sins.[8] Not only does Hashem forgive sins we committed intentionally, but He also forgives the satisfaction we had when we committed these sins.

Moreover, Rav Dessler explains that if a person doesn't take the severity of sinning seriously, he will never be able to improve. Having regret for the sin is what ensures that a person won't continue in that way.[9] The *Rambam* even says that one of the steps of *teshuvah* is that you must regret the sin you committed.[10]

The haftarah recited on the Shabbos after Tishah B'Av, the saddest day of the year, begins, "*Nachamu nachamu ami*—Be consoled, be consoled, My nation."[11] Rav Moshe Feinstein comments on the double "*nachamu*," saying that we need a double consolation because our sins were double: the Jewish People sinned against God, and on top of that they didn't realize they sinned. Rav Moshe explains that if a person believes that what he did was correct—when it wasn't—that is the worst form of sin, because then one is less likely to do *teshuvah*, and that itself is a sin.[12]

Rav Yitzchak Arama, the author of *Akeidas Yitzchak*, says that the homosexuality of Sedom was treated more severely than that of any

6   *Shemos* 34:7.

7   See *Rabbeinu Bachya* (*Shemos* 34:6), who does explain it to mean unintentional sins, as does the *Maharal* (*Nesiv Hateshuvah*, ch. 6). For additional approaches, see *Shiras David*, p. 48.

8   *Seforno, Shemos* 34:6.

9   Rabbi Eliyahu Eliezer Dessler, translated by Rabbi Aryeh Carmell, *Strive for Truth! Michtav Me'Eliyahu* (Feldheim, 2002), vol. 4, pp. 112–13.

10   *Hilchos Teshuvah* 2:2. See also *Taam Vadaas, Bereishis*, p. 22.

11   *Yeshayah* 40:1.

12   *Darash Moshe, parashas Va'eschanan*, p. 146.

other society, since it was ritualized there. He writes, "Removal of the repugnance associated with a transgression is even more serious a matter than the transgression itself."[13]

The Eretz Chemdah *beis din* was once approached by a non-Jew who had switched genders from female to male and wanted to convert to Judaism. The *beis din* outlined a number of reasons why it would not permit the conversion. One of the reasons was that there would be no regret for the sins involved in the transgender surgery, which the person would continue to violate by being in that state even after converting.[14]

Rav Moshe Sternbuch explains[15] the severity of promoting anti-Torah ideas by citing the *Zohar*, which says that before the sin of the Golden Calf, Hashem had said to take donations for the *Mishkan* from everyone, including the *eirev rav* (Egyptian converts who left Egypt with the Jews),[16] as the Torah says that everyone should donate to Hashem.[17] However, after the sin, Moshe told the Jewish People to take "from yourselves" to donate to the *Mishkan*—only the Jews should donate, not the *eirev rav*.[18]

Rav Sternbuch explains the difference. Before they sinned, the *eirev rav* had yet to publicize their heretical views, so their donations would have been accepted. However, after they sinned and publicized their views, they were not treated as part of the Jewish People, and their donations to the *Mishkan* would not be accepted.

SUMMARY

The celebration of sin is also a sin. In fact, according to the *Seforno*, the celebration may be considered worse than the actual sin. When a person is proud of his sins, he shows no regret for what he has done, which is the opposite of what it means to do *teshuvah*.

---

13   Rabbi J. David Bleich, *Judaism and Healing: Halakhik Perspectives* (Ktav, 2002), p. 71. Rav Yaakov Kamenetsky (*Emes L'Yaakov, parashas Noach*, p. 60) writes that a city or group that agrees or wants to uproot any single mitzvah has the status of an *ir hanidachas*, a city of idolatry, which the Torah says has to be destroyed.

14   See *Bamareh Habazak*, vol. 5, §87.

15   *Teshuvos Vehanhagos*, vol. 6, §167.

16   *Shemos* 12:37. See *Rashi, Shemos* 12:38. Rav Sternbuch (*Teshuvos Vehanhagos*, vol. 6, §167) notes that prior to the *chet ha'eigel*, the *eirev rav* had the status of Jews.

17   *Shemos* 25:2.

18   Ibid. 35:5.

THE DYBBUK EXORCIST

IN THE NEWS

One of the most famous and frightening movies ever produced was the 1973 horror film *The Exorcist*. Directed by William Friedkin, a Jewish American filmmaker born to Ukrainian immigrants, the film portrays the terrifying tale of a twelve-year-old girl who was possessed by an evil spirit that her mother tries desperately to expel by turning to doctors, psychologists, and religious leaders.[1]

At the 2016 Cannes Film Festival, Friedkin related the following story:

> *"I was invited by the Vatican exorcist to shoot and video an actual exorcism which...few people have ever seen and which nobody has ever photographed,"* and, he insisted, was very similar to his own film. *"I was pretty astonished by that. I don't think I will ever be the same having seen this astonishing thing. I am not talking about some cult; I am talking about an exorcism by the Catholic Church in Rome,"* he said. *"There must be something in there..."*[2]

Also, Rabbi Dr. Julian G. Jacobs, a rabbi for the United Synagogue of England and a prolific writer on Torah topics, notes that "in Italy

---

1   Roger Ebert, "The Exorcist Movie Review & Film Summary" (Dec. 26, 1973), www.rogerebert.com.

2   "Vatican Invites Exorcist Director William Friedkin to Meet a Real Dybbuk" (May 19, 2016), www.jewishpress.com.

no fewer than six hundred people a day appeal to the Roman Catholic Church for help because they are caught in the cult of Satanism. It was claimed the pressure was so great that the Pope was considering setting up a special Office of Exorcism."[3]

And finally, in a recent article in the *Washington Post*, Dr. Richard Gallagher, a board-certified psychiatrist and professor of clinical psychiatry at New York Medical College, shares his personal experiences with exorcism in the United States. He writes that at first he was highly skeptical that a person can be possessed by a demon—it didn't conform to any of the training he received at Yale and Columbia where he studied psychiatry. However, after being asked to analyze patients who claimed to be possessed by demons to determine whether their claims were merely the results of mental illness, he began to believe them. Based on his experience and training, Gallagher could find no other explanation than to say that they were indeed possessed by demons.[4]

According to Reverend Vincent Lampert, an Indianapolis-based priest-exorcist, there are around fifty exorcists designated by bishops to deal with the demonic issue in the United States.[5]

What does the Torah say about dybbuks and exorcism? Do they really exist?

A TORAH PERSPECTIVE

First, let's understand what a dybbuk is. It is the soul of a person who once lived and died that takes over the body of living person.[6]

The story is told that when the Satmar Rebbe, Rav Yoel Teitelbaum, visited Israel, a man approached him with his daughter and told him that a dybbuk had entered his daughter's body. He told the Rebbe that

---

3   Julian G. Jacobs, *Judaism Looks at Modern Issues* (Aviva Press, 1993), p. 193.

4   Richard Gallagher, "As a psychiatrist, I diagnose mental illness. Also, I help spot demonic possession" (July 1, 2016), www.washingtonpost.com. Note that this article presents some aspects of dybbuks that are contrary to the Jewish approach to this subject.

5   Ibid.

6   Rabbi Joseph B. Soloveitchik stated, "The concept of a dybbuk entering a person is an incisive Chassidic notion. The idea is that although an individual might outwardly engage in improper activities, the true inner person would never do so" (Debra and Robert Kasirer, *Rosh Hashanah Machzor: With Commentary Adapted from the Teachings of Rabbi Joseph B. Soloveitchik* [K'hal, 2007], p. 6).

his daughter had pains throughout her body and was speaking with a voice that wasn't hers. The Satmar Rebbe turned to the girl and said that she had lost her mind and should be taken to a psychiatrist.[7]

According to Rabbi Mordechai Torczyner, it is very possible that the *Rambam* would dismiss the idea of the dybbuk and exorcism as well.[8] The *Rambam* writes that believing in magic, astrology, demons, fortune telling, witchcraft, and superstitions is against the Torah and rooted in idolatry.[9] However, says Rabbi Torczyner, this is not conclusive because the *Rambam* was referring to dangerous spirits (demons), and these are not necessarily the same as souls that possess people (dybbuks).

On the other hand, there were many great people who did accept the concept of a dybbuk in Judaism.[10] Rav Avraham Simchah of Amtzislav told the following story in the name of his uncle, Rav Chaim of Volozhin, who was a student of the Vilna Gaon.[11]

---

7   Rav Shlomo Aviner, *Ner B'ishon Lailah*, pp. 96–98.

8   Rabbi Mordechai Torczyner, "Supernatural Judaism: The Jew and the Dybbuk" (Jan. 26, 2016), www.yutorah.org. See *Ner B'ishon Lailah*, p. 97, which records a story about a woman who many thought was possessed by a dybbuk and how the *Rambam* went to great lengths to explain rationally why, in fact, she was not. Similarly, the *Rambam's* son rejected the concept of *gilgulim* (souls reincarnated in new bodies)—see *Ner B'ishon Lailah*, p. 88.

9   *Peirush Hamishnayos, Avodah Zarah* 4:7.

10   Josephus Flavius writes (*Antiquities of the Jews*, vol. 7, 2:5) that God gave Solomon the ability to drive away demons using exorcism. Although Josephus mentions exorcising demons from one's body, he doesn't specifically mention a dybbuk. The *She'iltos of Rav Achai Gaon* (*parashas Eikev* §145) records an incident of a king whose only daughter was possessed by a demon and none of the doctors were able to expel it. When the king placed on his doorpost the *mezuzah* that had been given to him as a gift by Rabbi Yehudah HaNasi, the demon immediately left his daughter's body (see *Vehaarev Na*, vol. 3, p. 458; see also *Otzar Hayedios* [Rav Yechiel Michel Stern], vol. 2, pp. 535–38, regarding stories of the *Chasam Sofer* and others where items of holiness interfered with the dybbuk).

The *Me'am Lo'ez* seems to accept the concept of a dybbuk as well. In his introduction to *Avos* (pp. 10–11), he records the story of an Arab faith healer who said that in order to heal the patient, he needed to speak to the spirit inside her and get it to leave her body. The *Me'am Lo'ez* thinks that the Arab's strategy was prohibited because speaking to the spirit was considered praying to a foreign god (see *Shulchan Aruch, Yoreh Dei'ah* 179:8, with the *Shach* and *Taz*). However, he doesn't seem to reject the idea that a spirit could exist in someone else (i.e., dybbuk). See *Otzar Hayedios* (Rav Yechiel Michel Stern), vol. 2, p. 535, where the *Chazon Ish* also accepted the concept of a dybbuk.

11   Introduction to the Vilna Gaon's commentary on *Midrash Rus Hechadash*, cited in *Ner B'ishon Lailah*, p. 98.

> *One time an evil spirit entered a man in Vilna while he was in*
> *the courtyard of the shul and caused a tremendous commotion to*
> *the amazement of everyone there.*[12] *The Vilna Gaon opened the*
> *window of the shul to see what caused the loud noise. When the*
> *dybbuk saw the Vilna Gaon, the dybbuk said, "Rebbi, about you*
> *they say above, 'Be cautious with Eliyahu [the Vilna Gaon] and his*
> *Torah.' If you just decree that I leave this person's body, I would be*
> *forced to comply and exit the body."*[13] *The Vilna Gaon responded,*
> *"I want nothing to do with you nor speak with you at all."*

Additionally, Rav Tzvi Yehudah Kook told Rav Yaakov Moshe Charlap
that his father, Rav Avraham Yitzchak Kook, exorcised a dybbuk in Yafo in
the year 5672 (1911). Rav Charlap was excited by this story and said that
all the details of the story should be written and preserved as a permanent
remembrance. However, Rav Tzvi Yehudah Kook did not take this approach
and publicize the story. He preferred to publicize pure faith in Hashem,
fear of Hashem, and excellent character development. Furthermore, Rav
Tzvi Yehudah wrote that his father, too, underplayed the significance of
such stories, saying that a person is not praised for his ability to exorcise a
dybbuk, but rather for his *chessed* and knowledge of Hashem.[14]

However, there were great rabbis who felt that there were very important messages that one could learn from the stories of dybbuks and, therefore, felt the need to publicize and teach them.[15] In the introduction to

---

12   See *Otzar Hayedios* (Rav Yechiel Michel Stern), vol. 2, §252, where an entire chapter is devoted
     to this topic. See there in the name of Rav Chaim Vital for details on exactly how a dybbuk
     enters a body (p. 532), how it leaves the body (p. 538), and, citing the *Shaar Hagilgulim*, some
     reasons for choosing the specific body it enters (p. 533). See p. 536 about how sometimes a
     person possessed with a dybbuk speaks different languages and sounds different than usual.
13   Rav Chaim of Volozhin explained that it was because of the Vilna Gaon's tremendous dedica-
     tion to Torah that he had reached such a high level—a level of *ruach hakodesh*—that the dyb-
     buk had to obey. See the introduction to commentary of the Vilna Gaon on *Safra Ditzniusa*,
     cited in *Ner B'ishon Lailah*, p. 98. See *Otzar Hayedios* (Rav Yechiel Michel Stern), vol. 2, §252,
     p. 534, for the story in which the *Taz* decreed that a dybbuk leave someone's body.
14   *Ner B'ishon Lailah*, pp. 97–98.
15   Rav Shlomo Aviner writes that many of the students of the Arizal recorded surprising sto-
     ries involving the Arizal, in order to strengthen people's faith in Hashem (*Ner B'ishon Lailah*,
     p. 98). See *Otzar Hayedios* (Rav Yechiel Michel Stern), vol. 2, §252, p. 538, for instances
     where exorcising a dybbuk was publicized in order to make a *kiddush Hashem*.

the *Lev Eliyahu*, the *mussar shmuessen* of Rav Eliyahu Lopian, his student, Rav Shalom Schwadron, records an interesting story about a dybbuk.[16]

Rav Schwadron says that it is well known that Rav Eliyahu Dushnitzer was one of the ten men in the Kodashim Kollel in Radin whom the Chafetz Chaim sent to exorcise a dybbuk from a woman.[17] It is also well known that Rav Elchanan Wasserman was another one of the ten men to participate in that event, and he would tell that story at every Purim *seudah* in front of his entire yeshivah for almost two hours.[18] However, Rav Schwadron writes that he asked Rav Dushnitzer to tell him the exact story about that dybbuk, but Rav Dushnitzer responded, "What will come out of this story? It is just a story."[19]

Rav Dushnitzer said that he would tell him a different dybbuk story instead, one that has a powerful message. This story, said Rav Dushnitzer, is worthy of being publicized. Rav Schwadron prefaces the story by writing that Rav Dushnitzer told it over word for word the way he heard it from the great rabbi of Pinsk, Rav Elazar Moshe Horowitz. The story goes as follows:[20]

> *There was a Jew in Kelm named Reb Nota who married off his daughter to a talmid chacham. Reb Nota supported the*

---

16   Vol. 1, p. 15, and vol. 2, p. 85. Rav Schwadron writes that he heard this story from Rav Eliyahu Dushnitzer, who served as the *mashgiach* of Lomza Yeshivah in Petach Tikva.

17   In his work, *Making of a Gadol*, Rav Nosson Kamenetsky cites numerous members of the Chafetz Chaim's family who said that the woman had a mental illness and that the Chafetz Chaim was just treating her (Rabbi Dr. Natan Slifkin, "Ghosts, Demons, and Bacteria" [July 17, 2016], www.rationalistjudaism.com).

18   Rav Elchanan Wasserman wrote in the name of the Chafetz Chaim that this famous dybbuk story was likely to be the last such story in our times; see Rav Yaakov Kamenetsky, *Emes L'Yaakov*, *parashas Va'eira*, p. 264, and see there for Rav Yaakov's explanation of why we no longer have dybbuks.

19   Rav Schwadron writes there that his impression was that Rav Dushnitzer did not want to tell him the dybbuk story since he would then have to say what the dybbuk said, and perhaps the dybbuk's speech was inappropriate (*Lev Eliyahu*, vol. 1, p. 15). When students of Rav Moshe Twersky told him that they wanted to witness a dybbuk being exorcised, he wasn't excited by the idea and remarked, "I see more revelation of the Divine Presence in a *Tosafos*!" (Rabbi Yehoshua Berman, *A Malach in Our Midst: The Legacy of A Treasured Rebbi, Harav Moshe Twersky* [Feldheim, 2016], pp. 66–67).

20   *Lev Eliyahu*, vol. 1, p. 15, and vol. 2, p. 85.

young couple for three years, in addition to the large dowry he gave them, which allowed his son-in-law to sit and learn Torah without distraction. After the three years were up, Reb Nota's daughter complained about a lack of means of support, whereupon her husband responded that he wouldn't give up his learning. The wife suggested that they use the money from their dowry to open a store so that they could earn a living. She promised her husband that she would operate the store most of the day, while her husband would only have to run it for two hours a day. This way, he could still continue learning.

However, this plan lasted for only three months. The husband began manning the store for a much longer period of the day, to the point that he spent so much time involved at the store that he did not even open a Gemara.

One motza'ei Shabbos, the wife went out into the courtyard and suddenly began gagging and was unable to speak. She was brought to many doctors to cure her, but to no avail. People began suspecting that she was possessed by a dybbuk.

She was brought to a tzaddik and mekubal in the city of Shtutchin by the name of Rav Mendel, whom people went to for such matters. Rav Mendel asked her many questions, and she began to speak, but not in a normal way. Her stomach was swelled up and her lips did not move, while a voice emerged from her body. After questioning her, Rav Mendel said that it was in fact a dybbuk.

The dybbuk began screaming frantically, saying that five angels of destruction were waiting for it, and as soon as it would leave the body, they would destroy it (the angels couldn't punish it as long as the dybbuk was in a living being). Then the dybbuk began mentioning all sorts of inappropriate things, prompting bystanders to close their ears.[21]

---

21   There have also been instances where dybbuks revealed people's sins; see *Otzar Hayedios* (Rav Yechiel Michel Stern), vol. 2, §252, pp. 534–35.

Rav Mendel asked the dybbuk why he entered this woman's body. The dybbuk responded that the girl's mother and husband's mother, who had already passed away, desired that it enter her body and the resulting pain would prompt her to repent for her grave sin of taking her husband away from learning Torah. Otherwise, the dybbuk said, she would have no standing in this world or the next.

After hearing this, Rav Mendel told the woman's husband to promise that he would return to learning Torah, and Reb Nota promised to learn Mishnayos for the dybbuk, who had been a young man.[22] The woman was placed on a chair in the middle of the room, when suddenly she fell to the ground, and a loud voice emerged declaring, "Shema Yisrael." Then one of her fingernails burst open, and one of the windows shattered. After that she was peaceful and quiet.[23]

Rav Lopian concluded that this story is a great lesson in *mussar*, guiding us to serve Hashem properly.[24]

Are there any sources in classic Jewish texts for the idea of the dybbuk? How does this idea fit in with Jewish philosophy in general?

Jewish tradition teaches that after a person dies, his soul leaves his body and moves elsewhere. The Talmud relates some general facts about where the soul travels to receive its ultimate reward and punishment. With regard to the bodies of the wicked, the Gemara cites the *pasuk*,

---

22 See *Lev Eliyahu*, vol. 1, pp. 16–17, for details of the previous life of this dybbuk and the importance of *teshuvah*.

23 The way to exorcise a dybbuk is by using oaths to force it to leave the person's body. The Arizal told his student, Rav Chaim Vital, the proper oaths one should use in exorcising dybbuks (*Shaar Ruach Hakodesh*, p. 88, cited in *Ner B'ishon Lailah*, p. 97). See *Otzar Hayedios* (Rav Yechiel Michel Stern), vol. 2, p. 536, where he says that the Arizal taught his student Rav Chaim Vital that before using oaths to exorcise a dybbuk, one must first mention the name of the dybbuk. See also *Otzar Hayedios* (Rav Yechiel Michel Stern), vol. 2, pp. 537–38, about how a dybbuk was exorcised in the times of the *Chasam Sofer*.

24 *Lev Eliyahu*, vol. 2, p. 85. See also *Lev Eliyahu*, vol. 1, p. 18, and *Otzar Hayedios* (Rav Yechiel Michel Stern), vol. 2, p. 535, citing Rav Lopian regarding the importance of *teshuvah* derived from the concept of the dybbuk.

"God declares, 'There is no peace for the wicked!'"[25] With regard to their souls, the Gemara cites the *pasuk*, "And may the souls of your enemies be slung with the hollow of the sling,"[26] and interprets it to mean that an angel is at one end of the universe and another is at the other end, and they sling these souls to each other.[27] This Gemara seems to allude to the concept of a dybbuk as a form of punishment.[28]

Furthermore, the *Radvaz* accepts the idea of *gilgulim* and says that Hashem uses them as an opportunity for those who need to repent for sins they committed in a previous life.[29] The *Kaf Hachaim* also writes explicitly that a person's soul may enter another's body as a form of punishment.[30]

Therefore, based on the *Radvaz*, and certainly the *Kaf Hachaim*, the idea of the dybbuk is that it serves as a punishment for the sins of the person to whom the dybbuk's soul belonged while in this world, and possibly also as a punishment for sins committed by the person whose body it overtakes.[31] This fits into the general Jewish philosophy of reward and punishment.[32]

---

25   *Yeshayah* 48:22.

26   *Shmuel I* 25:29.

27   *Shabbos* 152b.

28   See *Otzar Hayedios* (Rav Yechiel Michel Stern), vol. 2, p. 537, where it says that sometimes the dybbuk reveals the sins it had committed in its previous lifetime in this world.

29   *Shu"t HaRadvaz* 8:87.

30   *Kaf Hachaim, Orach Chaim* 46:32. See there for the interesting context in which this statement was made.

31   The Arizal says that if someone caused others to sin, but he didn't sin himself, then the one who sinned will have to be a *gilgul*, and the one who caused others to sin will have to be a dybbuk within the *gilgul* (*Peninei Halachah, Sanhedrin* 50b). However, sometimes the dybbuk enters even a righteous person's body; see *Otzar Hayedios* (Rav Yechiel Michel Stern), vol. 2, §252, p. 532. See also *Maor Vashemesh, parashas Shelach*, where he explains the *parashah* of the *meraglim* based on the concept of a dybbuk and the ability of *tzaddikim* to actually decree for souls to enter the bodies of others. The *Pardes Yosef* (*parashas Pinchas* §7, 8) cites the *Zohar*, which says that Nadav and Avihu were dybbuks inside Pinchas. Rabbi Chaim Yehuda Pollack, Rosh Kollel of the Willowbrook Kollel in Staten Island, told me that with regard to *tzaddikim*, the term used is *ibur neshamah*, which is a good thing, because the extra *neshamah* helps, but a dybbuk is a foreign *neshamah* that disturbs the person it possesses. See *Halekach Vehalibuv Al HaTorah*, 5763, *parashas Bechukosai*, p. 213, for more on the topic of *ibur neshamah*.

32   Reward and punishment is number 11 of the *Rambam's* thirteen principles of faith, as stated in his *Peirush Hamishnayos*, ch. 10 of *Sanhedrin*.

Alternatively, the *Maharal* says that the *pasuk* in *Shmuel* as cited by the Gemara, "And may the souls of your enemies be slung with the hollow of the sling," teaches that the wicked souls are in a state of limbo.[33] The idea of a dybbuk may be based on the idea that souls of the wicked are in limbo after they leave this world.[34]

SUMMARY

The Satmar Rebbe seemed to be skeptical toward the concept of the dybbuk—at least in our times. However, many others, including the Gra, Chafetz Chaim, and Rav Kook, did believe in it. In addition, some rabbis, including Rav Avraham Yitzchak Kook, did not believe in publicizing dybbuk incidents, while Rav Eliyahu Lopian and Rav Elchanan Wasserman thought such stories were enlightening in one's *avodas Hashem*.

---

33   *Chiddushei Aggados, Shabbos* 152b.

34   The Gemara in *Shabbos* and the *Maharal* are mentioned by Rabbi Mordechai Torczyner, "Supernatural Judaism: The Jew and the Dybbuk" (Jan. 26, 2016), www.yutorah.org.

THE HONOR GUARDS

IN THE NEWS

What the Royal Guards are for Buckingham Palace, Secret Service agents are for the White House. While that is their role, unfortunately, the Secret Service didn't live up to expectations on September 19, 2014. Omar Gonzales, a former US Army combat soldier with a police record, succeeded in scaling the White House fence, sprinting across the lawn unabated, and entering the East Room before finally being subdued.

According to a Department of Homeland Security report on the incident, Secret Service agents on duty at the time were responsible for a series of grave errors. The mistakes included not reporting a suspicious person outside the gates, not visually spotting the intruder on the lawn due to construction in the vicinity, losing sight of the intruder when he entered the bushes, speaking on a personal cell phone while on duty, forgetting to bring a two-way radio to work, and attempting to stop the intruder with a flashlight instead of a baton.[1]

In 2015, Doug Hughes, a sixty-one-year-old Florida mailman, flew his gyrocopter onto the Capitol lawn, bypassing air-defense systems—one of the many embarrassments to the Secret Service.[2]

Following the Gonzales security lapse at the White House, Julia Pierson, director of the US Secret Service, resigned from her position.[3]

---

1 Michael S. Schmidt, "Secret Service Blunders Eased White House Intruder's Way, Review Says" (Nov. 13, 2014), www.nytimes.com.
2 Mike DeBonis and Marc Fisher, "Florida mailman lands a gyrocopter on Capitol lawn, hoping to send a message" (April 15, 2015), www.washingtonpost.com.
3 Erin Dooley, Pierre Thomas, and Jonathan Karl, "Secret Service Director Julia Pierson Resigns" (Oct. 1, 2014), www.abcnews.go.com.

While one lawmaker called it a "comedy of errors,"[4] the incident acted as a wake-up call for the Secret Service to focus on protecting the nation's most important domain and citizen.

After a number of blunders in guarding the White House, Secret Service Director John Clancy asked the US House Appropriations Committee for eight million dollars to construct a replica of the White House at their training site in Maryland. Clancy explained, "Right now, we train on a parking lot, basically. We put up a makeshift fence and walk off the distance between the fence at the White House and the actual house itself. We don't have the bushes, we don't have the fountains, we don't get a realistic look at the White House." However, with a full-scale model of the White House, Clancy claims they would have a "more realistic environment, conducive to scenario-based training exercises."[5]

Of course, when the Secret Service is doing its job, the average person may not simply enter the White House. A CNN article reports, "There are approximately 3,200 special agents and an additional 1,300 uniformed officers who guard the White House, the Treasury building, and foreign diplomatic missions in Washington."[6] Additionally, for the Secret Service, the requisite age is between twenty-one and thirty-seven.[7] Furthermore, the White House has been designated as a no-fly zone.[8] The Federal Aviation Administration's policy is that any pilot who flies in the prohibited area at an altitude below 18,000 feet without permission faces civil and criminal penalties.[9]

The central goal of all of this is to protect the president of the United States and his domain, the White House. For the Jewish People, the most important domain on earth is Hashem's "home on earth," the Beis

4   "Comedy of errors: Secret Service officer chatted on cell phone as intruder scaled White House fence" (Nov. 14, 2014), www.foxnews.com.

5   Alexandra Jaffe, "Secret Service asks for $8 million White House replica" (March 18, 2015), www.edition.cnn.com.

6   "Secret Service Fast Facts" (May 3, 2019), www.edition.cnn.com.

7   "Special Agent," www.secretservice.gov.

8   "Washington, DC Metropolitan Area Special Flight Rules Area," www.gpo.gov.

9   Mike DeBonis and Marc Fisher, "Florida mailman lands a gyrocopter on Capitol lawn, hoping to send a message" (April 15, 2015), www.washingtonpost.com.

Hamikdash. And just as the homes of our nations' leaders are protected by high-level security guards, we find that the Torah commands us to guard the Beis Hamikdash.[10]

How does the security system of the Beis Hamikdash compare with security systems of today's White House? More specifically, what is the purpose of protecting the Beis Hamikdash—is it to protect the building or to create a certain atmosphere? What were the consequences, if any, if a Beis Hamikdash guard was negligent in his duties? How many guards did the Beis Hamikdash have on duty at one time? How old did one have to be in order to join the Beis Hamikdash guards' team? If the Beis Hamikdash guards wanted to replicate the Beis Hamikdash in order to practice guarding it, would it be permitted for them to do so?[11] Are there any restrictions regarding the airspace of *Har HaBayis* (the Temple Mount)? And finally, does the commandment to guard *Har HaBayis* apply today?

A TORAH PERSPECTIVE

Rashi writes that the purpose of protecting the Beis Hamikdash is twofold: to prevent people who are not allowed to enter it from entering and to protect the holy vessels from being touched by people who are *tamei* (spiritually unclean).[12] The *Rambam*, however, says that the purpose of the guards is not to keep people out, but to act as Honor Guards, demonstrating honor to the holy edifice—in his words, "A palace with guards is different from a palace without guards."[13]

The Mishnah tells us that the *Mikdash* guards were on duty throughout the night,[14] even though the Beis Hamikdash was locked at night and no one could enter. According to *Rashi*, this is difficult to understand, since there shouldn't be any concern that someone would enter the Beis Hamikdash when it was locked. But according to the *Rambam*,

---

10   *Bamidbar* 18:1–7.

11   For a news story regarding recent plans to build a full-size replica of the Beis Hamikdash, see Alon Meltzer, "Vayakhel—Building the mishkan vs. building a fake temple" (Feb. 21, 2014), http://blogs.timesofisrael.com.

12   *Rashi, Bamidbar* 3:6, 8:19, 18:1.

13   *Hilchos Beis Habechirah* 8:1.

14   *Middos* 1:2.

it is clear—the guards were not there to "guard," but rather to give honor and majesty to this holy abode.[15]

To elaborate, Rav Asher Weiss suggests that the *Rambam*'s opinion could be based on the concept mentioned by the *Rosh*: that the guards were needed to remind people that they were standing in the presence of the Master of the universe.[16] Therefore, it was more important to appoint guards at night than during the day because, in the daytime, the very occupation of serving Hashem was the reminder, but at night, when there was virtually no service, Bnei Yisrael needed the guards to serve as the reminder.[17]

The difficulty with the *Rambam*'s approach is that the *pesukim* in the Torah seem to clearly state that the objective of the guards was to prevent unauthorized people from entering the Beis Hamikdash, as *Rashi* explains.[18]

The last Lubavitcher Rebbe, Rav Menachem Mendel Schneerson, proposed that perhaps *Rashi* and the *Rambam* don't disagree; each one is merely placing an emphasis on the one aspect that he felt was the primary reason for the guards, but each truly agrees that the other's reason is true as well.[19]

Concerning a guard of the Beis Hamikdash being negligent while on duty, the *Rambam* writes:

> *Guarding the Temple is the fulfillment of a positive commandment (mitzvas aseih)... And if they are remiss in guarding, they have violated a negative commandment (mitzvas lo saaseih), as it says, "And they should guard the security of the Temple," and the word shemar, "guard," implies a warning*

---

15   *Hilchos Beis Habechirah* 8:2. However, in his *Sefer Hamitzvos*, the *Rambam* seems to say that the mitzvah is to guard the Beis Hamikdash both day and night. For more on this subject, see the Lubavitcher Rebbe's comments in *Beminchas Chinuch*, p. 287.

16   *Peirush HaRosh* on *Maseches Tamid* 1:1.

17   *Minchas Asher*, *Bamidbar*, pp. 11–12.

18   *Rashi* says (*Bamidbar* 18:1) that the purpose of the guards was in order to keep out Yisraeilim—non-*Kohanim* and non-*Levi'im*—who would be punished with death for entering the restricted area.

19   *Likutei Sichos*, vol. 13, *parashas Korach*.

against transgressing a negative command. You have learned
[therefore] that guarding it is a positive commandment, and
being remiss in guarding it is a negative commandment.[20]

The Mishnah writes that the person in charge of *Har HaBayis*,
known as the *"ish Har HaBayis,"* would check on the guards of the Beis
Hamikdash at night to see if any were "sleeping on the job." If he caught
one sleeping, he would hit the guard with a stick; he was even permitted
to burn the guard's clothing, and such an incident actually occurred.[21]
Why would he burn the clothing? The *Tiferes Yisrael* says it was the
guard's outer clothing that kept him warm and made him drowsy.

Unlike the White House, which has 1,200 guards, the Mishnah at
the beginning of *Maseches Middos* states that there were twenty-four
guards stationed at twenty-four different points of entry of the Beis
Hamikdash; three were manned by *Kohanim*, and twenty-one were
manned by *Levi'im*.[22]

It's not clear how old Beis Hamikdash guards had to be. Apparently,
this is a matter of dispute between the *Minchas Chinuch* and the *Avnei
Nezer*, which is a result of the previously mentioned opinions of *Rashi*
and the *Rambam*. The *Minchas Chinuch* learns that the reason for the
guards was to demonstrate honor, not to keep people out, and therefore
even a minor was eligible to be a guard because that also shows honor.
But the *Avnei Nezer* learns that there is also a requirement to prevent
unauthorized entry, and a *katan* would not be qualified to do that.[23]

Shedding light on this, the Mishnah in *Maseches Tamid* says that
"rovim" and *"pirchei kehunah"* would participate in guarding the Beis
Hamikdash.[24] The *Mefaresh*, the *Raavad*, and the *Rosh* all say that *rovim*
refers to young *Kohanim* (from the word *"ravyah,"* child[25]) who were too

---

20   *Hilchos Beis Habechirah* 8:3.

21   *Middos* 1:2.

22   The *Aruch Hashulchan* (*Orach Chaim* 128:15) writes that the reason for having *Levi'im* wash the *Kohanim's* hands prior to *Birkas Kohanim* commemorates the service in the Beis Hamikdash, where the *Levi'im* guarded the *Mikdash* and served under the *Kohanim*.

23   See *Minchas Asher, Devarim*, p. 12.

24   *Tamid* 25b.

25   See *Chagigah* 13b where this term appears.

young to perform the *avodah* in the Beis Hamikdash (under the age of thirteen), and the *pirchei kehunah* were above the age of thirteen. These Rishonim lend strong support for the opinion of the *Minchas Chinuch*. The *Mishneh Lamelech*, though, argues; he objects to the idea that the important task of guarding the Beis Hamikdash was left to minors, which fits with the opinion of the *Avnei Nezer*.[26]

Concerning the question of replicating the *Mikdash*, the Gemara learns a number of halachos from the *pasuk*, "*Lo saasun Iti elohei chesef veilohei zahav lo saasun lachem*—You shall not make with Me gods of silver and gods of gold; you shall not make for yourselves."[27] One of them is that it is prohibited to replicate parts of the Beis Hamikdash. For example, one is not permitted to make a house in the shape of the *Heichal* (the holy section of the Beis Hamikdash), a porch in the shape of the *Ulam* (the area in front of the *Heichal*), or a yard in the shape of the *Azarah* (Temple courtyard).[28]

The prohibition of recreating the Beis Hamikdash is codified in the *Shulchan Aruch*,[29] but only in terms of one with the same dimensions of width, length, and height. Based on this, Rav Moshe Feinstein permitted building a miniature model for students to learn about the Beis Hamikdash.[30] However, Rav Yosef Chaim Zonnenfeld, the venerable *rav* of Jerusalem in the early 1900s, was against this.[31]

---

26   *Mishneh Lamelech, Hilchos Beis Habechirah* 8:5. See *Beminchas Chinuch*, p. 294, where the Lubavitcher Rebbe explains that the *rovim* were qualified to serve as guards along with the "*ish Har HaBayis*," the chief supervisor of all the guards, whose supervision gave the *rovim* the status of *ish omeid al gabav* (a minor who is supervised by an adult attains the status of an adult for certain halachos).

27   *Shemos* 20:20.

28   The Gemara seems to say the source for this halachah is "*Lo saasun Iti*," prohibiting the replication of objects that are used to serve Hashem. The *Rambam*, however, seems to offer a different source. The *Rambam* codifies this prohibition in *Hilchos Beis Habechirah* 7:10, along with the halachos of *mora Mikdash*, the mitzvah to have awe for the Beis Hamikdash. This context suggests that the *Rambam* held that building a replica of the Beis Hamikdash was forbidden because it diminished the awe we are supposed to have for the real Beis Hamikdash.

29   *Yoreh Dei'ah* 141:8.

30   *Igros Moshe, Yoreh Dei'ah*, vol. 3, §33.

31   *Salmas Chaim, Yoreh Dei'ah* §440. The *poskim* debate if it is forbidden to use a replica that was built by non-Jews. See *Torah Ladaas, parashas Terumah*, vol. 1, p. 332. See *Beminchas*

A final comparison between the White House and *Har HaBayis* involves the airspace above them. With regard to *Har HaBayis*, Rav Ovadiah Yosef says that the airspace above it is an extension of *kedushas Har HaBayis*, and therefore it is prohibited to fly over it by helicopter or plane.[32]

Discussing security measures of the Beis Hamikdash raises the question of whether the commandment applies to *Har HaBayis* today. Rav Yitzchak Zilberstein quotes Rav Ben Tzion Abba Shaul, who explained (citing the opinion of the *sefer Mishkenos Laavir Yaakov*) that the mitzvah of guarding the Beis Hamikdash does apply today.[33] Based on this, Rav Abba Shaul ruled that if a Jewish soldier assigned to guard *Har HaBayis* is a *Levi* and is stationed next to one of its gates, he is fulfilling the mitzvah of guarding the Beis Hamikdash and, therefore, should be careful not to fall asleep.[34]

Chinuch, pp. 194–95, where the Lubavitcher Rebbe discusses the opinion of the *Minchas Chinuch* (254:9), who says that the prohibition of replicating the *Mikdash* does not apply today.

32   *Yabia Omer*, vol. 5, §26. The *Or Letzion* (vol. 3, §30:4) agrees.

33   See Rav Avraham Moshe Avidan's *Masa Behar*, p. 174, where he relates that when Anwar Sadat, the president of Egypt (1970–1981) visited Eretz Yisrael, he wanted to pray at the mosque on *Har HaBayis*. The IDF purposely enlisted religious soldiers to provide security for him, based on the ruling of the *Gedolim* in Yerushalayim that it is preferable for religious soldiers, who are careful about the sanctity of *Har HaBayis*, to ascend, rather than irreligious soldiers, who would not be as careful about keeping the laws regarding the sanctity of the area.

34   *Upiryo Matok*, *Vayikra*, p. 301. *Shu"t Or Letzion*, vol. 3, §30:4, says that any soldier who is required to guard *Har HaBayis* should make sure to go to the *mikveh* beforehand, and he should also not wear any unnecessary clothing, as they are *tamei*. This is based on the *Chazon Nachum*, who says, citing *Tosafos* (*Shabbos* 16b), that the clothing of an *am haaretz* is assumed to be *tamei* for those who are careful with the laws of *taharah* (ritual purity). Therefore, one's clothing is presumed to be *tamei*, since we all have the status of *amei haaretz* in this sense (since we no longer need to be careful with the laws of purity).

The *Karnos Hamizbei'ach* argues that we are not considered *amei haaretz* nowadays, since we are not required to be careful with the laws of impurity. And even if we are considered *amei haaretz*, the decree was not on the *amei haaretz* but on the *chaveirim* (very observant Jews) vis-à-vis the *amei haaretz* (Rabbi Aryeh Lebowitz, "Visiting Har Habayis" [May 12, 2015], www.yutorah.org). See Rabbi David J. Bleich's article in *Tradition* (Spring 1973), "Survey of Recent Halakhic Periodical Literature," pp. 191–92; *She'eiris Yosef*, vol. 4, §62; and Rabbi Shlomo M. Brody, *A Guide to the Complex: Contemporary Halachic Debates* (Maggid, 2014), p. 281, regarding walking on *Har HaBayis* today.

However, the *Tzitz Eliezer* cites a number of Acharonim who argue with this, including the *Avnei Nezer*.[35] The *Tzitz Eliezer* cites the *Olas Hatamid*, which says that although the *kedushah* of *Har HaBayis* remains today,[36] the mitzvah of guarding the Temple only applies to the actual Beis Hamikdash.

The *Avnei Nezer* says that it depends on the reason for the mitzvah. If the reason for guarding the Beis Hamikdash is to keep out non-*Kohanim*, then it would also apply today. But if it is meant to prevent people from stealing or contaminating the *keilim* (holy utensils), or for the honor of the Beis Hamikdash, then it obviously does not apply today, since we don't have the Beis Hamikdash or the *keilim*.[37]

Another proof that the mitzvah doesn't apply today, according to the *Rambam*, comes from what he writes in his *Sefer Hamitzvos*. When discussing the mitzvah to be in awe of the *Mikdash*, he writes that it still applies today. However, when listing the next mitzvah, guarding the *Mikdash*, he doesn't mention that it applies today.[38] The difference is that the obligation to guard the Beis Hamikdash involves honoring and respecting the physical edifice, but the mitzvah of being in awe of the *Mikdash* focuses on the *Shechinah* that dwells there, not the actual building.[39]

---

35   *Yoreh Dei'ah*, vol. 2, §449.

36   This is actually a matter of debate in the Gemara; see *Megillah* 10a and *Zevachim* 107b.

37   *Avnei Nezer*, *Yoreh Dei'ah*, vol. 2, §449.

38   *Mitzvas aseih* §21, §22. Based on this, the Gemara in *Berachos* 54a says that certain inappropriate conduct is prohibited on *Har HaBayis*, such as using it as a shortcut, carrying one's wallet there, and wearing shoes. There is a debate if all shoes or just leather shoes are prohibited. Nowadays, religious soldiers who have to patrol *Har HaBayis* wear non-leather sneakers, instead of their regular boots, and also go to the *mikveh* first.

39   The Lubavitcher Rebbe, however, holds that when the *Rambam* wrote that the mitzvah of guarding the Beis Hamikdash is to honor it, he didn't mean the actual building, but Hashem's presence that is strongly felt there (*Sichos, parashas Shemini* 5750). To support his opinion, the Rebbe points out that when speaking of the mitzvah to build the Beis Hamikdash, the *Rambam* says the mitzvah is to have awe, not for the Beis Hamikdash but for the One (Hashem) who commanded that it be held in awe (*Hilchos Beis Habechirah* 7:1). And the *Rambam* writes that the *Shechinah* has never left the site of the Beis Hamikdash. Therefore, the Rebbe says, it follows that the mitzvah to guard the Beis Hamikdash should still apply today as a way of showing respect and awe for the *Shechinah* that rests there. (There are many levels of Hashem's presence; the *Rambam* refers to Hashem's presence that

While the Lubavitcher Rebbe thinks the mitzvah does apply today, he agrees that it is not practical to place guards around *Har HaBayis* today. However, there is an aspect of this mitzvah that the Rebbe says we can fulfill today. We can all be guards over ourselves, as each of us is a miniature Beis Hamikdash, thereby demonstrating that the *Shechinah* rests in all of us.[40]

SUMMARY

The reason for the mitzvah of guarding the Beis Hamikdash is either to keep *tamei* people from entering or to provide honor to the Beis Hamikdash. There were twenty-four guards stationed around it, comprised of *Levi'im* and *Kohanim*. It is a matter of dispute whether or not children were eligible to guard the Beis Hamikdash and if the mitzvah still applies today. Finally, while constructing an exact replica of the Beis Hamikdash is prohibited, building a miniature one is permitted by some.

---

is hidden. We pray that we should experience Hashem's revealed presence very soon [*Binyan Tzion* §3, cited in *Tzefunos Haparshah*, p. 41].) Rav Moshe Sternbuch says that according to the *Rambam*, who says that the *Mikdash* retains its holiness today, the obligation to ensure that anyone who is ritually impure is sent away from the *makom haShechinah* applies today, and we should appoint guards outside the walls of *Har HaBayis* to represent the Jewish People and make sure that no one enters *Har HaBayis* in a state of *tumah* (*Taam Vadaas, Bamidbar*, p. 14).

40 See *Shemos* 25:8, which says that the *Shechinah* dwells within each of us.

THE KABBALAH PHENOMENON

IN THE NEWS

On October 13, 2015, Yeshiva World News ran a paid-for article about an Israeli Kabbalist who would be visiting the US.[1] The article mentions how this famous *mekubal*, who is also a *talmid chacham*, would be available to meet people to offer advice and blessings to overcome challenges they might be facing. The article concludes with the dates of his visit and a phone number to arrange an appointment.

If you think that these visits are limited to faithful Jews, you should read the article in the *Daily Finance* (now part of aol.com) entitled, "The Mysterious Rabbi Who Gave LeBron James Business Advice."[2] According to this report, James paid the Kabbalist a six-figure sum in exchange for a meeting to advise him on a major marketing deal he was about to negotiate. The *Daily Finance* quotes another report in the *Real Deal*, a real-estate-industry publication, that said the rabbi, who "had no formal business education, only speaks Hebrew and won't meet with women, is considered by Israeli real estate professionals as well as people in other professions and of different faiths to be a holy man."

Similarly, there was an article printed in *The Jerusalem Post Magazine* regarding another Kabbalist with many followers. This *mekubal*, nicknamed

---

1   Dovid Grossman, "Miracles in Our Times: Rabbi Tzion Menachem Coming to Town" (Oct. 13, 2015), www.theyeshivaworld.com.

2   Jeff Bercovici, "The Mysterious Rabbi Who Gave LeBron James Business Advice" (Aug. 10, 2010), www.aol.com.

"the X-ray" for his apparent abilities to see what others can't, is credited by thousands with an amazing ability to cure and bless people.[3]

What does the halachah say about learning Kabbalah? Is it appropriate to seek advice and *yeshuos* (salvations) from Kabbalists? How does one know if the Kabbalist is genuine or a fake?

A TORAH PERSPECTIVE

First of all, we need to understand what, exactly, is considered Kabbalah. The Torah given to Moshe at *Har Sinai* consists of *Torah Shebichsav*, the Written Law (e.g., Chumash), and *Torah Shebe'al Peh*, the Oral Law (e.g., Talmud). Within *Torah Shebe'al Peh* there are four levels: *p'shat*, the simple meaning of the verses; *remez*, deeper meanings that are hinted to in the text; *derash*, homiletic exegesis; and *sod*, Kabbalistic interpretations. The most famous Kabbalistic texts are the *Zohar*[4] and the writings of the Arizal, which fall under the latter three categories.[5]

Rav Yaakov Hillel, the Rosh Yeshivah of Chevrat Ahavat Shalom, writes that

> *Kabbalah is the the study of Divine inspiration and prophecy; ways of approaching God and cleaving to Him; God's uniqueness, providence, and hanhagah—how He reacts to our deeds in this world through His attributes of Lovingkindess (Chessed), Stern Judgment (Din), and Mercy (Rachamim); how a human being perfects the worlds by performing mitzvot.*[6]

He adds that it also involves the study of how and why Hashem created the world and the inner meanings of the Names of Hashem. Additionally, Rav Hillel says that it is technically possible to manipulate our world through a part of Kabbalah called *Kabbalah maasit*, practical Kabbalah.[7] Rav Hillel also notes that Kabbalah involves the study of

---

3   Larry Derfner, "They Call Him 'The X-Ray'" (July 14, 2011), www.jpost.com.
4   Rav Elyashiv said that the *Zohar* is not Kabbalah, it is a *peirush* on Chumash (*Vayishma Moshe*, vol. 5, p. 237).
5   Rav Chaim Kanievsky would often relate that it says in the *sefarim* that there is value to learning the *Zohar* even if one doesn't understand what he is studying (*Hasefarim*, p. 57).
6   *Faith and Folly* (Feldheim, 1990), p. 32.
7   *Dialogue* (Fall 2013), p. 50. Rav Moshe Feinstein (*Igros Moshe, Orach Chaim*, vol. 4, §3) writes

abstract concepts that are not meant to be studied by everyone. Only those who have perfected their character, performance of mitzvos, and study of Torah should learn these secrets of the Torah.[8]

To illustrate, Rav Shlomo Aviner was asked why most yeshivos don't learn Kabbalah.[9] Rav Aviner responded that the *Rema* says one should not learn Kabbalah until he has completely filled himself with the knowledge of the entire Torah.[10] Rav Aviner added that when Rav Yosef Shalom Elyashiv was asked about learning Kabbalah, he pointed to his stomach, smiled, and said that "there is still room" (for learning Chumash, Gemara, and halachah).

The *Shach* wrote that some say one should not learn Kabbalah before the age of forty.[11] Rav Aviner[12] notes that the Arizal learned Kabbalah before that age, as he died at thirty-eight. However, Rav Aviner posits that during the time of Shabsai Tzvi, the false Messiah, many people studied Kabbalah when they were too young to understand it properly,

---

that the *Zohar* was written in the era of the Tanna'im and early Amora'im and therefore can be useful in resolving disputes among the *poskim*. On the other hand, even though the Arizal was a great Kabbalist and is considered an Acharon, his opinions aren't used to resolve disputes among the *poskim*.

8   *Faith and Folly*, p. 33.

9   See Torat HaRav Aviner, Short & Sweet—Text Message Q&A #290, www.ravaviner.com.

10   *Rema*, *Yoreh Dei'ah* 246:4. Rav Aharon Kahn, a Rosh Yeshivah at Y.U., explains that one could understand the *Rema* (246:4) to mean that "when the *Rambam* (whom he is quoting) speaks about *Maaseh Merkavah* (*Pardes*), he is not talking about (the study of the) *Zohar*, he is talking about philosophy; he is talking about an understanding of the Ribono Shel Olam's governing of the world, which borders on the philosophy of the gentiles" (Rabbi Aharon Kahn, "On Learning Zohar" [May 14, 2017], www.yutorah.org).

11   *Shach*, *Yoreh Dei'ah* 246:6. "When he would visit Kfar Chassidim, Reb Shalom Schwadron shared a room with Reb Elyah Lopian. Once during that period, Reb Elyah said to him, 'I would like to pass on to you the fundamentals of Kabbalah as I have received them from the Leshem (Rav Shlomo Elyashiv).' Reb Shalom Schwadron tactfully refused his offer. 'Although I am already over forty,' he explained, 'I don't feel that I have sufficiently filled my belly with Shas and Poskim.' Several years later, Reb Shalom met Reb Elyah in Kfar Chassidim, and asked him if he would still transmit to him the fundamentals of Kabbalah. 'I am sorry!' Reb Elyah lamented. 'You've come too late. I am no longer in a position to transmit all that I have learned in *chochmas hasod*'" (Rabbi David J. Schlossberg, *Reb Elyah: The Life and Accomplishments of Rabbi Elyah Lopian* [ArtScroll/Mesorah, 1999], p. 82).

12   *On the Air with HaRav Shlomo Aviner*, #3 [28 Tishrei 5768], www.ateretmedia.org. See *Kiddushin* 71a, which seems to say thirty-five is the age requirement for learning *Toras hanistar*. The Gemara in *Chagigah* 13a, as explained by *Rashi*, seems to say fifty.

which led them astray. Along these lines, Rav Aviner cites the Mishnah in *Chagigah*,[13] which says that those who know Kabbalah must be careful with whom they share it.

Rav Ovadiah Yosef was also asked about the Kabbalah phenomenon.[14] Rav Ovadiah writes that the study of Kabbalah is extremely important for those who fear God, as the *Zohar* writes that one who learns the secrets of the Torah will merit great reward,[15] and he cites a midrash that says Hashem will ask us if we learned the secrets of the Torah (i.e., Kabbalah).[16]

However, Rav Ovadiah also references the *Rema* cited above that says this only applies to someone who is God-fearing and has already mastered the Gemara and halachah. Rav Ovadiah cites another statement of the *Rema* rebuking the people of his generation for running to study Kabbalah when they did not fully understand what they were learning and hadn't even mastered the basics of Torah, like Chumash and *Rashi*.[17]

Rav Ovadiah then says that those who do learn Kabbalah must make sure that their teachers are genuine experts in Kabbalah, as Rav Chaim Vital (the Arizal's primary student) warned people not to be misled by mistaken approaches to Kabbalah. Rav Ovadiah concludes by addressing institutions in which teachers who are not God-fearing or Torah scholars call themselves Kabbalists and teach it. He said, in no uncertain terms, that one should be careful not to learn from them. He also quoted the Gemara, which says that one should learn Torah only from someone who is righteous.[18]

There are a number of Chassidic leaders who have said that in the years prior to the coming of Mashiach, the Kabbalistic texts should be taught to the masses. For example, Rav Chaim Elazar Spira, the Munkaczer Rebbe, argues this point explicitly.[19]

---

13   2:1.

14   *Yechaveh Daat, Yoreh Dei'ah*, vol. 4, §47.

15   *Zohar, parashas Pekudei* 247b.

16   *Midrash Shocher Tov, Mishlei* §10.

17   *Toras Ha'olah* 3:4.

18   *Chagigah* 16b.

19   *Minchas Elazar*, vol. 1, §50.

Often people will claim to be Kabbalists with the ability to bring salvation to others through their knowledge of *Kabbalah maasit*. Rav Hillel offers guidelines to determine if someone is a true Kabbalist or a fake.[20]

Rav Hillel cites Rav Chaim Vital, who says that the prerequisites to studying Kabbalah are being of great sanctity, having a profound knowledge of the revealed Torah (Tanach, Talmud, halachah), having an exceptionally refined character, and being meticulous in the fulfillment of mitzvos. Rav Hillel notes that many Kabbalists today not only have little knowledge of Kabbalistic texts, but are also ignorant of the revealed Torah altogether.

Additionally, Rav Hillel says that real Kabbalists distribute significant amounts to charity, spend their time learning and teaching Torah, and are not interested in publicity. Fake Kabbalists are motivated by a desire for power and wealth and seek out vulnerable people. They present themselves as Kabbalists who can fix people's lives, and at times even advise them to ignore doctors' orders, promising them that for a sum of money their problems will go away. Some of these Kabbalists can even be found on Forbes Israel's list of the top ten richest rabbis.

Lastly, true Kabbalists are first recognized by other Torah scholars and leaders and *then* they ultimately become known to the masses as well.[21] Moshe Rabbeinu is an example of this rule. The *pasuk* says, "Moshe was great in the Land of Egypt, in the eyes of Pharaoh's servants, and in the eyes of the nation."[22] The *Meshech Chochmah* there points out that Moshe was first noticed as a righteous, wise person by Pharaoh's elite and scholarly noblemen. Then, news of him spread to the rest of the Egyptians. This sets him apart from a person who stands out for his strange and wondrous acts that get the attention of the common people first, a phenomenon that would not prove that he is a genuinely great person.

The following story about Rav Moshe Feinstein clarifies who a true Kabbalist is:

---

20   *Dialogue* (Fall 2013), pp. 51–54.
21   *Faith and Folly*, p. 89.
22   *Shemos* 11:3.

A stranger claiming Kabbalistic powers had frightened some-one terribly by accosting him suddenly and announcing that it had been revealed to him that one of the man's close relatives was deathly ill. The stranger told the man that his relative's illness would soon become apparent unless the family followed an order of prayer and repentance that he would prescribe. The man accepted all the stranger had said as fact. However, he asked someone close to Reb Moshe to relate the story to the Rosh Yeshivah and ask if any additional repentance was neces-sary. After hearing the story, Reb Moshe was visibly upset. He said the man has nothing to worry about. The stranger's telling of his "revelation" in a manner that frightened the poor man so shows a total lack of sensitivity on his part. He is lacking in middos, and Hashem does not communicate with someone lacking in middos.[23]

At the end of the day, it's most important to remember, *"Tamim ti-heyeh im Hashem Elokecha—*Be wholehearted with Hashem, your God."[24] We ultimately place our faith in Hashem and pray to Him to help us. We must realize that blessing and salvation come only from Hashem.

SUMMARY

According to the *Rema*, one shouldn't learn Kabbalah until he has mastered the entire Torah (Gemara and halachah). Additionally, Rav Ovadiah Yosef writes that one should only learn Kabbalah from a teacher who is God-fearing, which, he notes, is unfortunately not easy to find. However, Rav Yaakov Hillel offers helpful guidelines in order to properly identify a true Kabbalist. Finally, Chassidic leaders have argued that in the generation prior to Mashiach, Kabbalah should be studied by the masses.

---

23   Rabbi Shimon Finkelman, *Reb Moshe: The Life and Ideals of HaGaon Rabbi Moshe Feinstein* (ArtScroll/Mesorah, 2012), pp. 473–74.

24   *Devarim* 18:13.

THE KOSHER SHABBOS GOY

IN THE NEWS

In March of 2016, the Jewish Telegraphic Agency ran a story entitled "These May Be America's Proudest Shabbos Goys."[1] The article reports about an interesting relationship between Samir Patel, a non-Jewish Hindu manager of Suhag Wine and Liquors in Kew Gardens Hills, Queens, and the local Jewish community. Patel volunteers as a *Shabbos goy* for the religious Jews of the neighborhood. The store even has a sign that reads, "Shabbos goy. If you need help on Shabbos, please ask us."

When Jews stop by for a *Shabbos goy*, he leaves his store and accompanies them to their houses. In the article, he explains what he does for them: "If someone needs anything, we go and do it for them. They might need us to turn off a stove. Or they left the fridge light on. Sometimes kids turn the light on by mistake." He said that he makes at least five such visits per weekend and doesn't charge for the help.

A local *Shabbos goy* like Patel isn't a rare occurrence; Jewish communities around the world have official *Shabbos goys*. Many famous politicians and celebrities, such as former New York governor Mario Cuomo, former US Secretary of State General Colin Powel, and singer Elvis Presley, once had the honor of being the local *Shabbos goy*.[2] Kareem Abdul-Jabbar's father, Ferdinand Lewis Alcindor, Sr., was also a neighborhood *Shabbos goy* in Brooklyn, New York.[3]

---

1   Uriel Heilman, "These May Be America's Proudest Shabbos Goys" (March 13, 2006), www. jta.org.

2   Raymond Apple, "Looking for a Shabbos Goy" (Feb. 24, 2016), www.jpost.com.

3   I heard this from Shlomo Katz, who heard it from Kareem's father.

Is it really permitted to make use of the services of a *Shabbos goy*? And, if so, are there any instances when it is prohibited?

A TORAH PERSPECTIVE

This subject is complex. To understand the issues involved, we are going to mention a few basic rules.

The primary rule is that it is a Rabbinical prohibition to *directly* ask a gentile to do any *melachah*, forbidden activities, for you on Shabbos.[4] This is known as *amirah lenochri*.[5] However, hinting to the gentile to do *melachah* is permitted under certain circumstances.[6]

There are at least two types of hints—one is permitted and the other forbidden. The forbidden type is when a command or request is made; this is called *remez derech tzivui*. For example, if the light is on and you want to go to sleep, and you say to the non-Jew, "Can you help me out?"—this is not considered a hint, but a request, and is prohibited on Shabbos just the same as *amirah lenochri*.[7]

Another type of hint is when it is not in the form of a command; this is called *remez shelo bederech tzivui*. An example of this is if you say to the non-Jew, "The lights are on, and I want to go to sleep." This is

---

4   There are three primary reasons given for this prohibition. *Rashi* in *Shabbos* 121a says that it is considered as if the gentile is a *shaliach*, an agent, of the Jew who told him to do the *melachah*, and therefore it is considered as if the Jew did the *melachah* himself. *Rashi* in *Avodah Zarah* 15a offers another reason, based on the *pasuk* where Chazal learn that it is prohibited to discuss forbidden activities on Shabbos (*Yeshayah* 58:13). According to this, telling a gentile to do a *melachah* is forbidden because the very mention of the *melachah* is *assur*. The *Rambam* (Hilchos Shabbos 6:1) says the reason is so you don't come to treat the Shabbos prohibitions lightly and ultimately violate the *melachos* yourself.

5   There are, however, a number of exceptions where it is permissible to ask a gentile directly to do a Rabbinically prohibited *melachah* for you, such as if there is a major financial loss involved (see *Mishnah Berurah* 307:22). It is even permitted to ask a gentile to do a *melachah d'Oraisa*—a Biblically forbidden activity—for someone who is sick (see *Shulchan Aruch, Orach Chaim* 328:17; *Mishnah Berurah* 328:47).

6   Even when it is permitted to hint, it is only permitted to hint to do a *melachah* that doesn't provide you any direct benefit. For example, you may not hint to a gentile to turn on the light in a dark room (*Shulchan Aruch, Orach Chaim* 276:1) because you directly benefit from the light, but you can hint to him to turn off the light, since the lack of light is an indirect benefit (ibid. 334:25; *Mishnah Berurah* 334:61).

7   *Rema, Orach Chaim* 307:22; *Mishnah Berurah* 307:76.

permissible, since you are not instructing the gentile to do anything for you, and you are not mentioning the intended *melachah*.[8]

There is another component to this subject that is very common, yet many people are unfamiliar with the pertinent halachah.

The *Shulchan Aruch* states that if one will suffer a financial loss (for example, Jewish-owned merchandise was left outdoors and it is about to rain, which will damage the merchandise), it is permissible to instruct a non-Jew to come to your house.[9] This is permissible even though it is clear that this instruction will lead the non-Jew to save the Jew's possessions, an activity a Jew is not permitted to do on Shabbos.[10]

The *Shulchan Aruch* then says that some only permit this in the case of a fire destroying one's possessions, but not for the sake of convenience. The rationale of the *Shulchan Aruch* is very clear: When the non-Jew arrives at your home, he will realize that you instructed him to come in order to do a *melachah*. In that case, the very instruction to come to your home is tantamount to instructing him to do the *melachah* for you, which is *amirah lenochri*, and Chazal only permitted this in a case of extreme property loss.

The *Rosh*, too, seems to say that one is not permitted to instruct a gentile to come to one's house if as soon as he comes he will understand what *melachah* it is he needs to do, since the act of instructing him to come is considered a command to do *melachah* (*remez bederech tzivui*).[11] Based on this *Rosh*, the *P'ri Megadim* says that unless there is a financial loss, one may not even instruct a gentile to come to one's house to hint for him to do *melachah*, since telling him to come to the house is *remez derech tzivui*.[12]

---

8   *Mishnah Berurah* 307:76.

9   *Orach Chaim* 307:19. See also *Orach Chaim* 334:26.

10   The *Mishnah Berurah* (307:69) says that Chazal were lenient in the case of monetary loss since they knew that people are very concerned about their money and without this leniency they would end up saving their possessions themselves, which could lead to Biblical Shabbos violations.

11   *Rosh, Shabbos* 16:10.

12   *Eishel Avraham* 307:27.

Rav Asher Weiss says,[13] in the name of Rav Shlomo Zalman Auerbach, that in accordance with these rulings, it should be prohibited to ask a gentile to come to one's house and then hint for him to do certain forbidden activities. Rav Weiss didn't want to publicize this ruling since it is contrary to the *minhag ha'olam*, common practice.

Rav Weiss himself concludes that instructing a gentile simply to come to your house is not a problem of *remez bederech tzivui*. He claims that this is only forbidden because of *remez bederech tzivui* if the gentile will immediately realize that he needs to do a *melachah* for you (such as if he arrives and sees a fire), because this would be like instructing him to do an obvious *melachah*. However, if you were to ask the gentile to come to your house, and upon arrival he will have no idea why you wanted him to come until you hint it to him, there would be no issue with asking him to come to your house.

On the other hand, the *Orchos Shabbos*[14] says, in the name of Rav Shlomo Zalman's son, Rav Shmuel Auerbach, that even if the gentile doesn't immediately understand what *melachah* is needed for him to do, it still might be prohibited to invite him to come to your house. This is because when you instruct the gentile to come to your house and he agrees, he is likely to do whatever you hint to him to do upon his arrival. For all intents and purposes, this is considered instructing him to do that *melachah* for you—*remez derech tzivui*.

Therefore, according to the *Orchos Shabbos*, one should not directly tell a *Shabbos goy* to come to his house, but rather he should hint to him to come. This way, the hint to come and the hint to do a *melachah* do not combine to be considered *remez bederech tzivui*. Therefore, similar to the earlier example, one should say the light is on in the house and you can't fall asleep, and the non-Jew will realize on his own what it is you need and will come to your house to turn off the light.

---

13   *Minchas Asher, parashas Bo* §18:2.
14   Vol. 2, pp. 440–41.

SUMMARY

It is generally prohibited for a Jew to ask a gentile to perform activities that are prohibited for the Jew on Shabbos. However, a Jew may use a hint to ask a gentile to perform a *melachah* if it is not in the form of a command, doesn't mention the *melachah*, and has no concrete positive benefit for the Jew.

The *poskim* debate whether or not it is permissible to ask a gentile to come to a person's home if he will subsequently hint that he should do *melachah* for him there.

THE LOST PARAKEET

IN THE NEWS

Once, in 2008, while a veterinarian was tending to it, a bird that had been lost said, "I'm Mr. Yosuke Nakamara." After the parrot provided Mr. Nakamara's address, as well, it was returned to its owner.[1]

In a similar story, another Japanese bird escaped and was found in a hotel, ultimately being turned over to the police. A few days later, Piko the parakeet told the police its address, enabling them to return it to its owner. Excited at the reunion with her pet, the owner told police that she had taught Piko to recite her address after having lost her first bird once before.[2]

It is a mitzvah to return a lost object to its owner. However, may one rely on a bird's recognition of its owner or the fact that it says its owner's name and address as evidence of ownership?

A TORAH PERSPECTIVE

Hashavas aveidah, returning lost objects, is one of the 613 mitzvos in the Torah.[3] Most of the halachos of *hashavas aveidah* can be found in the second chapter of *Bava Metzia*, entitled "*Eilu Metzios*."[4]

---

1   Meghan Neal, "Missing pet parakeet chirps his home address to police" (May 3, 2012), www.nydailynews.com.

2   "Lost Japanese Parakeet is Reunited with Its Owner after It Tells Police Its Address" (May 3, 2012), www.huffingtonpost.com.

3   See *Devarim* 22:3.

4   The *Ramban* (*Shemos* 18:15) writes that in the days of the prophets, people used to go to them for help locating their lost objects.

In his *sefer Chashukei Chemed*, Rav Yitzchak Zilberstein discusses a case similar to the one in the opening news story.[5] A person named Adam lost his parakeet. As he was walking down the street one day, his parrot spotted him and shouted his name.[6]

Does the fact that the parrot said its owner's name provide sufficient proof for him to reclaim it from the finder? Rav Zilberstein said that the answer can be found in discussions of the *poskim* on similar topics.

The *Rema* rules that if a bird flies away from its owner, and the owner is unable to retrieve it, the bird is considered ownerless, as it is assumed the owner gave up hope of finding it.[7] One would only be encouraged to return it *lifnim mishuras hadin* (going beyond the letter of the law),[8] provided that there is a valid *siman*, a distinguishing detail to verify ownership.[9] The question here is whether one can rely on the parrot's recognition of the owner as evidence of ownership.

There is a long passage in *parashas Naso* dealing with the halachos of a wife who disobeys her husband's warnings not to seclude herself with a specific man and does so regardless.[10] The Mishnah in *Maseches Sotah*, the tractate dealing with the intricacies of these halachos, says that if a bird reports that the wife secluded herself with that man, we believe the bird, and she is deemed a *sotah*.[11] The *Tiferes Yisrael* identifies this

---

5   *Chashukei Chemed*, Bava Metzia, p. 107.

6   See *Mesivta Shas, Peninei Halachah, Sotah* 48a, for a discussion of whether one is even permitted to have a parrot in his house. See also *Chukas Olam*, p. 411–13, for stringent and lenient opinions on this matter. Fascinatingly, Rav Yaakov Hillel (in *Faith and Folly* [Feldheim, 1990], p. 64) cites the *Nemukei Yosef* (to *Sanhedrin* 66a), who writes that the sages of the Talmud understood the language of birds and acted based on what they heard. The Gemara says that Rabbi Yochanan ben Zakkai understood the conversations of angels, demons, and trees (*Sukkah* 28a), and the Gemara in *Gittin* (45a) says that during the time of Rabbi Illish someone knew the language of birds. Rav Chaim Vital (*Shaar Hahakdamos*) says that the Arizal understood it as well. Also see *Upiryo Matok, parashas Shemos*, p. 78, where Rav Zilberstein cites Rabbeinu Avraham ben Shlomo, who remembers seeing a parrot in Egypt that was able to say many different *pesukim* from Tanach.

7   *Rema, Choshen Mishpat* 259:7.

8   *Shulchan Aruch, Choshen Mishpat* 259:5, 7.

9   See *Shulchan Aruch, Choshen Mishpat* 262, for what qualifies as a valid *siman*.

10   *Bamidbar* 5:11–31.

11   *Sotah* 6:1. This is how *Rashi* explains the Mishnah; some Rishonim explain it differently. This halachah is only the opinion of Rabbi Eliezer; Rabbi Yehoshua argues that one needs

bird as a parrot, whose nature is to report what it hears.[12] Therefore, with regard to returning lost objects, in our story the parrot should be believed and returned to its owner.[13]

The Gemara points out that we don't return money to people, even if there is a *siman* (distinguishing detail), since one who knows the identification marks may be a former owner who since spent the money, and it was lost by the new owner.[14] However, Rav Zilberstein says this concern only applies to coins, and therefore one need not be concerned that the parrot recognized Adam as being a former owner; it may be assumed that Adam is still the current owner, and it would be appropriate to return the parrot as *lifnim mishuras hadin*.

In fact, it would seem that there is an additional reason to obligate the finder to return the parrot to its owner, according to the letter of the law. In these cases, the parrots were trained by their owners to provide information in order to be returned in the event that they flew away. Therefore, it is likely that the owner never gave up hope of finding it, and the finder must return the parrot like any other lost object with a *siman*.[15]

In any case, because of *lifnim mishuras hadin*, it's appropriate to try to locate the owner of the pet. The idea of acting beyond the letter of the law might sound insignificant, but we find that Chazal considered it extremely important. The Gemara states that one reason for the destruction of the Beis Hamikdash was because the Jewish People did not act *lifnim mishuras hadin*.[16]

---

two witnesses to the seclusion. The *Rambam*, in his explanation of this Mishnah, says the halachah follows Rabbi Yehoshua, in which case the woman would not be a *sotah* based on the bird's testimony.

12   *Sotah* 6:1.

13   The *Rashash*, *Sotah* 31a, in explaining the *Rambam*, writes that parrots do not just repeat what they hear, but also sometimes understand what they see. Rav Zilberstein questions whether this *Rashash* can be relied on as halachah; see *Chashukei Chemed, Bava Metzia*, p. 108.

14   *Bava Metzia* 25b.

15   See *Me'iri, Bava Metzia* 24b, which says that we don't assume owners will give up hope on a domesticated bird, since they routinely return to their owners. See *Sefer Hashavas Aveidah Kehilchasah*, pp. 33 and 175, regarding how this mitzvah relates to gentiles.

16   *Bava Metzia* 30b.

SUMMARY

In general, if a bird flies away from its owner, it is considered ownerless, as it is presumed that the owner relinquishes hope of finding it. However, if there is a distinguishable feature on the bird that can verify ownership, returning it would be a fulfillment of going above the letter of the law (*lifnim mishuras hadin*). Therefore, if a parrot can recognize its owner, it seems that that would be sufficient proof, and it would be proper to return it. Furthermore, because the owner specifically trained the bird to identify and recognize him, he would be less likely to surrender hope of finding it.

THE MAGEN DAVID

IN THE NEWS

In August of 2014, Arutz Sheva reported on an anti-Semitic attack in Sweden.[1] While passing through a mostly Muslim neighborhood in Sweden, Anna Sjogren, a Swedish Jewish mother of four, was accosted, receiving multiple wounds to her body, head, and face.

"A Muslim girl saw that I was wearing the Star of David on my neck, and she started swearing at me and spat in my face. I got very upset and pushed her off," said Sjogren. Next, she felt something sharp strike her face, and, soon after, she was encircled and beaten by ten or more Muslims.

Sjogren added, "The Star of David is extremely meaningful and significant. I will never take it down no matter what happens."[2]

The Magen David—or Star of David—is the universal symbol of the Jewish People and deep emotions are connected to it. But what are the origins of this connection? Is there any reference to it in the Torah?

A TORAH PERSPECTIVE

The Gemara mentions the Magen David as a concept of shielding and protecting, but not as a six-pointed star.[3] It uses the term when describing Hashem's protection of David HaMelech and Mashiach, who

---

1   Ari Soffer, "Swedish Jewish Woman Savagely Beaten for Wearing Star of David" (Aug. 20, 2014), www.israelnationalnews.com.
2   The *Jewish Press* reported that Israel displayed a giant Magen David on Jerusalem's Light Bridge for Yom Hazikaron and Yom Ha'atzmaut in 2015 ("Raising the Star" [April 7, 2015], www.jewishpress.com).
3   *Pesachim* 117b.

will descend from David. Based on this, we conclude the third *berachah* after the haftarah, "*Baruch Atah Hashem, magen David*—Blessed are You, God, the shield of David."

An even earlier reference to the concept of Magen David can be found in *Nach*, where we find David praising Hashem for shielding him from harm.[4] But we don't find any clear source of a Magen David as a star there.

Rabbi Ari Enkin offers the theory that the Magen David refers to an actual star-shaped shield used by David in war,[5] but this is unlikely, as there is a tradition that there was a *menorah* on David's shield.[6]

With regard to the Magen David, Rabbi Yirmiyahu Ullman wrote on the Ohr Somayach website:

> A Shield of David has been found on a Jewish tombstone in southern Italy dating as early as the third century CE. A Tanach dated 1307 belonging to Rabbi Yosef bar Yehudah ben Marvas from Toledo, Spain, is decorated with a Shield of David. In 1460, the Jews of Hungary received King Mathios Kuruvenus with a red flag on which were two Shields of David. A Hebrew prayer book printed in Prague in 1512 has a large Shield of David on the cover with the phrase, "Each man beneath his flag according to the house of their fathers...and he will merit to bestow a bountiful gift on anyone who grasps the Shield of David." In addition, flags with the Shield of David apparently adorned the synagogues of Prague.[7]

The Gemara says that when David's life was in danger, Hashem performed two miracles to save him, one above ground (David was suspended in the air) and one below ground (the ground protected him).[8] The *sefer Otzar Hayedios* suggests that this may be the source for the

---

4   *Shmuel II* 22:36; *Tehillim* 18:36.
5   *Halachah Bilvad*, vol. 3, p. 264; see there for a great essay on this topic.
6   *Agra D'pirka* §176, cited in *Minhag Yisrael Torah, Orach Chaim* 90:4.
7   Rabbi Yirmiyahu Ullman, Ask the Rabbi, "Magen David" (April 5, 2008), www.ohr.edu.
8   *Sanhedrin* 95a. The ground miraculously softened, protecting David from being crushed by his enemy (*Rashi, Sanhedrin* 95a).

Magen David that has six points.[9] A human being can protect another from four directions; however, Hashem protected David from six directions (right, left, front, back, top, and bottom). Therefore, perhaps the Magen David, which has six points, alludes to Hashem protecting him from six directions.

Similarly, Rav Moshe Feinstein explains that although there is no known source for the Magen David, it represents the fact that Hashem rules in all six directions.[10] The reason it is associated with David, says Rav Moshe, is perhaps because David exhibited faith in Hashem as the Ruler of the universe and relied on Him when fighting wars. This faith helped David to not fear the kings he was battling.

Highlighting the significance of the Magen David as a Jewish symbol, Rav Yitzchak Zilberstein mentions a letter he received with a fascinating question:[11]

> *The letter was accompanied by a photograph of an Arab-looking man whose hand was tattooed with a Star of David... His mother, who was Jewish, had been abducted...and had been forced to marry a Muslim. To prevent her Jewish son from marrying a Muslim woman...the mother had tattooed a Star of David onto her son's hand, so that he would know that he was a Jew and would not be able to marry a Muslim. The man, who lived in an Egyptian village, had to conceal the tattoo on his hand all his life so that he would not be murdered...*

The halachic question that arose in connection with this letter was: In such a situation, was it permissible for a mother to tattoo her son's hand [a transgression of a Torah prohibition], in order to prevent him from intermarrying?

Rav Zilberstein responded that "it is certainly a great mitzvah to prevent a Jew from intermarrying among the gentiles. This was especially

---

9   *Otzar Hayedios* (Rav Yechiel Michel Stern), vol. 2, p. 7.
10   *Igros Moshe, Orach Chaim*, vol. 3, §15.
11   *Aleinu Leshabei'ach, parashas Kedoshim*, pp. 291–92; see also *Chashukei Chemed, Pesachim*, p. 427.

true because the tattoo of the Star of David was an image, not written with letters."[12] Also, since "the mother tattooed her son's hand so that he should not escape, i.e., from Judaism…her action would not be considered a violation of the Torah's prohibition."

SUMMARY

The Star of David has been a Jewish icon for centuries. However, the term is mentioned in the Gemara to mean a shield of protection for David HaMelech, not a six-pointed star. Elsewhere, the Gemara mentions Hashem miraculously saving David HaMelech from his enemies in all six directions, which may be a reference to the six-pointed star that is commonly referred to as the Magen David.

---

12   See *Pischei Teshuvah, Yoreh Dei'ah* §180, in the name of the *Me'il Tzedakah*, who says that the Biblical prohibition of tattoos is only when tattooing letters. See also "Removing Tattoos" above, where the issue of whether one is obligated to remove a tattoo is discussed.

THE REAL COMPETITION

IN THE NEWS

According to *The New York Times Magazine*, India has an obsession with world records. An article entitled "Why Is India So Crazy for World Records?" claimed that almost one-tenth of all world records submitted to Guinness World Records are from India. "In 2013, Indians applied for roughly 3,000 records, just behind the US and England."

A number of these records involved "mass participation," something "easy to come by" in India. Records include "the biggest blood drive (61,902 donors) and the largest motorcycle pyramid (201 men and 10 motorcycles)." Individual records include "the guitar performance on Mount Everest; the 103-character sentence typed out, in 47 seconds, with a nose; the limbo skating under a row of 39 parked cars."[1]

Nikhil Shukla, India's sole representative for Guinness World Records, theorized why India is more competitive than other countries. He explained that it stems from India's large population. Therefore, for example, people are always competing with each other—for "food-subsidy cards, train bookings, parking spots, public housing." Shukla believes that the daily contention among Indians has naturally led to competition for setting world records.

On a more somber note, on July 27, 2015, *The New York Times* published an article about the tremendous pressure on college campuses in

---

1   Samantha Subramanian, "Why Is India So Crazy for World Records?" (Jan. 23, 2015), www.nytimes.com.

the US entitled "Suicide on Campus and the Pressure of Perfection."[2] The article cites the Center for Collegiate Mental Health at Penn State University, which acknowledges that anxiety and depression, in that order, are more prevalent than any other mental health issues that university students face. Addressing the reason for this, the article states:

> *In 1954, the social psychologist Leon Festinger put forward the social comparison theory, which posits that we try to determine our worth based on how we stack up against others. In the era of social media, such comparisons take place on a screen with carefully curated depictions that don't provide the full picture...*
>
> *Gregory T. Eells, director of counseling and psychological services at Cornell University, believes social media is a huge contributor to the misperception among students that peers aren't also struggling. When students remark during a counseling session that everyone else on campus looks happy, he tells them: "I walk around and think, 'That one's gone to the hospital. That person has an eating disorder. That student just went on antidepressants.' As a therapist, I know that nobody is as happy or as grown-up as they seem on the outside."*

On a lighter note, let's turn to professional sports. The scene is Quicken Loans Arena in downtown Cleveland, Ohio, just before the beginning of game 3 of the 2015 NBA Finals. Cleveland Cavaliers superstar LeBron James approaches center court to start the game when he stops and bows to Jim Brown, the legendary Hall of Fame fullback for the Cleveland Browns, seated at the side of the court. Brown said of James's gesture, "It was one of my favorite sports moments of all time. He didn't have to be thinking about me, so for him to even have the brilliance to show that kind of respect... It doesn't happen too many times in my life."[3]

2   Julie Scelfo, "Suicide on Campus and the Pressure of Perfection" (July 27, 2015), www.nytimes.com.

3   Pat McManamon, "Jim Brown Honored by LeBron James Acknowledgment before Game 3" (June 11, 2015), www.espn.com.

Astonishingly, despite having had an extremely successful professional football career, Jim Brown felt that James's bow to him was one of his best sports moments ever. Clearly, Brown feels that the recognition of others helps make him successful.

What does the Torah say about competing and comparing ourselves to other people?

A TORAH PERSPECTIVE

In *parashas Vayishlach*, the Torah discusses the battle between Yaakov and the *saro shel Esav*, Esav's ministering angel. The *pasuk* describes the scene of the battle: "And Yaakov was left alone, and the man fought with him until dawn."[4] The term used by the Torah for Yaakov being alone is *levado*. The midrash brings another place where the word *levado* is used, this time in reference to Hashem: "And Hashem will be exalted alone (*levado*) on that day."[5] This midrash is very cryptic—what is the association between Yaakov being alone with the *saro shel Esav* and Hashem?

Rav Yerucham Levovitz, the famous *mashgiach* of the Mir Yeshivah in Poland, explains the connection between *levado* used in reference to Hashem and to Yaakov.[6] The lesson is that Yaakov was emulating this attribute of Hashem to be *levado*, independent. Yaakov developed the characteristic of independence in what he believed, similar to the independence of Hashem from all other beings in the entire world, and with this power he overcame the *saro shel Esav*. That is what it means that Yaakov fought when he was *levado*, alone—not that he was by himself, but that he was an independent person, following his own beliefs and fighting for them.[7]

Rav Yerucham develops this idea further. The Mishnah cites Ben Zoma, who said, "Who is a wise person? One who learns from all people.

---

4   *Bereishis* 32:25.

5   *Bereishis Rabbah* 77:1, citing *Yeshayah* 2:17.

6   *Daas Torah, parashas Vayishlach.*

7   Similarly, it says regarding Avraham Avinu, "Avraham was one, and he conquered the land" (*Yechezkel* 33:24). This can be interpreted in the same way: because Avraham had Hashem's power of independence, he was able to "conquer" the world.

Who is a strong person? One who conquers his [evil] inclination. Who is a rich person? One who is happy with his lot."[8] Rav Yerucham says that the Mishnah is teaching us that in order to achieve wisdom, strength, and wealth, we don't have to compete against other people. On the contrary, it all depends on our attitude. A wise person is not someone who gets the best grades in school or into the best universities, since that requires other people to compete against; the wise person is someone who learns from others simply because of his thirst for knowledge. Similarly, a strong person is not someone who can beat up someone else; it's someone who can conquer his own internal desires.[9] Likewise, the rich person is happy with what he has, whether it's a lot or a little, irrelevant of how much others have. Achieving success with our *middos* and *avodas Hashem* is dependent only on ourselves and not other people.

Another illustration of this idea is the relationship between Moshe and Aharon. It is written, "These are Aharon and Moshe whom Hashem said will take Bnei Yisrael out of Mitzrayim."[10] There, *Rashi*, quoting the *Mechilta*, points out that sometimes the Torah writes Moshe's name before Aharon's, while other times it writes Aharon's first, as in this *pasuk*, to show that they were both equal.

Rav Moshe Feinstein is bothered by this *Rashi*.[11] How could it be that Moshe and Aharon were on the same level? It was Moshe, and not Aharon, who spoke directly to Hashem and received the Torah on *Har Sinai*! Moshe was the greatest prophet of all time, as it says, "And another prophet like Moshe will never arise."[12] So how could it be that Moshe and Aharon were considered equal?

Rav Moshe answers that Moshe Rabbeinu was indeed endowed with greater talent than Aharon (which is why he was given more

---

8   *Avos* 4:1.
9   This idea is brought home with the concept of *nazir*. A *nazir* is someone who refrains from partaking of grapes and wine. Literally, the word *nazir* means "separation," but it can also mean "crown." The message is that someone who rules over his own inclinations is considered a king and deserving of a crown (Rabbi Yonasan David Arenias, *Journey of Faith* [Shaarei Torah, 2013], p. 94, based on *Ibn Ezra, Bamidbar* 6:2).
10 *Shemos* 6:26.
11 *Darash Moshe, parashas Va'eira*, p. 41. See also *Darash Moshe, parashas Vayeilech*, pp. 166–67.
12 *Devarim* 34:10.

responsibilities), but since Aharon met his potential just as much as Moshe did on his level, in that sense he was equal to Moshe. Thus, both Aharon and Moshe reached their potentials and fulfilled their roles to the greatest extent possible; therefore, in the eyes of Hashem they were considered equal.

Hashem judges us against ourselves, not against anyone else. And someone of lesser ability who reaches his potential is greater in the eyes of Hashem than someone of greater talents who doesn't reach his potential.

Rabbi Bernard Weinberger explains that the true measure of success in this world is not what secular society says makes one successful. Rather, true success is when we are able to fulfill our potential by serving Hashem with the talents He gave us.[13]

This concept is illustrated by the famous story Chassidim tell about Rebbe Zusha of Anapoli, who used to say, "When I appear before the Heavenly court, they will not ask me why I wasn't like Moshe Rabbeinu. They will ask me, 'Zusha, why weren't you like Zusha?'"[14] The point is not for us to compare ourselves to others but to concern ourselves with fulfilling our own potential. Zusha wasn't expected to be like Moshe, since he didn't have the spiritual capabilities of Moshe. He was expected to fulfill his own potential and become "like Zusha."

Likewise, Rav Zelig Pliskin, who was a *talmid* of Rav Mordechai Gifter, the late Rosh Yeshivah of the Telshe Yeshivah in Cleveland, recalls that

---

13   *Shemen Hatov*, vol. 3, *Bamidbar*, p. 159, and vol. 4, *Bamidbar*, p. 252. The *Biur HaGra*, *Mishlei* 16:4 (cited in *Or Gedalyahu*, *parashas Bamidbar*), says that the role of the prophets was to reveal to each person his unique role in life, what his abilities were, what his special strengths were, and what he should fix in his lifetime.

14   Rabbi Joseph B. Soloveitchik believed this anecdote never occurred since it seems to contradict what the *Rambam* writes in *Hilchos Teshuvah* (5:2): "Every human being may become as righteous as Moshe Rabbeinu or as wicked as Yaravam..." The Rav then said, "They will not ask me why I wasn't Rabbi Soloveitchik, but why I wasn't like Moshe Rabbeinu. It is a frightening thought, but this is what the *Rambam* means" (Shaul Weiss, *Insights of Rabbi Joseph B. Soloveitchik: Discourses on Fundamental Issues in Judaism*, p. 157). However, based on the idea of Rav Moshe Feinstein cited above, perhaps when the *Rambam* says we can all be like Moshe Rabbeinu, he doesn't mean that we have to be as great as him, but that we have to fulfill our potential just as Moshe and Aharon did, and then we will be equated to Moshe and Aharon. See also *Chiddushei Halev*, *Vayikra*, p. 1.

Rav Gifter would insist that each and every *talmid* be himself, but at the same time be certain to utilize his full potential. He emphasized this point with an example from the Torah:

> *Yeast and honey were not permitted in the offerings on the Altar, but salt was. Rav Gifter taught that yeast makes the dough rise higher and honey makes things sweeter, but both are external additives. Salt, however, only brings out the food's existing flavor. When serving Hashem, we should follow the model of salt: we should be ourselves, but bring out the best flavor in ourselves and make every effort to be all that we can be.*[15]

Rav Moshe, who felt the same way, once asked a senior student of his to help arrange a match between the daughter of an esteemed rabbi and a younger student in the yeshivah. The senior student did not think this match was appropriate and told Rav Moshe that the prospective boy was not an advanced Torah learner. Rav Moshe was clearly upset by this response. Shocked, Rav Moshe asked, "How does one speak this way about one who studies day and night?" Rav Moshe's message was that the student "carried out his mission" by studying day and night, which is the most important quality he could have possessed.[16]

The Torah writes, "Bnei Yisrael should encamp, each man by his flag, according to the sign of his father's household..."[17] *Rashi* there brings two explanations regarding the nature of the sign of his flag. The first explanation is that each tribe had its own flag in the color of its stone on the *choshen*, the breastplate worn by the *Kohen Gadol*. The other explanation is that they had a sign handed down to them by Yaakov Avinu before he was *niftar* so that they could carry it when they stood around his body to bring it to the Land of Israel for burial.

---

15   Rabbi Yechiel Spero, *Rav Gifter: The Vision, Fire, and Impact of an American-born Gadol* (ArtScroll/Mesorah, 2011), p. 278.

16   Rabbi Shimon Finkelman, *Reb Moshe: The Life and Ideals of HaGaon Rabbi Moshe Feinstein* (ArtScroll/Mesorah, 2012), pp. 153–54.

17   *Bamidbar* 2:2.

Rabbi Bernard Weinberger explains the meaning behind this "sign." He quotes the midrash, which says that when Bnei Yisrael were at *Har Sinai*, they saw the holy angels in their holy encampments, and they, too, wanted to have special encampments.[18] Rav Weinberger explains that the idea is that Bnei Yisrael saw that every single angel understood his mission, and Bnei Yisrael wanted to know their personal missions in life too. That desire to understand their mission was the *os*, sign, that Yaakov gave the tribes.

Before Yaakov passed away, he told his sons how each of them could identify with a different quality of Yaakov's—that each one of them would be unique in his mission, but that they would all unite by fulfilling his wishes for taking care of his burial. Through recognizing one's unique purpose and mission in this world, a person doesn't become jealous of anyone else. This message enabled the different tribes to be united. That is why, says Rav Weinberger, the tribe of Levi didn't need their own flag—they knew clearly that their purpose in life was to serve Hashem in the Beis Hamikdash.[19]

SUMMARY

We, too, must realize that Hashem only demands of us what we are capable of doing based on the abilities and strengths He gave us and that someone else's talents have nothing to do with us.[20]

---

18   *Midrash Tanchuma, parashas Bamidbar* 14.
19   *Shemen Hatov*, vol. 3, *Bamidbar*, p. 159, and vol. 4, *Bamidbar*, p. 252.
20   See *Darash Moshe, parashas Va'eschanan*, p. 146.

THE UPS MATCHMAKER

IN THE NEWS

In May of 2014, the CrownHeights.info website published an endearing story:

> *This shadchan wasn't your typical matchmaker, but thanks to his persistence and some divine providence, a young Jewish couple was brought together. Meet Terry, your friendly neighborhood UPS delivery guy...*
>
> *Since he is constantly dropping by homes and businesses in the neighborhood and gets to know quite a few single young men and women, Terry is known to often try and make shidduchim.*
>
> *After dozens of different suggestions, this time it actually worked out!*
>
> *After years of making deliveries to the Eastern Parkway home of the Goldin family, which is just one block over from where Mrs. Regina Simon works, Terry began to suggest that Mrs. Simon's daughter Chanah "go out" with the Goldins' son Zevi...*
>
> *Last week the Goldin and Simon families celebrated the l'chaim of the new couple, and Terry's presence was once again hard to miss.[1]*

The question is, were the Goldin and Simon families obligated to pay *shadchanus* (a matchmaking fee) to the UPS driver?

---

1   "The Shidduch that Terry the UPS Driver Made" (May 6, 2014), www.crownheights.info.

A TORAH PERSPECTIVE

Rav Yitzchak Zilberstein tells a similar story, where a non-Jew was working in a Jewish home and left information on the table about a certain boy he knew from his time working in a yeshivah, thinking the boy would be a good match for this family's daughter. In the end, they got married, and the gentile worker, knowing of the Jewish practice to pay matchmakers, asked for his payment. The father approached Rav Zilberstein to know if he had to pay the non-Jew for setting up the couple.[2]

The obligation to pay a *shadchan* is like the obligation to pay any hired worker.[3] The Vilna Gaon says that one must pay a matchmaker, even if the involved parties didn't turn to him for help, but he proposed the match on his own.[4]

This is based on a concept found in the Gemara.[5] The Gemara says that a gardener can demand payment from the owner of a garden for the plants that he planted, as long as the garden was eventually going to be planted, even if the owner didn't hire the gardener.[6] The same is

---

2   *Upiryo Matok, Chayei Sarah*, pp. 215–17.

3   *Rema, Choshen Mishpat* 185:10; see also *Rema, Choshen Mishpat* 87:39 and 264:7. Rav Moshe Feinstein (*Igros Moshe, Choshen Mishpat*, vol. 1, §49) discusses the case of a *shadchan* who set someone up and was involved for a few dates, and then someone else took over. Would the original *shadchan* be entitled to *shadchanus*? Rav Moshe says that the obligation of paying *shadchanus* is based on the obligation of *sechirus po'alim*, paying a worker, and one has to pay the *shadchan*, even if he didn't hire him and even though he didn't finish the job. We see this idea from Moshe Rabbeinu as well. Moshe was rewarded for starting the mitzvah of burying Yosef, even though he didn't finish the job (*Sotah* 13a). See also *Hanisuin Kehilchasam*, pp. 169–70.

4   *Biur HaGra, Choshen Mishpat* 87:117.

5   *Bava Metzia* 101a.

6   *Tosafos* (to *Kesubos* 107b) holds that one must pay a person that provides him with a tangible benefit, even if the beneficiary did not explicitly hire the worker. The *Ritva* (*Bava Metzia* 101a) says that when it is obvious to all that you would like someone to do something for you, then you have to pay him, even if you didn't ask him to do it. Rav Yitzchak Zilberstein (*Chashukei Chemed, Bava Kama*, pp. 341–42) ruled that one would be obligated to pay a midwife who came on her own to assist another woman give birth at her home, even though the woman was planning to give birth by herself. Rav Shlomo Aviner (*On the Air with Rav Aviner* [J Levine/Millennium, 2009], pp. 176–77) ruled that a person would not be obligated to pay a security guard for voluntarily watching his car for him, since the car owner didn't ask him to guard it, and he didn't receive any tangible benefit.

true with *shadchanus*; a matchmaker can demand payment for making a match and providing this service to both sides, even if he wasn't asked to do so.[7]

However, in the above case involving the non-Jew, Rav Zilberstein says that one would not be obligated to pay the gentile the matchmaking fee. The reason is that it is not clear that the non-Jew initially intended to be paid for his efforts in arranging the match between the boss's daughter and the boy. After all, the worker left the boy's information anonymously on the table, since he knew that if he would have approached the boss directly, he would not have been taken seriously. When the Gemara says that one has to pay the gardener for the benefit he provided, that is when from the onset he did the work with the intention of being paid.[8]

In our case, as a rule, gentiles don't require paying someone who made a match, unless they were specifically asked to do so, like a dating website. Therefore, if the gentile demanded payment, it would seem that we could tell him that according to secular laws we are not required to pay *shadchanus*.

Although one may not be obligated to pay the non-Jew, it's best to give him a nice gift to show appreciation for what he did. It is always important to have *hakaras hatov* for the good that others do for us.

SUMMARY

There is an obligation to pay a *shadchan*. This applies even if the *shadchan* approached the families or couple of his own initiative. In the case of the UPS driver, if he didn't make the match with the intention of being paid, one may not be obligated to pay him.

---

7   There are some halachic differences between soliciting a matchmaker and being approached by one. One such difference is whether the mitzvah of *bal talin* (paying workers on time) applies (*Shu"t Halichos Yisrael*, §1–2, cited by Rabbi Yirmiyohu Kaganoff, "The Spurned Shadchan" [Aug. 19, 2010], www.rabbikaganoff.com). In the Sephardic community, the practice is that one does not pay for *shadchanus*. Therefore, an Ashkenazi who suggests a successful match for Sephardim cannot demand payment because Sephardim don't generally pay *shadchanim* (Rabbi Shlomie Dickman with Rabbi Tzadok Katz, *Shadchanus in Halacha* [Israel Bookshop, 2017], pp. 21–22).

8   See also *Hanisuin Kehilchasam*, p. 159; *Shach, Choshen Mishpat* 391:2; and *Shitah Mekubetzes, Bava Kama* 11b, cited in *Vehaarev Na*, vol. 1, p. 75.

TORAH ON THE MOON

IN THE NEWS

A May 2014 Matzav news article reported plans to send a *Sefer Torah* to the moon.[1] The project, called "Torah to the Moon," plans on sending the *Sefer Torah* to the moon as part of the Google Lunar XPrize mission, which aims at sending relics from Earth to the moon for safekeeping in case Earth ever comes to an end.

In addition to the *Sefer Torah*, two other major texts will be sent: the Vedas (Hindu scriptures) and the I-Ching (an ancient Chinese philosophical work). Paul Aouizerate, the man behind the mission, said, "This is an incredible, beautiful project. These three texts are among Earth's most ancient documents, created over three thousand years ago. They are significant to billions of people."

Aouizerate and his associates set out to collect $20.5 million for their project. One small difficulty that the team is trying to overcome is protecting the *Sefer Torah* from the effects of extreme temperature swings on the moon.

Coming back down to Earth, while it's not a full *Sefer Torah*, the holiness of a *mezuzah* gives it special halachos too. Matzav reported in January of 2017 that the Whitefish, Montana, police department placed a *mezuzah* on one of their main doors as a sign of solidarity with the Jewish community in the face of neo-Nazi threats.[2]

---

1 "Israeli Team Plans to Send *Sefer Torah* to the Moon" (May 26, 2014), www.matzav.com.
2 "Mont. Police Display Mezuzah after Neo-Nazis Threaten Jewish Community (Jan. 26, 2017), www.matzav.com.

Is it permitted to send a *Sefer Torah* to the moon? And is it permitted to assist non-Jews to place a *mezuzah* on their homes or offices?

A TORAH PERSPECTIVE

Rav Yitzchak Zilberstein was actually asked a question similar to the *Sefer Torah* question above.[3] A wealthy American contacted a *sofer* (scribe) to have him write a beautiful *Sefer Torah* for him, and the remuneration that he promised was very significant. The wealthy man revealed to the *sofer* that his intention was to send this *Sefer Torah* to the moon, believing this would be a big *kiddush Hashem*. The *sofer* approached Rav Zilberstein to ask whether he was allowed to write the *Sefer Torah*, knowing that this gentleman planned on sending it to the moon.[4]

Rav Zilberstein responded as follows:

The *Talmud Yerushalmi* says that a Persian king once sent Rabbi Yehudah HaNasi (Rebbi) a gift of a very expensive jewel, and he told Rebbi to send him something of equal value in return.[5] Rebbi sent the king a *mezuzah*.

The king said, "I sent you something very expensive, and you sent me something worth so little?"

Rebbi responded that our values are not the same. Furthermore, Rebbi said, "You sent me something that needs to be guarded, whereas what I sent you protects you, as the *pasuk* says, 'As you go forth, it will guide you; as you recline it will guard you...'"[6]

The Netziv asks how Rebbi was permitted to send a *mezuzah* to the gentile king, because the halachah says[7] that it is prohibited to affix

---

3   *Vehaarev Na*, vol. 3, p. 458.

4   See *Betzeil Hachochmah*, vol. 4, §142, regarding sending a *Sefer Torah* on a plane, a boat, or by mail. See also Rabbi Ari Enkin, *Halachah Bilvad: Halachic Insights and Responsa*, vol. 4 (Dalet Amot Publishing, 2010), p. 131, on transporting a *Sefer Torah*.

5   *Pei'ah* 1:1.

6   *Mishlei* 6:22. The *She'iltos of Rav Achai Gaon* (*parashas Eikev*, §145) brings this story with a postscript. The king had only one daughter, whom a demon entered and possessed, and none of the doctors were able to exorcise it. Once the king placed the *mezuzah* on his doorpost, the demon immediately left his daughter's body. (See the chapter entitled "The Dybbuk Exorcist.")

7   *Shulchan Aruch, Yoreh Dei'ah* 291:2.

a *mezuzah* on a gentile's doorpost.[8] This lowers the sanctity of the mitzvah object (because gentiles are not commanded in the mitzvah) and is a disgrace to the *mezuzah*.[9]

The Netziv answers that this only applies when the *mezuzah* was written with the intent to use it to fulfill a Jew's mitzvah. In such a case, one cannot send it to a gentile, since it is lowering the *kedushah* of the *mezuzah*. But Rebbi wrote this *mezuzah* with the express intention of sending it to the gentile king and not for Jewish use, and therefore there is no issue of lowering the *kedushah* or disgracing the *mezuzah*.[10]

The Netziv brings support for this idea from the *Yerushalmi*, which says that a *Sefer Torah* that is housed in Eretz Yisrael should not be transferred to the Diaspora,[11] but if it was written with the intent to be taken out of Israel, then it is permitted to do so.

---

8   *Haamek She'eilah* §145.

9   The Gemara says, "*Maalin bakodesh velo moridin*—We increase the level of holiness, not decrease it" (*Menachos* 99a). For example, the Gemara in *Shabbos* 79b says one may not use *tefillin shel rosh* for the *tefillin shel yad*, since that is lowering it from a higher level of *kedushah* (*shel rosh* has the majority of Hashem's Name on it) to a lower level of *kedushah* (of the *shel yad*). However, the *Rema* writes (*Yoreh Dei'ah* 291:2) that if a gentile will hate you if you don't give him a *mezuzah*, then it is permissible to give it to him. According to this, some Acharonim explain how Rebbi was allowed to give the *mezuzah* to the gentile king—because he feared that otherwise the king would hate him.

The *Rema* (*Yoreh Dei'ah* 291:2) is based on the *Maharil*, who writes (*Maharil Hachadashos* §123) that the concern for giving a *mezuzah* to a gentile is that if he is injured or a tragedy befalls him, he will say that the *mezuzah* didn't protect him and will come to degrade the *mezuzah*, causing a *chillul Hashem*. Another concern is that after the gentile's death his children may not have the same respect for it that he initially had. The *Nachal Eshkol* (*Hilchos Mezuzah* §23) writes that Rebbi knew that the gentile would not degrade the *mezuzah*. See *Mesoras Moshe*, p. 340, where Rav Moshe Feinstein invokes the ruling of the *Rema*. Rav Moshe also says that if the gentile believes that the *mezuzah* serves as a protection for his home, then Hashem will protect him in turn. See *Igros Moshe*, *Yoreh Dei'ah* vol.1, §184, for another explanation of why Rebbi was permitted to send the *mezuzah* to a gentile.

10   Similarly, Rav Moshe Feinstein writes that it is permitted to sell a *Sefer Torah* to Conservative Jews who don't keep the Torah but will honor and read from it, provided that it is a new *Sefer Torah* (*Igros Moshe*, *Yoreh Dei'ah*, vol. 1, §174). The reason for this caveat is that if it had already been used, it may be considered degrading it or lowering its sanctity by having it placed in the possession of violators of halachah.

11   *Yerushalmi*, *Sanhedrin* 3:9. Almost all *poskim* don't cite this halachah, including the *Rif*, *Rambam*, *Rosh*, *Tur*, and *Shulchan Aruch*. The *Chayei Adam* in *Shaarei Tzedek*, however, does codify it. See also *Shevet HaLevi*, vol. 2, §137.

Rav Zilberstein said that perhaps, based on the Netziv, one could suggest that if the *sofer* doesn't write the *Sefer Torah* with intent for it to have the sanctity of a regular *Sefer Torah*, but for the sake of sending it to the moon, then he would be permitted to write it for this gentleman.

However, Rav Zilberstein says that one could differentiate between the cases. The prohibition against giving a *mezuzah* to a gentile stems from the fact that one is lowering it from a higher level of *kedushah* to a lower level. Therefore, if the *mezuzah* was originally written to be sent to a gentile, then from the start the *kedushah* is a lower *kedushah*, and it would be permitted to give it to the gentile. The same is true with regard to sending a *Sefer Torah* out of Eretz Yisrael. If the *Sefer Torah* was written to be used in Israel, it has a higher degree of *kedushah* due to the greater holiness of the land, and by sending it out, one is lowering its *kedushah*; therefore, it is forbidden to do so. But if it was originally written for the Diaspora, then it is not such a disgrace to send it out of Eretz Yisrael, since there is a purpose in it being used by Jews in the Diaspora to fulfill the mitzvah of having and reading from a kosher *Sefer Torah*.

However, sending a *Sefer Torah* to the moon—even if it was written specifically for that purpose—is a tremendous disgrace to the *Sefer Torah*, because one is taking a kosher *Sefer Torah* and sending it to a place where it will never be used.

In addition to the halachic question involved in sending a *Sefer Torah* to the moon, let's consider the philosophical significance of man landing on the moon.[12]

On July 21, 1969, Neil Armstrong and the *Apollo* 11 crew made history with their monumental landing on the moon. Much literature has been written about the significance of this moment from a Jewish perspective.

The moon landing was broadcast throughout the world. Some didn't want to believe it. They thought that it was a contradiction to the *pasuk* in *Tehillim* that says the heavens are for Hashem and the earth was given

---

12   See *Genuzos Haparshah*, p. 169, where he explains why a Jew should not be an astronaut.

to mankind.[13] Rav Yosef Scheinberger, then the secretary of the Eidah Chareidis, was in New York at the time and went to visit Rabbi Joseph B. Soloveitchik to discuss the matter with him. Rav Scheinberger told Rabbi Soloveitchik that many residents of Meah Shearim were dejected over the news and asked for guidance.

Rabbi Soloveitchik cited the *Ramban* at the very beginning of *parashas Bereishis*, who comments that when the Torah says Hashem created the heavens and earth, the sun, moon, and stars are all considered part of the earth. The angels are not mentioned at all in the story of Creation, since they belong to the sphere of the heavens and upper worlds. So when the *pasuk* in *Tehillim* says that the heavens are for Hashem and the earth is for man, the earth includes the sun, moon, and stars. Rav Scheinberger related this explanation to the residents of Meah Shearim, who were very happy with this explanation.[14]

Rav Elazar Menachem Shach, Rosh Yeshivah of Ponevezh and a leader of the Chareidi world in Eretz Yisrael at the time, noted that while people are focusing on this great accomplishment of mankind, or in the Torah's words, "*kochi ve'otzem yadi*—my strength and the might of my hands,"[15] in truth we should be taking this opportunity to contemplate how great and vast the world really is, and how small mankind is in relation to it. Rav Shach reminds us that no matter how accomplished and successful we may be in this world, we should never forget how great Hashem is and how dependent we are on Him.[16]

Similarly, the prophet Ovadiah's warning to the nations of the world not to become arrogant can be applied here as well. As Ovadiah said, "Though you soar aloft like the eagle, and you set your nest among the stars, from there will I bring you down, says God."[17]

---

13 *Tehillim* 116:16.
14 *Divrei Harav*, p. 243.
15 *Devarim* 8:17.
16 Rav Shach, *Michtavim Umaamarim*, vol. 3, §253. Rav Yechezkel Abramsky was once asked what he thought about the American accomplishment of sending a rocket to a faraway star. Rav Abramsky said, "If a human being is able to accomplish that, just imagine what Hashem is capable of doing" (*Aleinu Leshabei'ach, parashas Shelach*, p. 234).
17 *Ovadiah* 1:4. Rabbi Natan Slifkin writes, "When the *Apollo 8* spacecraft was sent for the first orbit of the moon, a different approach was presented. The astronauts, upon being the first

Rabbi Menachem M. Kasher, author of *Torah Sheleimah*, believed that the moon landing was a fulfillment of what the prophet Yeshayahu said, that in the end of the days the moon will be embarrassed.[18] *Rashi* comments that those who worship the moon will be ashamed.[19] Rav Kasher elaborates that man once worshipped the moon for its majesty, but now, with the lunar landing, mankind has humiliated it by demonstrating his mastery of it.

SUMMARY

One should not have a *Sefer Torah* written in order to send it to the moon, as this is a disgrace to the holiness of the *Sefer Torah*. Additionally, in general, it is best not to aid non-Jews in affixing *mezuzos* to their doors. If this causes animosity against Jews, however, according to the *Rema*, it would be permitted.

---

people in history to see the earth from the heavens, did not mock that they could not see God. Instead, they delivered an altogether more humble message: 'We are now approaching lunar sunrise, and for all the people back on Earth, the crew of Apollo 8 has a message that we would like to send to you: 'In the beginning, God created the heaven and the earth.' They continued to recite several verses from Genesis. Astronaut Gene Kranz related that he was overwhelmed by the beauty of the experience. It is a remarkable example of poetic justice that the Russians, who scorned God, did not make it to the moon, while the Americans, who humbly recited the verses attesting to God's creation of heaven and earth, landed safely on the moon in 1969. Yet that extraordinary accomplishment became in itself a potentially dangerous cause for undue pride. 'Though you soar aloft like the eagle, and you set your nest among the stars...' prophesies Obadiah; when the Eagle landing craft touched down upon the moon, many people felt that man had truly become the master of the stars. But even from there, God brought man's pride crashing down with the terrible *Challenger* disaster of 1986" ("Space Odysseys," www.jlaw.com). See also *Sanhedrin* 109a for its relevance here as well.

18   *Yeshayah* 24:23. See *Hapardes*, § 44, vol. 1 (1969), cited by Rabbi Dr. Norman Lamm in *Derashot Ledorot: A Commentary for the Ages* (Maggid, 2012), *Genesis*, p. 16. For more on Rav Kasher's view of the moon landing and other opinions, see Rabbi Gil Student, "Man on the Moon" (July 22, 2014), www.torahmusings.com.

19   *Rashi, Yeshayah* 24:23.

UNORTHODOX COLLECTORS

IN THE NEWS

The *New York Post* reported on a surprising phenomenon that happened in New York. Under the snood and long skirt, the lady with the outstretched hand begging for "sedaka" wasn't really Jewish.

Realizing that the Jewish People are the most benevolent in the world, a new wave of panhandlers has discovered how to make an easy buck: dress up like a Jew. In fact, the *Post* reported that Vincent Maurizio has been soliciting charity at 13th Avenue and 43rd Street in Boro Park for nearly twenty years and said he once collected $750 over the holiday of Pesach.

Bernard Vei, an Orthodox Jew, explained, "We're good people; we always give. That's the problem—they think we have all the money in the world!"[1]

Has one fulfilled the mitzvah of giving tzedakah if one inadvertently gave it to someone who is not truly deserving?

A TORAH PERSPECTIVE

The Gemara records a debate between Rav Huna and Rav Yehudah on whether we investigate a person who begs for clothing, money, or food.[2] The Gemara says that we follow the opinion of Rav Yehudah, who holds that if the beggar is asking for food, we give him right away, since

---

1   Tara Palmeri, "Panhandlers dress as Jews to beg from Orthodox" (July 5, 2014), www.nypost.com.

2   *Bava Basra* 9a.

he may be suffering (it may be a life-threatening situation), but if he asks for clothing (or money), we need to investigate to verify that he is truly needy. The *Shulchan Aruch* codifies the opinion of Rav Yehudah and says we don't turn anyone away when asking for food. However, when it comes to giving money, we do investigate if the person is truly in need.[3] According to the *Tur*, "truly in need" is defined as someone who lacks the money to invest in business ventures as a livelihood.[4] The *Shevet HaLevi*, though, ruled that someone with a fixed salary that is sufficient to support himself and his family with basic needs, would not be considered poor, even if he doesn't have enough money, at that moment, to sustain them for the entire year.[5]

The Gemara tells a story about Nachum Ish Gam Zu, who was punished with severe bodily afflictions for not responding immediately to a poor man's request for food, and as a result, the poor man died of starvation.[6] The *Menoras Hamaor* uses this story as support for the opinion of Rav Yehudah that when a poor man asks for food, one should give him the food right away without asking questions.[7]

When Rav Shlomo Aviner was asked if one should give money to the beggars at the Kotel or to collectors who come to one's door, he cited this ruling of the *Shulchan Aruch* that states that we don't give money to people unless they prove that they truly deserve it. Letters of acknowledgment written by rabbis can easily be forged or invalid, so one should not be quick to rely on them. Rav Aviner says that 90 percent of collectors are likely frauds. However, with regard to providing

---

3   *Shulchan Aruch*, *Yoreh Dei'ah* 251:10. The *Mishneh Halachos* (vol. 13, §173) writes that although one is not obligated to do so, it is permissible to provide for collectors without verifying that they are truly needy. See also *Pesakim Uteshuvos* §249, p. 348, n. 54, on whether the responsibility to verify that the collector is genuinely poor is the onus of the collector or the donor. See there (§251, pp. 402–3) for more on verifying if the collector is genuine. See *Pesakim Uteshuvos* §251, p. 401, regarding a case where the collector is suffering from very cold or very warm weather due to his lack of proper clothing. Would one be obligated to give him clothing in such a case?

4   *Tur*, *Yoreh Dei'ah* §253; see *Pesakim Uteshuvos*, *Yoreh Deiah* §253, p. 413.

5   *Yoreh Deah* 5:138, 2:120.

6   *Taanis* 21a.

7   Cited in *Mesivta Shas*, *Taanis* 21a, p. 140.

food, we do so without investigating since it may be a life-threatening situation.[8]

What about someone who is truly needy but has the ability to work and support his family and chooses not to? Rav Moshe Sternbuch cites the *Maharshdam*, who was asked this question. The *Maharshdam* says there is no difference between someone who has money but doesn't want to support his family or someone who doesn't have money and is able to work to support himself but doesn't—in both cases you don't have to give them tzedakah. Rav Sternbuch says that it is clear from here that if a person is able to work and chooses not to, he is not called poor, and you are not required to support him.[9]

However, the *S'mak* writes that when the *pasuk* says, "You shall not harden your heart or close your hand from your needy brother,"[10] it means that you should not refuse to support a poor man by stating that he should go and get a job.[11] Rav Sternbuch points out that the *S'mak* is referring to a case in which you don't know the poor person's capabilities. But if you know that the poor person is fully capable of supporting himself by working, then you can certainly turn him away.

---

8   "Giving Tzedakah to Beggars," www.ravaviner.com. The *Rambam*, in *Hilchos Matenos Aniyim* 10:19, points out that anyone who tricks the public into thinking he is poor and needs tzedakah when he isn't will ultimately truly need tzedakah. Rav Yisroel Belsky seemed to have a different response to donating money to collectors who came to his door. He believed that if one was in doubt regarding the veracity of a collector's need, he should give tzedakah due to the possibility that the collector is telling the truth, and avoid causing him embarrassment. Furthermore, Rav Belsky said, "And if you are right and he is a phony—so you have given money to someone who is emotionally unwell. You can daven for him as one would for any sick person" (Rabbi Shimon Finkelman, *Rav Belsky: The Life of a Multi-dimensional Gadol: Rosh Yeshivah, Rebbi, Posek, Genius, Adviser, and Friend* [ArtScroll/Mesorah, 2017], p. 435).

9   *Teshuvos Vehanhagos*, vol. 6, p. 385, citing the *Maharashdam, Yoreh Dei'ah* §166. Rav Hershel Schachter agrees and says there is no mitzvah to give tzedakah to someone who has the ability to earn a living (*Jewish Action*, Fall 2011). The *K'li Yakar* (to *Shemos* 23:5) says there is no obligation to give tzedakah to people who choose not to work, and that is why the halachah only requires one to help load another's donkey if the owner is loading it as well, but not if the owner is sitting down and watching. See Dovid Lichtenstein, *Headlines: Halachic Debates of Current Events* (OU Press, 2014), pp. 34, 39, for other implications of this idea. It is not considered tzedakah to support someone who has money but refuses to spend it due to mental instability (*Vayishma Moshe*, vol. 4, p. 215).

10   *Devarim* 15:7.

11   *S'mak*, Mitzvah §20.

If the person won't be able to make ends meet even by working, though, then you should support him.

Rav Sternbuch adds that even when it is permissible to turn away a collector, one should still give him a very small amount of money. This is based on the *Rambam*'s statement that quotes the *pasuk*, "Let not the dejected turn away in shame,"[12] and says that it is forbidden to turn away a poor person who asks for money empty-handed; even giving one fig is enough.[13]

Rav Sternbuch also says that if you know that the person collecting has a family, although he is undeserving of your donation, you should support him nonetheless—his family shouldn't be punished because of his sins.[14]

Rav Yaakov Blau, in his *sefer Pischei Choshen*, writes that Rav Shlomo Zalman Auerbach ruled that if you are approached by someone for tzedakah, and you know for a fact that he is not a needy person, it is forbidden to give him tzedakah, even if you decide to give it to him as a gift. His reasoning is very simple: Since the collector knows he is doing something wrong (he's stealing by misrepresenting himself as a poor person), if you give him the money, you are violating *lifnei iveir*—causing or facilitating others to sin. This *issur* applies even if the person is not

---

12   *Tehillim* 74:21.

13   *Hilchos Matenos Aniyim* 7:7. Rav Sternbuch's application of the *Rambam* is difficult to understand because the *Rambam* seems to be speaking about a genuinely poor person; if he is not truly deserving, maybe the *Rambam* would say you don't have to give him anything. Perhaps Rav Sternbuch's intention when invoking the *Rambam* is to say that you should at least give a little money just in case the collector is in fact truly deserving, since it is not always clear. See *Pesakim Uteshuvos* §249, p. 347, for additional situations when one is not obligated to give tzedakah to a poor person, but should still not turn him away empty-handed.

14   Rav Sternbuch cites the story of a great rabbi, the Tchebiner Rav, who was once asked the following *shailah* by a factory owner. The factory was located in a secular neighborhood and hired secular workers, but if he would move his factory to Bnei Brak, he could hire and support religious people. Should he move the factory? The rabbi answered that he should not move his factory, because even if his workers didn't observe the Torah, it didn't mean that their children should suffer financially. Rav Yisroel Belsky stated that although one is not obligated to support someone who is capable of earning a living, at times one should do so, since the needy person's health may be in danger from the financial pressure the situation causes him (Rabbi Shimon Finkelman, *Rav Belsky: The Life of a Multi-dimensional Gadol: Rosh Yeshivah, Rebbi, Posek, Genius, Adviser, and Friend* [ArtScroll/Mesorah, 2017], pp. 440–41).

actually sinning, for example, if one gives him the money as a present.[15] Rav Blau, however, in his *sefer* on *hilchos tzedakah, Tzedakah Umishpat,* disagrees with Rav Shlomo Zalman and says he is not violating *lifnei iveir* by giving him money.[16]

In light of all this, has one fulfilled the mitzvah of giving tzedakah if one inadvertently gave it to someone who is not truly deserving?

The Gemara in *Bava Kama* says that if a person gives tzedakah to someone who does not really need it, he has not fulfilled the mitzvah of tzedakah.[17]

We also find that when the prophet Yirmiyahu prayed for the death of those who tried to kill him,[18] the Gemara says that he asked Hashem that if those people try to give tzedakah, He should arrange it so that they give to those who are undeserving so that they won't receive reward for their good deed.[19] The *Rif* explains that tzedakah can save someone from the punishment of death,[20] so Yirmiyahu was asking that they not be given the opportunity to properly perform the mitzvah of tzedakah and merit salvation.

Rav Yitzchak Zilberstein asks regarding this *pasuk* in *Yirmiyahu*, when Yirmiyahu davened to Hashem that his adversaries should encounter people undeserving of tzedakah, what type of undeserving people is the Gemara referring to?[21]

Rabbeinu Yonah says it refers to actual needy people who were

---

15   *Pischei Choshen*, vol. 5, p. 298. See also *Kiddushin* 81b.

16   *Tzedakah Umishpat* 2, footnote 57. If one gave money to a collector and then realized that he was not really in need, he is permitted to take back the money (*Pesakim Uteshuvos* §252, p. 402).

17   *Bava Kama* 16b. The *Chiddushei Harim* (*chiddushim* to *Shulchan Aruch, Choshen Mishpat* 97) explains that there is no *berachah* recited before performing the mitzvah of tzedakah since there is a possibility that the person won't actually perform the mitzvah, for example, if the recipient is not actually poor.

18   See *Yirmiyahu* 11:21–23.

19   *Bava Kama* 16b. See *Yalkut Biurim, Shabbos* 63a, p. 101, where the question is asked that since we have a rule that if one intends to do a mitzvah but does not succeed, it is considered by Hashem as if he actually did the mitzvah, then in the case of Yirmiyahu, even if their tzedakah money does not reach true paupers, perhaps they deserve reward from Hashem as if they gave tzedakah.

20   Based on *Mishlei* 11:4.

21   *Chashukei Chemed, Pesachim, Peninei Halachah*, p. 51.

unscrupulous.[22] Similarly, the *Yad Ramah* says that if you give tzedakah to those who are not *hagun* (i.e., who are immoral[23]), you haven't fulfilled the mitzvah of tzedakah.[24] Rav Zilberstein adds that the *Yad Ramah* is also referring to truly needy people who are not *hagun* (otherwise it would be obvious that you haven't fulfilled the mitzvah of tzedakah). Thus, giving tzedakah to genuinely poor people who are immoral is not a fulfillment of the mitzvah of tzedakah, not to mention giving to those who are not actually poor.

On the other hand, the *Nemukei Yosef* says that when the Gemara states that you haven't fulfilled the mitzvah of tzedakah when giving to people who are not *hagun*, it means that you knew that they were not really poor. But if you thought the person was deserving of tzedakah, then you would be fulfilling the mitzvah, even if they are not really poor.[25]

Rav Zilberstein said that based on this statement of the *Nemukei Yosef*, if someone gave *tzedakah* to another thinking he was poor and deserving of the money and found out he is not actually poor, the person still fulfilled the mitzvah of tzedakah, since at the time he gave the money he thought he was fulfilling the mitzvah. Rav Elyashiv, however,

---

22 *Rabbeinu Yonah*, *Avos* 1:2. The *K'li Chemdah*, *parashas Re'eh* 231, discusses whether he was referring to a rich person pretending to be poor or an actual poor person who was evil and a sinner.

23 See *K'li Yakar*, *Bereishis* 18:4.

24 *Yad Ramah*, *Bava Basra* §119.

25 *Nemukei Yosef*, *Bava Kama* 16b. Rav Asher Weiss (*Shu"t Minchas Asher*, vol. 2, p. 14) cites *Rabbeinu Yonah* who believes that one fulfills the mitzvah of tzedakah even when given to those who are not worthy. See *Eretz Hatzvi*, *parashas Ki Savo*, p. 219, for a similar conclusion. The Gemara in *Bava Basra* 8a also indicates that if you didn't know that the person was not deserving of the tzedakah, then you do receive reward for giving. (See the Mishnah in *Shabbos* 19:4 regarding a mistake when performing a mitzvah.) There seems to be a contradiction between the *Rabbeinu Yonah* that Rav Asher Weiss quotes and the *Rabbeinu Yonah* that Rav Zilberstein quotes—one holding that if a person gave tzedakah to an unscrupulous person he has fulfilled the mitzvah, and the other holding he has not. The *Nemukei Yosef* seems to reconcile these two statements of *Rabbeinu Yonah* by differentiating between a case where one knew the person was unscrupulous (and so he does not fulfill the mitzvah) and a case where one didn't know (and so he does fulfill the mitzvah). Along these lines, Rav Aviner ("Giving Tzedakah to Beggars," www.ravaviner.com) says that although the *Rambam* (to *Avos* 3:15) says that it's better to give a smaller amount of tzedakah to many people than a lot of tzedakah to a few people, because each act of tzedakah refines your personality and develops your good character traits, that applies only if the recipients are actually poor and the money is beneficial to them.

ruled that if one gives to collectors who don't have proper verification that they are truly needy, and it is common for there to be dishonest collectors, these donations cannot count toward tzedakah.[26]

Commenting on the *pasuk*, "You shall surely give him and your heart shall not be grieved when you give him, for because of this thing, Hashem, your God, will bless you in all that you do,"[27] the Dubno Maggid explains that we learn from here that one should not overly investigate someone who asks for charity, but rather give him the benefit of the doubt. By doing this, Hashem will hopefully act the same way toward us and not be overly exacting to determine if we are deserving of reward for the mitzvos we perform.[28]

Rav Hershel Schachter says that in general we should recall the Mishnah in *Pirkei Avos*[29] that says that "we are only trustees of HaKadosh Baruch Hu's money. We shouldn't act as if it is ours. [We must always remember that] everything belongs to the Ribbono Shel Olam—our bodies, our souls, our wisdom, and our property..." and that we are required to follow the halachos of how and when to distribute tzedakah.[30]

SUMMARY

According to the *Nemukei Yosef*, as long as the giver thought the collector was poor, even if he was not, the giver fulfilled the mitzvah of tzedakah. On the other hand, Rav Zilberstein explains the *Yad Ramah* to mean that giving to those who are not poor does not fulfill the mitzvah. Rav Elyashiv agrees with this ruling. Because applying the definition of "truly in need" is complex, one should investigate the situation and consult with a Rav before deciding that a collector doesn't qualify to receive his tzedakah.

---

26   Cited in *Pesakim Uteshuvos* §251, p. 401.

27   *Devarim* 15:10.

28   *Torah Ladaas, parashas Re'eh*, vol. 2, p. 389. Someone once asked Rav Shlomo Yosef Zevin if it was permissible to pass a bill to prohibit people from collecting money in front of a shul. Rav Zevin based his response on a teaching from Rav Levi Yitzchak of Berditchev, essentially saying that such an attitude was the Sedom mentality of cruelty and selfishness, which banned providing for the needy (Rav Yisrael Meir Lau, *Rav Lau on Pirkei Avos*, vol. 3 [ArtScroll/Mesorah, 2007], p. 829).

29   *Avos* 3:8.

30   Rabbi Gil Student, "Charity In a Changed Economy: An Interview with Rabbi Hershel Schachter," *Jewish Action* (Fall 2011).

WHO CHOPPED DOWN THE CHERRY TREE?

IN THE NEWS

On July 30, 2012, *The New York Times* ran an article about a Boro Park resident named Sheya Weider, who ran into a problem when he tried to build an extension to his house: a "big, shady tree."[1] It's not that he couldn't hire men to cut it down. The problem was that it was a mulberry tree, and the Torah prohibits felling fruit trees. Instead, Weider built the staircase of his new house in a way that allowed him to save the tree. Weider explained that "the rabbis wouldn't let me take it down...They told me if there is any possibility, even if it costs you money, you should work around it." According to Weider, the expense of saving the tree was over $100,000.

A similar incident occurred in the Midwood section of Brooklyn on East 27th Street, between Avenue I and Campus Road, as reported by *Vos Iz Neias?*[2] A huge mulberry tree stood in front of a Jewish home. The homeowner and the neighbors despised this tree because it "dropped sticky fruit on neighbors' cars and littered the sidewalk with a tacky, dark-purple paste that made residents walk in the street to avoid stepping in the mess." Still, he wouldn't take it down out of respect for the Torah. But on Saturday, August 27, 2011, the nasty tree met its fate. Hurricane Irene arrived and knocked down the giant mulberry tree.

---

1 Elizabeth A. Harris, "Instead of Taking Down a Fruit Tree, Building Around It" (July 30, 2012), www.nytimes.com.

2 "Brooklyn, NY—Neighbors Cheer Act of Hashem In Toppling Fruit Tree After Irene" (Aug. 30, 2011), www.vosizneias.com.

One more story, but with a different ending: A Lakewood boys' school, Shaagas Aryeh, wanted to build a new building in the middle of their nine-acre property, and once again, fruit trees stood in their way. In this case, there were twenty apple trees. Rabbi Shloime Chaim Kanarek, the founder of the school, searched for a solution to his problem and found one. He hired a company that owned special machinery to dig up the trees with their roots and some dirt, and he had them replanted at the edge of the property.[3]

Where does the Torah say that it is prohibited to chop down fruit trees? Were the people in these stories truly required to go to such extremes to avoid chopping down the trees, or are there some leniencies that they could have relied on?

A TORAH PERSPECTIVE

The source for the prohibition of destroying fruit-bearing trees is found in *parashas Shoftim*. The Torah states, "When you lay siege to a city for many days…do not destroy its trees by swinging an ax against them, because from them you will eat…"[4] The *Sifri* counts the prohibition of cutting down fruit-bearing trees as both an *aseih* (positive commandment) and as a *lav* (negative commandment). Besides the punishment of lashes (which is the standard punishment for violating a negative commandment), there is an additional punishment of *misah bidei shamayim* (premature death).

The *Sefer Hachinuch* explains why it is prohibited for us to cut down fruit trees:

> *The reason for this commandment is in order to train our spirit to love what is good and beneficial and to cling to it, and as a result good fortune will cling to us, and we will move well away*

---

3   "School Moves Apple Trees To Make Way for New Building" (Jan. 19, 2012), www.thelakewoodscoop.com.

4   *Devarim* 20:19. However, destroying trees in order to create a siege or to stop the enemy from using them is permitted (*Hasagos HaRamban* on *Sefer Hamitzvos* of the *Rambam*, *Mitzvos Aseih Sheshachach HaRambam* §6). Rav Asher Weiss (*Minchas Asher*, *Devarim* §33, p. 225) cites a debate on whether pruning dead branches of a fruit tree is prohibited. See *Aruch Hashulchan*, *Yoreh Dei'ah* 116:13, who is lenient. See also *Ramat Hashulchan*, p. 224.

from every evil thing and from every matter of destructiveness. This is the way of the men of piety and the conscientiously observant; they love peace, are happy for the good fortune of others, and bring them near the Torah. They will not destroy even a mustard seed in the world, and they are distressed at every ruination and spoilage that they see. If they are able to rescue, they will save anything from destruction, with all their power. Not so, however, are the wicked, the brethren of destructive demons. They rejoice in the destruction of the world, and they are destroyers... He who desires good and rejoices in it, his spirit shall abide in good fortune forever...[5]

This prohibition, though, does have its limitations.

The *Rambam* writes that it is permissible to cut down fruit trees if they are damaging other trees, if the value of their wood exceeds the value of their fruit, or if they are old trees that produce very little fruit and it's not economically worth the effort to continue harvesting them.[6] In all of these cases, it is permitted to cut down the tree, since the prohibition is only to cut them down *derech hashchasah*—in a destructive manner (i.e., for no constructive purpose).[7] However, the *Pischei Teshuvah* says that in these situations it is best to have a gentile cut down the tree.[8]

According to the *Chasam Sofer*, even if the tree is producing adequate fruit, if the value of the land is clearly worth more than the value of the

---

5   *Sefer Hachinuch*, Mitzvah §529. The Netziv in his *Haamek Davar* (*Devarim* 20:19) suggests another reason: since this world was created for us to benefit from it, destroying fruit trees that were created to provide us that benefit is counterproductive.

6   *Hilchos Melachim* 6:8–9, based on *Bava Kama* 92a. However, the *Darkei Teshuvah* 116:51 says that one may not cut down a fruit tree even if the fruit is infested with insects or is too sour to eat, since it has other uses too.

7   The *Machaneh Chaim* 1:49 says this is only permitted in a case of need. The *Chavos Ya'ir* §195, however, says it is completely permissible.

8   *Pischei Teshuvah*, *Yoreh Dei'ah* 116:6. Rav Shmuel Wosner rules this way as well (*Shevet HaLevi*, vol. 2, §47). Usually it's not permitted to ask a gentile to do something that is prohibited for a Jew to do. However, as Rav Wosner points out, we are not just relying on the fact that it's a non-Jew that makes it permissible; there are other factors as well that make it permissible. See *Yabia Omer*, *Yoreh Dei'ah*, vol. 5, §12:5, for a similar point.

fruit tree, it is permitted to cut down the tree.[9] However, it's not always clear whether the land's value will be worth more without the tree.

The *Chasam Sofer* also cites the *Rosh*, who says that if you need the area where the tree is located, it is permitted to cut it down.[10] Based on this *Rosh*, the *Taz* permitted someone to cut down a fruit tree on his property in order to build a house in its place.[11]

Another leniency is given by Rav Yaakov Emden.[12] He says that it is permissible to uproot a fruit tree on condition that one removes the entire tree, including the roots and enough dirt to sustain it, and then replants it somewhere else. The *Chasam Sofer* adds that even where it is permitted to chop down the fruit tree, if it is possible to transplant it, then there is no permission to chop it down.[13] Rabbi Yair Hoffman points out that some *poskim* don't rely on this alone, which may be due to the fact that not every tree that is transplanted will continue to grow.[14]

Rav Wosner records another leniency: a tree may be cut down for a mitzvah.[15] His decision was related to a case where a yeshivah wanted to transfer a fruit tree in order to erect their building. Based on the mitzvah involved and the reasons cited by the *Rosh* and Rav Yaakov Emden above, Rav Wosner permitted them to take down the tree.[16]

Even when it is permissible to take down a fruit tree, Rav Ovadiah Yosef writes, like the *Pischei Teshuvah*, that it is best to hire a non-Jew to

---

9   *Shu"t Chasam Sofer, Yoreh Dei'ah* §102. But if it is possible to replant the tree elsewhere, then it must be done.

10   *Rosh, Bava Kama* 8:15.

11   *Taz, Yoreh Dei'ah* 116:6. Rav Asher Weiss (*Minchas Asher, Devarim* §33, p. 228) says that those Acharonim who permitted cutting down trees for the sake of other needs meant serious needs, not frivolous ones. For examples of what is considered a legitimate need, see *Chavos Ya'ir* §195 and *Aruch Hashulchan* 116:13, which say that making room to take walks is not a justified need.

12   *She'eilas Yaavetz,* vol. 1, §76.

13   *Shu"t Chasam Sofer, Yoreh Dei'ah* §102.

14   "New York—Halachic Analysis: Removing a Fruit Tree To Build a Yeshiva" (Nov. 8, 2010), www.vosizneias.com.

15   *Shevet HaLevi,* vol. 2, §46.

16   Another example is if the tree is being cut down to use the wood to build a *sukkah* (*Har Tzvi,* vol. 2, §102; *Yechaveh Daat, Yoreh Dei'ah,* vol. 5, §46). Rav Zilberstein (*Chashukei Chemed, Pesachim,* p. 582) said that a man could uproot a fruit tree to bring it to his father who was hospitalized and wanted to say *Birkas Ha'ilanos.*

cut down the tree, and even better to sell the tree to the non-Jew before he cuts it down.[17] Rav Asher Weiss argues on this that the prohibition to chop down a fruit tree exists regardless of whether it is owned by a Jew or anyone else. Rav Weiss contends that, after all, the context of the prohibition against cutting down fruit trees in the Torah was during a war, where the trees were presumably owned by the enemy nations or were altogether ownerless.[18]

There is also a degree of danger associated with cutting down fruit trees that may explain the extreme measures to which the people in the articles went to avoid doing so. The Gemara quotes Rav Chanina as blaming his son's premature death on the fact that his son had cut down a fruit tree.[19] Rav Yaakov Emden explains that the son must have been very righteous, since that was the only reason they could find for his untimely death.[20] But if he was truly righteous, why did he violate such a basic Biblical prohibition? It must be, concludes Rav Emden, that it was a case where it was permissible to chop down the tree for one of the reasons cited above, but nevertheless it is not a *middas chassidus*—it's inappropriate for a pious person to do so—and therefore he died prematurely. This is why many people avoid relying on leniencies to cut down fruit trees.[21] Rav Emden added that transplanting the tree is not considered cutting it down, and there would be no danger in doing so. Therefore, this may be a good option for one who needs to move a fruit tree.

The *Binyan Tzion* disagrees with this explanation. He argues that it cannot be that Rav Chanina's son was halachically allowed to cut down the tree yet was killed for doing so. Rather, he explains, Rav Chanina's

---

17   *Yabia Omer, Yoreh Dei'ah*, vol. 5, §12. See *Minchas Asher* (*Devarim* §33, p. 226), where Rav Asher Weiss distinguishes between a non-Jewish day worker and a contractor.

18   *Minchas Asher, Devarim* §33, pp. 226–27. See also *Shulchan Aruch Harav, Shemiras Haguf Vehanefesh* §14. See *Binah Basefarim*, p. 191, where it is discussed whether the prohibition against chopping down fruit trees applies to ownerless fruit trees.

19   *Bava Kama* 91b; see also *Bava Basra* 26a.

20   *She'eilas Yaavetz*, vol. 1, §76.

21   According to Rabbi Aryeh Lebowitz, "Rav Willig won't *pasken* cutting down tree questions based on this line" (Rabbi Aryeh Lebowitz, "Baba Kama Daf 92—Various Wise Sayings" [March 30, 2009], www.yutorah.org).

son erred in his judgment; he thought it was permissible to cut down the tree, but in reality it wasn't.[22]

Rav Ovadiah Yosef agrees with the *Binyan Tzion* and says that the punishment of premature death doesn't apply when it is permissible to destroy a fruit tree.[23] As support, Rav Ovadiah cites a number of *poskim* who permitted cutting down fruit trees (for specific reasons) without ever mentioning that there is still a danger in doing so.

However, Rabbi Yehudah HeChassid writes that a fruit-bearing tree should never be chopped down.[24] This means that, even in the permitted situations listed above, one should refrain from doing so since there is still a danger involved.[25]

There is a debate whether one is required to follow the writings of Rabbi Yehudah HeChassid. According to Rav Chaim Palagi, one of the greatest nineteenth-century Turkish rabbis, one who transgresses Rabbi Yehudah HeChassid's writings will not avoid punishment, and *chamira sakanta mei'issura*—one has to be more concerned about matters of mortal danger than the Torah's prohibitions.[26] Rav Yaakov Emden was also concerned about Rabbi Yehudah HeChassid's warning, even in a permitted situation, and therefore he only permitted transplanting the entire tree.[27]

Rav Ovadiah quotes the *Shem Aryeh*, which says that one who is not concerned about the statements of Rabbi Yehudah HeChassid need not be worried by them. After all, he says, Rabbi Yehudah HeChassid was offering warning for extremely far-fetched dangers. Likewise, the Maharam Mintz notes that Rabbi Yehudah HeChassid's instructions

---

22   *Binyan Tzion* §61.

23   Rav Asher Weiss, too, agrees; see *Minchas Asher, Devarim* §33, p. 224.

24   *Tzavaas Rabbi Yehudah HeChassid* §53.

25   Some say that even chopping down non-fruit-bearing trees will prevent a person from receiving blessing through his labor; see *Binah Basefarim*, p. 181. Rav Herschel Schachter said that it is best to be concerned for the opinion of Rabbi Yehuda HeChassid and sell the tree to a gentile and also have a gentile cut down the tree (Rabbi Shay Schachter, "Cutting Down Fruit Trees for Home Construction" [Aug. 23, 2017], www.yutorah.org).

26   Rav Chaim Palagi, *Chaim Beyad* §24.

27   *She'eilas Yaavetz*, vol. 2, §76.

have not been generally accepted.[28] Furthermore, the idea of *chamira sakanta mei'issura* doesn't apply here, where the danger isn't tangible.[29]

In practice, Rav Wosner maintains that even where it is permissible to chop down the fruit tree, one should *lechatchilah* (preferably) heed the opinions that are concerned about the possible danger that may arise. Therefore, he should sell the tree and the surrounding area to a gentile and have him cut it down. In this case, Rav Wosner feels that no danger will occur, which he notes has been the case on countless occasions.[30]

Finally, in explaining why Hashem chose *atzei shitim* (acacia trees) for the construction of the *Mishkan*, as opposed to another variety of trees, the *Bnei Yissaschar* writes that Hashem wanted to ensure that fruit-bearing trees would not be cut down. It was certainly permissible to cut down any tree that was necessary for the construction of the *Mishkan*, even a fruit-bearing tree, because the value of building the *Mishkan* was greater than the value of the fruit trees. However, Hashem didn't want to use fruit trees. This seems to model the importance of avoiding cutting them down for us. So too, when we want to cut down fruit trees because their value is less than that of our other needs, such as constructing a new building, we should take care to avoid doing so if possible.[31]

SUMMARY

The Torah prohibits us from cutting down fruit trees. Although there are a number of exceptions that would permit doing so, many

---

28   *Teshuvas Maharam Mintz* §79.

29   Rav Moshe Feinstein had two sons-in-law with the name Moshe, so he was obviously not concerned about Rabbi Yehudah HeChassid's warning that a father-in-law and son-in-law should not have the same name. However, my brother-in-law, Rav Moshe Pessin, pointed out that this proof is not conclusive since Rav Moshe Feinstein's sons-in-law each had two names, not just Moshe, which may render their names completely different than someone with just the name Moshe.

See *Mesoras Moshe*, pp. 500–1, for more about Rav Moshe's views on following the will of Rabbi Yehudah HeChassid. Rav Moshe Sternbuch (*Teshuvos Vehanhagos*, vol. 2, §728), however, holds that even where it is permitted to chop down a fruit tree, one should still bring the matter before a *beis din* for review because of the danger involved. See *Shu"t Minchas Asher*, vol. 2, §75, for more on following the *tzavaah* of Rabbi Yehudah HeChassid.

30   *Shevet HaLevi*, vol. 5, §95.

31   *Toras Bnei Yissaschar, parashas Terumah.*

poskim recommend avoiding cutting down these trees due to the danger involved, according to Rabbi Yehudah HeChassid. Nevertheless, Rav Ovadiah Yosef writes that when halachah permits chopping down fruit trees, one need not be concerned about any danger.

YEARNING FOR MASHIACH

IN THE NEWS

One of the universal tenets of our faith is the coming of Mashiach, but as people vary, so do the ways they display their belief in Mashiach.

Dr. Harold Goldmeier, a former research and teaching fellow at Harvard University who made *aliyah*, posted the following personal experience on the Life In Israel blog:

> We rent an apartment, rather than buy...[and] our lease has a clause that only appears in an Israeli document, and not many of them. It claims we have sixty days to vacate the premises "when the Mashiach comes."[1]

And Rav Shlomo Aviner told the following anecdote, quoting Rav Tzvi Yehudah Kook:

> A few years ago a Torah scholar told Rabbi Aviner that a few young men [from years before] wanted to avoid military service in a non-Jewish army and wasting time from learning Torah. They wanted to physically injure themselves in order to be disqualified from the Polish military. But the Chafetz Chaim opposed this: "A person is not permitted to injure himself. The body is not his. And why avoid practice in the army? The Messiah will arrive soon. There will be a State. And when there is a State, there will be a need for an army. Prepare here.

---

1   Dr. Harold Goldmeier, "Only in Israel: Some Stories from Daily Life of a New Immigrant" (Dec. 16, 2012), www.lifeinisrael.blogspot.com.

You have the opportunity to prepare for the army of the State of Israel."[2]

Yet another story was told at Rabbi Shlomo Carlebach's funeral how Reb Shlomo would often go around with bags filled with people's names and addresses, so that when Mashiach comes, he would be able to contact them.[3]

Likewise, on the wedding invitation of Rav Levi Yitzchak of Berditchev's son, it said that the wedding would take place in Yerushalayim, but if Mashiach had not yet arrived, it would then take place in Berditchev.[4]

It is told that when the venerable *rav* of the Old Yishuv in Jerusalem, Rav Shmuel Salant, would pray *Shemoneh Esreh* every day, just prior to reciting the blessing of *Es Tzemach David*, which is a request for the coming of Mashiach, he would pause, look right and then left, and then continue praying. One day, his students asked him why he did such an odd thing when he davened. He answered that he knew that Mashiach would come that day, and he didn't want to make an unnecessary blessing, so he paused to see if Mashiach had already come before making the blessing.[5]

---

2   *Sichot Ha-Rav Tzvi Yehudah, Devarim*, p. 263, cited in "Teachings from the mouth of our Rabbi from the Chafetz Chaim," www.ravaviner.com.

3   From video footage of the funeral seen by the author.

4   Rabbi Elchanan Adler, "Yearning for Salvation" (May 14, 2011), p. 6, www.yutorah.org.

5   Rabbi Shimon Schenker, "Awaiting the Arrival of Moshiach" (July 26, 2015), www.yutorah. org. See *The Lord Is Righteous in All His Ways: Reflections on the Tish'ah be'Av Kinot* (Ktav, 2006), pp. 132–33, where Rabbi Joseph B. Soloveitchik writes about being prepared for Mashiach and the custom that shuls had of placing their *Kinos* in *sheimos* (holy books that are no longer in use and require respectful burial) and not saving them for next year, believing they would not be needed.
    A number of years ago, Gilad Shalit spoke at Yeshiva University in Lamport Auditorium. After his address, he was quickly escorted out of the auditorium and followed by Rabbi Shay Schachter. Rabbi Schachter asked him what his message for American Jewry was. Shalit said, "When I was in captivity, every time they gave me napkins or a paper plate—something to write on—I always drew pictures of different cities in Israel to attach myself to Israel. I was yearning to get back, and if only everyone would yearn for Israel the way I did, the redemption would come" (Rabbi Moshe Tzvi Weinberg, "Longing for Home: The Centrality of Eretz Yisrael in the Life of a Jew" [May 6, 2014], www.yutorah.org). If only we would yearn for Mashiach the way Shalit yearned for Eretz Yisrael, Mashiach would surely arrive.

Finally, Joseph Telushkin tells the following story in his book, *Rebbe*:

A few years before Reb Moshe's [Rav Moshe Feinstein] death, he needed to have a pacemaker installed. Quite uncharacteristically, his son-in-law, Rabbi Dr. Moshe Tendler, recalled he was reluctant to accede to the doctor's orders.

When Tendler asked him to explain his hesitancy, given that a number of doctors agreed that the procedure was essential, Reb Moshe answered, "I know how unworthy I am. I know how little Torah I know. But I am also aware that if they are to pick seventy-one people to make up the Sanhedrin (the ancient Jewish High Court that tradition teaches will be reconstituted in the Messianic era), they most likely will pick me too. However, a ba'al mum (someone with a physical defect) cannot join the Sanhedrin. I am perturbed at the thought of doing something to myself that would make me unfit to join the Sanhedrin when the Mashiach comes."

Only after Tendler showed Reb Moshe diagrams illustrating exactly what would be done did he realize that the procedure would not render him a ba'al mum, and he agreed to have a pacemaker put in.[6]

Is believing in Mashiach a Biblical obligation? Is there any consequence for someone who doesn't believe in his imminent arrival? What exactly are we supposed to believe?

---

6   *Rebbe: The Life and Teachings of Menachem M. Schneerson, the Most Influential Rabbi in Modern History* (Harper Wave, 2014), p. 428; see also p. 492. Telushkin concludes, "Though Rabbi Feinstein was known for being a particularly humble person; his humility did not preclude him from thinking that his knowledge made him a likely candidate, if the Messiah came, to be appointed to the *Sanhedrin*." See *Mesoras Moshe*, vol. 2, p. 470, where this story is reported as a first-hand account. It is reported that Rav Elyashiv said that this story about Rav Moshe is not true, since Rav Moshe at the time was already very old, and that itself would have disqualifed him from being on the *Sanhedrin* (*Haggadah Shel Pesach Yisa Berachah*).

A TORAH PERSPECTIVE

The Gemara says that after a person departs from this world, he is judged by a Heavenly tribunal, and one of the questions they ask him is if he yearned for the ultimate salvation, which will be ushered in by Mashiach.[7]

The *S'mak* explains the source for this requirement to believe in the coming of Mashiach.[8] The first of the Ten Commandments says that Hashem is our God, who took us out of Egypt.[9] The *Sefer Mitzvos Katan* explains that Hashem wants us not only to believe that He redeemed us from Egypt, but also that in the future Hashem will once again redeem us from exile in the times of Mashiach.

The *Rambam* compiled a list of thirteen principles of faith, and the twelfth is the belief in the arrival of Mashiach.[10] A Jew who doesn't fully believe in these principles is considered a *kofer* (heretic). The *Rambam* adds that a person is deemed a *kofer* not only if he denies the coming of Mashiach, but also if he doesn't yearn for it.[11] Furthermore, the era after Mashiach's arrival will be one of universal recognition of Hashem.[12] If a person is comfortable with his present situation and doesn't yearn for Mashiach, he is demonstrating that he doesn't appreciate how much Hashem's Name is disgraced in our times.[13]

The *Rambam* also states that Mashiach will be a very righteous person with the spirit of God resting on him.[14] His primary goals will be to restore the monarchy of David HaMelech, build a new Beis Hamikdash, and gather all Jews from the Diaspora.[15] The *Navi* says

---

7   *Shabbos* 31a. For more on this topic, see Rabbi Ari Enkin's *Amot Shel Halachah* (Urim, 2009), vol. 2, pp. 235–37.
8   *S'mak*, Mitzvah §1.
9   *Shemos* 20:2.
10   *Peirush Hamishnayos, Sanhedrin*. The *Chasam Sofer* (*Yoreh Dei'ah* §356) seems to disagree with the *Rambam* and rules that believing in Mashiach is not one of the fundamental principles of Judaism, although a person must believe it to be true, since it is stated in the Torah and *Neviim*. See Rav Shimshon Pinkus, *Galus Venechamah*, pp. 177–78.
11   *Hilchos Melachim* 11:1.
12   Ibid. 12:5.
13   See *Hilchos Melachim* 12:4.
14   *Yeshayah* 11:2–5. See *Rambam, Hilchos Melachim* 11:4.
15   *Rambam, Hilchos Melachim* 11:1.

that Mashiach will also bring peace to the world and an increase of devotion to God.[16]

Along with Mashiach's arrival will come *techiyas hameisim*, revival of the dead. The *Ritva* says that there will be two stages of *techiyas hameisim*—the first will be at the time when the rebuilding of the Beis Hamikdash has begun and will only be for those who yearned for the redemption from *galus*. The second *techiyas hameisim* will be at the end of the era of the days of Mashiach.[17]

Rav Aryeh Tzvi Frumer, Rosh Yeshivah of Yeshivas Chachmei Lublin until his untimely death at the hands of the Nazis, *yimach shemam*, quotes the *berachah* of *Nacheim* on Tishah B'Av, which states that "with fire Hashem will rebuild the Beis Hamikdash." What does it mean that Hashem will build the Beis Hamikdash with fire? He explains that it is the fire and passion of the yearning of the Jewish People to be redeemed from exile and rebuild the Beis Hamikdash that will fuel the actual events.[18]

Along the same lines, Rabbi Yitzchak Mirsky explains, in his commentary to the Haggadah, that our very faith in the *geulah* is a condition for the *geulah* to transpire.[19] Those who don't have faith won't merit the *geulah*. He brings a number of proofs for this. One of them is from the Netziv, who says that the *dor hamidbar* (the generation who traveled in the desert for forty years) did not believe that Hashem would take them into Eretz Yisrael, and that is why, when the time came to enter the land, they did not enter.[20]

The rabbis of the Gemara understood the importance of yearning for Mashiach. In Rav Yosef Zvi Rimon's commentary to the Haggadah, he explains why the story of the Seder mentioned in the Haggadah was held in Bnei Brak.[21] Why did the great rabbis go to their student, Rabbi Akiva, in Bnei Brak to conduct the Seder? The reason, he says, is because

---

16   *Yeshayah* 2:3, 2:4, 11:6; *Rambam, Hilchos Melachim* 12:5.
17   *Ritva, Taanis* 30b, s.v. *"kol ha'ochel"*; see also *Taam Vadaas, parashas Haazinu*, p. 233, where he brings support for the *Ritva*.
18   *Eretz Tzvi, Parashas Hachodesh*, p. 235.
19   *Hegyonei Halachah*, p. 63.
20   *Haamek Davar, Shemos* 4:9.
21   *Haggadah for Pesach: Shirat Miriam* (Ktav, 2014), p. 150.

Rabbi Akiva was known to be an optimist, even in the most difficult times.[22] This Seder took place during a time of harsh Roman persecution. Rabbi Akiva understood that even in a difficult exile, we have to yearn and speak about the joy of the redemption. Therefore, on the night celebrating our freedom, the rabbis wanted to come to the person who would offer them the most encouragement—Rabbi Akiva.

While it may feel difficult to maintain faith that Mashiach is coming in our long exile, the Chafetz Chaim points out that the fact that we are so close to the redemption means that it is that much easier for it to arrive.[23] He explains by bringing the *pasuk* that says, "If you redeem [the land] close to *Yovel*, [the redemption money] is less than if there are many years until *Yovel*."[24] The Chafetz Chaim applies this to Mashiach. He writes that because the earlier generations were so far from the *geulah*, they needed to do much more to bring it close; for us, even though we are on a lower level, since we are so much closer to the *geulah*, we don't need to do as much, so we should not be discouraged.

Hashem told Yaakov, "Your children will be like the dust of the earth, and you will go forth to the west, east, north, and south."[25] The *Seforno* comments that it is specifically after we are at the lowest state imaginable (as low as the dust of the earth) that Hashem grants us the power to burst forth in tremendous growth. This, says the *Seforno*, is how the ultimate salvation will unfold.[26]

Parashas Shemos offers support as well. Rabbi Baruch Simon, a Rosh Yeshivah at Yeshiva University, explains the concept of yearning for Mashiach with the story of Moshe's rescue after his birth.[27] Yocheved, Moshe's mother, could no longer conceal baby Moshe at home, so she placed him in a basket in the Nile. All were skeptical that he would be saved. After all, no Egyptian would want to save a Jewish boy, and no Jew would risk his life to do so either. Yocheved abandoned him at the

---

22   See *Makkos* 24b and *Pesachim* 116b.
23   *Taam Vadaas, parashas Behar*, p. 166.
24   *Vayikra* 25:50.
25   *Bereishis* 28:14.
26   See *Taam Vadaas, parashas Vayeitzei*, p. 136.
27   *Imrei Baruch, parashas Behaalosecha*, p. 121.

Nile, and his father, Amram, rejected his daughter Miriam's prophecy that Moshe would one day lead the Jewish People out of Egypt. Yet Miriam firmly believed in her prophecy and waited until Moshe was saved—the most improbable scenario, which came true. Thus, Rabbi Simon says that when the Gemara says that we will be asked if we yearned for Mashiach, it means we will be asked if we yearned for Mashiach even when it seemed like he would never arrive.[28]

Although we must believe in and anticipate the arrival of Mashiach, the Brisker Rav says it's not enough to say, "I want Mashiach." We have to learn Torah and do good deeds so that we are prepared for his arrival.[29] Furthermore, Rav Yitzchak Zilberstein cautions a person against saying, in a sarcastic tone, "Sure, that will happen when Mashiach comes," because this shows one's disbelief and lack of yearning for the coming of Mashiach.[30]

While we must yearn for Mashiach and believe that he can come any day, we must still live in the present reality until that point. Rav Zilberstein told a story about a patient who needed surgery and, without it, the doctors said he would certainly die within ten years. The patient, however, didn't want to have the surgery, since he had faith that Mashiach would come soon, and then he would be healed. His question to Rav Zilberstein was, did he have to undergo the surgery?

Rav Zilberstein asked his father-in-law, Rav Yosef Shalom Elyashiv, who said that the person must have the surgery, since at that moment he had a mitzvah to stay healthy,[31] which he was not fulfilling by relying on Mashiach's arrival and his subsequent cure.[32]

---

28   Similarly, the Netziv (*Haamek Davar, Shemos* 4:1) says that Mashiach can come in any way, even one that we cannot imagine.

29   *Taam Vadaas, parashas Vayeitzei*, p. 187.

30   *Vehaarev Na*, vol. 2, p. 265.

31   *Devarim* 4:15.

32   *Peninei Halachah, Chashukei Chemed, Pesachim*, p. 252. Rav Elyashiv also cites the *Rambam* (*Hilchos Melachim* 12:5), who says that in the times of Mashiach nature won't change, and it's not clear if this person will automatically be healed at that time. The Gemara in *Shabbos* 63a records a dispute between Shmuel and Rav Chiya bar Abba regarding what changes there will be between our times and the times of Mashiach. Interestingly, those changes already affect the halachah now.

Interestingly, Rav Zilberstein was asked another similar question. A man required surgery on his leg—should he have the surgery before Pesach or wait until afterward?[33] Rav Zilberstein answered that since we believe that Mashiach could come at any moment, perhaps he will arrive before Pesach, the Beis Hamikdash will be rebuilt, and he will have a mitzvah of *aliyah laregel*—walking to the Beis Hamikdash on Yom Tov to bring special *korbanos*. In order to fulfill the mitzvah of *aliyah laregel*, he needs to be able to walk,[34] and if he has the surgery before Pesach, he will be in the process of recuperating and unable to fulfill the mitzvah. Therefore, Rav Zilberstein ruled, he should wait until after Pesach to have the surgery.[35]

Similarly, Rav Zilberstein advised someone who owned a herd of sheep that he should demonstrate his anticipation for Mashiach by marking the birth dates of each animal.[36] This way, when Mashiach arrives and people will need sheep that are within their first year for the *Korban Pesach*, as the halachah requires, he will be able to demonstrate that they are indeed a year old, kosher for the *Korban Pesach*. Rav Zilberstein also told him that he should keep track of events that would invalidate the sheep from being used as a *korban*, such as being born through caesarean section or being exchanged for a dog.

Rav Ephraim Greenblatt, a close *talmid* of Rav Moshe Feinstein, says that one recites *Birkas Hagomel*, the *berachah* for long-distance airplane travel, only after completing one's round trip.[37] For example, someone flying from Israel to Chicago would recite the *berachah* only upon returning to Israel. However, Rav Shmuel Fuerst, a *dayan* in Chicago, reports that Rav Moshe Feinstein held that if one flies from Chicago

---

33   *Peninei Halachah, Chashukei Chemed, Pesachim,* p. 165. Here there was no health concern in delaying the surgery.

34   *Rambam, Hilchos Chagigah* 2:1.

35   In contrast, Rav Yaakov Kamenetsky maintains that a person is required to continue all daily routines and responsibilities even though he anticipates Mashiach's arrival at any minute. He reasons that spontaneity is an integral part of the redemption process (*Emes L'Yaakov, parashas Vayeishev,* p. 202, and n. 32).

36   *Chashukei Chemed, Haggadah,* p. 81. For a similar story, see *Aleinu Leshabei'ach, parashas Bamidbar,* p. 57.

37   *Rivevos Ephraim,* vol. 1, §155.

to Israel, one recites *Birkas Hagomel* upon landing safely in Israel, not upon his return to Chicago, since the hope is that Mashiach will arrive and he will stay in Israel.[38]

Each of us should try to find our own best way to show our anticipation of Mashiach's arrival.[39] The *Meshech Chochmah* points out that Chazal say that the Jewish People were redeemed from Egypt because they had a unique style of dress and speech.[40] What is special about these practices is not that they helped keep them separate from the Egyptians, since they were already segregated in their own section of the country. What is significant about them is that they helped the Jews stay focused on yearning for redemption.

Halachically, we incorporate the concept of yearning for Mashiach in our daily lives. The *Shulchan Aruch* writes that every Jew should feel pained over the loss of the Beis Hamikdash.[41] Therefore, the *Mishnah Berurah* says that on weekdays, before *bentching*, one should recite *Al Naharos Bavel* (psalm 137) as a reminder of the destruction of the Beis Hamikdash, and on Shabbos, Yom Tov, and other happy occasions one should say *Shir Hamaalos* (psalm 126), which expresses our desire for the rebuilding of the Beis Hamikdash (without referring to its destruction).

The last Lubavitcher Rebbe, Rav Menachem Mendel Schneerson, would often quote the Chafetz Chaim, who said, "It is crucial for Jews to actively appeal to God for the Messiah's coming."[42] The Rebbe anticipated the arrival of Mashiach so much that audio tapes from *farbrengens* (Chassidic gatherings) show that when everyone would sing the *Rambam*'s principle of faith, *Ani Maamin*, "I believe in the coming of the Mashiach, and even though he may tarry, I shall wait for him every day to come," the Rebbe would clearly say the opening words, "I believe in

---

38   Rabbi Yisroel Langer, *"Birchas Hagomel"* (April 3, 2009), www.cckollel.org.

39   Rav Moshe Feinstein once told a woman that she should not worry about doing specific mitzvos to bring Mashiach, since it is not in our hands; she should just yearn that Hashem brings Mashiach (*Mesoras Moshe*, p. 583).

40   *Meshech Chochmah, Shemos* 6:6.

41   *Shulchan Aruch, Orach Chaim* 1:3.

42   Rabbi Joseph Telushkin, *Rebbe: The Life and Teachings of Menachem M. Schneerson, the Most Influential Rabbi in Modern History* (Harper Wave, 2014), p. 431.

the coming of the Mashiach," but would not sing "even though he may tarry…" It seems that due to his great desire for Mashiach to come right away, he couldn't articulate the possibility that he would tarry.[43]

Finally, the Gemara says that one should not calculate when Mashiach will arrive, since if the date arrives and he doesn't come, a person might think that he will never come.[44] Rather, a person should wait and anticipate his arrival.[45] So, in practice, we should learn more Torah and perform more mitzvos, to show that we are actively preparing for the arrival of Mashiach at any time.[46]

May it be soon!

SUMMARY

The Gemara writes that one of the questions we will be asked in the next world is whether or not we yearned for Mashiach. The *Sefer Mitzvos Katan* teaches that just as we must believe that Hashem redeemed us from Egypt, we must believe that He will redeem us from the current exile in the times of Mashiach. More categorically, the *Rambam* remarks that one is considered a heretic if he doesn't believe in and yearn for Mashiach.

---

43   Ibid., p. 114.

44   *Sanhedrin* 97b; *Rambam, Hilchos Melachim* 12:2.

45   See ArtScroll Gemara, *Sanhedrin* 97b, n. 29, for a good summary regarding the idea that throughout the centuries many great sages have tried to calculate the arrival of Mashiach.

46   The sixth Lubavitcher Rebbe, Rav Yitzchak Yosef, cited in *On the Air with Rav Aviner* (J. Levine/Millennium, 2009), p. 230.

ABOUT MOSAICA PRESS

Mosaica Press is an independent publisher of Jewish books. Our authors include some of the most profound, interesting, and entertaining thinkers and writers in the Jewish community today. Our books are available around the world. Please visit us at www.mosaicapress.com or contact us at info@mosaicapress.com. We will be glad to hear from you.

ABOUT THE AUTHOR

Rabbi Simcha Lauer received his Rabbinic ordination from Yeshivas Rabbeinu Yitzchak Elchanan and holds a master's degree in Jewish Education from the Azrieli Graduate School of Jewish Education and Administration. He currently lives in Ramat Beit Shemesh, Israel, with his wife and children.

Rabbi Lauer welcomes questions and comments to his email address: learningthenewsbook@gmail.com.

ציידי נאצים

נושא בחדשות:

בינואר 2016 כתבה הופיעה ברשת הCNN תחת הכותרת: "לציד נאצים אמריקאי נשאר מקרה פעיל אחד".[1] הכתבה מתמקדת ביאקב פאליג' בן התשעים ושתים המתגורר בג'קסון הייטס, קווינס. פאליג' שמש כשומר במחנה ההשמדה הנאצי טרווינקי, אלא שבמקום להענש על פשעיו הוא התגורר רוב ימיו כאדם חופשי בביתו האמריקאי.ב-2004 שופט פדרלי צווה על גירושו של פאליג' לאחד משלוש מדינות אירופיות, אך אף לא אחת מהן הסכימה לקלוט אותו.

אלי רוזנבוים ,צייד הנאצים הנודע של המחלקה האמריקאית לצדק, עזר לעלות על עקבותיהם של 137 נאצים במהלך שלושים שנות פעילותו. מאה ושבע מתוכם אבדו את אזרחותם או גרשו בזכותו. רוזנבוים הפך את לכידת הנאצים למשאת חייו. פאליג' היה האחרון ברשימתו, לפי הCNN. בנוגע לפאליג' התבטא רוזנבוים: "מר פאליג' מנע מאחרים להגיע לגבורות. הוא שרת במחנה האמונים והתשתיות של ה—SS, טרווניקי ששמש למעשה כבית ספר להרג המוני..."

עוד כתבה בנושא התפרסמה ב"מצב" בנובמבר 2013 תחת הכותרת:"הייקינד זועם על כך שפושעים נאצים חיים בארה"ב.[2] חבר מועצת מדינת ניו יורק דב הייקינד אומר: "לאנשים יש את העזות לומר, הם מבוגרים למה לעורר דובים מרבצם? אבל מה אם אותם מאות ואלפים חפים מפשע שנטבחו ועונו בידי חיות אדם אלו? האם אין לנו כל מחויבות כלפיהם?.. אנחנו לא רוצים לראות את הרוצחים הללו חיים בתוכנו בין הצאצאים של אותם גברים נשים וטף

1   איון פרץ, אלבסנדר רוזן, וסלי ברר, ג'רמי מורהד, אלכס לי "U.S. Nazi Hunter has one active case" (28, יוני 2016) www.edition.cnn.com

2   "Hikind is furious that Nazi war criminals are living freely in U.S." (5, נובמבר 2013) www.matzav.com

שעונו על ידם. מדובר פה על מעבר לזריית מלח על פצעים, זו פשוט חרפה.
אם ארצות מוצאם של הפושעים מסרבות לקלוט אותם העמיסו אותם על
אוניות ושלחו אותם החוצה. אין להם זכות להנות מחרות אותה הם שללו
מאחרים.

ומזווית אחרת על העניין ניתן לציין שזמן קצר לאחר השואה התארגנה
קבוצה של יהודים בשם ה"נוקמים" והציבה לעצמה מטרה להרוג כמה שיותר
נאצים. הקבוצה חפשה אחריהם בספרד, ארגנטינה, קנדה ובארצות נוספות
שנודעו כקולטי נאצים. משימה מרכזית שלהם התבצעה בסטאלג' 13 מחנה
מעצר לאנשי SS בנירנברג. הקבוצה גלתה כי הלחם לעצירים סופק על ידי
מאפיה בודדת והתארגנה על מנת להרעיל משלוח לחם יומי. הם מרחו רעל
על כשלושת אלפים כיכרות.[3] דיווחים מציינים כי הם הצליחו להרוג קרוב
לאלף נאצים בדרך זו. הם תכננו גם להרעיל את מערכת אספקת המים בברלין,
וויימאר, המבורג , מינכן ונירנברג, אך נתפסו לפני שצלחו בכך.

מהי השקפת התורה? האם אנו צריכים לתפוס פושעים נאצים? ואם לוכ-
דים פושעי מלחמה נאצים האם מותר להוציאם להורג?

ממבט תורני:

הרב אפרים אושרי, בשו"ת השואה שלו נשאל האם אדם מחויב לרדוף
אחר רוצחים נאצים על מנת להעמידם לדין.[4] השאלה התעוררה בעקבות
אדם שנגש לרב אושרי וספר לו כי ידוע לו שהשרת הליטאי של בניין מגוריו
הרג את הוריו אחיו ואחיותיו. הוא גלה לאחרונה כי אותו אדם מתגורר
במאריפל ליטא. האם הוא מחויב להוציא כספים על מנת להוציא את הצדק
לאור ולשלוח בכך מסר לשונאי יהודים אחרים? הרב אושרי השיב כי מצד
אחד אסור לאדם להפגין אדישות כלפי אותם רוצחים ועליו לעשות בכל
יכולתו לנקום את נקמתם של בני משפחתו ולהשתמש בכל האמצעים הנד-
רשים להביאם למשפט. אך בו זמנית הוא חייב לוודא שאינו מעורר תגובה
אנטישמית.[5]

---

3   יונתן פרידלנד, Revenge (יוני 25, 2015) www.theguardian.com

4   Responsa from the Holocaust (Judaica Press, 2001) ס' 75. הרב אושרי נולד בקופיסקיז, ליטא,
       ב1914. כאשר השואה פרצה, הוא כבר נודע בשערים. ב1941, כאשר הנאצים פלשו לליטא, הוא
       נשלח לגטו קובנה, שם השיב על שאלות הלכתיות רבות בנושאי חיים ומוות, אותם היא תעד והדפיס
       לאחר המלחמה. הוא נפטר בניו יורק ב2003.

5   ראה את הערתו של הרב יוסף ב. סולוביצ'יק, Faith and Destiny: From the Holocaust to the
       State of Israel (Ktav, 2000) בו הוא מציין כי דם יהודי אינו הפקר, הוא מדבר על השמדת נאצר או
       המופתי, ומתי נקמה מותרת ומוצדקת על פי דעת תורה.

כמה שבועות מאוחר יותר דיווח האיש לרב אושרי כי הוא זרק רימון יד
לתוך ביתו של הנאצי והרג אותו. הרב אושרי מיד המליץ לאיש לברוח מליטא
על מנת שקרוביו של הנאצי לא יפגעו בו ובכדי שהממשלה לא תאסור אותו
על לקיחת החוק לידיים.

בהזדמנות אחרת הרב אושרי כתב: "מצוה גדולה לכל יחיד לעשות בכל
שביכולתו לחשוף את הרוצחים הללו ולהעמידם למשפט, ובוודאי אסור לע-
זור להם לחמוק מהגמול המגיע להם על מעשיהם."[6] באופן דומה מתבטא
הרב אושרי על החשיבות שבזכירת הצרות אותם גרמו לנו הנאצים והנלווים
אליהם.[7] כמו כן כאשר אישה פעם נגשה לרב אושרי ושאלה אותו האם מותר
לה למחוק קעקוע המסמן אותה כזונה, עבור החיילים של היטלר ימ"ח? הרב
אושרי השיב כי היא וכל הנשים האחרות במצבה צריכות "לשאת את הקע-
קוע שלהן ולשמור עליו, לא כאות של חרפה אלא כאות כבוד וגבורה—עדות
לאשר סבלו על קדוש שמו". הקעקוע הזה ודאי יזכיר לנו את הנכתב בתורת
משה: "הרנינו גויים עמו כי דם עבדיו ינקום ונקם ישיב לצריו".[8] הרב אושרי
האמין בחשיבות הזכרת הפשעים הנוראים שעוללו הנאצים, ובמניעת האפ-
שרות מרוצחים לשכוח אותם. וזאת על מנת להוציא את הצדק לאור למען
הנרצחים.

מה שמחייב מחשבה מעמיקה בנושא השאלה היא האם מותר לאדם לקחת
את החוק לידיו ולהרוג מישהו עליו ידוע לו כי היה רוצח נאצי.

כדוגמא לכך יובא משפט אייכמן, כאשר אדולף אייכמן ימ"ש נתפס ונשפט
ע"י הממשלה הישראלית, הוא הפך להיות היחיד שהוצא להורג אי פעם
במדינת ישראל.[9]

האם היה בסיס הלכתי למעשיה של המדינה? אחרי הכל הרמב"ם כתב כי
בלא הסנהדרין אין לנו אפשרות לדון דיני נפשות.[10]

כמה אפשרויות הוצעו כדי לענות על השאלה מדוע היה מותר להוציא את
אייכמן להורג.

---

6 Responsa from the Holocaust (Judaica Press, 2001), ס' 104.

7 שם, 99.

8 דברים (ל"ב, מ"ג).

9 ראה הרב ד"ר נורמן לאם, Derashot Ledorot: A Commentary for the Ages (Koren, 2013), פ'
כי תשא, עמ' 194-195, שם רב לאם מגלה את דו-פרצופיותם של אלו שגנו את ישראל על משפט
אייכמן.

10 הלכות סנהדרין י"ד, י"ג.

הראשונה מבוססת על הכלל של "גואל הדם". הפסוק אומר כי קרוביו של אדם שנרצח יכולים לנקום את נקמתו ולהרוג את הרוצח.[11] בנוגע לשואה, בה נרצחו מליוני יהודים, כל יהודי נחשב כקרובם של הנרצחים.[12]

אבל הרמב"ם[13] מסתייג וכותב שגואל הדם הינו רק אדם שמהווה יורש הלכתי של הנרצח. אם אין כזה בי"ד יוציאו להרוג את הרוצח. לפי כך משמע שרק אלו שהם קרובי משפחה (ויורשים) של הנרצחים רשאים להרוג את הרוצחים. הצמח צדק לעומת זאת כותב כי אין הגבלה, הקרוב החי בעל הקרבה המשפחתית הגדולה ביותר יכול לשמש כגואל הדם.[14]

עוד אפשרות מבוססת על דברי הרמב"ם הנוגעים ליכולתו השיפוטית של מלך.[15] הרמב"ם מסביר שמלך בשל סמכותו המלכותית רשאי להוציא להרוג רוצחים שבית דין אינו צפוי לדונם וזאת על מנת לשמור על חיי חברה תקינים.[16]

---

11 — במדבר ל"ה, י"ט (סנהדרין מ"ה, ב' ד"ה "גואל הדם") משמע שמצוות "גואל הדם" רק נוגעת לאדם שנרצח בשוגג לא במזיד. הרמב"ן (הגהות הרמב"ם על ספר מצוות לרמב"ם מצוות עשה ששכח הרמב"ם מצוה י"ג) מתווכח ואומר כי התורה מציינת במיוחד שהלכות גואל הדם נוגעת ברוצח במזיד. מרש"י (במדבר ל"ה, ט"ז) משמע כי הוא מסכים שגואל הדם נוגע אף לרוצח במזיד. רב הראשונים (הרמב"ם הלכות רציחה, א', ב', יד רמה על סנהדרין מ"ה, ב', ורבינו פרץ (שם)) מבינים כי המצווה של גואל הדם יכול להרוג את הרוצח כאשר הרוצח רצח במזיד ונשפט ע"י בי"ד. הרמב"ן (ספר מצוות שם) מוסיף כי גואל הדם יכול להרוג את הרוצח רק במקרה שבי"ד אינו יכול לשפוט ולהוציא להרוג את הרוצח קודם לכן. בנוסח הרמב"ם (הלכות רציחה שם). ע"פ הבנת הכסף משנה כותב כי גואל הדם אינו יכול להרוג את הרוצח אלא אם כן בי"ד הרשיעו אתו. אך אפילו הרמב"ם (הלכות רציחה פרק ו', ה') מסכים כי אם גואל הדם הלך והרג כבר את הרוצח אינו חייב על רציחה. הקצות (ב', א', מצוטט באנציקלופדיה התלמודית כרך ה', עמוד 223). לעומת זאת כותב כי לגואל הדם מותר לכתחילה להרוג את הרוצח גם אם הוא לא נשפט. ראה אנציקלופדיה תלמודית (שם) לעוד דעות בסוגיה זו. הקצות מסתפק האם המושב של גואל הדם קיים בזמנינו, ראה הרב צבי שפיל, Cases in Monetary

12 — Halacha (Artscroll/Mesorah, 2001) עמ' 34. הקצות מסתפק מכיון שיתכן שזקוקים לעדים לוודא כי החשוד בצע את הרצח, והיום אנחנו איננו רשאים לקבל עדות לדיני נפשות. התומים אומר כי גואל הדם למעשה איננו קים בזמנינו מאחר ואין בית דין שיקבע זאת. החוות יאיר (קמ"ז) מסכים לדעת התומים, אבל מסתייג ואומר שמותר גם בימינו להשתמש בהלכה של גואל הדם. ראה אוצר הידיעות (הרב מיכל יהודה שטרן כרך ב' פרק ר'). הצמח צדק (הקדמון קי"א) כותב כי מצוות גואל הדם קים גם בימינו, גם כאשר הרוצח רצח בלא עדים. הצמח צדק מציין נקודה (שם) המצוטטת רבות ע"י חבר מועצת מדינת ניו יורק דוב הייקינד כי יש להביא רוצחים על עונשם בכדי שאחרים לא יחשבו שהם יכולים לעשות ככל העולה על רוחם. ראה משנה ברורה (ש"ו, נ"ח) בנוגע לגואל הדם בזמננו.

13 — הלכות רציחה א', ב'.

14 — צמח צדק הקדמון, קי"א מובא ב"דף על דף" מכות י', ב.

15 — הלכות רציחה (ב',ד').

16 — בספרד המוסלמית, לקהילה היהודית היתה הסמכות לגזר עונשי מוות ואכן עשו זאת, בייחוד במקרים בהם מסרו את הקהילה לידי השלטונות. (ג'ולין ג' ג'ייקובס, Judaism Looks at Modern Issues [Aviva Press, 1993] עמ' 34). הריב"ש, שחי בספרד במאה הארבע עשרה כותב (שו"ת ריב"ש 234) כי על אף דברי הגמרא (סנהדרין מ"א, א) המורים כי אין סמכות לדון דיני נפשות בימינו, ישנם

מספר פוסקים סוברים כי לממשלה הישראלית כיום סמכות של מלך. הרב עובדיה יוסף מצטט את הרב אברהם יצחק קוק[17] שאומר כי אף היום שאין מלך בישראל לממשלה הנבחרת יש סמכות של מלך בנוגע לעניינים לאומיים.[18] הרב אליעזר וולדנברג סובר כך גם הוא ואומר כי בימינו ראש הממשלה, הממשלה והכנסת שנבחרו על פי רוב יהודי ארץ ישראל משמשים במקום מלך לכל נושא לאומי. (אך במקרה שדעתם נוגד את דעת תורה, היא לא תקפה).[19] לכן אם הממשלה החליטה שלצורכי חוק לאומיים ובין לאומים יש להוציא להורג רוצח נאצי, הדבר מותר.

אפשרות שלישית מציעה כי לרוצח נאצי יש דין של רודף. הגמרא מביאה מקור מן התורה המתיר להרוג אדם הרודף אחר אדם אחר במטרה להורגו.[20] למרות שבהעדר סנהדרין בלשכת הגזית אסור לגזור דין מוות הלכות רודף עדיין תקפות בימינו.[21]

במבט ראשוני נראה כי קשה להכיל את הלכות רודף במקרה שלנו, של הוצאה להורג של רוצחים נאצים קשישים, אשר כרגע אינם יכולים לסכן איש. אולם מדברי הרב יוסף אנגל[22] ניתן להבין את הסיבה לכך. הרב אנגל כותב כי ישנם שתי מטרות המושגות כאשר בי״ד מוציא להורג רוצחים. הראשונה: הוצאת הצדק לאור. והשניה: הרתעת רוצחים עתידיים מלבצע את זממם.[23]

הסיבה השניה מתבססת על הפסוק בדברים שכותב כי על כל עם ישראל להיות נוכחים במעמד ההוצאה להורג של רוצח "למען ישמעו ויראו"[24] מדבר ד'. הרב אנגל מביא כי שאם בי״ד אינו מוציא להורג את הרוצח הדבר יגרום לאחרים ללכת בעקבותיו, ולכן הגדרת רודף חלה עליו. היות ואם יותר בחיים

בתי דין בספרד בסערת המבצעים הוצאות להורג כצורך שעה, בהיתר מהמלך. ראה סנהדרין מ״ו, א, רמב״ם הלכות רציחה ב', ד', שולחן ערוך, חושן משפט, ב', א', ושו״ת ריב״ש, 251. הרא״ש כותב בתשובתו (הרא״ש י״ז, ח' ראה גם שו״ת הרא״ש כ״א, ח' ופניני הלכה בסנהדרין (שם)) כי מה שהסבירו הקהילה בספרד, על שהוציאו להורג—דבר שלא עשתה שום קהילה יהודית אחרת בעולם, היה כי הם מתבססים על הרשות שנתנה להם מהמלך ולא על העיקרון שלבית דין מותר להוציא להורג בשעת צורך גדול. התומים (ב', ראה גם בית יוסף על חושן משפט ס' ב' ד״ה "אף על פי") מתנגד לריב״ש ופוסק כי לבית דין בזמננו לעולם אין סמכות להוציא להורג. ראה גם פניני הלכה סנהדרין כ״ז, א'.

17   תשובת משפט כהן קמ״ד, ט״ו.
18   יחווה דעת כרך ה', ס״ד.
19   ציץ אליעזר כרך י', א'.
20   סנהדרין ע״ג, א'.
21   רמב״ם הלכות רציחה א', ו'-י״ג, שלחן ערוך, חושן משפט, תכ״ה, ב'-ה'.
22   גליוני הש״ס, פסחים, צ״א, ב'.
23   בנוגע לגישת התורה לעונש מוות, מציין הרב משה פיינשטיין (אגרות משה על חושן משפט, כרך ב', ס״ח) כי למרות שבימינו ללא הסנהדרין הגדולה של שבעים ואחד דיינים אין אפשרות לגזור עונש מוות, במקרה של השתוללות רוצחים, יהיה מותר להוציאם להורג על מנת להגן על המדינה.
24   דברים (כ״א, כ״א).

הוא יסכן חיי אנוש הגם כי בעקיפין. ובכך גם מובן שאם נאצים (בייחוד אייכמן, האחראי לרצח כ"ב הרבה יהודים). לא יענשו על פשעיהם הדבר יוביל לעוד רוע ורצח על ידי אחרים. כך, שהוצאתו להורג של אייכמן בידי הממשלה הישראלית שמשה למעשה כגורם הרתעה מרצח עתידי.

הטענה של גואל הדם ורודף יכולה גם להסביר מדוע ליחיד במקרה של הרב אושרי היה היתר הלכתי לעשות את מה שעשה ולהרוג את רוצח משפחתו.

תקציר:

הועלו מספר אפשרויות מדוע היה מותר להוציא להורג את אדולף אייכמן, ביניהם המושג של גואל הדם ורודף וכן העובדה כי הנאצים הם מסתבר מזרעו של עמלק.[25] כל אלו רלוונטים בהסבר מדוע מותר ליהודים לצוד אחר נאצים.

---

[25] אפשרות שונה לחלוטין מתבססת על דבריו של הגר"א כי לגרמנים יש דין של עמלקים, ואותם צוותה התורה להשמיד. עין שמות, י"ז, י"ד, ודברים כ"ה, י"ט. הרב יוסף ב. סולובייצ'יק (קול דודי דופק, פרק י') מביא כי ישנם שני רובדים בנוגע לחיוב למחות את עמלק. על כל יחיד מוטלת החובה למחות את זכר עמלק, ועל עם ישראל בכללותו מוטל החובה למחוק את עמלק. אך חובתו של היחיד הינה רק כלפי זרעו הביולוגי של עמלק, לעומת זאת, מחובתנו כעם למחות כל עם המנסה להשמיד אותנו מאחר והם נחשבים לעמלק. לפי דברי הרב, משמע כי כאומה עלינו להרוג את אותם עמים המתקיפים אותנו, אבל החיוב אינו נופל על כל יהודי כיחיד. לכן, לאדם פרטי אין סמכות להרוג נאצים. בדומה לכך, הבריסקר רב (חידושי הגרי"ז ק"ס) פוסק כי החיוב למחות את עמלק חל על עם היהודי במהלך יציאה למלחמה ולא על יחיד. עוד נושא היוצא לכאורה מדברי הגר"א הוא הנידון האם מותר לאדם מזרע עמלק להתגייר. הרב שמואל וואזנר (שבט הלוי חלק ה', קמ"ט) כותב כי מותר לקבל גרים מעמלק. ראשית, הרמב"ם (הלכות מלכים ו', ד') מתיר לקבל גרים מזרע עמלק. שנית, הגמרא בברכות (כ"ח, א') מלמדת כי סנחריב מלך אשור בלבל את כל האומות וגרם לכך שלא ידוע מי מקורו מכל אומה, היוצא מכך: יתכן שישנם גרים בימינו מזרע עמלק, אך היות ואי אפשר לדעת מי הם, מותר אף להתחתן איתם. כך גם לא ברור כי הגרמנים הם מעשה עמלק, והמסורת שיש לנו מהגר"א על כך שגרמניה היא עמלק אינה מספיקה בכדי למנוע את גרותם ובודאי שאי כדי להרגם.

תפילה על גויים

מתוך החדשות:

ביוני 2016, אקדחן רצח לפחות 50 איש ופצע 50 נוספים במועדון לילי באורלנדו. קודם הירי התקשר היורה ל-911 והצהיר אמונים לדאע"ש (ISIS). כתבים הכתירו את האירוע בשם "הטבח באורלנדו".

בתגובה לאירוע, מנהל תיכון דתי בריברדייל, ניו יורק, מסר שיחה לתלמידיו בה הרחיב במספר מסרים המחנכים מהי ההתייחסות הנכונה לאירוע שכזה. לאחר מכן, התלמידים קראו פרקי תהילים והתפללו עבור הקורבנות.[1]

ביוני 2016 הופצה חדשה נוספת, ה"טיימס אוף יזראאל" פרסם ידיעה תחת הכותרת: "נוצרים מבקשים מרב להתפלל עבורם בעיר אוקראינית".[2] הכתבה מדווחת כי נוצרים מכל רחבי אוקראינה, ספרד, פורטוגל, איטליה, מולדובה ורומניה, מבקשים מהרב נח קופמנסקי מצ'רניבטסי, אוקראינה, להתפלל עבורם. הכתבה מציינת כי אותם נוכרים מחפשים יהודים שיתפללו עבורם מתוך אמונה כי תפילתם של יהודים רצויה יותר לפני אלוקים. אנשים מבקשים מהרב קופמנסקי שיתפלל בשביל כל מיני דברים, החל מניתוח כלייתי מוצלח ולא כלה בה־צלחה במבחני כניסה לאקדמיה משטרתית. הרב מציין כי הוא מאמין שהקשר המוצלח בין הקהילה היהודית והנוצרית בעיר נובע ממאמצם להתפלל בעדם. השאלה היא, האם מותר להתפלל עבור גויים?

ממבט תורני:

הרב עובדיה יוסף דן בהרחבה האם מותר לגר להתפלל עבור רפואתו של אביו הגוי.[3] הוא פוסק כי במקרה של הגר הוא מוסלמי, הבן ודאי יכול

1   רחל דליה בנאים, How a Principal's Speech About Orlando is Comforting—Students in Orthodox Schools (יוני 24, 2016) www.tabletmag.com

2   ג'ולי מאסיס, In a Ukrainian city, Christians ask the Rabbi to pray for them (יוני 14, 2016) www. timesofisrael.com

3   יחווה דעת, כרך ו' ס'.

להתפלל על רפואתו, מאחר ומוסלמים אינם נחשבים עובדי עבודה זרה.[4] הרב עובדיה מוסיף כי אפילו אם אביו הגוי הינו נוצרי ומאמין בשילוש עדיין מותר לרפואתו ולהתפלל לרפואתו, אף אם לא תוצר איבה מאחר ואמונתם אינה נח־שבת עבודת אלילים. הדבר מבוסס על תוספות המביא כי אין איסור לנוכרים להאמין בשילוש.[5] יתר על כן כי תפילה עבור ההחלמה יכולה לגרום לקידוש ד'.[6] כמו כן הרב עובדיה קובע כי גם אלו הסוברים שנצרות היא בגדר עבודה זרה יסכימו שתפילה עבור הרפואתם מותרת.[7] סברתו היא מאוד פשוטה: אם הנוכרי אינו ראוי לרפואה, ד' לא ירפא אותו, כך שתפילות לא יכולות להזיק. בנוסף אם הנוכרי עצמו מבקש שיתפללו עליו, הרי זה מוכיח שהוא מאמין שד' כל יכול. בהתבסס על הנאמר לעיל יהיה מותר להתפלל עבור הרפואתם של גויים בימינו גם אם אין איבה.[8]

אולם ספר חסידים[9] פוסק שאין להתפלל לרפואתם של אלו שהחטיאו אח־רים.[10] ספר חסידים מצביע על כך כי לפני שהנביאים התפללו עבור חוטאים

---

4   עין ברמב"ם הלכות מאכלות אסורים י"א, ז' ואחרים המובאים ביחווה דעת כרך ו', ס'. הרב עובדיה מסביר כי זו הסיבה שהרמב"ם שימש כרופא עבור מוסלמים במצרים—מאחר ואין להם דין של עובדי אלילים, ולא משום חשש איבה.

5   תוספות, סנהדרין ס"ג, ב' (ד"ה אסור) ראה גם רמ"א על אורח חיים קנ"ה, א'. פסקי תשובה על יורה דעה קמ"ז, ב', שואל ומשיב מהדורה תנינא כרך א', נ"א, עשה לך רב כרך ט', ל'. הבנת הרמ"א של התוספות היא, כי התוספות סובר כי אמונה בשיתוף אינה נחשבת עבודה זרה עבור גויים. אך אחרים חולקים עליו (שער אפרים כ"ד, מעיל צדקה כ"ב) ומסבירים כי כוונת כתובתם היתה שגרימה לנוכרי להישבע בשם השיתוף אינה בגדר האיסור "לא ישמע על פיך". מאחר ונוכרים אינם מחשיבים את קדושיהם (ע"פ"ל) לאלוהים, אבל התוספות אכן סובר ששיתוף נחשב עבודה גלולים אפילו עבור נברים.

6   הרב שלמה אבינר נשאל: "האם מותר לשאת תפילה בבית כנסת עבור השוטר הדרוזי שנרצח כאשר הגן על יהודים במתקפת הטרור בהר נוף?" הרב השיב: "בודאי! הוא הקריב את חייו עבור עם ישראל ונחשב אחד מאותם חסידי אומות העולם. זהו גם הפסק של הרב עובדיה יוסף בנוגע לחייל הדרוזי שנפל במשמרתו במהלך שירותו בצה"ל. אחד מהאריות שלו לפסק היה מהירושלמי (מגילה ג', ז') המביא כי בפורים אנחנו אומרים "וגם חרבונה זכור לטוב"—מאחר והוא דבר נגד שונאו של ישראל, המן. הדבר נכון עוד יותר עבור אותם חיילים דרוזים המסכנים את חייהם על מנת להגן על עם ישראל, בודאי שמצווה להתפלל עבור נשמתם. (חזון עובדיה, אבלות, כרך ג', 238) ראה Q&A on Terrorist Attacks in Jerusalem—www.ravaviner.com

7   יחווה דעת, כרך ו' ס'.

8   הרב משה פיינשטיין מתיר גם להתפלל עבור רווחתו של גוי הוא מביא את שלמה המלך בתור ראיה, ראה מסורת משה כרך א', עמ' 504. הנביא (מלכים א', פרק ח, מ"א—מ"ג) כותב כי שלמה התפלל שכל תפילותיהם של הגויים בבית המקדש יתקבל.

9   ספר חסידים, תרפ"ח. חתם סופר (אבן העזר ס"ט מובא בילקוט פארים, סוטה י, ב') כותב, לעומת זאת, כי ע"י הנלמד מהגמרא בסוטה (שם) מותר לאדם להתפלל אפילו עבור רשע שדוד המלך התפלל עבור רשע—בנו אבשלום. ספר החסידים (תש"ץ) חולק על הראיה, הוא מסביר כי דוד התפלל עבור אבשלום מאחר והיתה לו אחריות חלקית למעשיו הרעים של אבשלום.

10   התורה כותבת כי פרעה בקש ממשה רבינו שיתפלל עבורו שיעצרו המכות. למעשה, במהלך מכת ברד משה עזב את העיר ופנה להתפלל בשדה מאחר והעיר היתה מלאה בע"ז. החזקוני (שמות, ט' כ"ט) כותב שמשה עזב את העיר ויצא לשדה מאחר והמכה היתה מורגשת שם ביותר וממילא ממלא התפילה

הם דרשו מהם שיחזרו בתשובה. בדומה לכך צדיקים היו מבקשים מהבאים
אליהם שיעשו תשובה לפני שיתפללו עבורם. הסיבה לכך היא שאחרת יתכן
ותפילתם של הצדיקים לא תתקבל ועלול לגרום חילול ד'.[11]

אבל הרב זילברשטיין מביא כי עשויה להיות סיבה מוצדקת לצדיקים לא
להתפלל עבור חוטאים, סיבה שאינה מונעת מאחרים להתפלל עליהם.

יותר מכך היו זמנים בהם יראי ד' התפללו עבור פושעים ומזידים. המעם
לועז בפרושו על הפסוק "רחוק ד' מרשעים ותפילת צדיקים ישמע".[12] מסביר כי
למרות שד' רחוק מרשעים הוא מקבל את תחינתם של צדיקים בעדם. ה"מעם
לועז" מבאר כי זו הסיבה שאברהם ברך את ישמעאל והקב"ה ענה לו.[13] בדומה
לכך אומר התומר דבורה כי מתאים לרחם גם על רשעים מאחר: "סוף סוף
הם בני אברהם יצחק ויעקב".[14] בהתבסס על ההבנה של המעם לועז, משמע
שמותר להתפלל עבור פושעי עכו"ם. על פי התומר דבורה הדבר פחות ברור
מכיון שיתכן וכוונתו היא רק כלפי רשעי ישראל.[15]

הרב חזקיהו מדיני בספרו ה"שדי חמד"[16] כותב שמותר להתפלל עבור גויים
ישרי דרך אך על גויים המרשיעים כלפי אלוקים ואדם אין להתפלל מלכת-
חילה. אבל בהעדר ברירה אחרת, במקרה בו המנעות מתפילה תוביל לאיבה
מותר להעתיר עבורם. הדבר דומה להתירה של הגמרא לפרנס עניי עכו"ם עם
עניי ישראל במקרה שהתנהגות שונה תגרום לאיבה.[17]

במקום ההוא תנבע מעומק הלב. ניתן לשאול: האיך היה יכול משה להתפלל עבור פרעה הרשע?
יתכן וניתן לומר שתפילתו של משה היתה עבור עמ"י מאחר ופרעה הבטיח "העתירו אל ה' ...ואשלח
אתכם". כך שלא בהכרח מדובר פה בתפילה עבור גויים או פושעים.

11 ספר חסידים תשנ"ד, תשנ"ה לעוד בנושא תפילה עבור תשובתם של חוטאים ראה חשוקי חמד,
ראש השנה, עמ' 170 ה' 41, במראה הבזק כרך ד', י', הרב יעקב מונטרוס Halachic World
כרך 2 (Feldheim, 2006), עמ' 86, הרב ירמיהו קגנוף 'From Vanishing Importers to Vultures
Wings: More Fascinating Expositions on Contemporary Halachic Issues (Feldheim, 2014)
The Rav Thinking Aloud on the Parsha: Sefer Shemos (Laor Ltd.) דוד הולצר, עמ' 136-140
עמ' 67, ושירת דוד, עמ' 95.

12 משלי (ט"ו, כ"ט).

13 בראשית (י"ז, י"ח, כ').

14 תומר דבורה א', י"ב.

15 בספרו לב שלום (עמ' 150-151), הרב שלום שבדרון מסתייג מתפילת אברהם על סדום כדוגמא
לתפילה עבור חוטאים. הוא מביא את המדרש המספר כי אברהם אבינו קלל את דור הפלגה (בוני
מגדל בבל) ושואל מדוע הוא התפלל עבור אנשי סדום ולא עבור דור הפלגה. בדור הפלגה, אברהם
ראה את דרכיהם הקלוקלות והרגיש שהתגובה הנכונה היא לנזוף בהם ולקללם, בתקוה שהדבר יוביל
לחזרתם בתשובה. אצל סדום לעומת זאת, ה' גלה לאברהם שהוא הולך להחריב את העיר. בנקודת
הזמן הזאת, תפקידו של אברהם לא היה להשפיע עליהם להיטיב את דרכם. התגובה המצופה היתה
לרחם עליהם ולהתפלל בעדם.

16 כרך ג'.

17 גיטין ס"א, א'.

תקציר:

הרב עובדיה יוסף מתיר להתפלל עבור נוכרים במקרים בהם הדבר מסוגל לגרום לקידוש ד'. הרב עובדיה אפילו מתיר להתפלל עבור גויים עובדי אלילם. לעומתו השדי חמד קובע כי ישנה עדיפות לא להתפלל עבור פושעי עכו"ם. בהעדר ברירה אחרת ובתנאים מסוימים אפשר להתפלל עליהם.

שימור מינים

מתוך החדשות:

בדצמבר 2013, בנאשיונאל ג'אוגרפיק הופיעה כתבה תחת הכותרת: "20,000
מינים בסכנת הכחדה: הגיע הזמן לשקלל מחדש, איך מחליטים את אלו
לשמר". הכתבה מציינת כי "מדענים וממוחי שימור נותנים עדיפות בהתבסס
על תפיסות ציבוריות והחשיבות הכלכלית של המין. האם מדובר על מאכל ים
פופולארי או במין המספק כסף תיירותי למדינה". הכתבה ממשיכה להסביר כי
בריכוז המאמצים להצלת מינים נבחרים אנחנו מצמצמים מאוד את יכולותינו
להציל רבים אחרים. לדוגמא, עלות השימור של טיגריס בלבד היא שמונה
מיליון דולר בשנה אחת. בסך הכול, אנו נוטים לדאוג על מצוקתם של מינים
הנמצאים בסכנת הכחדה.[1]

מהי דעתה של התורה לגבי שימור מינים?

ממבט תורני:

בפרושו על מצוות שלוח הקן (שליחת הציפור הנקבה לפני לקיחת ביציה)[2]
מסביר הרמב"ן:[3] הקב"ה רוצה בקיומם של כל המינים ולא בהכחדתם של אף
אחד מהם. מהסיבה הזו, הוא משווה בין הציוויים האוסרים על הריגת הציפור
הנקבה ובנה ועל שחיטת אם הבהמה ובנה באותו יום, כיון שמעשים כאלו
הם מעין הכחדה למין הנשחט. כמו שהרב אברהם גורדימר מגדיר[4] "ההיתר
לחסל "משפחת" בעלי חיים במכה אחת עלול לאיים על יכולת הקיום של
המין כולו." אנחנו רואים מהרמב"ן פה כי התורה מבקשת מאתנו לשמר את כל

---

1   כריסטיאן דלמור, 20,000 Species are Near Extinction: It's Time to Rethink How We Decide Which to Save (דצמבר 16, 2013) www.news.nationalgeographic.com

2   דברים (כ"ב, ו').

3   (שם).

4   הרב אברהם גורדימר, Torah Lessons from a Cruel Hunt (אוגוסט 1, 2015) www.blogs.timesofisrael.com

מיני החי.[5] רבנו בחיי[6] מסביר כי שכר אריכות ימים שהבטיחה תורה על מצוות שילוח הקן הוא ביטוי להנהגת ה' בעולם מידה כנגד מידה. האדם עזר לשמר את קיומם של מיני החי והקב"ה משיב לו כגמולו באריכות ימים.[7]

יתכן שתעלה מחשבה כי תכליתה של מצוות שילוח הקן היא הגברת הרחמים, אך הגמרא בברכות מוכיחה אחרת.[8] "האומר על קן ציפור יגיעו רחמיך ... משתיקים אותו." חזיונות הרמה מסביר שאם תכלית המצווה הייתה חמלה, היה טוב יותר להרוג את האם וגוזליה על מנת שאף אחד מהם לא יראה במות האחר. אלא שאין זו התכלית, סיבת המצווה היא לשמר את קיומו של המין.[9]

ומכיוון אחר: המשנה באבות מספרת כי העולם נבנה בעשרה מאמרות. רבנו יצחק בן רב שלמה מסביר את חשיבות הדברים: הבורא הקדיש אמירה לכל מין על מנת ללמד אותנו עד כמה הוא מחשיב את העולם.[10] הרב ישראל מאיר לאו בפרושו לפרקי אבות[11] מעיר על הדברים: לכן, גם אנו מחוייבים להאריך את היופי והשפע של היקום ומשם נובעת חובתנו לשמר על עולמו של הקל. כמו שאמרו חז"ל (קהלת רבה ז', י"ג) "בשעה שברא הקב"ה את אדם הראשון נטלו והחזירו על כל אילני גן עדן ואמר לו: 'ראה מעשי כמה נאים ומשובחים הן, וכל מה שבראתי בשבילך בראתי. תן דעתך שלא תחריב ותקלקל את עולמי.'"[12] סביר להניח כי צוויו של ה' המתואר כאן יחול על שימור כל המינים בעולמו.

בעוד שהמקורות המובאים עד כה דברו על חשיבות השימור של מיני בעלי חיים בכללותם, כאשר מדובר בבני אדם לכל יחיד יש ערך עצום.

הרב יוסף דוב סולוביצ'יק[13] מנגיד בין מותו של בעל חי בודד למותו של אדם יחיד. הרב מסביר כי מותו של בעל חיים בודד אינה טרגדיה[14] כיון שסוגו

---

5   ראה אמת ליעקב (נח, עמ' 67-68 ה' 34) שנה לא היה מודאג מהאפשרות של גרימה להכחדת העורבים.

6   דברים (כ"ב, ז')

7   מעבר להקיפה של עבודה זו להקיף כמה גלויה יד ה' בשכר על מצווה זו.

8   ברכות ל"ג, ב'.

9   נחשוני פרשת כי תצא עמ' 1, 340-341, האברבנאל (דברים כ"ב, ו') מציין כי מטרת המצווה אינה לדאוג להמשכיות המין מאחר והיא אינה חלה על ציפורים לא כשרות, וכן מותר לשחוט צפור נקבה ובנה ממין כשר באותו יום כאשר הם נמצאים בביתו של אדם.

10   לאו עמ' 725.

11   ה', ב'.

12   לאו, עמ' 725.

13   The Rav Thinking Aloud, Parshas Chukas עמ' 165-166.

14   למרות שאובדן בעל חיים בודד אינו טרגדיה, אנחנו מצווים דלא לגרום צער לבעלי חיים, אלא אם כן יש לנו מכך תועלת—שחיטתם לצורך בשרם. צער בעלי חיים לדעת רבים הוא איסור דאורייתא. ישנו סיפור מדהים המובא בביאוגרפיה של הרב מרדכי גיפטר (עמ' 317) המראה אותו של הרב גיפטר לבעלי חיים: "הייתי בחור צעיר בישיבת טלז וביום גשום אחד, עשיתי דרכי לביתו של הרב, כאשר צפרדע קטנה קיפצה לתוך הכביש. מכונית התקרבה. הרב גיפטר עצר את המכונית, והנהג פתח את החלון ושאל: 'האם ראש הישיבה צריך נסיעה?' 'לא,' השיב ראש הישיבה, 'אבל יש

ומינו ממשיכים להתקיים. אצל אדם לעומת זאת המוות הוא טרגי זאת מפני שאדם אינו רק אורגניזם או אחד ממין. אדם הוא הוויה רוחנית ויש לו זכות קיום בלתי תלויה בסובבים או בנסיבות.

הוכחה לכך נמצא מגמרא בתענית[15] האומרת כי בזמן רעב אדם אינו רשאי לקיים תשמיש המיטה עם אשתו. אך משמע מן הגמרא שעל מנת לקיים מצוות פריה ורביה (הבאת ילדים לעולם) הדבר מותר. אולם הט"ז אומר שאף אם כבר יש לאדם ילדים, אם כתוצאה מהאיחוד הזה הוא יוכל להביא עוד ילד לעולם התשמיש מותר. אפילו בזמן רעב.[16] כל זאת אם המטרה היא שמירה על קיומו של המין האנושי. אך מסתבר שהט"ז אינו מדבר על מצב בו יכולת הישרדות האנושות בסכנה. הרעיון פה הוא שכל בן אנוש הוא בעל חשיבות. הבאתו של ילד אחד לעולם שקולה לשימור כל המין האנושי.

למרות ששימור כל בעלי החיים ויחס נכון אליהם משמעותי. אין לבלבל בין חשיבותו של אדם שנברא בצלם אלוקים לבין זו של חיה.

על נושא זה כתב פעם הרב משה גורליק מעיתון משפחה "הרב משה מרדכי אפשטיין ראש ישיבת כנסת ישראל (חברון) באירופה ואחר כך בארץ ישראל. בקר פעם בגרמניה וראה אישה יושבת על ספסל בגינה ומנשקת את כלבה. בתדהמה, הוא ניבא 'בארץ הזאת עוד יטבחו אנשים ביום מן הימים כמו שנאמר בפסוק: 'זובחי אדם עגלים ישקו'".[17] הרב גורליק מביא עוד דוגמא של תפיסה מוטעית כלפי ערכם של בעלי חיים הוא מביא את סיפורה של נערה אמריקאית מבית רפורמי לה כלב בשם "מאם" (אימא). הנערה שהשתתפה בסמינר להכרת הזהות היהודית נשאלה על ידי מרצה שומר תורה ומצוות: "מה יקרה אם תראי את כלבך טובע בנהר וסמוך לו תראי אדם טובע, את מי תצילי קודם?" בת השש עשרה השיבה: "ודאי שאציל את מאם היא הכלבה שלי, אני מכירה אותה".

תקציר:

הקב"ה רוצה בקיומם של כל המינים. בנוגע לבעלי חיים מדובר בהכחדה של מין רק כאשר כל בעל חי מאותו מין מומת. אך כאשר מדובר בבני אדם כל אחד נחשב במובן מסוים למין בפני עצמו ולכן כל פרט הוא מוערך ובעל משמעות.

צפרדע על הכבש.' ובכך הוא התכופף והניס את הצפרדע כשהוא מסביר כי היה צער בעלי חיים לתת לנהג להמשיך בנסיעתו. הצפרדע יצאה מכלל סכנה, הרב גיפטר סימן לנהג לנסוע, והמשיך ישר לביתו."

15	י"א, א'.
16	מתיבמא תענית י"א, א'.
17	הושע (י"ג, ב').

כמו שכותבת הגמרא:[18] "המאבד נפש אחת מישראל מעלה עליו הכתוב כאילו אבד עולם מלא וכל המקיים נפש אחת מישראל...כאלו קיים עולם מלא"

ולבסוף עלינו לזכור ששימור המין הייחודי שלנו, את עצמינו פירושו הרבה יותר משמירה על גופינו. במציאותינו כהוויה רוחנית מחייבת ציות מדוקדק לתורה ומצוות—הגדרים שהקב"ה טבע על מנת להבטיח את קיום העולם. וכאשר נזכור את הנכתב כאן נזכה להגן על בריותיו של הקב"ה ברמה העולמית, שמור מינים בכלל וברמה האישית עבודה על עצמינו כפרט.
